Queens of Academe

Queens of Academe

Beauty Pageantry, Student Bodies, and College Life

KAREN W. TICE

OXFORD
UNIVERSITY PRESS

OXFORD
UNIVERSITY PRESS

Oxford University Press, Inc., publishes works that further
Oxford University's objective of excellence
in research, scholarship, and education.

Oxford   New York
Auckland   Cape Town   Dar es Salaam   Hong Kong   Karachi
Kuala Lumpur   Madrid   Melbourne   Mexico City   Nairobi
New Delhi   Shanghai   Taipei   Toronto

With offices in
Argentina   Austria   Brazil   Chile   Czech Republic   France   Greece
Guatemala   Hungary   Italy   Japan   Poland   Portugal   Singapore
South Korea   Switzerland   Thailand   Turkey   Ukraine   Vietnam

Published by Oxford University Press, Inc.
198 Madison Avenue, New York, New York 10016

www.oup.com

Oxford is a registered trademark of Oxford University Press

Library of Congress Cataloging-in-Publication Data
Tice, Karen Whitney, 1955–
Queens of academe : beauty pageantry, student bodies, and college life / Karen Tice.
     p.   cm.
Includes bibliographical references and index.
ISBN 978-0-19-984278-0 (cloth : alk. paper)—ISBN 978-0-19-984280-3 (pbk. : alk. paper)
1. Women college students—United States. 2. Beauty contestants—United States.
3. Beauty contests—United States. 4. Universities
and colleges—United States—Sociological aspects. I. Title.
LC1757.T53   2011
378.0082—dc23   2011031972

1 3 5 7 9 8 6 4 2

Printed in the United States of America
on acid-free paper

For my mother, Jennet Crocker Tice

CONTENTS

ACKNOWLEDGMENTS

Much like beauty pageant contestants whose advisors and coaches have helped them to prepare and preen for campus pageants, I am indebted to the numerous people who have helped me along the way with their ideas, questions, stories, and humor without which this book could not have been written.

First, I would like to acknowledge those who were essential to the birth of this project. I would like to thank members of my immediate and extended family including my father Norman Tice, Elaine Liberto, and Barbara Wood for their wonderful archives of family clippings, memories, photographs, and stories. I also want to thank my students for alerting me to the need to pay attention to life outside of the classroom and educating me about student rituals and the world of campus pageants, especially Terri Seay, Charliese Brown, Jenny Jones-Goodwin, and Dawn Offut, who were particularly helpful in the early phases my research. I am also grateful to numerous students who have taken my seminars in Gender & Education, Popular Culture, and Feminist Theory over the years, for their incisive questions and ideas. They have been excellent scholarly tour guides and interpreters of the nuances of popular culture, media, and student life. Aretina Hamilton and Courtney Brooks are due special thanks for arranging pageant outings and for giving me opportunities to be both front and back stage. Thanks also to Dave Block and Sandra Kryst for their photographs and keen observations at the Kentucky Mountain Laurel Festival.

I give my heartfelt thanks to my friend, colleague, and "book coach," Srimati Basu, who read the manuscript in its entirety on an airplane en route to India (when she could have been reading a novel) and who provided keen and insightful comments for sharpening my arguments. Without her prodding, I would still be reworking this book, kneading it like overwrought bread dough. A constant source of encouragement, Srimati was crucial in helping me weather my extended bouts of doubt throughout the writing and submission processes.

I am indebted to David Ruccio for his feedback on my prospectus and his sage advice along the way. I also want to thank those who have read and reacted to an earlier article on campus queens, especially Sandra Gunning. Thanks go to Monica Udvardy and Francie Chassen-Lopez for late night phone conversations and dinners, and for their tough questions about feminism and empowerment, and to Patricia Rieker, Mary Anglin, my writing group (Ellen Rosenman, Ellen Furlough, and Suzanne Pucci), and Virginia Blum, Anna Secor, and other participants in the University of Kentucky Social Theory Working Paper Series. Special thanks also go to my friend, conference buddy, shopping partner, and co-author Brenda Weber. Working with Brenda on a *Genders* article about the makeover/pageant show *The Swan*, along with our numerous discussions of beauty, bodies, and makeovers, undoubtedly helped to sharpen the arguments in this book. I also want to thank Rusty Barrett (with whom I co-taught a seminar on Gender, Sexualities, and Performativities) for sharing his wonderful insights on sexualities and gay men subcultures, and for his riveting tales of southern small town beauty pageants. I am especially indebted to the fine work of Maxine Craig on black beauty pageants and I have relished our conference and Cape Cod conversations. I also wish to thank Ruth Crocker in Gender and Women's Studies at Auburn University, Richard Wilk in Anthropology at Indiana University, Jim Gruber, Lars Bjorn, and Suzanne Bergeron at the University of Michigan-Dearborn, the Center for Research on Women and Gender at the University of Michigan, the Women and Gender Studies program at the University of Massachusetts at Boston, Boston University Sociology Department, and Sherry Rostosky at the University of Kentucky for inviting me to give talks on their campuses or in their classes. I also thank the Women, Gender, and Sexuality Studies program at Northeastern University for offering me a visiting scholar position in 2007. Also thanks go to Steve Wrinn, Director of the University of Kentucky Press, for his early encouragement and advice as well as to the University of Kentucky College of Arts & Sciences for supporting this project with a College Research Activity Award.

I am deeply grateful to Dale Williams and Saida Grundy for sharing their passionate and profound commitments to, and understandings of, racial legacies, communal solidarities, black colleges, and the pervasive ways that racism permeates college life and how it can be challenged. I hope that this book conveys the deep respect I have for their wisdom and struggles.

Out-of-town weekend writing retreats at other people's kitchen tables, often prompted by cats in need of a live-in nanny while their humans were traveling, have afforded me the alone-time and space for complete immersion and word wrestling. Special thanks go to Betsy Zeldin and Polly Grant for the use of their "Sea Cabin" on the Isle of Palms, South Carolina; Norman Tice for the use of his Corn Hill cottage in Truro, Massachusetts; and to John and Rhonda May and Ronnie and Grace Cary for the use of their idyllic farmhouse in Nancy, Kentucky. Also thanks go to Susan Brand, Gail Horowitz, and their frisky felines for their bayside condo in Provincetown, Massachusetts, and to Lisa Markowitz and her acrobatic felines for their house in Louisville, Kentucky (even if the kitties insisted on frolicking on my computer keyboard).

Thanks are also due to those dear friends who reminded me to stretch and play and who provided needed diversions and encouragement along the way including kayaking trips, clamming and oystering excursions, dinners, breadmaking, dog walks with my dear companion Bravo and his friends, and queen-themed parties, especially Frank Doring, Wallis Miller, Merle Rosen, Richard Angelo, Susie Seligson, Hillary Angelo, Thomas Hakansson, Stephanie Cramer, Lisa Cook, Lisa Markowitz, David Ruccio, Lucinda Ramberg, John LaForte, Suzanne Pucci, Susan Brand, Gail Horowitz, Joan Smart, Judith and John Cumbler, Kathleen Fluhart, Srimati Basu, Mary Patten, Tiku Ravat, John Erikson, Chris, Kathleen, Maggie, and Caroline Pool, Kelli Carmean, Stephanie Tice, Mike Chinquee, Beth Goldstein, Dave Block, Sandra Kryst, Patty Cooper, and my colleagues in the University of Kentucky departments of Gender and Women's Studies and Educational Policy Studies and Evaluation.

Julie Tongue at Morehouse College, Sharon McGee at Kentucky State University, Bradley Cook at Indiana University, Glenn Lewis at Grambling State University, and Deirdre Scaggs at the University of Kentucky were invaluable in granting permissions for photographs. "Thank you" as well to Skip Mason at Morehouse College for inviting me to the Miss Maroon and White pageant and the splendid Homecoming Crowns and Gowns exhibit he curated. I also want to thank Veleashia Smith for sharing her programmatic initiatives for African American students and to so many queens, kings, and their advisors for generously sharing their experiences and dreams in interviews.

I would also like to thank my editor, James Cook, who has made the entire publishing process a true pleasure, as well as the anonymous manuscript reviewers for their helpful suggestions for revisions.

Further, I owe special thanks to Richard Angelo, whose love of ideas and mentorship have been an ongoing and steady source of inspiration and intellectual nourishment throughout the years. I would like to thank *Feminist Studies* for permission to excerpt portions of my article "Queens of Academe: Campus Pageantry and Student Life," 31, 2 (Summer 2005), and Ashgate Press for permission to excerpt ideas from my chapter "The After-Life of Born-Again Beauty Queens," in Michael Bailey and Guy Redden (Ed.), *Mediating Faiths: Religion, Media, and Popular Culture* (Ashgate, 2010).

Finally, and most important, my love and gratitude go to my life partner, Dwight B. Billings, for the incredible generosities, sustenance, and ideas he has given me throughout the life of this project. Without his presence, pep talks, insights, and help, this book could not have been written. I promise no more 11:00 PM dinners.

Queens of Academe

Beauty and the Boar

In 2002, Georgetown College—a Baptist liberal arts college in Kentucky—held its annual "Belle of the Blue" beauty/scholarship pageant, continuing a tradition that had begun in 1950. Throughout the decades, the format for this pageant had been modified. The practice of sending contestants' photographs to celebrity male judges had been dispensed with and the swimsuit competition had been dropped altogether. Thanks to these makeovers, Sara Ramsey, chair of the Association of Georgetown Students, stated that the Belle of the Blue now "represents what is best about the Georgetown College" since it evaluated contestants on the basis of "scholarship, talent, and poise."[1] She observed that the Belle of the Blue was selected in accordance with Georgetown's mission of "providing an environment for intellectual, spiritual, and social growth, and a commitment to Christian values."[2]

Then, as now, the Georgetown student association received support from the Office of Student Activities for the Belle of the Blue pageant. The Director of Student Activities told me that helping with the pageant was her favorite part of her job; although, generally, she claimed not to be a big fan of beauty pageants. She explained, however, that "this pageant is different since poise and appearance only count for ten percent of the total score."[3] Hearing of my interest in the pageant, as well as my plans to write about campus pageantry, she arranged a front row seat for me and we made plans to meet in person at the pageant.

On the night of the pageant, a steady stream of students filled the campus chapel to capacity and I took my seat next to the pageant judges, one of whom was a Catholic priest. His job, like that of the other judges, was to rank the fourteen white student contestants on their "scholarship, interview, talent, poise and appearance, and communication skills." Surprisingly, the seat for the student affairs director remained empty, but I assumed that she was busy helping back stage.

The pageant opened with a chorus line dance number, "I'm a Star," performed by all fourteen contestants, who wore tight black pants and short strapless tops. To stoke up applause, the emcee asked the audience, "Aren't these girls wonderful?" Then the competition for the campus crown began in earnest as each contestant performed her individual routines. A $1,000 scholarship, a title, and a tiara were on the line for the winner as well as the opportunity to compete in the Kentucky Mountain Laurel Festival, a statewide pageant for women attending Kentucky's universities and colleges.

Those in attendance were treated to typical pageant fare including women clad in shimmering evening gowns pirouetting before the judges to show their curves and cleavage and a Q&A session to assess contestants' academic prowess and communication skills. For the talent portion of the pageant, the majority of contestants choose to sing Gospel and Broadway songs, although some danced or played the piano. However, first-year student Stacy Keaton Brown's talent and attire were unconventional and, to some, heretical. Yet at this time, I did not imagine that it would engender a media blitz. Dressed as a cowgirl, Brown galvanized the crowd with her energetic gymnastics and her lasso. However, the audience mood became even more electrified when Brown threw her lasso backstage and rolled out on stage a life-sized, stuffed pig that had been hidden behind the curtains. The crowd roared its approval for Brown and the portly boar she had corralled. Despite her crowd-pleasing performance of cowgirl prowess, Brown did not win the crown although she was named Miss Congeniality. Meanwhile, an announcement had been made that the director of student affairs had been unable to attend the pageant, although no reasons were given for her absence.

Subsequently, I found out why her seat had been vacant. Sensational newspaper headlines proclaimed: "Pageant Pig Hell," "Miss Adventure," "Miss Congeniality Loses Catfight," "Catfight at the Belle of the Blue: Contestants Go Ape Over a Stuffed Pig," and "Pageant Rehearsal Turns Ugly When Miss Congeniality and Official Scuffle." Satirical coverage soon followed on NPR's *Morning Edition* and the *Jay Leno Show*. It was reported that the Director of Student Activities had been arrested and charged with fourth-degree assault after allegedly dragging Miss Congeniality off the pageant stage and intentionally causing her physical harm at the pageant dress rehearsal. According to one contestant, tensions had been simmering for weeks between the two women over pageant proprieties. She stated that the "controversy was over whether or not her talent was *ladylike*. It had never been done before"(emphasis added).[4] After hiring a lawyer, the Director of Student Activities left her position at Georgetown College.

When interviewed on NPR, Ashley Sample, the 2001 Miss Belle of the Blue, explained that the pageant feud had sparked so much media frenzy because "it is hard to pass up a story about a stuffed pig."[5] Despite its brief notoriety, the Belle of the Blue pageant continues to be held annually. Miss Congeniality's cowgirl rodeo performance helps to reveal the potential for gender troubles and disruptions in campus pageant spaces. Brown's performance reveals some of the tensions and complexities of class, religion, race, gender, and region that characterize campus pageants and student cultures more generally. Brown and her pig troubled middle-class and racialized norms for self-presentation, propriety, and stylization in this historically white pageant. On the Belle of the Blue stage, "ladylike" meant

Gospel or Broadway songs, ballet dances, or classical music on the piano—more indicative of middle-class pursuits and performances. Although Brown's boisterous, circus-like performance was a crowd pleaser for many students at the pageant, her talent choice offended official prescriptions for taste and refinement. Brown's legacy appears to have influenced other women at Georgetown College to defy expected norms for gender and class performativity. Choosing to step outside of conventional scripts for the talent competition, the 2009 Belle of the Blue pageant featured several "unique" talents including a chemistry major who used beakers of liquids to produce a rainbow and a contestant who chose to demonstrate traditional culinary arts by making a ham and cheese quiche appetizer. Another student performed a jump rope routine, but she did not include a stuffed animal in her act.[6] As we shall see, contenders for academic crowns, on both historically white and black campuses, sometimes go much further in attempts to stretch the boundaries of the pageant template and its platformed performances of racialized femininity by using pageants as forums to challenge racism, ethnocentrism, and homophobia on campus.

I begin with this beauty and the boar pageant vignette because it not only reveals the investments made in campus pageantry but also introduces some of the paradoxes and fractures that accompany the bestowing of jeweled coronets on college women. As we shall see, campus pageant sponsors, organizers, contestants, and audiences bring divergent personal and political agendas to pageants. Campus pageants and contestants themselves differ across time and space and serve as barometers for generational differences in the affirmation, destabilization, and remaking of race, class, and gender norms in campus cultures. Contestants express widely different understandings of personal and/or collective empowerment that campus pageants promote as motivations for their participation. The Belle of the Blue pageant, like all campus pageants, has been an alterable site subject to numerous makeovers to enhance the project of academic upgrading and pageant modernization throughout the course of the twentieth century. Some campus pageants, but by no means all, have like the Belle of the Blue eliminated the swimsuit spectacle. Likewise, similar pageants have refashioned conventional pageants protocols to showcase new performative constellations of religiosity, self-maximization, and gendered collegiate excellence on campus catwalks—themes I will explore in greater depth throughout this book.

Campus beauty pageantry has been surprisingly durable and elastic. The 1960s and 1970s movements for civil rights and feminism along with the growth of Christian evangelism have produced new facelifts for campus pageants. Most recently, personal choice "post-feminism," "girl power," and neo-liberal discourses on personal responsibility and self-improvement (image and body makeovers) have lent new legitimatization and form to contemporary campus pageants. New strategic uses of campus pageants have emerged as well. Pageant supporters are re-scripting and revitalizing longstanding queen traditions by employing widely variant secular and spiritual discourses of scholarship/achievement, self-improvement, and personal empowerment and choice, as well as grammars of racial solidarities, homeplaces, and cultural education to justify their paradoxical campus presence.

Popular collegiate pageant reforms today include proclaiming new competitive criteria and expanding the ambassadorial, marketing, and recruitment responsibilities of campus queens. Today's queens of academe are typically expected to be much more than "campus cuties" parading in tiaras, sashes, and gowns. While campus queens still walk the runway in heels, gowns, and even bathing suits, they now must project discipline and self-enterprise and demonstrate an unwavering commitment to careerism and self-advancement to prove their academic suitability and justify their presence on campus. Accomplishment, as well as appearance, is now valorized on the runway since pageants typically require knowledge quizzes, essay competitions, and interviews with faculty and staff. Contestants are expected to share publicly their relationship to God, family, nation, culture, success, education, and global problems. They must adopt "platforms" of good works and appear determined, enterprising, socially savvy, and confident—driven to seek professional careers, middle-class futures, and prosperity. And an increased number of contestants on both Christian-identified and non-Christian campuses use their pageant performances and platforms to publicly affirm their Christian commitments and to spread God's word.

Despite these overall patterns, vast differences and contradictions exist within and among campus contestants and pageants. Pageants rarely lend themselves to a single coherent narrative. This is especially pronounced in campus pageants since these pageants are not professionally managed or scripted for national TV audiences. Typically, they are less orderly and more amateurish productions. Some campus pageants reflect decades of university tradition and ritual and are governed by official protocols and administrative oversight. Yet others are less rooted in tradition and official sanctioning as student organizations from Greeks to LGBT groups have established pageants to advance their particular agendas. Campus pageants help to reveal both the diversity of student cultures and institutional missions, and they also implicate staff and faculty in the messy politics of beauty and bodies and their presence in campus life. Although they rely on paradigms of national pageantry, campus pageants, as locally particular expressions of student life, student cultures, and institutional politics, channel both the tensions of beauty, image, and popular culture and the norms of academic recognition and distinction. This is why college pageants provide rich cultural sites for exploring shifting configurations of race, class, region, sexuality, and gender, as well as the display of both normative and even occasionally transgressive identities and projects on campus. They help to bring to the surface the ways beauty and embodiment infiltrate all aspects of higher education including its student body and academic relationships in and out of the classroom. Although not focused on campus beauty pageants, David Perlmutter's 2004 article in the *Chronicle of Higher Education* "Are We Grading on the Curves?" poses the question of how "lookism" and student beauty potentially impact teaching and grading.[7] He reminds us that the ivory tower does not always sequester the life of the mind from that of the flesh. Patrolling, training, assessing, and assigning value to student appearances through dress codes, etiquette training, and beauty pageantry has been and continues to be a facet of higher education.

Campus contestants and pageant organizers invest much time and money in not only producing pageants but preparing and preening for competition. Their labors have maintained these collegiate rituals over the course of the twentieth century. Not only do contestants work hard to win the title but, if crowned, they often find themselves constantly in the limelight, expected to act and look the part. As we shall see, many queens even attend boot camps for class-coded training in style and etiquette. Dr. Tonea Steward, a former campus queen and a speaker at a 2004 national training conference I attended for black college queens, reminded the newly crowned queens that they were now part of a regal lineage that required them to be accountable.

> The fact that you are campus queen is going to follow you for the rest of your life. Someday, somewhere, you'll hear somebody say, "I remember you!" Some queens are remembered more than others, simply because they were about the business of being that school's queen. The first person I had to represent was the college. I had to get my lessons. I had to balance my calendar. I had to learn how to say no and when to say yes. You have to make sure your alumni are aware of who you are. You have to give your time. You have to keep your face out there, knocking on the corporate door. You have to let them know what you are doing. And you don't let them know like you are asking them. You let them know like you have done something. You are the queen.

Black college queens are especially revered on historically black U.S. campuses (HBCUs). Several black college queens have told me that they are remembered long after their reigns ended. I recently had a first-hand experience of this. After having attended the 2009 coronation of the first white queen at Kentucky State University (KSU), a historically black campus, I was traveling through Mississippi when I stopped in Lorman, Mississippi, to eat fried chicken at the famous Old Country Store Restaurant. Arthur Davis, its owner, asked me where I was from. When I told him I live in Kentucky, he beamed and proudly told me that his sister had been the KSU campus queen in 1962. Having not yet downloaded the photographs I had taken at the KSU coronation and its retrospective photographic exhibit of the seventy past black campus queens who had served as Miss KSU, I was able to show Mr. Davis a photograph of his sister on my camera.

Thrilled, he called his sister who was living in the area to tell her about our encounter. What surprised me was not that a photograph of Mr. Davis's sister would be displayed at KSU nearly a half century after her reign, but that I had a copy of it that I could share with a stranger in another state who had identified himself to me as the brother of a campus queen on my mere mention of being from Kentucky.

This project has produced numerous such surprises. I discovered, for instance, that some of my faculty colleagues and many of my students are former beauty contestants. Even more astonishing was finding a photograph of my mother, Jennet Crocker, in the University of Connecticut archives. She had competed for and won the title of Cotillion Queen in 1952. In retrospect, I suspect that my fascination with exploring beauty pageants begins with my mother. While I did not know that she had been a campus queen when I began this project, I was well aware that she had won a beauty contest in the 1960s at an amusement park in Agawam, Massachusetts—the Miss Riverside pageant. I can remember feeling a range of conflicting emotions including embarrassment and envy. (As a plump child, I had always envied her beauty and stature.) I also recall wishing that she was rotund and that she would devote herself to making homemade cookies for me and my siblings instead of her other activities. I often cringed when she modeled her latest outfits but would mumble the expected compliments. At the same time, I was drawn to her makeup table since I found it to be a treasure trove of mysterious and wondrous tools and color palettes that provided endless possibilities for making a fantasy face. We both eagerly awaited the regular visits of the Avon saleslady, a Lady Bountiful it seemed to me, who would freely dispense sample lipsticks shaped like golden bullets. My first career choice was to follow in her footsteps and become an Avon sales lady so that I too could drink coffee all day and give out magic potions that would bring smiles to many faces. Such were my preliminary emotional excursions into the swamp of beauty.

I am left perplexed by the contradictions of my mother's relationship to pageants and by my own reactions. Why did my guitar-playing and unconventional mother, who lived in a small working-class industrial valley, plaster our family station wagon with women's liberation bumper stickers, attend protest marches, and dress flamboyantly (including a purple Afro wig and white patent leather go-go boots), but also compete in conventional displays of beauty, poise, and femininity? How did she reconcile these seemingly contradictory allegiances? What was the cover story that my mother used to iron out the wrinkles and paradoxes in her relationship to beauty and feminism? These are questions that I wish I could have asked my mother, now deceased.

When I went to college in Binghamton, New York, in 1973, I again confronted the morass of beauty pageantry. Given my feminist proclivities, I did not broadcast to friends that my mother and her best friend were in town to attend the Miss World-USA pageant as chaperones for the contestants. I slinked to the restaurant where we had agreed to meet for dinner. At the same time as the pageant, the Binghamton NOW chapter was holding a forum, "Beauty Pageants: What Do they Promote," an event I was sorry to have to miss. Alfred Patricelli, the director of the Miss World-USA pageant was part of the panel. The local newspaper had described Patricelli as having "more guts than a lion-tamer smelling of catnip" since he "singlehandedly did battle with a group of feminists bent on convincing him that beauty pageants are for the birds." Patricelli told the audience that he believed that beauty pageants were "an extension of the competition between women that begins at birth. All women are in competition with other women to get themselves a good husband."[8] How could I understand my mother's seemingly contradictory behavior in attending women's liberation marches but also supporting events that generated feminist protest? How are we still to make sense of this not uncommon fusion of beauty pageant devotion and feminist identifications and appropriations?

Teaching courses on gender, education, and popular culture has helped to propel me back into the world of beauty pageants. During one of my classes, students, incredulous that I was not aware of the popularity of campus pageants, invited me to attend the Mr. and Ms. Black University of Kentucky (UK) pageant that was being held that evening. I was surprised to find that the pageant was packed with students. It was, in fact, the largest gathering of African American students that I had ever seen on our campus. While I had always considered myself student-centered and interested in gender and student cultures, at that moment, I had to admit that I knew far too little about student life.

This book attempts to redress a lack of attention and understanding of the dynamics of race, gender, and class in variant student cultures by exploring campus beauty pageantry on both historically black and predominantly white campuses. Although much needed work has been done on gender and higher education—especially focusing on women's colleges, women's access to higher education, and women as academic professionals—far less attention has been devoted to media, popular culture, student life outside the classroom, and informal educational spaces. Only recently has scholarship begun to examine the intersections of popular culture, schooling, and student subjectivities as well as how student cultures maintain and sometimes challenge gender, class, and race hierarchies.[9]

Within the past two decades, we have seen an extraordinary rise in plastic surgery options and age and weight reducing technologies. Televisual before-and-after makeover spectacles have engendered a complicated chorus of scholarly feminist debates about beauty, body modification, discipline and pleasure, consumption, objectification/victimization, subjectification/empowerment, performativity, class mobility and status enhancement, post-feminist and neo-liberal logics, and even the contours of feminism itself. Many feminist academics denounce beauty ideals as objectifying women although some point to the possibility that beauty practices can be understood in the context of a pervasive beauty culture as a means of self-expression, pleasure, and group identity making. As significant student rituals, campus pageants likewise raise thorny questions concerning the empowering and emancipatory aspects of body and beauty work as well as their damaging, disciplinary, and regulatory effects. Such questions have often polarized feminist scholars as they debate the interplay of beauty, style, consumption, commodification, pleasure, agency, empowerment, performance, display, and representation. Additionally, scholars have also considered how race, ethnicity, class, and sexuality complicate these matters. They leave us asking important questions on how best to enhance the pleasures of our bodies while interrupting damaging patterns in their global trafficking and regulation.This book is thus situated within the wide-ranging feminist project of theorizing gendered, classed, and racialized bodies and debates about beauty.[10] A rich literature has studied beauty pageants, especially the Miss America pageant, and more recently, diasporic and non-Western pageant traditions to examine the politics of nationalism, globalization, assimilation, and modernization.[11] Despite the upsurge in beauty pageants on college campuses across the globe, especially ethnic-specific pageants, these academic pageants and their queens of academe have not been studied at all.

Popular Culture and Pageant Economies

Despite the recently sagging ratings and ongoing misfortunes of the Miss America pageant in securing a stable TV niche, beauty pageants today remain a significant part of the national imaginary that champions a consumerist and self-improvement cultural economy that is beauty and body-centered. Popular culture has nourished the beauty trade and helped to orchestrate pageantry across the globe. In addition to national and transnational pageants such as Miss USA, Miss Black USA, Miss Universe, Miss World, Miss America, and Miss Black America, numerous global pageants have welded preened bodies to a variety of national and diasporic political projects and gendered identities including Miss Latina US, Miss Africa US, Miss Asian America, and Miss India America. New beauty competitions — such as the "Miss HIV Stigma Free" pageant held in Botswana, the "Miss Beautiful Morals" in Saudi Arabia, the "Miss Earth Beauty for a Cause" pageant, and the anti-assimilation gay "Miss Les" pageant—and even labor union and prison pageants have debuted onto the pageant scene.[12] Academic queens even proliferate in cyberspace. Numerous online competitions have been established including "Dr. America," a competition for women who have completed their doctorates. Boasting that it is 100 percent achievement-based, Dr. America's lofty mission is to "create a new societal standard of beauty" by "glamorizing achievement."[13]

Reality television TV, for example, also features numerous beauty pageant competitions including *King of the Crowns*, in which a South Carolina pageant business proprietor helps to make women pageant savvy. Many series feature behind-the-scenes looks at pageant preparation including *Miss America: Reality Check* and *Pageant School: Becoming Miss America*. The latter featured the fifty-two contestants for the Miss America crown, living together for a month under the tutelage of pageant coaches as they prepare for the national competition. The most improved contestant is crowned Pageant School Queen and given a $23,000 diamond necklace. *Pageant Place* is another behind the scenes look at the winners of the Miss Teen USA, Miss USA, and Miss Universe pageants while they are living together in an apartment owned by Donald Trump. Other shows focused on the family dynamics of pageantry including *Crowned* (a pageant for mothers and their daughters) and *Tiara Girls*, which showcased high school girls and their families as the girls prepared for pageant competition. *Instant Beauty Pageant* fused beauty and consumption by giving contestants money and three hours to shop and dress for a beauty pageant. ABC's *True Beauty* featured women and men living together in a mansion who were unaware that their "inner beauty," rather than their physical appearance, was being evaluated. Three reality TV series featured beauty pageants for children, including *Painted Babies*, *Painted Babies at 17* (a retrospective look at baby beauty contestants), and TLC's long-running *Toddlers and Tiaras*. Fox's *The Swan* merged plastic surgery and pageantry: contestants underwent extensive plastic surgery and then competed in a beauty pageant in which the winner was crowned the Swan. Shows such as *Wife Swap* featured the ever-popular melee between feminists and beauty queens by having the two switch places in their respective homes. New series featuring beauty queens as drill sergeants continue to debut such as the Style Network's *Wicked Fit*.

In a particularly bizarre twist, some reality TV pageant shows have been marketed as a means of feminist teaching and recruitment. According to the producers of the British series *Miss Naked Beauty*, this pageant was designed to subvert "beauty fascism" and to introduce feminism to young women "by stealth."[14] In this pageant, all forms of artifice including makeup, hair dye, and "punishing and corrective clothing" are banned. Sue Murphy, the director of features for a British TV station, says that she commissioned *Miss Naked Beauty* because "feminism has gone out of fashion . . . new generations of women are afraid to call themselves feminists or learn its politics, a fear that has left them without the tools they need to stand their ground against the pressure." "It occurred to me," Murphy added, "that I could subvert the traditional pageant format with the image that there's not one image of beauty."[15] As we shall see, numerous contestants flock to campus pageants in hopes of subverting normative iterations of beauty, bodies, and distinction. Rightly or not, many college contestants believe that pageants can be a means to further racial and gender empowerment on their campuses.

Reality TV shows also feature beauty queens as teachers in *My Fair Lady*–style boot camps that aim to refine unruly working-class women through etiquette, life skills, and beauty culture. This "pull yourself up by your bras and bootstraps" television genre of instruction in grammar, manners, and glamour is designed to mute markers of class and race and to produce the sophisticated, affluent, and whitened bodies expected of middle-class ladies. Such shows include *Ladette to Lady* and *Asbo Teen to Beauty Queen* (where working-class British teens, some of whom had been given "antisocial behavioral orders" by the courts, were coached by a beauty queen to compete in the Miss Teen International beauty pageant). In *The Girls of Hedsor Hall*, U.S. working-class women were sent to England to attend a charm school. This program was produced by Donald Trump and featured Tara Connor, a Miss USA recently released from a rehabilitation program, as one of the trainers. *Flavor of Love Girls: Charm School, Rock of Love Girls: Charm School*, and *American Princess* each featured beauty pageant consultants or former beauty queens and/or borrowed pageant protocols as part of their charm curricula. I learned to keep sponges or socks on hand to throw at my TV when I watched these shows with friends.

There are many other indicators of the cultural and commercial power of the tiara. Over the course of the twentieth century, numerous movies have featured beauty queens and pageants. Pageant film fare includes crooked beauty contests and promoters (*Goldie Gets Along*, 1933); the exploits of pageant coaches (*Juke Joint*, 1947); beauty queens in space (*Missile to the Moon*, 1959); fruit queens (*Waikiki Wedding*, 1937, and *Duchess of Idaho*, 1950); murder and mayhem (*The Case of the Lucky Legs*, 1938, *Wicked As They Come*, 1956, *Carrie*, 1976, and *Prom Night*, 1980); southern and regional pageants (*Miss Firecracker*, 1989, and *Muskrat Lovely*, 2005); mobility and comeuppance stories (*Free and Easy*, 1930, and *Miss Mink*, 1949); pageant spoofs and critiques (*The Beauty Jungle*, 1965); offbeat and unconventional pageants or contestants (*I Wanna be A Beauty Queen*, 1979 (starring Divine), *Little Miss Sunshine*, 2006, *Miss Congeniality*, 2000, and *Miss Congeniality 2: Armed and Fabulous*, 2005); and the feminist infiltration of beauty pageants (*The Great American Beauty Contest*, 1973).

Former beauty queens author memoirs, cookbooks, diet and fitness books, and self-help manuals designed to impart tips for achieving pageant success. Pageant guides include *Pretty Smart: Lessons from a Miss America, Catching the Tiara, The Crowning Touch, Producing the Beauty Pageant: A Director's Guide, How to Win Your Crown: A Teen's Guide to Pageant Competition*, and *Under the Crown: 51 Stories of Courage, Determination and the American Spirit*, which features interviews with the 2001 Miss America delegates about their decision to participate in the pageant in the wake of 9/11 as an "inspiration to a grieving nation." Magazines such as *Crown and Sash, Tiara*, and *Pageant Life* cater to the widespread pageant public. *Pageantry* magazine enjoys a readership of over 2.5 million and its introduction of to school-age readers via the American School Directory's Computers for Education program was recently heralded.

Pageantry sometimes provides a stepping stone for mobility and lucrative business careers. Contestants need both regalia and coaching to produce the winning look. On numerous websites, former queens peddle pageant wear including body duct tape, bikini glue, silicone push-up pads and cleavage enhancers, swimwear, evening gowns, rhinestone jewelry, and hair extensions. Surprisingly perhaps, some beauty queens combine beauty commerce and religion to establish themselves as televangelists and launch faith-based beauty ministries to help women revitalize both their sagging bustlines and spirits. Some queens even use winning the tiara as a prelude to successful political careers, including, most dramatically, Sarah Palin.

Campus Pageants

In our ubiquitous cultural economy of beauty, style, makeover somatics, consumption, and self-enterprise, it is perhaps not so surprising after all that even college campuses offer catwalks for gendered distinction. Campus beauty pageantry has been surprisingly limber throughout the decades. Surviving various challenges from women's clubs, churches, second-wave feminists, and in the 1970s, the diminished influence of Greeks on campus, pageantry has enjoyed a remarkable resurgence on college campuses in the past two decades. Over forty U.S. universities and colleges conduct official, campus-based feeder pageants for the Miss America Pageant that include mandatory swimsuit competitions. Additional campuses have recently renewed their affiliations with the Miss America system as did the Miss University of Kentucky pageant in 2011.[16] Beauty pageants for African American, Native American, Latin American, Asian American, and African college women as well as pageants for men have become especially popular. New legitimations and strategic uses of campus pageantry have emerged in the past twenty years as pageant supporters have rescripted and revitalized queen traditions by employing discourses of achievement, leadership, upward mobility, cultural education, and professional development to justify their campus presence. Some campuses crown more than fifty women a year to represent and market college life. Many of these local campus pageants have been scaled up to national pageants such as the National Black Alumni College Hall of Fame and Mr. Historically Black College and University.

We have witnessed an explosion of campus pageants across the globe, fueled by global market economics since the 1980s that mobilize complex configurations of gender, race, ethnicity, class, and nationhood. Campus beauty queens are thus not only a phenomenon of American student cultures. Western images of beauty and success are globally influential. For example, the *East African Weekly* reported in 1999 that the proliferation of universities in Uganda "naturally led to a proliferation of Miss This and Miss That campus pageants." The reporter noted "only the Islamic University of Mbale and the serious Mbarara University of Science and Technology have not so far held beauty contests."[17] The Russian "Miss Akademia" pageant aspires to "develop alternative forms of student activity and a civilized attitude towards beauty."[18] A Miss University is elected each year in the

Philippines and in Venezuela, a country famous for its success in international beauty contests, it has been noted that pageants can be found at "every university, school, and neighborhood, . . . even jails and hospices have beauty queens."[19]

Besides campus and national level pageants, international collegiate competitions have also proliferated. The 2000 international Miss Malaika pageant, sponsored by the Thurgood Marshall Scholarship Fund for college women who view themselves as being of African origin, was broadcast to 380 million viewers worldwide. In 1986, the World Miss University Contest was established under the auspices of the International Association of University Presidents, a United Nations–affiliated NGO, to celebrate "beauty and intellect" and "spread a message of love and peace throughout the world by appointing a public service delegation of outstanding women university students." [20] In 1993, the UN Secretary General granted these contestants the status of international peace emissaries.

Campus queens currently enjoy numerous symbolic and material rewards including visibility as campus spokeswomen, free tuition, money for wardrobes and programming, elaborate coronation ceremonies, instruction in etiquette and image enhancement, and marketing and recruitment responsibilities. Not surprisingly, given these rewards and the challenge of reconciling the incongruity of simultaneously celebrating the cerebral and the corporeal, campus pageants have generated numerous conflicts over representation and objectification, race and ethnicity, commercialization, sexuality, gender, feminism, racism, and homophobia. As we shall see, one especially significant source of campus beauty strife is racial politics as African American students have continually challenged the color of beauty in campus pageants. Nor are campus beauty pageant conflicts confined only to the U.S. Campus pageants such as the Miss University London, for example, have become mired in conflicts between feminist protesters challenging the commercialization and objectification of women students and contestants evoking post-feminist rationales of choice and personal empowerment. Japanese universities are also mired in pageant politics. Some Japanese campus queen pageants have been organized by voluntary student groups, often with corporate backing, including the prestigious Miss Keio University, whose sponsors include Japan Airlines. Whereas Keio University defends its campus pageant as a "voluntary student activity," Shoichi Inoue has stated that "the reason Keio has managed to keep its pageant going is because everybody involved is invested in the university's brand image."[21] Waseda University, however, banned the use of its name on student pageants and students were prohibited from staging them on campus. Tohoku University eliminated its campus pageants altogether when students protested that they were discriminatory. Akita University, however, recently revived its campus pageant after a twenty-year hiatus but banned swimsuit competitions since organizers feared another round of protests.

Campus beauty pageants have inspired religious strife between Christian and Muslim students in Nigeria. Christian students at the University of Maiduguri organized a beauty pageant in 2003, the year after the Miss World riots in Nigeria. But when Muslim students protested the exhibition of scantily dressed women as offensive to Ramadan, the university banned the pageant. In spite of the ban, Christian students staged the pageant privately on campus, but Muslim students attacked the contestants and beat them with clubs. Christian students responded by attacking the campus mosque during prayers, resulting in the death of a Muslim student and the closing of the university until the end of Ramadan.[22] Few corners of the globe seem untouched by the wand and club of academic beauty pageantry, if not always with such violent repercussions.

In the chapters that follow, I dissect this complex world of campus pageantry through interviews, case studies, and field work on both historically black and predominantly white campuses. In order to analyze the barrage of racially and class-coded pedagogies of gender that are promoted and performed in pageants, I conducted field work at over twenty-five campus pageants in the U.S., attended a national training conference for African American campus queens, and interviewed more than thirty-five pageant contestants and sponsors. I have also done archival research on several campuses and analyzed the websites of countless queens and student pageant associations. My fieldwork and archival research have included a diverse range of campuses including Spelman College, Morehouse College, Clark Atlantic University, Morris Brown College, the University of Georgia, KSU, Purdue University, Pennsylvania State University, Indiana University, Georgetown College, the University of Connecticut, and the University of Minnesota. I have attended state wide extra-mural pageants for college women including the Kentucky Mountain Laurel Festival and the Black and Gold pageant for African American women sponsored by the Alpha Phi Alpha fraternity. Among the campus queens and kings I have interviewed are winners of the National Black Alumni College Hall of Fame pageant, Morehouse College's Miss Maroon and White, Miss Indiana University, Mr. and Ms. Black University of Kentucky, Miss Pride of Kentucky State University, the queen of the Kentucky Mountain Laurel Festival, the Miss Kentucky Derby Princess queen, Miss Purdue University, and Miss Kentucky State University. I have also watched countless hours of campus pageant videos.

Building upon previous scholarship on performativity and the processes for the making and remaking—the staging—of gender, race, and class, I read the stories of pageant participants to see how gender, class, and race are not only structural locations but are also ongoing projects, things done and undone.[23] I focus on ongoing gendered, racial, and classed negotiations as strategies and/or subversions of advancement and distinction, passing, and boundary-making that occur in campus pageantry. In the chapters that follow, I extend the commonplace notion of pageant "platforms"—typically, in pageant parlance, community service projects—with the verb "platforming," to capture the deliberate and ongoing process/project of self-making, sculpting, and performing normative class, race, and gender competencies—on stage and off. I explore contestants' strategies for gendering, classing, and racializing themselves as well as the ongoing cultural performances they enact. I also use "platforming" to probe not just the reaffirmation of normative constructions of collegiate femininities and masculinities but also their destabilization. I attend to the diverse iterations of class, race/ethnicity, and culture mobilized in campus pageants and, more generally, the possibilities and limits for the resignification of traditional, white Western beauty pageants.

In her insightful study of diasporic beauty pageants in Central America, Lok Siu explores the degree to which Judith Butler's notion that performance and reception can foster "subversive confusion" is operative in pageants.[24] Butler's notion is useful for analyzing both the reaffirmation and destabilization of normative constructions of collegiate femininities and masculinities in campus pageants, as well as the contradictions in the use of pageants as a seditious means for promoting ethnic solidarities. Do the narratives of campus contestants really generate "subversive confusions" about race, ethnicity, class, and femininity? Or do they merely reaffirm the normative?

In my interviews with contestants and organizers and my pageant fieldwork, my guiding questions include the following: How do contestants and sponsors account for their participation in campus beauty pageants—despite pageants' incongruous location in higher education—and what gendered/racialized/ classed meanings do they attach to their experiences? How do contestants appropriate or mute discourses of feminism and post-feminism, racial solidarities, cultural affirmation, and class mobility into their justificatory narratives as well as reconcile these goals with the body-centered and classed dimensions of distinction rewarded in campus pageants? How do pageants help to construct an inner group elite and generate otherness, desire, and discontentment? What forms of meritocracy are normalized in campus pageants?

Maxine Craig has aptly argued that "women negotiate a sense of self through beauty work and in relation to beauty standards, but they do so as socially located women positioning themselves in relation to socially located beauty standards."[25] Beauty pageants are not just about normative self-crafting and individualized choice and mobility but are also rooted in racial legacies, allegiances, and obligations. Throughout my interviews and field work, I analyzed not only the diffusion and defiance of dominant white and middle-class beauty idealizations but also how contestants draw from multiple beauty standards forged within socially located student cultures to create campus politics. As a result, I explored the following areas: How do assimilation, citizenship, ethnic pride and preservation, pleasure, power/discipline, personal and collective empowerment, achievement, and inclusion/exclusion operate within campus beauty pageants? How do the traditional pageantry components—talent, swimsuits, evening gowns, and platforms—both authorize and truncate the performances of ethnicity, culture,

class, and religion? How is class mobilized in pageants and campus queen training, and how does class complicate contestants' desires for enhancing racial solidarities?

Finally, new contestants and new grammars of motive can be seen and heard
on campus runways in light of emergent socio-economic transformations on and
off campus, which also have shaped the questions of this analysis. What lies
behind the recent intensification of religious fervor, prayer, and testimony among
campus beauty queens? What are the interfaces between campus pageantry and
the marketing of universities and civic, corporate, and national endeavors? What
are the recent impacts of neo-liberalism and makeover technologies on contemporary campus pageants? Why are increasing numbers of college men suddenly
taking to the pageant stage? How, more broadly, do pageants illuminate gendered
and racialized landscapes of higher education, popular culture, and the multiplic-
ity of today's student cultures?

In chapter 2, "Cleavage and Campus Life," I begin by tracing the scope and roots
of campus pageantry in nineteenth-century public exhibitions of women's bodies.
Contexts include circuses, dime museums, industrial fairs, community festivals,
May Day rituals, and photographic newspaper and magazine beauty contests. I also
examine the increased popularity of national beauty pageants for black and white
women, such as the Miss America pageant and the Miss Golden Brown pageant.
Here, I discuss how cultural anxieties surrounding suffrage and women's proper
place, migration and immigration, and the increased presence of women in public
spaces, including on campus, paradoxically helped to popularize beauty pageantry.
In order to understand why so many college women sought not only diplomas but
tiaras, I explore the genealogy of campus pageants in the 1920s. This period witnessed fierce debates over women's education and fears that college attendance
would result in the loss of "natural" feminine virtues and undermine matrimony
and childbearing, especially for white women. African American college women, in
contrast, faced the burden of rewriting powerful texts about their presumed immorality and inferiority. I show how both groups used campus pageantry to respond to
these anxieties. Finally, I trace the supervision and training of college women in the
arts of middle-class deportment, prudence, and heterosexual desirability.

In chapter 3, "Pride and Pulchritude: Campus Pageant Politics, 1920–1980," I
examine the changing contours of campus pageants through two in-depth case
studies of a historically black university and a predominantly white institution in
the Southeast from the 1920s through the 1980s, including the impact of civil rights
organizing, black power student movements, and second-wave feminism. Then,
using Indiana University as a focal point, I examine the several eruptions that
occurred there beginning in the 1960s when African American students repeatedly
challenged normative iterations of beauty on that campus.

In chapter 4, "Making the Grade in the New Millennium: Beauty, Platforming,
Celebrity, and Normativity," I explore the contemporary world of campus pageantry

across diverse university contexts as well as the discourses of primarily white contestants and organizers as they attempt to accommodate and negotiate celebrity, corporeality, and the cerebral. I then examine the staging of pageants themselves, the campus activities and responsibilities of various queens, contestants' "vocabularies of motive" for their participation, and the defense of pageants as representing more than a vacuous world of sprays, gels, and silicone artifice. I examine assertions of the academic relevance of beauty competition, and I probe the increasing reliance on post-feminist discourses of choice and empowerment as well as neo-liberal discourses of self-enterprise in contestants' accounts. Finally, I examine the recent surge of male pageants, which, paradoxically, showcase racialized masculinities, leadership, and swagger in a venue originally created for the display of women's bodies.

In chapter 5, "'We Are Here': Pageants as Racial 'Homeplaces' and Ethnic Combat Zones," I focus on racial/ethnic pageants on historically black colleges and universities as well as racially separate pageants that have been imported to predominantly white campuses. As the result of racist legacies and the injuries to black women imaged as flawed in body and behavior, to this day black queens have invested in etiquette, fashion, and beauty pageantry as collective symbols of racial progress and pride. Often rooted in notions of legacy, communal preservation and progress, and cultural education, many of these pageants are distinguished from the emphases on personal pride, ambition, and the acquisition of life skills that are typically platformed by white pageant contestants. Contestants in ethnic pageants commonly assert distinctive aspirations for beauty pageantry, including the advancement of racially and culturally specific agendas that promote black colleges, the cultivation of community and racial solidarities, homeplaces, and cultural education. Here, I explore the problems of presenting cultural complexity and healing racialized wounds and exclusions through beauty pageants. Are claims of difference adulterated by the wearing of traditional Native American tribal dress and clothing from various African nations when followed by high heels, evening gowns, and even swimsuits? Can the corset of beauty pageantry be stretched to accommodate cultural and racial agendas without replicating hierarchies of distinction based on heterosexual desirability and class? Do they allow for the expression and reception of "subversive confusion" or simply platform the normative?

In chapter 6, "Class Acts and Class Work: Poise and the Polishing of Campus Queens," I unpack the aesthetic and moralized competencies that queens are expected to master by using three case studies to explore the class-coded "platforming" of campus queens as scholarly, enterprising, and socially savvy women. First, I highlight neo-liberal makeover technologies in popular culture and their diffusion on college campuses. I then analyze the class-coded instruction in etiquette, style, and personal packaging that is championed at national training conferences for black college queens. Finally, I examine the different micro-politics, investments, and performances of class at two state wide, predominantly white collegiate pageants, the Kentucky Derby Princess Festival and the Kentucky Mountain Laurel Festival. Here, I examine how campus queens are expected to perform class-coded signifiers of genteel and sophisticated ladyhood as indexed by poise, social skills, comportment, and etiquette.

In chapter 7, "Flesh and Spirit: Beauty, Bibles and Bikinis," I look at the recent fusion of religiosity, spirituality, and beauty pageantry wherein many contestants increasingly use college beauty pageants for divine purposes. Body stewardship, God's design, and inner spiritual beauty are increasingly platformed on campus runways. I explore how these efforts to merge the spiritual and the sacred with secular, body-centered transformation and materiality are reshaping evangelical bodies, sacred femininities, and Christian identities as well as campus pageantry itself. The corporeality of bikinis and Speedos and the display of cleavage and curves in evening gowns continue to present quandaries, however, for all contestants who claim spiritual and/or cerebral motives for participation. Thus, I probe how contestants attempt to navigate displays of the flesh while neutralizing the ever-present reality of body politics in campus beauty pageantry.

In a short afterword, "Class Work/Homework," I discuss the diverse effects of campus beauty pageants for affirming and disrupting restrictive gender/race/ class dynamics on campus. I also examine the effects of neo-liberalism, post-feminism, and new media technologies not only on student cultures but on universities themselves. I analyze the recent escalation of marketing discourses, corporatization, and branding of higher education and the effects on governance and quotidian practices. Finally, I explore recent patterns of consumption, "buzz" marketing, self-maximization, image enhancement, and body regulation among students, and the growing phenomena of using students as "brand ambassadors" and "style scholars" as well as student-generated fashion webzines and blogs that groom, package, and manage student bodies. I end by suggesting strategies for enhancing critical awareness of the problematic ways in which gender, class, race, and beauty are continually braided and embodied in student culture and higher education.

2

Cleavage and Campus Life

Dating perhaps as far back as ancient Greek times, the tradition of choosing a queen for major affairs is not a new one; nor is it likely to become extinct, for it is a practice continued with much success by most colleges and universities.

—*Nutmeg Yearbook*[1]

One local—and largely overlooked—U.S. site where the cultural power of beauty pageants has long been expressed is in higher education. On first consideration, colleges and universities would seem to be unlikely venues for showcasing beauty and cleavage, yet colleges have been in the business of sponsoring student beauty pageants for almost ninety years. Since the 1920s, the bestowing of jeweled coronets on college women has been a prominent aspect of U.S. campus life. Campus pageants have crowned college women as May Day, homecoming, prom, fraternity, and even academic department queens. Many queens of academe were also sent off-campus to represent their universities at extra-mural civic and industry festivals. Especially for women, who lacked the wide array of extracurricular opportunities and honors available to college men, social appeal, etiquette, and pulchritude became significant elements in a gender-differentiated status system. Beauty, charm, heterosexual desirability, poise, and popularity were key components of campus queen competitions. Helen Horowitz has aptly noted that "college men vied for positions on the field or in the newsroom; college women gained their positions indirectly by being asked out by the right man. Their primary contests became those of beauty and popularity, won not because of what they did, but because of how and to whom they appealed."[2]

Beauty queen contests thus became popular and, in many cases, the primary sources of visibility and symbolic prestige afforded women students on college campuses. A University of Wisconsin "Badger Beauty" described her exhilaration with the attention she received after being selected as one of the six most beautiful women on campus in the 1950s.

In the 1956 yearbook, there I am, in my borrowed finery, seated up top of the UW president's grand piano! The ultimate thrill of this fairy-tale experience was at the military ball, where the Badger Beauties were presented. It was an era of beautiful ball gowns, long, white gloves, and handsomely uniformed escorts. We swept down the stairway of the Great Hall in the Memorial Union, and under a military sword arch.[3]

One woman asserted that being selected as a Badger Beauty had contributed to her "confidence and belief" in herself while another gushed that her beauty victory had opened doors to numerous career opportunities since several potential employers told her in interviews that they had "always wanted to meet a Badger Beauty."[4] Although many pageant sponsors sought "a curvy queen" who could "boost their sales curve," some Badger queens expressed reservations about the mercantile and promotional aspects of their reign.[5] One, for example, noted that while the "ball and the attention were fun," she was nonetheless "upset to find myself in my formal adorning a car dealership."[6]

Throughout the twentieth century across the U.S., the Wisconsin Badger Beauties were joined by thousands of other campus queens, sweethearts, and beauties representing dorms, student organizations, fraternities, yearbooks, student newspapers, military programs, and academic departments on their campuses. In a feature on fraternity queens in the 1950s, *Jet* magazine observed that no other "scholastic social title" offered college women a year long reign of homage and such rewards as free shoes, hosiery, evening wear, and even boyfriends.[7] Campus queens were presented at balls, proms, and sporting events and featured in campus publications, and their photographs decorated the hallowed hallways of academe as well as car lots and department stores. Off campus, college queens traveled great distances to participate in extramural competitions, such as the "Campus Queen of New York City" pageant, the National Miss Negro College pageant, the Miss United Negro College Fund pageant, and the National College Queen Pageant. The National College Queen Pageant, sponsored by the Best Foods Division of Corn Products, Inc, for example, expected its contestants not only to possess beauty but knowledge of "blouse-ironing, cooking hamburgers, cake decorating, and doodling designs with colored pens on electric blankets."[8] The winner received a convertible, a trip to Europe, ten shares of Corn Products stock, and cash each time she appeared as a "royal saleslady" to promote the company.[9]

By 1950, it was observed at the University of Minnesota that "no campus event is complete without the selection of a princess, sweetheart, or dream girl."[10] In that same year, UK students confirmed the widespread popularity of their campus queens by declaring, "We have queens for everything."[11] After the debut of three new campus queen contests at the University of Connecticut in 1956 (Miss Fashion Plate, Miss Dairy Queen, and Queen of the

Arnold Air Society), it was noted that undergraduates were continually seeking "new opportunities to crown some comely Miss as the matriarch of their
organization."[12]

Each year, for example, UK sponsored homecoming and yearbook queens, a Little Miss Kentucky Derby Queen, a Pershing Rifles Queen, a Pushcart Queen, a
Mardi Gras Queen, a May Day Queen, and various fraternity sweethearts. Each
week, the *Kentucky Kernel* (student newspaper) featured a new campus sweetheart.
In addition to these competitions, numerous clubs, such as the UK Kittens, selected
women students as "hostesses" and "escorts" to help to woo potential basketball and
football recruits to the university. Kentucky State University, a historically black
campus, went even further. It bestowed titles on its women students on the basis of
academic department affiliations including Miss Biology, Miss Math, and Miss
Sociology.

Despite KSU's nod to academics, beauty—not brains—was the primary
basis for awarding campus distinction and honors through queen contests
throughout most of the twentieth century. Judging guidelines for the University of Wisconsin Badger Beauties contest, for instance, were based on the penetrating and exhaustive scrutiny of body parts, racialized and classed-coded
self-presentation, and social skills. In 1961, its judges were directed to dissect
the following traits of women students seeking campus distinction:

> Figure proportions—The relationship of the feet, ankles, legs, hips,
> waist, bust, and shoulders; Facial balance—eyes, nose, mouth, chin, and
> ears—See if the total adds up to a beautiful face, a face to be remembered
> and envied by others; Personal appearance—Look at the girls' hair,
> clothes, and makeup—See if they have done the most they could to
> enhance their natural beauty; Poise—Are they at ease? Do they present
> the best possible picture of themselves? Would they be able to tackle a
> strange situation without being unduly nervous? Ability to converse—
> Can the girls carry on an intelligent conversation?

Microscopic inspection of body proportions were often registered in yearbook
photographs of disembodied queen parts.

Conferring homage on campus beauty so defined contributed to a body- and
style-centered climate of exclusion and, for many women students, shame and
self-reproach. One University of Wisconsin student wrote:

> With long, straight hair that hung just below their shoulders, these
> women [Badger Beauties] were everything I was not. Midwestern and
> beautiful, their striking smiles, and straight white teeth were attributes
> I did not have, nor could ever hope to strive for. True, the braces I

Men agree "there is nothing like a dame." The female has many attributes, not the least of which is this abstract called beauty. Women, like many things in nature, are often endowed with characteristics universally accepted as pleasing. These physical attributes are the showcase by which a girl's personality is expressed. The way she dresses, the way she smiles, the way she walks, talks, and gestures . . . all these things offer clues to her personality. The next few pages are concerned with five pretty coeds. Each girl is strikingly different; each is pretty in her own way. Taken as a group they offer proof that there is little in nature to rival the American coed.

89

Figure 2.1 Frontispiece of "Beauty" section in Indiana University's 1955 *Arbutus* Yearbook showing microscopic inspection of body parts. Courtesy of Office of University Archives & Records Management, Indiana University, 1955.

wore until leaving for college did help to make my prominent under bite quite presentable, yet it was light years away from their dazzling smiles. A freckled-face, frizzled-hair brunette from the city streets of Bronx, New York, stood not a chance of standing among the six beauties that were chosen every year on the UW-Madison campus.[13]

Figure 2.2 Dissection of body parts of the 1955 Indiana University queen. *Arbutus* Indiana University Yearbook. Courtesy of Office of University Archives & Records Management, Indiana University, 1955.

Nonetheless, innumerable college women aspired to gain glory and popularity as campus queens spent countless hours preening their bodies and perfecting their "performing selves" in order to improve their chances of winning a coveted campus beauty title.[14] In addition to middle-class norms for bodies, fashion, and style, poise (a fluid assemblage of classed behaviors including self-confidence, composure, and the ability to navigate social occasions, conversations, and public displays) was also an essential component of campus beauty competition.

Poise and self-assurance were necessary for the 150 white college women who took to the catwalk at the Miss Indiana University pageant in 1939. Before an audience of over 1,000 people, they were appraised by three judges and an audience applause meter. Much like the Badger Beauties, they too were ranked on "poise, facial features, smile, and general beauty."[15] Photographs of the winner were featured in the student newspaper and the yearbook as well as in the *Chicago Tribune*. Miss Indiana University was also "presented" at a Chicago shoe store and a state wide ball for Indiana "beauties." A decade later, the 1948 Miss Indiana University's victory package had become even more elaborate, including free modeling lessons and the opportunity to audition with the Metro-Goldwyn film studio. Not all contestants, however, sought such fame and stardom. Some women participated in pageants as evidence of assimilation, belonging, and cultural citizenship. A contestant in the Badger Beauty contest, the daughter of Polish and Russian immigrants who lived in the "unofficial Jewish girls' house on campus," said that "being in the Badger beauty contest meant I was part of Americana, and that was amazing to me!"[16]

As we shall see, until recently campuses tended only sporadically to bestow titles on college men. Rarely evaluated themselves, male students ranked the attributes of campus queen contestants as did faculty, staff, and celebrity male judges. Some campus contests barred women students from voting altogether. For many years, only male students, for instance, could vote on the selection of May queens at UK. Male celebrities, such as Clark Gable, Bing Crosby, Jerry Lewis, and Dean Martin, prestigious modeling moguls such as John Powers, and even the illustrator Norman Rockwell regularly judged campus beauty pageants across the country. In 1964, thirty Indiana University male students responded to a call soliciting judges for a pageant sponsored by the yearbook. One potential judge boasted that he was well qualified to appraise campus beauties since he had "a long tenure in observing female pulchritude . . . and had developed sufficient criteria for perusal of our coeds."[17] Another pointed to his experience in choosing majorettes and Playboy bunny queens.

University deans and presidents were sometimes called upon as judges, but more commonly they played ceremonial roles, often kissing the winners. In 1962, for example, University of Connecticut president Albert Jorgenson lamented that during his retirement he would most "miss the opportunities to kiss all of the campus queens."[18] He stated that he would have liked to have seen even more queen contests on his campus but the board of trustees had vetoed his recommendations.

Distinction and acceptance for women students thus rested not just on intellectual achievement but also on how they disciplined and displayed their bodies, how they performed a constellation of middle-class norms for poise and charm, and how these efforts were judged by men. Margaret Lowe has observed that when college women began to claim the life of the mind by entering colleges in large numbers in the late nineteenth and early twentieth centuries, it was their bodies that drew the most scrutiny.[19] Facing highly charged gendered and racialized landscapes both on and off campus, college women were confronted by a barrage of class-coded instructions and expectations for how to improve their bodies and cultivate feminine charm, heterosexual desirability, and respectability. In addition to beauty pageants, both black and white college women have participated in a gender-differentiated set of extracurricular activities that has included charm schools, etiquette training, and fashion shows. Throughout the course of the twentieth century, campus beauty contests and royalty rituals have undergone extensive modernization and makeover and, for many participants, they are much more than clichéd relics of the past. Many students, staff, and alumni still view campus pageants as venerable traditions that enshrine idealized versions of campus beauty, femininity, self-hood, desirability, and distinction.

Precursors to Campus Beauty Pageants: Setting the Stage

Established in the 1920s, campus beauty pageants inherited the numerous debates and discord that had accompanied the growth of public exhibitions of women's bodies throughout the nineteenth century. Indeed, campus beauty contests have been magnets and barometers for conflicts about respectability, distinction, modesty, virtue, propriety, race/ethnicity, class, beauty, style, and the cerebral and corporeal. Always subject to symbolic usage and public scrutiny, women's bodies have long been utilized to advance a variety of political, civic, commercial, and nationalistic projects across the globe. As beauteous figureheads, queens have been exhibited and performed on a variety of staged venues including floats, catwalks, tents, boardwalks, and tableaux as they have presided over a jumble of rituals, commercial fairs, and community festivals.[20] Calibrations of class and racialized femininity in these beauty competitions have differed greatly over time and place. Some pageants have evoked mythic representations of Greek, Elizabethan, aristocratic, and southern plantation traditions, others have portrayed civic pride and business enterprises and commodities, while still others can be traced to less genteel roots in seaside resorts, circuses, carnivals, and dime museums.[21] These divergent class-bound and racialized pageant genealogies have continued to haunt debates about and justifications for campus pageantry. Class-coded discourses of social refinement, culture, poise, taste, and respectability are used to elevate and differentiate among various pageants. Many contestants use class-coded interpretive repertoires to defend their participation in pageants by asserting that their pageants are "high"-class events because they are university affiliated and they receive refined scholarly prizes such as educational scholarships as opposed to the modeling contracts, furs, and cars associated with contests perceived to be low-brow, working-class spectacles of flesh.

In 1854, entrepreneur P. T. Barnum held one of the first American beauty pageants in which contestants paraded in the flesh before a panel of judges. Moral outrage over the live display of women's bodies pushed Barnum to devise an alternative, the photographic beauty contest, which by the 1920s had become a regular feature in many white- and black-owned newspapers and magazines, including even the decorous *Ladies Home Journal*, which had previously denounced beauty pageantry as crass commercialism.

Photographic beauty contests became increasingly popular in both mainstream magazines and newspapers as well as in circuses and fairs. In 1888, circus entrepreneur Adam Forepaugh advertised in national publications in order to recruit women to compete for a chance to appear in his circus. More than eleven thousand women submitted photographs in order to compete for $10,000 and a chance to star in a dramatic production featuring skimpy costumes and circus elephants. The search for a queen of the 1905 St. Louis Exposition likewise generated widespread interest. Promoters contacted major newspapers around the country and, reportedly, over forty thousand entries were received. Even though there was no swimsuit competition, the wrath of the many religious leaders was aroused nonetheless. Reverend Thomas Gregory protested that the St. Louis beauty contest was obscene and indecent, urging the public "to imagine a really refined and innocent girl sitting upon a platform at a great exposition to be gazed at and ogled and discussed and commented upon by the great mixed multitude. . . . No truly refined young girl would submit to such a thing. The mere thought of it would drive her mad."[22] As we shall see, such battles between flesh and faith in beauty pageantry would periodically erupt throughout the twentieth century.

Despite religious revulsion at what many characterized as flesh-peddling, the popularity of pageants mushroomed in a variety of locales including dime museums. Modeled after Barnum's American Museum and catering to working-class and immigrant audiences, dime museum beauty contests offered training in crafting assimilated and appropriately gendered bodies. Lois Banner has observed that "they were significant sources of transmitting to immigrant men and women American standards of physical appearance."[23]

The post–Civil War period also witnessed the growing popularity of showcasing women's bodies at agricultural fairs and its acceptance by the middle class and industry. The Chicago Columbian Centennial of 1893, for example, included a Congress of Beauty where women from around the world posed on stage in the dress of their homelands, much like P. T. Barnum's original beauty contest, which earlier had been labeled risqué. The 1895 Atlanta International Cotton Exposition included a beauty pageant and in 1898, the producers of the Ohio Elks Mid-Summer Street Carnival and Industrial Exhibition went to great lengths to recruit beauties for their pageant by offering a prize to the town that sent the most attractive wagon load of local women to compete.

Community queen festivals also gained popularity throughout the nineteenth century as a way to promote tourism and trade. Beginning in 1699, the New Orleans Mardi Gras, the nation's prototypical festival, had helped to spawn subsequent community festivals including the Pasadena Tournament of Roses established in 1889 and the St. Paul Winter Carnival, which was established in 1885 by business -men to counter unfavorable publicity about Minnesota's weather. After the fanfare of the 1905 Lewis and Clark Centennial Exposition in Portland, Oregon, many business leaders feared that their city would no longer continue to enjoy the profitable business and tourist climate that the exposition had generated. In order to protect tourism and trade, they established the annual Festival of Roses, which still selects a festival queen today.[24]

Numerous businesses and civic groups crowned beauty queens not only to market their products, including cotton, coal, apples, and peanuts, but also to adorn community celebrations of spring and the fall. Unlike the dime museum contests, many of these civic festivals tended to select queens from among the daughters of the local elite. While such queen festivals clearly violated Victorian prohibitions against the public display of women, elite organizers managed to minimize condemnation by championing their pageants as essential for nation-building, trade, tourism, civic pride, and the maintenance of traditional social hierarchies. Lois Banner has observed that such queen festivals helped to moderate social tensions by bringing "all classes together to perform a ritual of community solidarity."[25]

With their curious entanglements of commercial and prurient agendas and, sometimes, elite participation, nineteenth-century beauty competitions helped to choreograph twentieth-century campus beauty pageants. As women in increasing numbers sought diplomas, tiaras, the vote, and careers, their visibility increased in a variety of public spaces in the 1920s, including on college campuses. The expansion of visual technologies, commodity consumption, urbanization, immigration, and "spectacularization" ushered in a multitude of new occasions, sites, and ways for women's bodies and behaviors to be displayed and evaluated in the glare of the public eye.[26] Yet a myriad of tensions accompanied this enlargement of women's public presence in that era. Alongside new opportunities for emancipation, leisure, self -expression, and feminine identities, new technologies for the regulation and normalization of women's bodies and behaviors also emerged. Liz Conor notes that Western modernity intensified the importance of the visual, of self-display, and the pairing of commodity consumption with social mobility, self-care, and gendered success—new cultural emphases that restyled Victorian idealizations of female modesty, dignity, and self-restraint. Conor asserts that "modern women understood self-display to be part of the quest for mobility, self-determination, and sexual identity."[27] Supplementing and, in some cases, superseding more modest and effacing

Victorian appearances, new visual taxonomies and subject positions for racialized feminine identities proliferated—among them, the city or business girl, blues jazz singer, the flapper, the screen star, the beauty contestant, and, of course, the college queen.[28] Women were increasingly encouraged to look, display, and spend, that is, to become more beholden to the world of consumption, fashion, body aesthetics, and the commodity form. Importantly, however, since access to commodity transformation was restricted by race and class, longstanding patterns of inclusion and exclusion were perpetuated as well.

Campus pageants were also shaped by cultural anxieties about the emergence of impudent and brazen women, as well as by the unsettling and breaching of conventional gendered, classed, racialized, and national borders. Numerous social reformers spoke of the escalating dangers posed by women's heightened sexuality, boldness, and independence as well as new perils wrought by migration and immigration. The increasing presence of women in dance halls, movie theaters, department stores, and public places—as well as the specter of women with vermilion lips, rouged cheeks, and flashy clothes—were taken as ominous signs of a shattered gendered order and moral decay. Social reformers engaged in the relentless scrutiny and refinement of working-class and immigrant women judged to be in danger of falling into depravity. New taxonomies of gendered, racialized, and class-specific dysfunction based on women's appearances and conduct were constructed including "prostitutes in the making," "sex weakness," "incorrigibility," and "aggressive self-direction."[29]

Similar inter-class tensions emerged around the bodies and behavior of African American women as well. Between 1890 and 1920, over 1.2 million African Americans migrated from the South to the North and West, creating what Hazel Carby has termed "moral panics" on the part of the northern black elite.[30] The wide-scale migration of presumably poor and inferior rural blacks to northern cities spawned a variety of intra-racial, class-based improvement projects, including beauty contests and fashion shows. W.E.B. Du Bois famously asserted that "the race must train and breed for brains, for efficiency, for beauty."[31] Images of refined and attractive black women and girls graced the covers of the NAACP magazine, the *Crisis*, under the leadership of DuBois, representing "a visual and literary blueprint for the ideal, modern, black individual." [32] As an antidote to the destabilizing specter of brash college women, suffragettes, flappers, screen stars, and "new women," as well as the perceived menace of crude working-class, immigrant, and rural women, numerous attempts were made to repackage beauty queens as icons of feminine gentility and modesty. Soon after women procured the right to vote, numerous national beauty pageants were established including the Miss America pageant in 1921, the super bowl of white beauty pageants. In 1923, over 300,000 people attended the Miss America pageant to watch seventy-five women compete in front of a panel of judges. Kimberly Hamlin has argued that the popularity of Miss America was due in large part to fears that the

Nineteenth Amendment, along with women's increased mobility and presence in public life, were undermining conventional understandings of white middle-class femininity and gendered boundaries. The first Miss America winners epitomized the obverse of bold "new women." They were "small, passive, non-threatening women with little or no interest in remaining in the public eye."[33] Contestants were expected to uphold traditional feminine virtues and attend church as well as abstain from makeup, alcohol, and tobacco. Pageants rules banned married or divorced women and women who had been pregnant from participating in the contest. Armand Nichols, Director General of the Miss America pageant, predicted a "return to pre-flapper days," asserting that the "sweet modest girl of old is coming back."[34]

Such assurances, however, did not mean that beauty pageantry escaped criticism and opposition. Despite their promotion of gendered conventionality, bathing beauty contests, such as Miss America, ignited an inferno of opposition from both churches and women's organizations that condemned beauty contests. One of the numerous battles between beauty pageants and organized religion occurred in New Jersey in 1923, when the Ocean City Camp Meeting Association, a Christian group, denounced the Miss America pageant for "taking girls of tender years and dressing them in attire that transgresses the limit of morality. . . . The saddest feature of this affair is the willingness of a few businessmen to profiteer on the virtues of those tender years."[35] In 1925, Paul Volcker, city manager of Cape May, New Jersey, said that his town would not send "charming young women" to "be measured, weighed, appraised, and gazed upon by a curious multitude."[36] In 1927, Bishop William Hafey fumed that the pageant was simply the "exploitation of feminine charm by money-mad men."[37] Throughout the 1920s, a wide spectrum of religious and women's organizations ranging from the Southern Baptist Convention, the Vatican, the YWCA, and the General Federation of Women's Clubs joined together to vilify Miss America for its pernicious effects on the morality of the contestants and the public at large.[38] Many contestants themselves also complained that Miss America "reeked of commercialism."[39] Ironically, as I suggest in chapter 7, feminists would continue to oppose the objectification of women in beauty contests, while many religiously identified contestants would begin to embrace pageantry as a divine opportunity to promote Christian evangelism.

To help cushion Miss America from condemnation as merely the tawdry, flesh-peddling exploitation of women, the pageant underwent many makeovers in the ensuing decades. In doing so, the Miss America pageant helped to forge lasting connections between college and cleavage, scholarship and swimsuits. In 1937, Lenore Slaughter became the director of Miss America, a position she held for over thirty-five years. Slaughter made numerous attempts to minimize the pageant's prurient roots as merely a bathing beauty leg show by successfully aligning the pageant with civic organizations such as the Junior Chamber of Commerce, the National Association of Colleges and Universities, the U.S. military, and a variety of corporations. In order to navigate the contradictions inherent in promoting conflicting gender ideologies of modesty and sensuality, flesh and virtue, decency and titillation, the Miss America pageant attempted to link its beauty contest with athleticism, wholesomeness, and domesticity in the 1920s; higher education, scholarships, and Junior Chambers of Commerce in the 1940s; and, more recently, careerism, evangelicalism, and post-feminist empowerment to subvert opposition to the public display and appraisal of women's flesh. Lenore Slaughter was especially proud of the pageant's collegiate connections, noting, "I knew I could not build the pageant and recruit a better class of contestants without the background and recognition of colleges and universities."[40] Consequently, she approached Guy Snavely, executive director of the Association of American Colleges and Universities, in 1944 to head the pageant's scholarship program. Slaughter boasted that this association "opened the door to anyplace I wanted to go to talk to a college, so that universities would understand that we were not a leg show and would encourage their girls to participate in the pageant."[41] Although initially the scholarship was not supported by other board members, who according to Slaughter "were geared too much to Hollywood," Slaughter's goal "to give every girl in America who had ambition the chance to study and have the education to be what she wanted to be" was eventually accepted and became the pageant's primary legitimation.[42]

The first recipient of a Miss America college scholarship, Bess Meyerson, asserted, "I needed a scholarship. However, all the free money for education that year had been allocated to returning GIs who deserved assistance. Nobody was thinking about what girls needed in 1945 except this beauty pageant in Atlantic City."[43] Despite the particularities among beauty pageants, the Miss America pageant did institutionalize many pageant orthodoxies including the scholarship justification that continues to unify many disparate beauty competitions today.[44] It also spawned a national web of feeder pageants across the U.S., including scores of local Miss America competitions on both predominantly white and historically black college campuses.

Miss America not only attempted to uphold traditional codes of femininity but also defended white superiority. Initially, only white women were allowed to participate in Miss America pageants. Until 1950, Miss America contestants had to complete forms detailing their racial heritage and ancestry. Pageant rules stipulated that "only members of the white race" could compete as contestants.[45] African American women, however, were allowed to participate in 1923 as slaves in the "Oceanic Majesty's Court." Native American women were selected as princesses throughout the 1920s and in 1926 Norma Smallwood, a Cherokee, was crowned Miss America.[46] Many state preliminary pageants for Miss America, however, prohibited Native American women from participating. In 1952, for example, Native American students were barred from competing in the South Dakota State College campus preliminary pageant for Miss America. Three former

Miss America winners, Bess Meyerson, BeBe Shopp, and Yolande Betbeze supported the efforts of campus protesters to allow their participation.[47]

Puerto Rican and Asian American women did not compete in Miss America until 1948, and it was not until 2001 that an Asian American woman won the title. African American women were banned from competition until 1971 and it was not until 1984 than an African American woman was crowned Miss America. Throughout its history, most Miss America contestants both nationally and on college campuses have been white women and the few ethnically and racially diverse entrants have tended to closely approximate and re-inscribe white standards for beauty, body type, skin color, attire, hairstyles, and conduct.[48] Despite dropping its official prohibition against African American women, a variety of racial barriers remained operative and many African American college women choose not to compete in historically white pageants such as Miss America and its offshoots.

As beauty pageantry gained popularity among middle-class white women, middle-class African Americans, in part due to their exclusion from white-only pageants such as Miss America, created separate but parallel contests to showcase black beauty, class, virtue, and racial advancement. Maxine Craig has argued that the links among racial dignity, class, self-presentation, grooming, and manners were institutionalized by the National Association of Colored Women when each club member was urged to be an "ocular demonstration of the swift advancement of the race," an impulse that soon spread to black college women.[49] Likewise, Noliwe Rooks has observed that African American migration, urbanization, and consumerism helped to shape the mission of many elite African American women who urged migrant and working-class black women to adopt "redemptive skills" including "demeanor, clothing, behaviors, and attitudes . . . to signal an embrace of dominant cultural understandings of womanhood and gentility."[50] Fusing desires for middle-class distinction, racial advancement, and commercial interests, black newspapers, black colleges, cosmetic and hair companies, black social and fraternal organizations, and groups such as the NAACP became sponsors of black beauty pageants and fashion shows.

The first national black beauty pageant, the Golden Brown National Beauty Contest, was held in 1925. Like many white pageants, commercial interests were behind this pageant. It was sponsored by the white-owned Golden Brown Chemical Company, a maker of cosmetics for black women. Widely promoted by black newspapers, approximately 1,400 women entered the contest. Since then, middle-class African Americans have created a variety of beauty pageants to display black beauty and gendered excellence.[51] In 1952, *Jet* magazine observed that "upwards of 3,000 Negro beauty queens [had been] deified during the past ten years by fraternal organizations, schools, labor unions, sausage companies, beer and pretzel firms, and burial associations."[52] A 1956 *Ebony* editorial concluded that "because we live in a society in which standards of physical beauty are most often circumscribed by a static concept of whiteness of skin and blondeness of hair, there is an aching need for someone to shout from the housetops that black women are beautiful."[53] Campus queens regularly appeared in the black press. For example, Miss Maroon and White of Morehouse College was featured in the society pages of the *Atlanta World Daily*.

Just as white beauty pageants differed from each other on many dimensions including class politics, so too did black pageants. Although often designed to counter white representations of black women's presumed immorality and inferiority, black beauty contests sometimes reinforced intra-racial hierarchies of class and color. Many black queens have been deeply mired in class politics since they often are positioned as levers, escalators, and leaven for class work within their communities. Maxine Craig argues that black contests varied according to whether or not they were "explicitly framed as displays of racial pride, whether or not they incorporated images of Africa or Europe, whether or not they promoted explicitly middle-class images of women, and whether or not they challenged or reinforced the African American pigmentocracy."[54] As a result of the contradictions of class and color within many black pageants, Craig concluded that black beauty pageants have been "symbols of both defiance and conventionality."[55]

Similar tensions about assimilation, cultural preservation, pride, national identities, class, mobility, and exclusion have also characterized the numerous ethnic beauty pageants that were established in the mid-twentieth century including Miss Chinatown, USA, Nisei Week Queen, the Hawaii Cherry Blossom Festival, and Miss Indian America.[56]

In 1938, the University of Hawaii pioneered an avant-garde campus pageant, the Miss Ka Palapala, in which college women from six different racial/ethnic groups competed in both ethnic dress and swimsuits. Each ethnic group was allowed a winner since "it was felt that each race has its own distinct type of beauty and therefore should not compete against each other."[57] A decade later, the editors of the yearbook *Ka Palapala* explained that they wanted "an ethnic rainbow to illustrate the point that, in spite of all these traditional artifices emphasizing ethnological differences, peoples of different heritages can form as beautiful a harmony as that of the spectrum of the rainbow. The time has come for us not merely to recognize these differences but to understand them."[58] As we shall see in chapter 3, rainbow harmony, however, would not always prevail in other campus pageants across the U.S.

As beauty pageantry became increasingly respectable throughout the 1930s, the number of queens continued to mushroom. Even the Democratic National Convention staged a national beauty pageant in 1936. Many public school systems recommended beauty pageants as a means to create "greater interest in personal care among girls of the school and for giving the girls profitable training to take the place of strenuous exercises during hot days."[59] Chambers of Commerce and business councils eagerly sponsored beauty contests to promote their products and enterprises. However, as more middle-class and elite groups began to sponsor beauty pageants, class indexed as an assemblage of micro-skills such as self-presentation, demeanor, poise, conversational fluency, savvy, and confidence was increasingly incorporated into beauty contests. In 1939, for example, the Maid of Cotton contest was established by the National Cotton Council of America. Promoters claimed that "every word and gesture of the Maid of Cotton counts in winning friends for the nation's leading textile fiber. She is instrumental in increasing the sale of women's apparel and makes a solid public relations contribution that is important to all cotton products."[60] Not only did successful contestants need "culture and refinement" but also family pedigree, educational prowess, and self-restraint. To be chosen as the winner they "should come from a home where other members of her family are a welcome asset, they should be easy to manage, and they should possess enough education to assure a disciplined mind; one that can absorb and master basic facts regarding the cotton industry." As we shall see, college campuses regularly sent their campus queens to such industry festivals to represent their universities and market a variety of commodities.

Campus Gender Genealogies

Besides its indebtedness to off-campus beauty pageants, the genealogy of campus beauty pageants also encompasses nineteenth- and early twentieth-century debates about women's fitness and place in higher education as well as racial and class-coded norms for student life. Emergent cultural discourses on beauty, fashion, and consumerism, as well as increasing spectacularization of the female body, helped to elevate campus pageantry and with it, the intense surveillance of students' bodies. Both black and white college women helped to revise and reconfigure nineteenth-century collegiate notions of femininity, identity, body image, and the performing self—corporeal legacies that have helped to choreograph our contemporary body fixations and desires.

Margaret Lowe has argued that college women displayed their readiness for college life in the late nineteenth century by "repeated demonstrations of gaining: weight, inches, and athletic skills for white women and virtue for black women."[61] White college women, presumed to be fragile and unfit for the rigors of academe, were encouraged to gain weight to counter popular and scientific discourses about "race suicide," and "lost femininity" that many feared would accompany their invasion of academic spaces.

Against a national climate of increasing divorce rates, declining birthrates, eugenics, and nativist fears of immigration, white women students in the early decades of the twentieth century were pressured to affirm that the development of their intellectual potential would not undermine matrimony and childbearing or threaten conventional gendered practices. A 1915 *New York Times* article, for instance, blamed both the women's movement and higher education for creating high rates of celibacy and sterility among white women, thus allowing for the multiplication of an inferior stock of "dull-faced, semi-civilized victims of Europe's oppression who are now landing at Ellis Island" and creating a crisis characterized by "an unnatural selection of the fittest to die and the unfit to survive."[62] Educators such as M. Cary Thomas, president of Bryn Mawr College, countered such sentiments, however, by noting that more marriages and children occurred when men and women were educated together.[63]

Despite the early resistance to women's education, nearly half of all college students were women by the 1920s, and most of them attended co educational institutions. As space invaders in traditionally male enclaves, white college women were considered especially at risk for losing their natural feminine virtues and heterosexual desirability and thus more vulnerable to fears of lost femininity. In coeducational institutions, fears of women students surpassing men in enrollment and academic achievement also shaped the gendered norms on campus. Ritualized displays of hyper-femininity, such as beauty pageants, promised to bolster traditional constructions of proper white femininity and help to maintain gendered boundaries on campus. Elaborate homecoming rituals celebrating male prowess on the football field and female beauty at halftime were thus established in the first decades of the twentieth century at numerous universities.

At the same time, African American women students faced an altogether different set of expectations for managing their student bodies. Primarily attending segregated black colleges established by white missionaries, African American college women faced the burden of rewriting powerful texts of their presumed immorality and inferiority. Black women were imaged in racist ideologies as excessive and hypersexual, deficient in the "natural" feminine virtues of restraint, modesty, and respectability. Black college women were therefore expected to embody racial progress by refining and purifying their characters, appearances, and conduct. They had to prove that their educations would result in dignified middle-class morals and manners, virtues historically coded and reserved for white women. As result of such racist legacies and injuries, black queens to this day have had very distinct histories of investment in etiquette, fashion, and beauty pageantry as collective symbols of racial progress and pride. Many have felt the burden to prove that college educations would tame their bodies, refine their characters and manners, and serve as collective symbols of racial progress and pride.[64] The litmus test for black academic fitness was not based on a scale measured in pounds of body weight but on more piercing examinations demanding ocular evidence of inner virtue, self-control, and "class" as indexed by style, grooming, and appearance. While paralleling many aspects of the corporeal displays of white women on white campuses, black queen pageants, as we shall see, also entailed distinctive racial and cultural demands and missions.

Etiquette and Campus Ladies

> On most campuses, there is still a great deal of apprehensive attention to girls' manners and worry over deviations from cut-and-dried conventions.
> —Eunice Fuller Bernard[65]

In addition to the scrutiny and showcasing of cleavage and curves on campus, etiquette and refinement became important components of the beauty curriculum. Etiquette experts, such as best selling author Emily Post, became important social arbiters of taste, decency, deportment, and social advancement as technologies to ensure the moral temperance, prudence, and social refinement of women proliferated. College women were taught that the cultivation of not only well-tended bodies but also middle-class codes for self-presentation, poise, manners, and heterosexual relations were vital for college success and proper collegiate ladyhood.[66] Newspapers, magazines, and conduct books flooded women with gendered prescriptions for self-improvement, proper public conduct, personal fashion, domesticity, and consumption. Many etiquette books devoted whole chapters to college women and, increasingly, over the course of the twentieth century, entire books were written for them, including Kate Jameson and Frank Lockwood's *The Freshman Girl: A Guide to College Life* (1925), Elizabeth Eldridge's *Co-ediquette: Poise and Popularity for Every Girl* (1936), and Gulielma Alsop and Mary McBride's *She's Off to College: A Girls' Guide to College* (1940).[67] Magazines such as *Mademoiselle*, established in 1935, bombarded college-bound women with advice for how to make the most of their college years.

We have already seen that middle-class African American women were forced to work hard to overcome damaging representations in popular culture and white imaginary by embodying the virtues of prudence, restraint, and respectability in public. Black magazines likewise extolled the importance of middle-class etiquette. In 1920, Katherine Williams, editor of the *Half-Century Magazine for the Colored Home and Homemaker*, lamented that "many members of the race lack respect for conventionalities, decorum, and even common decency in public places. When the weather is hot, half naked men and women, some minus their shoes and stockings, sit around windows, on their porches and steps, or lounge on the curbstone in front of the house."[68] According to Katharine Capshaw Smith, decorum became a political tool the black aristocracy used to "push for assimilation by embracing the cultural codes of whiteness and, at the same time, censure racism and advocate for black solidarity."[69] Entrepreneurial black women in the beauty and hair business, such as Madame C. J. Walker, took advantage of this push for refinement and appearances by marketing grooming products as integral to racial progress.[70] Charm and modeling schools sprang up in many African American communities to enhance self-presentation skills.[71] As Shirley Lim has observed, the visual performances of "class-inflicted respectability" through beauty practices, etiquette, and fashion were part of the arsenal used by many Asian American women as well to combat immigration restrictions, fight ongoing racism, and claim the rights of cultural citizenship.[72]

Numerous authors, speakers, and teachers urged embodied projects of upward mobility and cultural assimilation onto African American women. E. Azalia Hackley, author of *The Colored Girl Beautiful* and a popular speaker on beauty and self-control at boarding schools for African American girls, counseled young black women to think of themselves as in a "beauty parade all the time."[73] She encouraged the young woman to be "an Esther to her race . . . especially in all matters of cleanliness, manners, and self-sacrifice to advance and change the prevalent opinion of the Negro."[74] Two decades later, African American educator Charlotte Hawkins Brown, head of the elite Palmer Memorial Institute, emphasized the importance of "polishing off the rough edges" of her students and instilling in them the fundamentals of proper etiquette and self-presentation to inspire other blacks. Author of *The Correct Thing: To Do—To Say—To Wear* in 1940, she asserted that "manners must adorn knowledge and smooth its way in the world." She urged African American students to be discreet and fastidious and to avoid all forms of loud, boisterous, and excessive behavior.[75]

The stress on middle-class ladyhood, hyper-femininity, modesty, self-control, and character-building thus shaped official discourses for regulating student life on both black and white campuses. In the 1920s, for instance, Auburn University women students were advised to be "ladies at all times" by dressing respectably and refraining from parties that were not properly chaperoned, while Columbia University's Teachers College held a series of fashion shows to encourage its "careless and indifferent" students to develop "economy and good taste" in their dress.[76] At the end of the decade, UK women students living in residence halls were given a handout delineating "Standards of Good Taste" which asserted that "augmenting personal charm and social ease is of eternal interest to women."[77]

Although the chaperonage of college women declined on northern college campuses throughout the 1920s and 1930s, women attending southern and black colleges continued to encounter strict guidelines for their conduct on and off campus. In 1921, the dean of women at UK described the social life of women students as much "too strenuous" and limited the number of dances and opportunities for women and men to meet without chaperones. In 1931, UK student newspaper reported that Dr. Ronald Lair, a psychology professor at Colgate University, had warned women students who were the "life of the party" that they were "destined to make a dull wife ten years later" since a girl in her "early twenties reaches the peak of her personality, [and] slowly burns out the activity of the thyroid gland, which directly controls such activity."[78] As late as 1939, women students at UK still needed permission from their parents and the dean of women to attend out-of-town dances, football games, and horse races. If their requests were approved, the university appointed special chaperons to accompany them to such events. University women were also prohibited from talking to men out of their windows or seeing them before noon. They were encouraged to attend only entertainments that were "simple, free from ostentatious display, and inexpensive."[79]

Such litanies of prohibitions were typically accompanied by specialized training. College deans and house-mothers encouraged women to date, but offered finishing-school-style instruction designed to enhance the propriety of heterosexual encounters. The University of Kentucky Dean of Women's Office, for example, helped to establish a campus dating bureau in the 1930s and offered numerous marriage training conferences, teas, and receptions to ensure opportunities for women to learn how to properly socialize with men.

Often, more stringent disciplinary policies were enacted to regulate the conduct and appearances of African American students. Stephanie Shaw has noted that the promotion of "circumspection and decorum" were important to both white missionaries who founded many black colleges throughout the South as well as the parents of students who attended them.[80] Atlanta University students, for instance, were trained in "those little outward signs of good breeding" and Scotia Seminary for Girls forbade all behaviors perceived to be "unladylike and disorderly."[81] Many white faculty and administrators at historically black campuses enacted a labyrinth of strict regulations designed to govern manners, morals, and appearances. Spelman College officials urged its students to join the White Shield Society, which sought to "develop purity of the heart, which shall manifest itself in conversation, dress, and conduct."[82] The White Shield Society required students not only to uphold the "laws of purity" and modesty but also to police the purity of their friends. Many college students themselves also affirmed the importance of official gendered criteria for collegiate cachet that were highly dependent upon visual appeal, poise, and self-presentation, and they policed themselves and their peers.[83]

Equating dress with racialized gendered integrity and moral character, dress codes were established to attempt to regulate student fashion on black campuses. Women at Fisk University, for example, were required to have "plain and becoming" clothing, and they were prohibited from wearing clothing with elaborate trimmings and gaudy jewelry. The Fisk University president also addressed the issue of men's fashion and manhood in at least one campus address. Evoking the modest and middle-class male as the ideal of visual assimilation against the specter of the unmanly and uncivilized "feathered Indian" and working-class Mexican immigrant, he stated that "the successful man of the world moves about inconspicuously and you would never recognize him by any outward and distinguishing mark. The real man is too busy to pose and too well-bred to attract attention."[84] Curfews and chaperones were common as many campuses policed and restricted opportunities for women and men to socialize. Men and women at Fisk University, for example, were prohibited from walking together on campus and women students were allowed to receive only one male caller for a half hour each week. Most student clubs at Fisk were gender-segregated. Likewise, women and men students at Atlanta's Morris Brown College could not socialize without official permission, and Spelman College women were allowed only twenty minutes a month to socialize with men under the watchful eye of the house matron. In 1927, male visits were extended to two hours a week.[85]

Despite university efforts to regulate and refine the bodies and behavior of college women, post–World War I transformations tied to consumerism, advertising, leisure, and emergent youth cultures helped to refigure and revamp collegiate conventions for respectability, sexuality, and self-expression. The pace and extent of these transformations in student cultures were, of course, dictated by region, race/ethnicity, and institutional setting. However, one can not assume student compliance with official prescriptions for gendered conventionality and respectability. Throughout the 1920s students on numerous campuses protested the labyrinth of gendered regulations that governed student life, including mandatory chapel attendance, military training, dress codes, and the supervision of women's and men's leisure and extra-curricular pursuits, as well as bans on smoking, drinking, fraternities and sororities, jazz and blues, and dancing.[86]

While gendered codes of conduct and dress persisted then as now, for many women, college would mean an exhilarating whirlwind of social activities including teas, proms, fashion shows, and pageants. More than thirty college dances and eighty fraternity and sorority dances were held each month at the University of Wisconsin in 1925.[87] Women students at Syracuse University in the 1920s identified "daily social contacts" as the most important aspect of their college experience.[88] Many people heralded the socially polished and fashionable college women of the 1920s by contrasting them with an earlier generation of college women represented as manly and dour "Bluestockings" who lacked true feminine appeal and desires. In 1933, the *New York Times*, for example, ran a series of articles describing the advent of a new generation of debonair and dashing college women. Based on surveys and interviews with representatives from fourteen college campuses, the report described a new era for college women in which "the once timid, despised bluestocking who crept into the back rows of the male classroom, and lived in drab boarding houses that she might vindicate her intellectual urge with a degree, has become the dashing college girl whose clothes and manners, are only less than those of movie stars."[89] Dean Sellery of the University of Wisconsin likened college women to social butterflies, noting that the "old-fashioned blue-stocking is pretty scarce nowadays."[90] As we shall see, these binaries of fashionable and flawed femininity and of pleasure and restraints would reappear in later decades in the clashes between student feminists and beauty contestants, and again in post-feminist rationales for participating in beauty contests.

The widespread venerations of fashionable and socially savvy college women in popular magazines, newspapers, advertising, student organizations, and, of course, in campus beauty pageants ushered in new types of gendered dysfunction such as the "socially awkward" college woman. Some deans of women developed programs to assist "socially inept women" at the same time that they maintained the traditional vigilant policing of college women to promote and protect respectability and moderation. Social success was considered by some deans and housemothers to be so vital that one dean asserted that there was "no problem more acute than that of the lonely left-out girl." [91] Many deans subscribed to the position that there were indeed new generational norms for gendered college success impelling them to ensure that "even the shyest modern college girl has her place in the social sun, as their predecessors worked to establish her in the academic shade."[92]

Training in middle-class modes of poise and social desirability would increasingly become part of the gendered curriculum as the undertow of regulation and constraint collided with a surge of new social pressures and opportunities. Attempts to reconcile the often contradictory agendas of gendered regulation with the promotion of panache and heterosexual allure would shape the experiences of women students at both historically black and predominantly white campuses throughout the twentieth century. As we shall see in the next chapter, campus beauty contests can serve as windows on shifting idealizations of scholastic femininity, tensions between self-restraint and self-display, the commercialization of college women, and the continuing impact of racially distinct educational legacies. Shifting patterns of segregation and integration on college campuses, in particuliar, would exacerbate these quandaries about successful collegiate womanhood as well as generate numerous battles over how collegiate coronets and honors were to be conferred.

3

Pride and Pulchritude

Campus Pageant Politics, 1920–1980

Beginning in the 1920s, numerous beauty contests were established on both historically black and white campuses. Throughout the ensuing decades, these pageant rituals were continually restyled in light of the changing demographics of college student bodies, especially shifting patterns of racial segregation and integration and the rise of feminist, civil rights, and black power student mobilizations. Campus pageant traditions were a continual flashpoint for campus conflicts, especially in the 1960s, when pageants encountered a barrage of critiques, including objectification of women and racial exclusion. Appraisals of campus pulchritude, respectability, and desirability have been historically variable and fluid. Generational differences in the investment, meanings, and performance of racialized and classed respectability, visual assimilation, and feminine distinction, as well as institutional and regional micro-cultures, impacted campus pageant protocols and oppositions.

In this chapter, I compare the founding of campus pageantry in the 1920s at KSU, a historically black campus—a higher education institution common throughout the South—and the predominantly white UK. After examining the differences and similarities between these racially segregated campus pageant traditions in the pre–civil rights era, I will trace the beauty battles that erupted on college campuses in the 1960s when increasing numbers of African American women began to challenge campus color barriers by entering formerly "white only" campus beauty pageants as a strategy to foster racial pride and challenge marginalization. I will also highlight the protracted racial turmoil that accompanied campus racial struggles at Indiana University throughout the 1950s and 1960s as black women sought not only to compete in historically white campus pageants but also to broaden the parameters for performances of student "beauty" itself.

Finer Womanhood and Racial Pride

Beauty pageantry is by no means a collegiate phenomenon restricted to a single region. College pageant rituals have been sites for performing regionally specific understandings of changing racialized gender relations throughout the U.S. Southern states, nonetheless, sponsor more local preliminaries to national pageants, such as Miss America, than do northern schools, and they host more county and commodity queen competitions as well.[1]

While Kentucky is a part of what has been called the southern "pageant belt," Kentucky differs from its more southern neighbors in having only a relatively small African American population. In the antebellum era, Kentucky had a significant number of slaves, but after Emancipation, many African Americans left the state. The largest concentration of African Americans today is in the state's two largest cities, Lexington and Louisville. A "border South state" during the Civil War, Kentucky is said to blend both southern and midwestern patterns of cultural and social life. If southern academic pageants have been barometers of regional differences in culture and history, that is, localized expressions, they nonetheless reflect shifting national articulations of gender and racial politics. Kentucky's college pageants have served as forums on race, class, and gender relations as well as for campus-based activism in eras of changing patterns of segregation and integration.

Kentucky State University, is an HBCU, was established in 1886 with a small state appropriation as the State Normal School for Colored Persons in Frankfort, Kentucky to train teachers for the state's segregated public schools. Although the nearby and privately funded Berea College had enrolled black students before the Civil War, with the passage of a 1904 state law prohibiting interracial education at both state and private colleges in Kentucky, KSU became a pivotal part of a Jim Crow educational system.[2] Racial segregation was not overturned until 1948 when African Americans won the right to attend UK (for graduate studies only) and again, in 1954, when white students were allowed to enroll at KSU. By 1975, KSU had become the most racially integrated university in Kentucky, raising fears that KSU would lose its black identity.[3] However, white students at KSU were primarily non-residential, part-time, and night students who tended not to participate in campus life. For the college's black students, campus pageantry has served to fortify KSU's African American identity and legacy.

KSU established its homecoming queen competition in 1929, and since then hundreds of queens and sweethearts have been crowned as exemplars of black beauty, middle-class respectability, and proper femininity. By 1975, over forty different queens reigned annually at KSU, including queens representing numerous academic departments and programs such as Miss African Studies, Miss Nursing, Miss Chemistry, Miss Gospel Ensemble, and Miss Criminal Justice.

Today, pageantry continues to play a significant role in KSU's student life, especially its "Miss Pride of KSU" contest, an official preliminary pageant for the Miss America competition, and the Mr. and Miss Kentucky State University pageant.[4] A lavish coronation ceremony is held each year for the newly crowned Miss and Mr. KSU. Queens are presented with the accoutrements? of royalty, including crowns, scepters, gold medallions, and billowing velvet robes. They are also given lavish gifts from student organizations and administrative staff, including the university president. Each Miss KSU queen has a royal court that includes her first and second attendants, "Lords and Ladies of Regalia," and numerous sub kings and queens who represent dormitories, Greek letter organizations, and student organizations such as the Baptist Student Union. Extravagant coronation spectacles for HBCU queens, and sometimes kings, have become customary as black campus pageants remain key venues for performing and showcasing racialized and classed accomplishments, as well as for challenging distorted white representations of black women and, more recently, black men.

KSU's pageants reflect the campus norms of other predominantly black southern colleges that have emphasized the development of middle-class manners, good grooming, and dignified self-presentation, especially for their women students.

In 1934, for example, several chapel colloquia at KSU were devoted to the importance of manners for racial advancement. In the same period, the university also sponsored etiquette weeks to enhance campus gentility and the "hostess skills" of its women students. The student newspaper served as a forum for social instruction in refinement and civility as well. The importance of adhering to dominant middle-class gender and class norms for manners, dress, deportment, leisure, and self-presentation—a redemptive strategy to counter damaging racial representations in popular culture and white racist attitudes—has been termed "the politics of respectability . . . a fluid and shifting position along a continuum of African American resistance."[5] Such a strategy entails constant body discipline as well as the adoption of class-coded norms for self-presentation to refute structural racism. African American college women have faced the complex burden of defying white racist myths and representations of their purported deficiencies in culture and subjectivity, asserting their own self-affirmations and definitions, and serving as gendered icons of middle-class blackness, racial uplift, and collective pride.[6] As Mary Helen Washington has argued, "burdened by the race's morality, black women could not be as free to think outside the boundaries of racial uplift; every choice they made had tremendous repercussions for an entire race of women already under the stigma of inferiority and immorality."[7] Throughout the twentieth century, black campus pageants have provided an opening to discern generational differences in performances of, and investments in, various anti-racism strategies including uplift, respectability, assimilation, separatism, civil rights, and Afro-centrism. Especially in the 1960s, racialized understandings of black collegiate beauty and performances of

Figure 3.1 Portrait of Miss Kentucky and her attendants embodying dignity and respectability. *Thorobred* Kentucky State University Yearbook. Courtesy of Kentucky State University Special Collections & Archives, 1953.

respectable womanhood were significantly altered by social movements for civil rights and black pride, which restyled the politics and aesthetics of campus pageants. But even then, as we shall see, restrictive gendered and classed norms for black women's bodies and behaviors continued to script beauty pageant performances and campus life.

Figure 3.2 Portrait of Kentucky State University queen signifying the importance of middle-class status and its accoutrements for racial pride. *Thorobred* Kentucky State University Yearbook. Courtesy of Kentucky State University Special Collections & Archives, 1953.

Nationally—beyond the confines of campus and across many decades—a variety of black educators and leaders have championed the internalization of middle-class behaviors and appearances to further the project of racial uplift and resistance. Black women's bodies, etiquette, and deportment became key signifiers of inner moral virtue and racial dignity. Black women's duty to their race thus included daily vigilance in dress and deportment. In 1922, for example, the *Half-Century Magazine for the Colored Homemaker* featured a story by a reporter, a.k.a. "The Investigator," who posed as an undercover fashion agent to ferret out the best and worst dressed black women on city streets. Lamenting the fashion atrocities she witnessed, the writer described one woman as being "so badly dressed that she made the investigator wonder whether or not her house had any mirrors in it."[8] Concerns about the public gaze were carefully registered on black campuses.

Just as today's women's magazines and reality TV makeover shows often dispatch undercover fashion detectives who ambush and transform sloppy and tasteless women, by the 1940s KSU had installed its own fashion operatives who regularly policed and published their verdicts on the outfits worn by women students and faculty to campus social occasions and even off campus to church. Good grooming, classy clothes, self-control, and politeness were integral to the ongoing class project of performing black collegiate ladyhood to elevate the race.

Fashion columns were thus regular features in KSU's student newspaper throughout the 1940s. In a long-running fashion column, "Correct, Collegiate, and Casual," student columnist Gwen Sherard provided a steady diet of advice for upgrading students' appearances. For example, in one column she warned that "stockings to a lady are essential to her apparel and her decency."[9] Clothes were described as just as important as academics for social mobility. In another column, in response to a dean's observation on sloppy dress in the university's dining halls, Sherard admonished students to avoid slovenly attire since such neglect signified an uncultured working-class disposition.

> Let us cooperate with her since she is right. One should finish college having added not only to his [sic] literary knowledge but also to his [sic] cultural knowledge. We may know what to wear and when but if we do not apply this knowledge it may be forgotten through disuse. Untidiness, sloppiness, and weird color combinations of solid colors and plaid and striped twosomes are displays of bad taste, neglect, and lack of attention.[10]

The conjoining of clothes, class, and character were at the heart of Sherard's fashion surveillance and her cultural policing of the KSU student body.

A 1941 newspaper column admonished women students of their perpetual responsibility to be tastefully dressed, especially in public, in order to avoid confirming racist stereotypes. To counter the panoptic white gaze, women students were expected to conduct themselves as if they were always on stage. They were warned that "when you leave your room for any occasion be sure your apparel is casual or collegiate and correct for the event. The eyes of Kentucky are upon YOU."[11] KSU women were thus bombarded with fashion and etiquette tips. Fashion columns such as "Correct, Collegiate, and Casual," were followed in later years by "Campus Attire," and in the 1960s by "Are You in the Know?" each extolling the virtues of fashion savvy and labeling fashion failures as racially reckless.

A 1960s student fashion columnist, Phyllis Stovall—a graduate of Nina's Beauty Salon and Modeling School before attending KSU—reminded her student peers that grooming and fashion require discipline and self-appraisal. She wrote:

In the feminine world, an attractive appearance is essential if you are going to deal successfully with the complexities of modern living. With good grooming goes self-confidence that helps you make the most of your personality and abilities. Your clothes are more than mere covering. To do justice to your appearance, you need knowledge of clothes and what they can do for you. Your first duty is to analyze yourself. You must give careful attention to every detail from the arrangement of your hair to the style of your shoes.[12]

In a later column, Stovall again emphasized that style and grooming were obligatory for black women, noting, "There is no such thing as a hopelessly ugly female. Beauties are made, not born. Your face is always on stage. Treat it well."[13] Women students were urged to be diligent in their beauty and grooming practices in order express racial dignity and elevate the collectivity. Beauty salons in women's dormitories and campus charm schools for women contributed to a gendered and racialized instructional landscape. Campus sororities regularly staged style shows featuring professional models, such as Miss Fashionetta, to help students in their image-making.

The student newspaper subjected faculty members and staff to fashion scrutiny as well, on and off campus. Columnist Sherard reported that

Mrs. C. J. Michaels was the subject of innumerable compliments for her two piece suit in a new shade of green with a stunning fur-trimmed plaid top coat at the homecoming game. Miss Ludye Anderson represented simplicity and dignified taste in black with a gorgeous set of silver fox furs. . . . Miss Anna Todd caused a rather loud murmur of admiration in church since she looked so ultra smart and striking in a black and red two piece suit. The top was bright red with black fur lapels. Her accessories were black except for her turban which matched the top of the suit.[14]

In 1942, Sherard again reported that while at church she "got a close-up of Miss Thelma Coleman's coat which is definitely new. The lines of the sleeves and yoke are this year's variation. Mrs. Lynem's coat of a bluish gray with black fur trimming was very becoming to her."[15] A reader of these fashion columns today cannot help but appreciate how deeply style and appearance were invested with racial significance on the KSU campus.

In such a campus culture, where composed bodies and temperaments signified class, gendered virtue, and racial advancement, it is not surprising that KSU queens and their attendants faced even more pressures to be visual exemplars of racial gentility, dignity, and charm than regular students. In the 1940s, KSU queen candidates were expected to be in "good standing morally" and to possess "finer womanhood, culture, charm, personality, and scholarship."[16] The 1958

Miss Kentucky State was admired for "her careful grooming, her genteel bearing, her quiet good sense, and her ever-readiness to be of service to others."[17] The 1962 Miss KSU was described as a lady-scholar embodying "womanhood, culture, charm, personality, and scholarship," descriptors that had been prevalent since the 1920s. This particular queen, seemingly aware of the representational and performative burdens of her reign, responded by saying that she hoped she "could live up to the attributes that Miss Kentucky is supposed to possess. I will try to carry myself in such a manner that the students will be proud of their selection."[18]

Alongside these pressures, however, KSU queens also enjoyed a great deal of veneration on campus. They were presented to large crowds at the halftimes of football homecoming games, received gifts, and represented their schools at a variety of ceremonies. They often traveled with the football team to represent KSU on other campuses. In 1941, several KSU queens participated in a national competition sponsored by Howard University to select the most beautiful women attending a black college. Former queens were often invited back to homecoming games for ceremonial reunions.

The reverence that queens at HBCUs receive is manifest in multiple ways including the lavishness of their coronation ceremonies, which has intensified throughout the twentieth century. In 1953, the coronation of Miss KSU was marked by a procession that included members of the varsity football team dressed in dark suits and white shirts, followed by numerous male and female representatives of student organizations, also dressed in formal finery. At the sound of a bugle, Miss KSU walked down the aisle wearing a white formal gown that contained thirty-five yards of satiny material and a purple cloak. She was given a key to the university by the president and a silver pitcher by the representative of a local chain store. She also received numerous feminine accessories, including handkerchiefs, compacts, bracelets, perfume, earrings, mirrors, and necklaces from various student groups and university officials, a gifting tradition that still exists today.

In 1954, a KSU student who had attended the coronation of Great Britain's Queen Elizabeth II initiated a new campus tradition of formally installing the new queen with a Grande March (which included university dignitaries) and a coronation ball to add glamour and dignity to the queen crowning. In 1971, the KSU coronation was again modified and, much like the presentation of Miss America, a ramp was added so that the queen and her court could enjoy a promenade before an approving crowd. Biographies and photographs of KSU campus queens have decorated campus publications and hallways for many years. Still today, many queens are revered and remembered long after their reigns including in retrospective hall of fame exhibits and queen reunions.

Most significantly, however, KSU queens have enjoyed much more than brief moments of adoration and fame at their coronations. Unlike the ephemeral attention usually given to white homecoming queens, black campus queens typically were—and are still—expected to be role models and inspirational campus leaders. KSU queens were not restricted to yearbook and student newspaper photographs as mute bodies on display. Instead, their prestige and expectations went far beyond the decorative.

Sarah Banet-Weiser has characterized some elements of the Miss America pageant as "subject-defining opportunities" that have allowed contestants some room to be "active thinking subjects," not just objectified bodies showcased in the swimsuit competition.[19] Black college queens were given even more opportunity to be vocal student leaders by writing columns in the newspaper, attending official functions, and speaking at college assemblies. Advice columns represented an important forum for queens to address their fellow students, a major departure from the lesser expectations for their queen counterparts at predominantly white educational institutions. KSU queens regularly urged students to think of them as friends and advisors and encouraged them to seek them out if they encountered any difficulties. Miss KSU 1970, for example, greeted incoming students with these words of advice on campus etiquette and gender relations:

> You are now a college student. Please act like it. Be a mature individual concerning your education. . . . Fit into our family. A little smile and hello isn't bad for anyone's system. Have respect for yourself and others. Men, please be gentlemen. Opening doors and carrying an extra tray may help you strengthen your muscles. Respect your beautiful black women and show us you're proud to be black. Have school spirit and show it. Women, act your part. Thank you's are always in order. You'll be respected if you act accordingly.[20]

Miss KSU 1974 counseled incoming students to "get involved" and to be proactive in crafting their life course, including finding a marriage partner. She told them that KSU offered many "outlets for students to enjoy. If one's main goal in college was to find a compatible spouse, we have an ample amount of males and females to go around. Kentucky is known for its fast horses and beautiful women. . . . Choose your majors wisely and consider the long range effects and job prospects."[21]

As we shall see more fully in chapter 5, queens at many historically black colleges and universities today continue to carry on highly visible activities as ambassadors of their campuses, helping in student recruitment, alumni relations, and college fund raising. They also attend extra-mural football games and compete in the Miss Black Alumni Hall of Fame pageant, and some have programming budgets at their disposal. As the result of the attention and leadership opportunities showered on KSU queens, contestants have typically taken royalty elections very seriously. In 1950, each candidate for Campus Sweetheart was represented by a male manager who presented her publicly and helped her to solicit votes.

One candidate placed poems and jingles written in her honor at every student dining table. In 1957, Frances Wilson, a Campus Sweetheart candidate, made her presence known on campus through "posters, show cards, candy suckers, kisses, and public appearances at dinners, lunches, and ball games," campaign practices that persist more than a half century later at KSU. [22] Not only did women work hard at wooing votes, but many contestants also attended special campus charm schools to help prepare them for their pageant performances and enhance their chances of winning campus thrones. [23]

While black campus pageants sought to showcase racial pride and black beauty standards, they were also tightly structured by conventional class and gender discourses. Indeed, black campus queens were expected to personify black middle-class codes of appearance and respectable conduct as part of the arsenal of strategies available to challenge the hegemony of racist caricatures. Visual markers of middle-class status including demure demeanor and elegant attire were especially significant elements in the staging and stylization of black campus royalty in photography. Markers of class distinction and refinement were consistently evident in the staging of KSU queens, who were photographed clad in finery evocative of white debutante balls, including white strapless satin gowns, pearl and rhinestone necklaces, elbow-length white gloves, and high heels. Given the meager funding of KSU, however, its queens were posed sitting on vinyl sofas and coffee tables, not before fine horse farms and mansions with their grand pianos, fireplace mantles, and wingback chairs signifying the genteel drawing room culture of the plantation South that frequently served as the opulent back-drops for the photographs of white queens at UK during the same era. Another noteworthy absence in most of the KSU as well as UK photographs was that of any academic accessories including books, except for one queen pictured in front of a bookcase and another who conveyed her student status by being photo-graphed carrying books on her way to class. Rarely were academic accomplish-ments or career goals highlighted; instead, the KSU photographs suggest that a finishing school culture would further racial progress.

Throughout the decades, KSU campus pageantry has served as a barometer for shifting racial and gender politics. Popular descriptors of the queens' attributes thus provide clues about the shifting politics of color and class operative in appraisals of black beauty and distinction. The physical measurements of pageant entrants were often splashed across the pages of the student newspaper, including height, weight, darkness of complexion, hair length and texture, and eye color as well as sorority membership and family background. In 1944, for instance, the campus newspaper detailed the charms of the contestants for Campus Sweet-heart by emphasizing their long straightened hair and light complexions. Indi-vidual contestants were described as having "a peaches and crème complexion," "a pretty face framed by long brown hair and a very winning smile," "a pretty, light complexion, big brown eyes, a cute pug nose, and a pretty little round face framed by long, long beautiful black hair—the kind that ripples and falls around in curls."[24] Although the practice of reporting physical measurements and skin tones of KSU queens in the student newspaper eventually disappeared, light-skinned women with straightened hair dominated the KSU queen competitions until the 1970s.

The advent of the 1960s and civil rights organizing, however, brought dramatic changes to the KSU campus and to other black colleges throughout the South as students and, in some cases, campus queens themselves, participated in sit-ins at segregated lunch counters and white businesses.[25] KSU students joined in these sit-ins and challenged campus regulations and norms that restricted the mobility of black women on and off campus.[26] Emergent representations and strategies for racial equality and pride that accompanied civil rights organizing, black power, and later Afro-centrism, began to modify facets of black campus beauty pageantry including the relaxing of some of the traditional hierarchies of colorism operative in black beauty pageants.[27] Manifest in such historical practices as paper bag tests for skin tone and flashlight tests (where one is positioned in profile to see if one's mouth or jaw extend beyond one's nose), colorism had often shaped black queen contests. One Howard University student observed "you could not be on the court unless you were very fair," and the queen was "always the whitest of the fair women on campus."[28] Yet queens began to challenge such colorism. Saundra Williams, for example, described her mission as Miss Black America 1968 as one where she could show that "black women could be beautiful even though they have large noses and thick lips."[29]

Nonetheless, conventional gender and class understandings were retained alongside these emergent representations of black beauty. Maxine Craig has observed that black women continued to face social pressure to conform to pre-vailing standards for appearance and manners. Feminist theorist Barbara Christian, coming to the U.S. from the Virgin Islands in 1959, for example, had been told by other African American students when she arrived at Marquette University that her failure to straighten her hair would make people "think of us as country," marking not only herself as unsophisticated, poor, and rural but all black women students. Straightened hair was a signifier of class and dignity since it "represented access to hair products, sanitation, leisure, and relative prosperity."[30] Clashes over the hair styles of campus queens have been ongoing ever since. Shampale Williams, Miss Voorhees College 2009, felt pressured by college administrators to relax her hair and Miss University of Maryland Eastern Shore reported that numerous students assumed she would get a weave or perm now that she was a queen.[31]

Yet in response to transformations in racialized practices and symbols wrought by the black power movement in the 1960s, many HBCU campus queens began to challenge normative conceptions of black beauty and distinction on their campuses and some queens broke the hegemony of processed hair and in-group colorism as well as the whiteness of their attire and their pageant performances. In 1973, several KSU queen contestants had Afros and refused to wear the traditional white gloves and dresses since they were "too much of a white image." They chose to compete in African-inspired clothing instead. The coordinator of the KSU charm school for queens, however, lamented this disruption of pageant traditions.[32] Subsequently, however, darker-skinned women with natural hairstyles were more likely to be chosen as queens at KSU. The 1972 Miss KSU pageant also dramatized these changing racial politics by including a narration about the significant presence of black women in struggles for equality. This particular pageant featured a tribute to black students who had recently lost their lives in student unrest at Southern University in Louisiana. It included a "Pan-Africanist lying-on of hands" ceremony, and after being carried down an aisle by four men, Miss Black Student Union was presented with gifts symbolizing "black ideology and aspirations."[33]

Although KSU's black beauty pageants have challenged white disparagements of black beauty and culture and have provided spaces for communal re-representation, affiliation, pride, and respectability, they have perpetuated conventional class and gender norms nonetheless and thus may have limited the range of possibilities for campus visibility and merit as well as strategies for racial re-definitions available to black college women. By the late 1960s, increasing numbers of black college students in the South were attending predominantly white institutions such as UK. At such institutions, they encountered distinctive pageant traditions for the performance of racialized understandings of femininity that had been constructed in formerly white-only spaces. African American students not only began to compete in these historically white pageants but they also imported black-only pageants that had been forged on historically black campuses to these once-segregated institutions.

The University of Kentucky "Campus Cuties"

The University of Kentucky is located only thirty miles from KSU. Its pageant history provides a rich opportunity for tracing similarities and differences in the constructions of class, race, and gender at a predominantly white university. Established in 1865, as a public land grant university, UK opened a normal department in 1880, which paved the way for the first enrollment of women students. Like their counterparts at KSU, white women students at UK faced normalizing conventions for determining their place in higher education, including a barrage of gender differentiated instruction and expectations. Although white women had the privilege of not having to challenge racial stereotypes, they did have to prove that their presence in a formerly men's educational world would not undermine their heterosexual desirability or future motherhood responsibilities.

If attending coeducational institutions threatened traditional constructions of southern white femininities, such fears might be neutralized by ritualized displays of hyper-femininity in beauty pageants. Consequently, campus beauty pageants played a role in constructing campus women as merely "campus cuties" and ladies, softening their intellectual presence and constricting their participation in campus life.

In rapid succession throughout the 1920s, a series of UK queen pageant traditions was inaugurated. In 1921, male students of the College of Agriculture elected a Fall Festival Queen, and in 1924, the first May Day Queen was selected by a vote of male students. In the 1920s, an annual beauty and popularity contest was initiated by the UK student yearbook, The *Kentuckian*, which soon became the most visible and popular pageant on campus. Wearing white gowns and gloves and with their contestant numbers hung like long necklaces around their necks, thirty to fifty women competed annually to be Miss Kentuckian by parading in front of panels of male judges. As described in the 1943 UK yearbook, "some 40 cuties, dressed in their finery and preened to perfection, paraded across the stage to be viewed.... Pictures of the seven finalists were then sent to a group of military men and these men had the task of choosing the queen and her attendants in order of their pulchritudinous appeal to military men."[34]

Picking the most beautiful coed for the Kentuckian Queen and her seven royal attendants soon became serious university business. Invitations to Hollywood producers and modeling agency representatives to help select UK queens indicated the complicity of campus pageantry in the commercialization of collegiate beauty. In 1929, Cecil B. DeMille came to UK to judge contestants. The *Kentucky Kernel* cheered this event, asserting that it was "essentially feminine to want to be beautiful and to have that beauty accepted as such by associates."[35] The 1930 contest for Miss Kentuckian was judged by Earl Carroll, editor of *Vanities* magazine, who proclaimed that he was searching for women students who possessed "charming physiques." He contended that the judging process would be easier if "each candidate would put their weight, height, neck, bust, waist, hips, thigh, calf, ankle [measurements] ... on the back of their photographs, risking disqualification if the measurements were not correct."[36] In 1939, UK men were complimented on their abilities to differentiate between true beauties and ladies and "artificial slinky vamps and baby-faced dumb-bells" for inclusion "on the university's glamour list."[37] The 1964 Kentuckian Queen contest continued this longstanding hunt for natural beauties and ladies when contestants were judged on their "natural beauty, manners, gracefulness, carriage on stage, and the ability to conduct oneself properly and with becoming composure."[38]

Explicit attention to ladyhood and body proportions thus shaped Miss Kentuckian queen contests for decades. In 1944, John Robert Powers, director of the Powers Modeling Agency, a judge for the Miss America pageant and a popular campus pageant circuit judge, noted that the photographs of that year's candidates were all exceedingly attractive but that his choice for queen was based on her "apparent alertness, intelligence, and innate charm—as well as features and contours of the face. My interest in and admiration for the natural girl has, of course, been the main criterion in judging this contest."[39] Ongoing invitations to Hollywood producers and modeling agency representatives to help in the selection of UK queens indicate both the investment of campus pageantry in mainstream gender norms and beauty ideals as well as the commercialization of campus pageantry. Mercantile trends accelerated in subsequent years when UK campus queens assumed modeling and marketing duties, both on campus and off, including selling shoes, clothing, and industrial and agricultural products and appearing in department store fashion shows, precursors to today's campus "brand ambassadors."[40]

Class and gendered desirability were tightly trussed and, as a result, UK offered women many opportunities to enhance both their class and sexual appeal. Even non-title-seeking students were expected to make the most of themselves through beauty and charm instruction. Deans of women encouraged them to participate in charm schools, dating bureaus, marriage conferences, and those extracurricular activities that affirmed the importance of heterosexual appeal, romance, marriage, and the acquisition of various "standards of good taste in appearance and hospitality" associated with southern ladyhood.[41] Like universities elsewhere, UK hired staff not only to oversee women's conduct but also to address deficiencies in their appearances and in their performances of social graces. In 1934, for example, Mrs. Ethel LeBus was appointed as the "official hostess" of the Women's Building, a central gathering place for women students. Serving as an official campus hostess—and by exuding "her charm as a gentlewoman"—LeBus was expected to be a "social confidante and arbiter" helping women students become refined and cordial ladies.[42] The imperative for campus women to enhance their desirability was also reinforced by a beauty salon for women in the student center that advertised itself with the proclamation "There is nothing more pleasing than having people admire your appearance."[43]

Dating bureaus were also seen as useful ways to increase the social competencies of women students as well as provide opportunities for finding a mate. In order to provide women students in the residence halls with an "opportunity to develop social graces and social intercourse," the "Hitching Post" was established in 1939 to afford "students an opportunity to mix with students of the opposite sex under strictly supervised conditions making it possible for ordinarily timid students to make acquaintance of attractive companions."[44] A subsequent article in the student newspaper promoted this dating service by pointing out that "a man may look over qualifications of prospective dates and decide whether to choose a blonde, a brunette, a sphinx, or a chatterbox."[45] In 1956, UK women were told that if they were "really desperate," they would have the best chance of finding men by enrolling in engineering courses and staying away from education.[46] UK was not alone in such endeavors to transform timid students and facilitate their hunt for men. Many campuses sponsored similar programs throughout the U.S.

In addition to these efforts to enhance women's appeal to men through dating and social savvy, their attire was closely monitored, although white UK women did not have the added burden of racism to overcome with their apparel. Although not as frequent as the fashion columns written for KSU's black women students, columns such as "Co-Ed Corner" did sometimes appear in UK student newspapers throughout the 1950s. Later, in response to the upheavals of the 1960s, an editorial in the UK student newspaper bemoaned the new manliness of female attire on campus and the scarcity of "ladies." Observing the "masculine appearance in the dress of UK coeds," the editors asserted that "no coed dressed in slacks can possibly have the admiration of her peers or her superiors" or compete with a woman "who looks like a lady and acts in a manner becoming her sex."[47]

The escalating visibility and commercialization of campus pulchritude went largely unabated, except during the late 1930s, when the practice of sending UK campus queens to compete in numerous commercial and industry festivals off campus was challenged by the UK dean of women's office. In 1936, two events set off a campus commotion. After photographs of UK women appeared in the magazine *Physical Culture*, Dr. Sarah Blanding, who later became the first women president of Vassar College, wrote the UK president saying that such exposure was "cheap and sensational" and that the magazine was known for its promotion of sex.[48] Soon thereafter, the organizers of the Shenandoah Apple Blossom Festival in Virginia requested a student beauty to compete in its pageant and Blanding again wrote the UK president saying: "I am wondering if the time has come to curtail this sort of activity. Although students like to go, I feel it is the kind of exploitation which we should discourage." Three years later, the UK dean of women's office took direct action to reduce the number of campus queens competing in the pageant and festival circuit. Declaring that too many demands were being made on the university "to supply beauties" to beer carnivals, civic festivals, and bathing beauty contests, Blanding organized a state wide Campus Queen Committee at the 1939 annual meeting of the Kentucky Association of Deans of Women to evaluate queen activities.[49] Her committee strongly rebuked the practice of supplying women students to local festivals. It issued a report concluding that "the use by commercial interests of our institutions and their representatives for the furtherance of purposes that have no direct relation to educational objectives" was distasteful, and that they intended to do "everything within our power to discourage the exploitation of our women students for commercial purposes."[50] For Blanding, the most explicit commercialization of such commodity-based pageants, such as the tobacco festival, threatened to undermine more refined notions and performances of southern campus beauty.

UK did stop sending its campus queens to the Kentucky Tobacco Carnival but Transylvania University, another Lexington college, sent three students to represent that university at the carnival dance and coronation. The practice of sending beauty queens to other civic/commodity festivals did not abate, however, despite the strong stance taken by Sarah Blanding and the Kentucky Association of Deans of Women in regard to the tobacco festival. The dean of women's office, for instance, continued to ensure that UK's beauties were represented at other festivals, including the Kentucky Mountain Laurel Festival held annually in Pineville, Kentucky, since 1931. In 1940, Blanding wrote to UK President Frank McVey that she had selected a student to represent UK at the Kentucky Mountain Laurel Festival who was not only related to some festival supporters but was also "considered one of our campus beauties. She is an able student and she will be a dignified and charming representative for the university."[51] The decision to withdraw UK queens from the tobacco festival created unfavorable press, however. For example, the *Cincinnati Enquirer* asserted that the decision was illogical since "Lexington depends more upon tobacco for its prosperity than upon mountain laurel or rhododendron."[52] It would not be until the late 1960s that queen contests at UK would again face significant criticism and modification.

This concern over commercialization and exploitation of women students did not extend to campus publications. With greater access than KSU students to luxurious Bluegrass mansions, UK queens were frequently featured in these rarefied spaces in campus publications.

Such photographs provided the main source of visibility and acknowledgment of women's presence on this southern campus. Despite an abundant photographic presence, however, UK queens were rarely given opportunities to be speaking subjects, unlike their African American counterparts at KSU. Instead, they were merely displayed as mute, ornamental bodies and praised for their desirability and decorum with descriptors such as "genteel and ladylike," "ravishing, sultry type of beauty," "unpretentious charm," "fragile beauty," and "sweetness." Rarely was academic prowess mentioned. The 1950 yearbook characterized one campus queen as a "well-established campus cutie . . . she has a smile which keeps you guessing, . . . quiet but quick-witted, . . . our vote for the girl we'd most like to have for a secretary." In a rare reference to intellect, however, one queen was described as "something new in the classroom . . . soft hazel eyes which bespeak brains as well as beauty." Depictions of UK queens such as these that characterized them foremost as beauties and not as scholars attest to women's intellectual diminishment on UK's post-war campus.

In addition to traditional displays of feminine beauty and charm, white regional identities, connected to a slaveholding past and southern womanhood, were conspicuously woven into UK campus activities throughout the 1950s.[53] The spouse of Margaret Mitchell was a UK graduate, an association that was touted in local media. The publication of Mitchell's book *Gone with the Wind* in 1936 provided a blueprint for subsequent campus pageantry and racial politics. Bell-shaped white

Figure 3.3 The 1959 Kentuckian Queen. Opulent display of southern white ladyhood. *The Kentuckian* Yearbook. Courtesy of the University of Kentucky Special Collections and Digital Programs, 1959.

dresses became popular among UK queens along with white parasols and wide-brimmed hats. The Kappa Alpha fraternity held an annual Old South Ball where male participants wore Confederate uniforms. Other fraternities sponsored "Dark Town Strutter Balls" where brothers wore blackface. A white contestant in the 1952 "Ugly Man" competition wore blackface and a dunce cap, displayed protruding lips, and wore ropes around his neck. Slave auction parties were also part of campus life. The annual Lances Carnivals, sponsored by a junior men's leadership society, exhibited white women students on a platform and then auctioned them to slave dealers to raise money for a men's scholarship fund throughout the 1950s.[54] Although the Lances slave auction went unchallenged, the dean of women did pronounce the student newspaper's weekly series the "Kentucky Kernel Kuties," which featured women students in a variety of suggestive poses, an affront to good taste in 1958.[55]

Although African Americans were employed on campus, it was not until 1936 that African American women were allowed to serve meals in UK's women's dorms and then only after they had submitted themselves to physical examinations. African American students were not permitted to attend UK until 1949, when a group of twenty-nine African American students were allowed to enroll in graduate programs at UK. Tables were reserved for these students in both the cafeteria and library, and they were banned from social functions and campus housing.[56] By the late 1960s, however, the increased presence of black students on white campuses, along with the civil rights and women's movements, had begun to significantly impact pageant traditions at UK and other universities. As we shall see, desegregation generated new anxieties at UK and elsewhere, just as the increased attendance of white students at KSU also proved threatening. National struggles against racism and sexism began to permeate and modify the scripts of many traditional campus pageants, generating widespread beauty bashing as well as the establishment of numerous new beauty pageant traditions on campuses throughout the U.S. Some campuses such as UK, however, maintained the whiteness of their primary beauty pageants long after other campuses were embroiled in racial battles about the complexion of their pageants.

Contesting the Color of Campus Pulchritude: Beauty Battles at Indiana University

Beginning in the 1950s, as more women of color began to attend formerly segregated universities, a few of them were victorious on campus catwalks. In 1950, for example, a woman of part-Asian descent was crowned Miss Football at the University of California at Berkeley after competing against queens from eight other universities. In 1951, Clarice Davis was the first African American woman to win the homecoming queen contest at the University of Illinois. Nominated by her black sorority, Davis said "I know that it won't be me standing there. It is a symbol of something we've always worked for. . . . Our school has the reputation of being the most prejudiced of all of the Big Ten schools. Now all of these impressions are broken."[57] However, such victories produced backlash.

In 1959, Nancy Streets, an African American student, was chosen by her sorority, Alpha Kappa Alpha (the first black sorority), to enter the Miss Indiana University pageant, a preliminary feeder pageant for Miss America. Her sorority sisters told her, "Don't worry about it—we know you won't win, but we want to be represented."[58] She competed in a bathing suit competition that was closed to the public in front of five white judges, which included the Bloomington mayor, three faculty members, and a representative of Merle Norman cosmetics. Subsequently, Streets and fourteen white finalists paraded and performed in front of a crowd of 700 people. Streets won the competition and her victory was heralded as a racial victory in many quarters, including *Ebony, Jet,* and *Tan* magazines and black college student newspapers. The *Indiana Daily Student* reported that "crowning of queens at IU is almost a weekly chore for someone. In this case, we do not think that Miss Streets will soon be forgotten since she is a Negro. We extend sincere congratulations to her and hope she becomes Miss Indiana and goes on to win the prize plum of them all, Miss America."[59]

Not everyone celebrated this racial breakthrough, however. Subsequently, as queen, she was barred at gunpoint from entering a skating ring and rode in a segregated float in the pageant parade. She later said: "If I ever came close to a nervous breakdown, it was that summer. I felt scrutinized, as though I was being controlled by someone else."[60] Even though it was typical to devote ten pages of the yearbook to various campus queens, the Miss IU pageant was not featured that year although numerous other less prestigious queens such as the Sweater Queen received ample coverage. In a later interview about her exclusion from the yearbook, she stated: "When my picture did not appear in the yearbook, it felt like I just didn't exist as a human being. It still makes me angry. I just wanted the university to recognize that I was a human being."[61]

Streets' victory inflamed many white alumni and Indiana University president Herman Wells received numerous letters expressing outrage, disbelief, and fears that her victory would lead to no less than the extinction of the white race. In one tirade, a man wrote:

> You must have a mighty sorry looking batch of white girls over there (which I doubt) forasmuch as it would not be possible for a thick lipped, flat-nosed negress to be given such acclamation. In the first place sir, it is not normal for white people to look at Negros as objects of beauty. It is for this reason that we have a white race at all. . . . You may look at the nations of the world who have integrated with the blood genes of Africa and measure their backwardness. Take a look at Brazil and Portugal, . . . the story is always the same. These people have a biological blight upon them. Once you scramble an egg—and once we are mingled—those blue eyes are gone forever.[62]

Wells replied to this letter by saying, "I dare say you are more than correct in your assumption that we have many very beautiful white girls. In this contest, however, the five judges deemed the negro girl most beautiful and talented."[63] A former Indiana University alumna, herself a former beauty queen contestant there, wrote that although she had taught her children to be "tolerant" of other races, she would never allow them "to sleep or eat with or to date other races." She concluded by saying "Now, Mr. Wells, just what is Indiana University trying to encourage, if not all of this, by electing a colored girl as the campus queen?"[64]

By the 1960s, campus pageants across the country were increasingly vulnerable to critiques that they were elitist, sexist, and racist. Attempts to legitimate and redesign beauty pageantry on college campuses would escalate in light of changing gender and race politics and student demographics. As black students began to attend predominantly white universities in greater numbers, pageants slowly began to mirror these changes and become sites for racial contestation. Black student organizations on predominantly white campuses across the country regularly sponsored candidates for campus crowns in the late 1960s.[65] Maxine Craig has observed that beauty pageants offered a "highly symbolic and easily organized focus" during the 1960s for the liberal integrationist strategies associated with the NAACP.[66] Nationally, the NAACP protested the exclusion of black women from the 1968 Miss America pageant and staged its own separate pageant, while women's liberation groups protested Miss America as both a sexist and racist spectacle degrading all women. In regard to these racial strategies, Craig aptly notes that black contestants challenged "the content of contests but not its form. On the contrary, their demands for inclusion reinforced the legitimacy of beauty contests as institutions that celebrate women."[67] Although the inclusion of a few light-skinned African American women, such as Nancy Streets, crossed pageant racial borders, their resemblance to white queens with light skin and straightened hair served to reinscribe racialized standards of beauty.[68] Challenging prevailing definitions of beauty itself, however, would soon become the focus of many campus struggles.

In 1968, Indiana University became the scene of yet another beauty battle that produced widespread turmoil on and off campus. After Indiana University eliminated the classist and racist rule that homecoming queen candidates had to be related to an alumnus of Indiana University, five African American students and forty-one white women entered the 1961 homecoming queen competition. Each contestant submitted a photograph and an application reporting their height, weight, complexion, bust, and hip measurements. The forty-six entrants were then judged on beauty (70 percent), personality and charm (20 percent), and interview skills (10 percent) by a panel of all white judges. Ten finalists were then selected from the pool. None of the African American women made the top ten list, and they subsequently filed suit with the University's Joint Committee on Discriminatory Practices (JCDP), arguing that white standards of beauty were operative in the pageant and that relying on one standard of beauty automatically discriminates against students of other ethnic groups with differing standards of beauty. Former Indiana University basketball coach Branch McCracken, one of the judges, reported that "one of the black women he had rated highly had not made the top ten." He then raised questions about the sizable percentage given to beauty in the homecoming pageant and asked "what is beauty and does beauty differ between black and white women?"[69]

As a result, the JCDP opened an investigation into the matter of what is campus beauty. Campus hearings were held and members of the JCDP received numerous letters, including a statement from the seven faculty members of the Department of Anthropology who opposed campus beauty pageants on the grounds of cultural bias. In their statement to JCDP, these anthropologists argued:

Concepts of beauty, like all other cultural things, are learned and therefore peculiar to each society. In this regard no one has been able to establish an acceptable, universal set of criteria to evaluate beauty among all
people. This is because such criteria are totally arbitrary: beauty is what
people say it is at a given moment and in a given place, nothing more,
nothing less. Consequently we regard any attempt to select beauty
queens as an exercise in cultural selectivity in which the criteria for judgment have been predetermined in the minds of the judges simply because
they, like everyone else, have been brought up to see and appreciate some
things more than others. Such cultural bias is perhaps one of the most
profound and subtle of human characteristics everywhere in the world.
People favor that with which they are most familiar and what they have
been taught to prefer.[70]

They further argued that,

given the racial climate in the United States, an all-white panel of judges
could not possibly be expected to act in a totally unbiased fashion given
the inter-group relations in the country as a whole. Moreover, it is
grossly unfair to encourage participation of representatives of any single
sub-cultural group within the society in such contests when there is no
way of controlling subtle biases; when cultural standards of beauty are
not made explicit beforehand; and, when most of the judges are, in a
sense, representatives of the majority group in society.[71]

Subsequently, the members of the JCDP ruled unanimously that the homecoming queen contest was void. In their recommendation to President Wells,
they wrote that "white physical characteristics were the standard and Black candidates could not compete on the basis of selection weighted towards physical
beauty of a certain type . . . no beauty contest can fairly consider entrants of different races or ethnic groups whose physical and behavioral characteristics
depart materially from the standard of the dominant segment of society, which
in this case means an American white standard." Furthermore, since "honors,
distinctions, and rewards" were not available equally to all students, white students enjoyed advantages not available to others. Although the committee recognized that there might be "ethnic group preferences for certain kinds of
performances and styles of communication," in order to minimize the discriminatory effects, the category of "general appearance which included poise, posture, and grace" should be reduced to only 10 percent of the competition and 90
percent should be based on talent and interviews, ignoring how these forms of
competition are also racialized and classed. Even though the JCDP felt that significantly different group standards existed with respect to general appearance,

"it appears improbable and perhaps not desirable to eliminate this criterion from the contest."[72] To reduce bias on the part of judges, it was suggested that a pool of judges should be familiar with the "various styles of communication and styles of appearance of the student body."[73] They also asserted that such modifications were especially urgent "in a time when social, political, and educational institutions stand in need of new and bold approaches for eliminating all vestiges of racism."[74] Notably, the committee left untouched the questions of sexism and classism in such contests and did not ban campus pageants indefinitely. Instead, the committee scrambled to accommodate pageant forms to new standards of racial inclusivity.

When President Wells concurred with the decision to annul the 1968 pageant, pandemonium ensued. Other campus queen contests were cancelled the same year and many interested parties spewed their fury in heated exchanges with Wells and in the press. An editorial in the *Lebanon Reporter* shrieked: "A homecoming football game without a homecoming queen is like a pancake house without pancakes, a campaign without any candidates, or a war with no Bob Hope." Furthermore, the editor raged that any beauty contest is "discriminatory by virtue of the fact that not everyone is beautiful. Drawn to its logical conclusion, the contest, could never be held because men could not enter being inferior in looks to females. And then there probably cannot be adequate representation of Eskimos or Chinamen, or women from the Ubangi tribe of Africa."[75] Two faculty members of the Indiana University School of Law wrote Wells as well as the local newspaper to protest the decision to have an empty throne. They stated that "we are not black racists, we are not supporters of George Wallace and Lester Maddox, and we do not believe that the Confederacy will rise again. We are our own minority group, in that we have a puerile belief in the effectiveness of common sense and fairness when brought to bear on such problems. That is, we believe that the future of the University should not be dictated by a dissident handful."[76] Another man wrote simply that "there must be more Commies, Bohemians, left-wingers, and plain stupid asses at IU than I even suspected. The place stinks."

Wells carefully responded individually to each of the letters he received. For example, he told one angry critic that "the one great hope of America, from the earliest settlers on, has been to find a country in which achievement is not limited by barriers of class, race, color, or religion."[77] In other letters, he apologized for his delay in answering by noting that the deluge of mail he had received regarding the queen conflict had overtaxed the capabilities of his office.

The conflict over beauty queens spread like wildfire to other Indiana University campuses, such as South Bend, where battle lines were drawn over whether or not to hold the Miss IUSB contest in March 1969. Dean Lester Wolfson wrote President Wells as well as local newspapers stating his belief that the IUSB contest should be held as scheduled even though he was not a fan of campus beauty contests. He asserted defensively that although he did not think the "question of racism in beauty contests is trivial," he believed that "in the stresses of these difficult times, some forget that many people whose motives are being questioned have spoken out against or worked for the removal of racism (and the human diminishment of women) in our society long before it became a part of public style to do so." He also argued that the Miss IUSB contest was different from the Miss Indiana University contest since it was a scholarship/talent pageant. He also noted that the contract between its two sponsors, the IUSB student government and the Michigan City Chamber of Commerce, did not mention the word "beauty" and stipulated that the scoring was based on talent (50 percent), personal grooming and poise (25 percent), and character (25 percent). He pointed out that the Chamber of Commerce had agreed "to conduct a fair and open pageant without discrimination relative to race, religion, and color of the participating contestants." In short, he contended that the pageant was designed "primarily as a talent and scholarship event" and thus anticipated a pageant rhetoric that would become increasingly prevalent among subsequent participants and defenders.[78]

The IUSB Student Affairs committee also pondered the racial politics of the Miss IUSB pageant and whether or not the competition should be held. One member of the committee said that no pageant judge could fairly rate "poise, charm, wit, and talent" since any evaluation of femininity and beauty was "culturally dictated." Another said there was prejudice even in a poetry contest and no judge could make "an impartial judgment without particular cultural overtones even between two black groups singing Gospel songs or dancing."[79] In a contrary decision to Dean Wolfson, the committee recommended that the pageant no longer be sponsored by student government. However, because it was too late to modify the pageant that year, it was allowed to take place.

The battle continued, however, when R. Scott Madison, representing the Students for a Democratic Society, wrote the JCDP in Bloomington saying that "the SDS has for some time opposed the staging of this pageant on the grounds that it tends to foster both economic and racial discrimination. . . . (Dean) Wolfson has termed the matter trivial and does not appear to be disposed to act. We insist that the concerned parties move with all speed to enforce university policy and stop the pageant."[80] The JCDP then held an emergency meeting to consider the charges of "unlawful racial and economic discrimination and male chauvinism" brought against the Miss IUSB contest. The committee noted that it was not part of its mandate to consider "expressions of male chauvinism apparent in the pageant and would consider itself paternalistic and parietal to suggest judgments in this regard." However, it did insist that "equitable provisions be made for the multi-ethnic character of the university." The committee applauded the use of sponsors for funding contestants as well as providing pageant garb gratis to help equalize economic barriers. It also ruled that the procedures for judging multicultural talent by relying on a panel of five "well-cultured judges" (white) was discriminatory and that judging procedures must thus be modified to account for "multicultural manifestations in talent."[81] However, classist and racialized assumptions embedded in appraisals of poise, talent, and self-presentation were not interrogated.

Indiana University campuses, however, did not remain without campus queens for long. The JCDP aptly observed that although a "beauty contest will never be free from some trace of discrimination, the strong desires on parts of the university community to sponsor contests that feature some manner of selection involving a judgment based on physical appearance" is a deeply rooted tradition. Although innumerable tiaras have been bestowed on Indiana University students since the 1960s, it was not until 1996 that Erica Hart was crowned as the first black homecoming queen at IU. After her reign, Hart said she "felt pride and fulfillment about another opportunity to serve. It gave me multiple opportunities to speak publicly about the university as well as the high quality of students we have in our African American student body."[82] However, her victory, too, was marred by racial politics. An alternative student publication, the *Griot*, chastised the *Indiana Daily Student* for its failure to cover the crowning and a heated volley occurred in print between the two newspapers.[83]

Indiana University was not the only campus where pageants became lightning rods for racial strife, but it was the scene of one of the earliest clashes. Campuses such as UK, with its regionally distinctive traditions of racial segregation and campus ethos, proved to be more impervious to efforts to challenge the color of beauty in its pageant traditions. It was not until 1979, long after numerous universities had crowned black homecoming queens, including the University of Michigan, San Jose State University, and even its neighboring Morehead State University, also in Kentucky, that racial challenges were made to white hegemony in UK pageants.[84] In that year, the UK Black Student Union protested that its contestants had not been judged fairly in interviews and that none of the sixteen African American women who competed had been selected as finalists in the historically white homecoming contest. Members of the BSU argued that although African Americans constituted only 2 percent of the student population at UK, they should have had at least one group representative in the finals.[85] After a meeting between the Black Student Union and university officials, the homecoming finalist field was enlarged to include an African American student, a decision that prompted subsequent editorials in the student newspaper that chastised the administration for "weakness" in caving in to "special interests" and giving black students "special treatment."[86] To date, UK has never elected an African American homecoming king or queen. Well into the new millennium, many campus pageants continue to spark contestation when historical racial boundaries are trampled. This has been most noteworthy at the University of North Carolina, where black contestants won a majority of homecoming titles in the 1990s, as well as the recent wins of non-black queens at HBCUs, including KSU, in 2009.[87]

At the same time that efforts were being mounted to integrate pageants on traditionally white campuses, black-only pageants were also imported from HBCUs. Black-only pageants on predominantly white campuses were less likely to encounter white resistance since they often received less official backing and attention from the university and the student body. Thus the late 1960s ushered in the establishment of new black-only pageants, such as the Miss Black Student Union queen competition at UK in 1969. The 1970 UK yearbook published a section on black beauty that featured a dark-skinned queen with unstraightened hair that embodied an emergent black aesthetic that challenged both white standards of beauty and the former supremacy of lighter skin contestants in traditional black pageants, such as those at KSU. The popularity of racial and ethnic pageants on predominantly white campuses would continue to grow in popularity, as we shall see in chapter five.

Pageants and Liberation

Racial inclusion was not the only minefield that historically white pageants had to navigate as traditionally white campus pageant supporters and participants were increasingly required to defend queen contests by modernizing pageant protocols and discourses. New legitimization strategies were needed to deflect the flood of students critiquing and mocking white pageants as shallow displays of physical charm and popularity. White pageants were especially vulnerable to critiques of chauvinism, racism, and objectification of women's bodies spearheaded by second-wave women's liberation groups spawned by the famous 1968 feminist protests at the all white Miss America pageant in Atlantic City that included skits protesting the use of Miss America as a military mascot, a life-size Miss America puppet, and the "Freedom Trash Can" which contained trappings of female enslavement including padded bras, girdles, corsets, high heels, and *Playboy, Ladies Home Journal*, and *Cosmopolitan* magazines.[88] (Significantly, no bras were burned because of a city ordinance although feminists have been branded and dismissed as bra burners and anti-beauty ever since these 1968 protests.) Also, on the same day in Atlantic City, the NAACP sponsored the Miss Black America contest which was spared of all the protest that accompanied Miss America earlier in the day. However, one beauty pageant protester, Robin Morgan was reported to have said that "Basically, we are against all beauty contests. . . . We deplore Miss Black America as much as Miss White America but we understand the issues involved."[89] Saundra Williams, the winner of Miss Black America and student organizer of a protest march against the "white business community," dismissed the protesters saying "they are expressing freedom, I guess . . . to each their own."[90]

Ironically, one result of feminist agitation was that some college men began to compete for, and then mock, the crown. For example, Vince Statens, a humor columnist for *The Daily Beacon*, ran for homecoming queen at the University of

Tennessee in 1970 as a joke. Staten said "If the students want to elect a boy, a sponge, or a tube of toothpaste as Homecoming Queen, they should be able to."[91] Wearing a paper bag, he received the support of many students who voted for him in order to counter the Greek dominance of homecoming activities. He won the election but was later disqualified because he was not an officially recognized candidate. Some of the queen contestants that year reported that they were distressed by Staten's mockery of tradition. One contestant reportedly said that "she had worked her whole college career to be queen."[92] There would not be another homecoming queen at University of Tennessee until 1983.

In 1975, UK boldly considered dropping its entire homecoming queen contest "as a sexist institution that had outlived its usefulness," but decided instead to "de-sex it." The student body president announced "that males would be judged equally with female contestants, according to overall appearance, poise, and their ability to answer the judges' questions," despite the fact that several fraternity presidents said they "would be disappointed if a male took the spotlight from women."[93] Two men entered UK's competition that year. One, a member of the Gay Students' Coalition, became the target of harassment and death threats, including ones from the KKK. Neither made the final round and their loss sparked editorials charging anti-gay and anti-male bias in the judging process. It was noted that since all of the judges were connected to the university public relations department whose role it was to make the university "look good," the prospects of a gay male homecoming queen would not only anger university administrators (who did not at the time allow gay students to have official student organization status) but also taint community and alumni relations.[94] Rules barring males were subsequently enacted, and it was not until 1991 that a separate pageant for men was established.

Until the 1960s, female pulchritude remained the primary criteria for all University of Kentucky queens. Thereafter, however, beauty was no longer enough to win crowns and silence critics as the parameters of pageant performances were elaborated in attempts to make them more scholastic at UK and on many other campuses. These changing standards typically resulted in more penetrating evaluations of contestants' social competencies and personalities. Contestants had to demonstrate that they could exude class, ease, and composure not only in the ways they presented their bodies but also their social fluency. Educational "rigor" was introduced into quests for the tiara primarily by the addition of new pageant competition protocols including talent, essay, and off-stage interviews with judges. In 1962, for example, the forty college women competing for the title of Miss Little Kentucky Derby had to perform in a talent show and attend a formal tea so pageant judges could rate their social skills. They were also were tested in an onstage question and answer competition that was, however, far from academically challenging. In order to assess their stage presence, one candidate was asked "With whom would you most want to be caught in a spaceship with?" while another was asked "What method would you use to teach the twist?" Further, the five finalists were required to talk privately with the judges so that their "intelligence and personality" could be evaluated more fully.[95]

Beauty, however, was by no means totally eclipsed by these new factors of distinction that arose in the 1970s and 1980s, including an energetic and proactive approach to self-making that included leadership, campus and community involvement, and career aspirations. Contestants were increasingly required to package and platform themselves as upwardly mobile and goal-directed as well as committed to charitable service to others. In response to student criticism at UK in 1979 that too much emphasis was being placed on sorority membership in choosing queens, the staff advisor for the homecoming queen committee told judges that to offset such criticisms they were to look for candidates possessing "poise, personality, goal directedness, general appearance, and leadership" in order to democratize the field.[96] In 1984, UK queen candidates were sought who possessed "leadership, poise and appearance, communicative ability (articulation and self-assurance), scholastic ability (demonstrated and potential), attitudes, warmth, and interests."[97] Despite the less explicit touting of "beauty," in the selection criterion for campus queens during these decades, beauty nonetheless remained embedded in UK's campus pageantry. In 1985, for example, the homecoming queen selection process included a fashion show hosted by the wife of the university president where queen finalists modeled clothes from local department stores.

The ensuing decades, however, would demand a further series of extreme makeovers on the part of supporters of competitive collegiate contests for beauty and distinction. Surviving and accommodating student mockery, apathy, lawsuits, and attacks from men and feminists, campus queen contests nonetheless remain a prominent feature of campus life today. In the next two chapters, based on numerous interviews with pageants' promoters and contestants as well as my observations of a variety of campus pageants, I analyze the continual "upgrading" of contemporary campus pageantry and the ongoing wounds and exclusions it continues to foster. I discuss the oscillations of power, post-feminist, and neoliberal discourses of self-advancement and regulation; class, careerism, and advancement; personal and collective empowerment; racial legacies; and their import for performing on campus runways in the 1990s and into the new millennium. I also focus on the different ways that black and white contestants and university staff still struggle to construct what Sarah Banet-Weiser has termed an "architecture of respectability" around beauty pageantry. I probe how contestants and their supporters justify their participation and sponsorship, platform enterprising subjectivities, adopt new internet and makeover technologies for self-promotion, and, in general, perpetuate pageantry as an enduring cultural form on college campuses.[98] As we shall see, historical tensions among beauty, bodies, and brains continue to haunt the selection and crowning of contemporary queens despite extensive efforts to smarten them up with academic trimmings.

4

Making the Grade in the New Millennium

Beauty, Platforming, Celebrity, and Normativity

> Behind that curtain is the best of the university.
> —Frank Brogan, Lt. Governor of Florida[1]

New forms of racism and color-blindness, neo-liberal and post-feminist logics for self-advancement, discourses of consumerism, personal responsibility and make-over, body-centered self-hood, and the escalating costs of higher education have each contributed to the reformulation of student bodies and identities. Campus queens are deeply responsive to race and class politics that regulate not only bodies but subjectivities. Queens often play starring roles in campus dramas, mediating traditional signifiers of feminine distinction as well as new forms of academic excellence. In 2009, Cody Kees, a University of Arkansas student reporter, observed that queens on her campus continue to play pivotal roles as campus luminaries since "every great business needs its celebrity endorsement, and though Chancellor Gearhart is doing a great job in that capacity, he just wouldn't look good wearing a crown and high heels."[2] The associate director of student activities at Howard University asserted that the campus queens and kings are "poster children" for the university and should act accordingly.[3] At the same time that supporters affirm their importance, fierce critiques of beauty pageants have prompted extensive facelifts of the campus queen scene that are visible on both historically black campuses and predominantly white schools, if to differing degrees. Merely being lady-like and refined is now touted as passé as contestants must also demonstrate sharp minds, fit bodies, academic accomplishment, assertive personalities, and strong commitments to careerism and leadership.

Despite the seeming incongruity of beauty and body displays in higher education, as well as the time investments needed to win contests, hundreds of college women continue to don glamorous evening gowns, high heels, and, often, swimsuits to compete each year on red-carpeted campus runways. They seek the rewards, privileges, and attention, material and symbolic, that have accrued to queens of academe since the 1920s, rewards that have been modernized as well. Additionally, buff heterosexual college men sporting tuxedos and Speedos are increasingly competing in campus pageants, as are gay men. Students who are attempting to modernize traditionally gendered pageant practices by championing discourses of post-feminism, neo-liberalism, and self-improvement point to the importance of the Q&A and their service platforms as evidence of a new era of enlightened campus pageantry. Other contestants go much further in their attempts to stretch pageant traditions as a strategy to challenge heteronormativity and racism in campus life.

In this chapter I begin by examining the structural renovations and the changing constitutions of class and gender performativity that are apparent in contemporary campus pageants. I focus on campus-based Miss America feeder pageants as illustrative case studies of efforts to "modernize" and legitimate pageants in light of critiques that they are exploitative and/or trivial—in either case, relics of a bygone era. I also examine the range of legitimation narratives that contestants themselves offer to explain their interest and investment in pageants as pathways to campus celebrity. Contemporary campus pageant protocols and contestants' rationales have been, in part, reinvented in response to feminist critiques of pageants as sites of objectification. In response, contestants assert post-feminist discourses to position themselves as empowered women who freely choose pageants as a venue to showcase their modern enterprising subjectivities and desires. Next I look at several instances of recent campus battles that have flared up over beauty pageants in the U.S. and England. Here, I focus on the brawl between feminist critics of the Miss University London pageant and its contestants, who asserted that they were not anti-feminist but rather adherents to a more flexible and modern feminism that allows a greater range of options for women's empowerment. Finally, I take a brief look at how and why black and white college men are becoming increasingly drawn into this historically feminized performative space as contestants, not just as judges and producers. As will become increasingly apparent in the following chapter on racial and ethnic college pageants and African American queens of academe, the pageant forms and legitimations I discuss in this chapter are primarily, but not wholly, characteristic of pageants on traditionally white campuses and among white participants. When it comes to understanding the surprisingly complex world of campus beauty pageants, race matters.

Vintage and Modernity in Campus Pageants

Tied to shifting gender idealizations and cultural politics, contemporary campus pageants showcase fit bodies, middle-class competencies, and professional career aspirations. The scholarship narrative pioneered by the Miss America organization has provided the suturing for modern campus pageant facelifts. Since 1944, when its scholarship fund and local feeder pageants were established on many college campuses, Miss America has continually trumpeted itself as the largest scholarship program for college women in the United States. Since then, Miss America has continued to strengthen its academic credentials—for instance by changing its name to the Miss America Scholarship organization in 1993 and establishing Miss America Scholar awards in 1996 for contestants demonstrating outstanding academic achievement. The Miss America Scholarship Organization boasts that it has a long "tradition of empowering young women to achieve personal and professional goals, while providing a forum in which to express their opinions, talent, and intelligence, working on issues of importance to society, enhancing personal and professional skills, and developing performance-related and other talents."[4]

Taking cues from Miss America strategists, college promoters now refer to their contests as "scholarship pageants," not "beauty pageants." They boast that contestants face "grueling" knowledge quizzes, interviews with faculty and staff, biographical essays, and that they devote themselves to socially significant service platforms. Queens are now expected to articulate lofty professional aspirations and assume an active and assertive presence in campus life and beyond. Quiet beauty, respectability, and charm no longer suffice. Instead, contestants must demonstrate academic rigor, self-discipline, and proactive postures. In my interviews, many campus contestants tout their academic and charitable accomplishments and minimize the body and beauty labor involved. Brains have become beautiful. The Howard University coordinator of a School of Engineering pageant, for example, proudly noted that its theme, "A Beautiful Mind," stressed that "true attractiveness in a person stems from their intelligence."[5] Again taking the lead from Miss America, many campus pageants award titles such as "Miss GPA" and "Miss Academic Excellence." Others have modified apparel requirements to include both evening gowns and business suits and they bestow such titles as "Miss Career" on contestants who show the most "confidence and intelligence" in their outfits.[6]

Many universities continue to offer college women a gateway into the Miss America pageant system, a pageant system that stubbornly insists on swimsuit competitions and restrictions on sexuality, pregnancy, and marriage. Both predominantly white and historically black campuses as diverse as Pennsylvania State University, the University of Georgia, Hampton University, the University of Florida, the University of Louisville, Auburn University, the University of Alabama, KSU, and Jacksonville State University each host annual Miss America local preliminaries. As we shall see, these campus pageants are amalgams of gender traditionalism and modernism. Since they lavish winners with celebrity, attention, and money, a diverse group of college women with variant agendas continue to compete on campus catwalks.

The changing anatomy of Miss America campus feeder pageants was evident in the recasting of the 1999 Miss Purdue University contest when nine white women vied for the opportunity to become Miss Purdue University. Each hoped to win a scholarship of $1,100.00 and the chance to compete in the state wide Miss America pageant. The pageant emcee began the evening by pointing out the potential for celebrityhood among the contestants, proclaiming "so many Miss Americas have launched successful careers in television and show business, and it all starts on a stage like this somewhere in America."[7] Once the competition began, all the contenders appeared on stage wearing black form-fitting dresses and high heels. As a group they danced to the song *I Feel Like a Woman*. After this traditional group display of contestants, the swimsuit competition was held. Following that, contestants were then expected to switch gears from those mute corporeal displays to perform as agentic and empowered women who could make a difference in the world beyond the pageant stage. They were expected to avoid any signs of sagging bodies or sluggish attitudes as the new pageant ethos demanded not only firm bodies but proactive personalities.

Modernization has also been evident in the elaboration of service platforms and in the Q&A portions of pageants, both of which were purportedly designed to evaluate the composure, charm, and personal efficacy of contestants. In recent decades, service platforms have become an integral part of pageant performances. Miss Purdue University contestants, for example, celebrated their benevolent activities and their dedication to combating such social problems as clinical depression, illiteracy, lack of parental involvement in schools, and ironically—given the body politics of pageants—eating disorders. One contestant was asked to discuss how she would advise a child victim of domestic violence while another was probed about how she would motivate low-income students to aspire to post-secondary education. This same contestant extolled the virtues of self-determination as a way to overcome income inequalities. Reducing class differences to a matter of reforming one's subjectivity, she responded by saying that she "would just tell them [low-income students] it can be done if you put your mind to it."[8] The incongruity of women clad in satiny strapless gowns with rhinestones and pearls pledging to help end poverty and educational inequality is jarring.

In addition to stressing the scholarships they had received, winners of the Miss Purdue University title extolled the therapeutic virtues of pageantry for helping them increase their affective potency and social power as women. They pointed to the importance of pageants as training vehicles for enhancing self-esteem and giving women a wider range of life options and experiences. One former Miss Purdue University, for example, said that pageantry "really prepares you for real life," and that she had learned "to challenge myself and to communicate. The interviews prepared me for job interviews."[9] Miss Purdue 2000, Breanne Rhoton, claimed that the pageant helped her to strengthen her psychological core and "come out of her shell" since both the Miss Purdue and Miss America pageants stress the "theme of self-expression and really trying to know the contestant. This holds true from the opening number to the interview." They are, she asserted, "making an effort to show that each woman has something important to say and that there is more to this pageant than an evening gown."[10]

Far across the country, Pepperdine's Meagan Winings also believed that pageants were crucial for women's affective empowerment and increasing women's abilities to act in the world. Winings noted that pageants helped her to step outside her comfort zone and, in her words, "taught me to push myself and to always believe in myself."[11] Even women who do not win the crown often remain steadfast in their support of beauty pageants. Udoka Omenukor, for example, a contestant in Southern Methodist University's 2008 Omega Psi Phi's Miss Purple and Gold pageant, said she was glad she competed since pageants "make you think about yourself."[12]

Many of the Miss Purdue contestants were well-experienced in the traditional scripts for smart bodies as well as in the modern art of platforming enterprising femininities since many of them had already competed in other contests including county fairs, teen pageants, and community festivals, such as the Blueberry Queen Festival. Many contestants, however, had sought out additional training. In order to boost her self-presentation skills and personal efficacy, Miss Purdue University 2001, Krista Kober, reported that she had hired a pageant coach since they "know how you should stand and what your personality should be."[13] As a result of her pageant experiences, she proudly noted that she had "learned how to be in the spotlight and present herself," skills she perceived as essential for future success. Pageants, she said, "teach you to act happy even if you are not since people do not want a snotty queen. One is going to encounter situations like that at work and in daily life." For Krista, the benefits of being a queen were largely about self-advancement and finding the means to realize her personal ambitions. Krista is also proud of the heightened sense of self-efficacy that led her to galvanize pageant supporters to express their outrage at an *Indianapolis Star* reporter who had disparaged beauty queens as mere "mannequins."[14]

Therapeutic rationales for pageantry as pathways for heightening the power of women are anchored in grammars of individualism and personal transcendence, not the systemic causes of women's collective disempowerment. The purported psychic/affective/professional benefits that accrue to women, however, provide many contestants with an empowering cover story for their participation that helps to conceal and minimize the import of the body-centered labors they perform in order to be competitive and desirable on stage. As we shall see, in doing so, some contestants claim feminism as a rationale for their efforts.

The internet has been an important venue for self-conscious platforming and self-promotion by campus queens, who increasingly make use of websites, blogs, YouTube, and Facebook to market themselves as icons of enterprising modern womanhood. In 2008, for example, a Miss Purdue University website urged "school assemblies, business organizations, trade shows, sales and product promotions, festivals and parades, fashion shows, and church groups" to schedule an appearance with Miss Purdue.[15] The same year, the reigning Miss Purdue University spoke at the Lafayette Business Expo, rode in the Grand Prix Parade, and visited numerous public schools.

The Miss PU website also featured a queen's activity blog and an advice column for students considering competing in the Miss Purdue contest. It included advice for improving one's catwalk literacy by choosing socially appealing platforms as well as how best to enhance one's corporeal charms.

> Work with what you have and what makes you comfortable and confident. Bridal stores and pageant consulting sites can be helpful. . . . Your swimsuit can be a one or two piece suit. Avoid "boy shorts" and *make sure you are comfortable showing it off* [emphasis added]. Heels add height and make legs look longer. Platform statements should be short and to the point. Some examples include promoting healthy lifestyles and volunteerism, sexual abuse, fine arts education, and organ donation."[16]

As we shall see, some campus queens turn student coaching into future careers in the thriving subculture of image, style, and pageant coaching, where they provide surgical-like dissection of the perceived flaws of contestants' bodies and behaviors and dispense remedies for correction.

Campus queens on other campuses have also used the internet to keep a public diary of their post-pageant activities, to offer advice for self-management, and to reinforce their commitment to social benevolence. Liza Pitts, the 2008 Miss University of Georgia (also a Miss America feeder pageant), noted the seriousness of her responsibility to represent the university through volunteerism and charity. She wrote:

> The day after the pageant, my mother, my sister, and I went around campus taking pictures. As we were driving around campus, I was looking at all the students and buildings. I made the comment that "I represent all of this." My mother and sister both giggled because that probably sounded like, as I call it, a "World Peace" comment. I meant what I said, however. I take my job that serious.[17]

Since she outshined thirty other contestants for the title of Miss University of Georgia (Miss UGA), Pitts regularly informed readers about her "charitable" acts. She reported a range of contradictory activities that include tiara tea parties and beauty pageants for young girls and speaking out about the global sex trade. The Miss UGA Tiara Tea party for young girls was a fundraiser for the Children's Miracle Network, an official Miss America charity.[18] Here, Pitts invited "little girls to meet Disney princesses" and then spend the afternoon learning "how to be true princesses." She added: "I was so excited to see it make the front page of the *Athens Banner Herald.*"[19] Pitts also used her position as a queen to speak to a local civic group about the problem of "sex trafficking in Africa" to benefit the Women to the World organization.

Pennsylvania State University [Miss PSU pageant] is another major U. S. campus that hosts Miss America preliminary pageants and blends tradition and modernization. Like other Miss America preliminaries, this campus-based pageant follows the guidelines issued by the Miss America organization, which stipulate that contestants must be "single, well spoken, poised, socially conscious, interested in higher education, and physically fit."[20]

The 2001 Miss PSU pageant was a blend of traditional and modern forms. The pageant began with drum rolls, pink pulsating spotlights, and a performance by a men's dance troupe. Fifteen women nervously waited for the curtains to open so they could compete for a chance to represent PSU in the state finals for Miss America, as well as win a prize package that included a rhinestone crown and pin, a plaque, a subscription to the pageant magazine *Turn for the Judges*, and a tuition scholarship. Soon, the outgoing Miss PSU, dressed in a hot pink gown, was carried on stage on the shoulders of a male dancer so she could emcee the pageant. The curtains parted and the audience got its first peek at the contestants in their opening dance number. After this routine, the contestants changed into spike heels and business suits, a recent pageant innovation, to present their various service platforms including domestic violence, music education in the public schools, AIDS, friendship with the elderly, and self-esteem programs for college students. Then the Q&A followed. Like their counterparts at the Miss Purdue University pageant, each of these contestants promoted education, positive thinking, and a can-do, self-assured posture as key ingredients for personal advancement. One contestant said, "If you are sure of yourself, you can do anything," reducing failure and inequality to matters of flawed subjectivities.

Contestants exhibited perky self-confidence, even as they shed their business suits for scanty swimsuits and began the bathing suit revue. Defensively, the emcee reminded the audience that this bodily display had merit because it offered contestants opportunities for self-expression since each "girl picks out her own swimwear and footwear to reflect her own unique personality."[21] Next up was the talent competition and the emcee once again instructed the audience that this competition was important because the "interpretive skills, stage presence, and poise" of the contestants would be evaluated. Finally, the evening gown competition began and, as they strutted in their glamorous finery, the women were serenaded by an all-male musical band. After the outgoing queen made her farewell walk, winners were chosen in various categories including the traditional category of Miss Congeniality as well as recent didactic upgrades such as Best GPA and Best Platform. As the drums increased in intensity, the top four candidates were chosen and a new queen of academe was crowned.

The director of Penn State's campus competition told me that she was proud to be associated with a university-affiliated pageant like Miss PSU since she believes that such pageants command more respect than non-campus-based pageants such as "Miss Covered Bridge." Even though Miss PSU is nearly identical in form and function to many non-academic pageants, she believed that being a queen of academe is an especially distinguished collegiate honor. [22]

The emphasis on platforming upbeat, confident, and ambitious pageant personalities rooted in neo-liberal logics for self-advancement differs from the quiet and constrained gendered performances prized in earlier college contests, especially in historicaly white pageants where queens rarely had speaking roles. Then as well as now, however, the importance of showcasing class-laden affective dispositions remains a key feature for both white and black pageant contestants. A contender for the 2005 Miss Maroon and White crown at Morehouse College, for example, described her viewpoint on mobility by saying: "Life is like a card game. Everyone's hand is different so you just have to play your best game with what you are dealt"—an approach that minimizes the challenges wrought by the unequal distribution of classed resources. [23] Queens rarely articulate their insecurities about their class performances including their affective and bodily challenges. Annette Kuhn notes that "class is not just about the way you talk, walk, or dress . . . it is not about the job you do or how much money you make doing it . . . nor which university you went to. Class is beneath your clothes, under your skin, in your reflexes, in your psyche, at the very core of your being." [24] The insecurities about one's ability to master collegiate class proficiencies (bodily dispositions, taste, lifestyle, food, art and culture, travel, etiquette, grammar, style, etc.) faced by many first-generation and working-class students must be hidden in the pageant world. Instead, contestants must project confidence and optimistic futures for themselves and those who make the necessary commitments to self-improvement regardless of social background. Pageant platitudes of self-help through willpower and attitude help to patrol the student body.

Participating in campus pageants can be costly, especially Miss America feeder pageants, since competition apparel is highly regulated. However, campus queens point to the numerous perks and privileges attached to being a university queen that they believe offset their investments and labor. Prize packages have been upgraded from the modeling lessons, shoe sales, and spots in the college yearbook that were once the only rewards of being campus royalty. In 2006, Miss Clark Atlantic University, for example, received over $23,000 in prizes in the form of tuition and room and board. She represented her university on BET's *Road Show* and was pictured in *Ebony* magazine's annual presentation of black campus queens. However, this queen reported that she "is constantly selling and marketing Clark Atlantic University," in a new cultural economy of branding campus life. [25]

Miss Alabama State University is given a campus office in addition to money for tutition and a wardrobe makeover. Queens on other campuses receive money to fund various campus programs. At Spelman College, for instance, they are automatically appointed to be head of the community service program of student government. Queens also enjoy opportunities to travel on behalf of their universities, often accompanied by an entourage of royal attendants and advisors.

Former queens are regularly invited back to their campuses for reunions and recognition ceremonies, and many have been enshrined in Hall of Fame exhibits, helping to ensure their continued celebrityhood.

For example, forty-five homecoming queens returned to the University of Alabama in 2001 to be honored at a homecoming pep rally and presented at halftime of the homecoming football game. They were photographed at the presidential mansion and helped to design a campus garden dedicated to their honor. To celebrate the 75th anniversary of Morehouse College's homecoming queens in 2005, university archivists mounted an extensive exhibit, "Crowns and Gowns: The Legacy of Miss Maroon and White," to display the coronation gowns, homecoming suits, crowns, and photographs of its former queens.[26] A documentary film was also released that featured interviews with former Morehouse queens regarding their perspectives on status hierarchies due to skin color, class divisions in the black community, their civil rights activism, and their post-queen careers. More than ninety queens and their attendants returned for the three-day reunion as part of that year's homecoming festivities.[27]

Campus pageants often bring out large crowds and thus represent what is still one of the most visible showcases for college women. The 1996 Ole Miss homecoming queen noted that "after weeks of anticipation, the crowning day is here.... I can't believe 47,000 eyes will be watching me; ... this is almost like a dream. This is such an honor, and never in a million years would I have imagined this."[28] Even smaller campuses provide ample opportunities for queenly display. At Tuskegee University, more than 2,000 faculty, staff, and students attend the Miss Tuskegee University pageant annually. The Miss Vincennes University pageant is broadcast live on the campus's public television station and streamed on the university website.

Being a campus queen can thus be a source of visibility as well as a stepping stone to eminence, opportunities, and cash. Many queens have told me that they felt like "brides" or "celebrities" during and after their coronation ceremonies. A former Morehouse College Miss Maroon and White told me her victory had been "like winning an Oscar."[29] She also observed that some Morehouse students date their matriculation by naming who was the reigning queen at the time and reported having recently met a Morehouse alumnus who could name queens going back three generations. She also told me that queens at nearby Spelman College were treated like "congresswomen." Another HBCU queen affirmed having at least a modicum of power when she told university officials that she would refuse to have her photograph appear in Ebony's annual feature on black college queens unless the university paid to have her hair and nails done professionally. The university complied with her request.[30]

Figure 4.1 Homage to the legacy of African American queens of academe. Kentucky State University Coronation and Hall of Fame Exhibit. Photograph by Karen W. Tice, 2010.

Campus queens typically serve their institutions as hostesses, role models for the student body, ambassadors, advocates, and symbolic figureheads at student and alumni activities, student recruitment drives, parting ceremonies, convocations, football games, and extra-mural activities including state and national scholarship pageants. Their photographs decorate campus calendars, university websites, and presidential and administrative offices and are often used in student recruitment. Singled out for special recognition, they remain a significant element of collegiate visual fields and in the reward and recognition structures on many campuses.[31]

In Defense of Pageants: Queenspeak

While many students seek and sanction campus crowns, pageant critics have been no less vociferous, forcing pageants to undergo numerous academic makeovers and accommodations. Whatever their backgrounds or motivations, royalty participants must navigate complicated terrains of contradictory forces when they enter campus contests. In the case of non-academic community queen festivals, Robert Lavenda has concluded that such rituals are "ideologically hybrid rather than totalizing and unified, susceptible of several different possible interpretations for outsiders, for organizers, and especially for participants."[32] Campus pageant participants and their sponsors likewise articulate a wide array of meanings to justify their involvement in campus pageants. My interviews with student contestants and event sponsors, especially white supporters, suggest that pageants are largely viewed as vehicles for self-promotion and advancement. Unlike the African American women I have interviewed, white contestants tend to valorize personal empowerment, self-improvement, skill enhancement, and social networking as justificatory motifs. The commonplace deployment of these particular motifs resemble what Gerth and Mills termed a "vocabulary of motive"[33] a socially distributed set of rhetorics of explanation for participation in pageantry that anticipate what others might see as misguided. Many of these contestants see themselves as intentional agents who can actively help redirect narrow understandings of campus pageants by sharing their accomplishments on stage. Occasionally, however, some of their stories fall outside the standard motifs typically offered by white heterosexual contestants to include more rebellious and explicitly oppositional explanations for their participation. However they are justified, pageants celebrate and construct both the normative and the exceptional. In the following sections, I examine the patterns of accommodation, negotiation, and re-signification in the discourses of contestants and organizers, and how contestants attempt to neutralize the criticism, contradictions, and anxieties they face as college women competing for campus distinction and celebrity on pageant runways.

Struggling against representations of beauty queens as nothing more than "performing monkeys in heels," pageant supporters attempt to preserve the legitimacy and dignity of the gendered throne by emphasizing the cerebral and the cultural.[34] Miss Purdue University 2001 acknowledged that even though "we do have to wear a lot of makeup and dress nicely when we go in public . . . we are not prisses and anorexics." As further evidence for this, Krista Kober reports that participants at pageants are frequently given lots of food, including dessert. She asserts that pageants do not require one to go hungry to lose weight but rather provide an "incentive to stay fit."[35] Fear that longstanding beauty pageant stereotypes will tarnish their tiaras and victories haunt some contestants—so much so that a few camouflage their involvement in pageants. Miss University of Georgia 2006, for example, told a reporter that "it is not the first thing I tell people," yet at the same time she planned to compete again in the Miss Georgia contest, a gateway to Miss America.[36] A few queens, however, admit that some of the popular characterizations of the world of beauty queens as one of adhesives, hairspray, gels, Vaseline, duct tape, and artifice are apt. One of the reigning queens at the University of Georgia in 2009, for example, said that despite the many benefits of modern pageantry, numerous stereotypes still ring true including the fact that contestants must have "butt glue." She continued by noting that "spray adhesive from Wal-Mart will work, but if you have a wardrobe malfunction on stage, that is probably the worst thing ever."[37]

A recent UK homecoming queen told me that although it is hard to "erase the fairy tale image" surrounding campus contests, there "should be more awareness that it is not just image-based, but that there is substance behind it." She added: "One can see this by looking at where winners are now and what they are doing career wise."[38] Her justification promotes the idea that personal ambition and careerism invalidate the criticism that queens are merely decorative. Nonetheless, she also divulged to me that she had recently coached a queen hopeful by consulting with her on her wardrobe and self-presentation and she acknowledged that such fashion instruction does indeed contribute to the persistent characterization of homecoming royalty as beauty queens. Another former UK homecoming queen likewise admitted that "it is unlikely that one would see an ugly queen, though this is less true for male royalty."[39]

The infusion of a scholarly veneer of educational and career aspiration, however, has not displaced the corporeality of academic pageants. Requirements for the 2008 Miss Mississippi State University Scholarship pageant, for instance, state that since Miss MSU is a "celebrity, a name, a public servant, she must maintain personal grooming whether on campus, going shopping, or on any personal errands." A Miss MSU must "maintain her body to be free from any tattoos and body piercing (except ears) and to maintain personal fitness and maintain her wardrobe in a cleaned and pressed condition."[40] Alongside the many renovations to modernize and smarten up the throne, keeping up ladylike appearances remains paramount.

Campus newspapers regularly herald the modernization of royalty rituals and queen traditions. The University of Minnesota student newspaper, for instance, has asserted recently that it no longer matters "if a candidate has the prettiest face on campus" since the selection process now emphasizes "leadership."[41] A letter published in the University of Southern California student newspaper likewise notes that while USC's homecoming pageant was once "guilty" of the "superficiality" of celebrating mere physical appearance, it has undergone an "evolutionary process," transforming it into a pageant that now celebrates "academic achievement, leadership, initiative, and accomplishments."[42] Some faculty claim that campus pageants enhance academics. David Hazinski of the University of Georgia School of Journalism, for example, has argued that pageant stage experiences, including public speaking, provide excellent training for future TV reporters, adding that "most of the women who do this are very motivated. They're going to succeed in a lot of different areas. I used to look at them as Twinkies. Now that I know some of them, not anymore."[43]

Despite tensions surrounding the evaluation of women performing on stage before audiences and the defensiveness of pageant partisans about charges of appearance-based distinction and triviality, a surprisingly diverse group of college women and men still choose to enter American collegiate beauty/scholarship pageants. Many of them are active in student government, sororities, honor programs, women's studies, racial/ethnic cultural centers, and LGBT groups. They enter campus pageants with diverse agendas and justifications, including winning scholarship money; gaining fame; enjoying the pleasures of attention for the public display of talents, bodies, and achievements; making oppositional political statements; expressing racial/ethnic solidarities; empowering women; maintaining campus traditions; giving back to the community; fundraising for charity; seeking opportunities to enhance poise, self-esteem, career skills, and self-branding; furthering professional goals and their social causes/platforms; affirming spiritual and inner beauty; doing God's work; and enjoying the prestige and spotlight of being university spokespersons. As we shall see, however, some of the white heterosexual men who participate in pageants confess to less lofty goals, such as wooing women and getting free food.

Many campus queens champion pageants as vehicles for women to be heard, downplaying the ocular, spectacular, and aesthetic aspects of pageantry. Instead of acknowledging the male gaze, they emphasize women's voice and empowerment. Miss University of Arkansas 2007 claims that "the Miss University of Arkansas pageant is the only stage many girls will ever be given to display the talents they have been blessed with."[44] Elsewhere, another contestant reports that "I had something in me that wanted to get out. So why not a pageant? It is a way for me to get my voice out."[45] Miss Silliman College contends that queens use their titles "as necessary shortcuts for a beloved cause, as a means to be heard in a society that entertains mostly male voices."[46] The 2009 Miss University of Georgia queen feels her crown gave her access to push her platform, noting, "I can't just walk into a school and say, 'Hey, I want to talk to you about Alzheimer's disease,' and have people listen to me. But apparently, when I have a crown on my head, I have something important to say."[47]

The most commonly given justifications for pageant involvement, however, include the pursuit of scholarship money, self-determination, and personal choice, especially among participants in historically white pageants. A contestant in the Miss Pennsylvania State University pageant, for example, observed that "it's a way for women who may be unable to win sport scholarships to win other scholarships." She went on to describe beauty pageants as strategic pathways for women's empowerment on campus.[48] In addition to scholarship money, job opportunities are also commonly given as a reason for participation. Queens often point out that winning competitions has proven to be a useful gateway into subsequent careers. For instance, a former UK homecoming queen told me that when the local newspaper reported that she was looking for a job after graduation, she received an offer the next day to work in the campus admissions office.[49]

The common strategy of legitimating campus pageants by pointing to what they are not appears in many guises in the accounts of participants who insist that their chosen pageants are more honorable, substantial, or respectable than those lacking rigorous criteria for competition. By far, the most popular marker of respectability is academic achievement. Pageant supporters stress the importance of high GPAs, active campus service, and interviews with faculty as the most decisive factors that differentiate contemporary campus pageants from their less admirable ancestors and cousins. Sponsors of the Miss Georgia State University pageant, for instance, justify their Miss America feeder pageant by arguing that its focus on appearance is counterbalanced by "scholarship opportunities and public speaking opportunities that enhance women's positions in the community."[50] Part of the cost of this pageant, funded by the Student Leadership Recognition budget, is justified by the argument that such pageants promote the "development of leadership skills through rehearsing, competing, and winning."[51]

It is also common for queens of academe to distance themselves from the embodied and visual aspects of campus pageantry by reporting that they do not, in fact, think of themselves as "beauty queens," nor do they consider contemporary campus pageants to be predominantly about normalizing hegemonic beauty standards. Instead, they argue that pageants are about affirming upwardly mobile and disciplined modern college women, celebrating academic accomplishment, shattering traditional pageant norms for collegiate femininity, disrupting traditional gender and race politics, and, more generally, transforming the meanings of pageants from the inside out. Xavier University's 2001–2 Miss Black and Gold winner Chakita Holmes proudly proclaimed that with a "mocha complexion, shagged hair, full-figure, I broke the norms at Xavier. Not having a brown paper bag complexion and long flowing hair, I broke the stereotypes set by people like Halle Berry."[52] She extolled the virtues of initiative and self-making, urging students to "be different and if there is something (personal or academic) out there that you want to do, 'Like Nike, Just Do It.'"[53]

Some contestants thus believe they subvert traditional pageant norms for bodies and beauty. Miss University of Georgia 2009, for example, asserts it is not necessary to have Barbie-like breasts to win campus titles. She proudly notes that "breaking the Barbie mode has been something she has talked to her mother about since she first began her involvement with pageants" and asserts that "I have never considered myself a pageant girl. You don't need measurements, you don't need platinum blonde hair, and you don't need a boob job."[54] The 2004 Miss Spelman College, who believed she could politicize the pageant through her choice of a platform, reports:

> When I set out on this journey, it was important for me to revolutionize the role of Miss Spelman and to engage my fellow sisters in a process that I hoped would incite involvement, participation, and give new meaning to the role of Miss Spelman. "Leaders for the Neo-Underground Railroad To Liberate a Whole People" was intended to rally my fellow sisters around an important and relevant cause for the purpose of bringing focus and attention to vital issues that impact women everywhere on a daily basis [breaking the chains of mental slavery in today's society].[55]

Her evocation of the history of slavery and her call for continued resistance to oppression by African American women students as a justification for her pageant participation, however, are quite distinct from the rationales typically offered by white queens, who are far more likely to focus on the acquisition of personal assets such as poise, confidence, and career skills as well as individualized investment strategies to enlarge their academic portfolios.

A member of a recent UK homecoming court told me that she was critical of beauty pageants such as Miss America and that she had designed an exhibit on the 1968 feminist protests at Miss America for one of her women's studies classes. She believes, however, that homecoming queen contests de-emphasize beauty and bodies since they do not include swimsuit competitions. An honor student and self-described "serious nerd," she claims to have brought alternative qualifications to the contest, receiving accolades for her academic honors, her work as a student ambassador, her poetry, and for not being a "big blonde hair type." She is proud that she does not "fit" the traditional homecoming beauty and body mold and feels that her presence has been "beneficial" to the contest. She asserts that homecoming selection rewards "well-rounded students who represent the university well," and in her case is an "affirmation of what I did, not that my legs are nice."[56] Other students, however, are more instrumental in platforming themselves. One contestant told me that since she knew that pageants do not want to hear from "fiery radicals" in the interview component, she had prepared herself to engage in "preferred forms of lying" if questioned about the war in Iraq and September 11 in order to help her achieve her personal and political goals by winning the throne.[57]

Regardless of how they legitimate pageants, contestants often minimize the heavy costs of pageant competition. Not only are the financial costs of competition apparel quite high, but contestants must work hard to be eye-catching and well-informed. When pressed, interviewees catalog a wide range of pre-pageant labors, including selling advertisements for the pageant program as a qualification requirement, campaigning and marketing themselves on campus and the internet, attending rehearsals, devoting time to their platforms, shopping, exercising, watching what they eat, practicing grace while walking in high heels, reading the *New York Times* to stay current on world events for Q&A competitions, and rehearsing their talent. Much like athletes in training, queen contestants work with friends, families, or paid coaches to improve their interviewing skills and poise, as well as to get advice on refining their hobbies, platforms, talents, and clothing, all of which involve much time and expense. Some admit that their grades suffer as a result. Several participants have told me that they have missed classes in order to compete in pageants, but, in some cases, are excused by their instructors since they are representing the university. Florida A&M University contestants report having spent hundreds of dollars on free food, t-shirts, radio, television, and billboard advertisements to win coveted spots of campus queen and king.[58] Lori Spivey, a finalist for Miss University of Florida, confesses that "girls say they do it to get scholarships, but I don't understand that if you are paying $2,000 for a dress."[59] Even after being crowned, queens have to maintain the competitive edge to represent their campuses in state and national collegiate pageants. In 2010, *Ebony* magazine, for example, intensified the pressures on HBCU queens by instituting a new policy of selecting the top ten vote getters in a national online poll to feature in the magazine. Each queen developed a promotional video posted on YouTube in order to platform herself and woo voters. Miss North Carolina Central University's, video, for example, included endorsements from the chancellor of the university as well as the mayor of Durham, North Carolina.

Women students not only spend considerable time and money to participate in campus pageants but also shoulder much of the work to organize them. Sorority women sponsoring the 2003 Mr. UK pageant drove male contestants to all rehearsals, treated them to free dinners, and paid for their competition tuxedos. By contrast, when asked why his fraternity sponsored an annual UK Black and Gold Pageant on the same campus for African American women, the president told me that his fraternity had to participate in a certain number of service activities approved by the national fraternity to remain in good standing, and that a pageant is one of the easiest ways to comply since the "women contestants did most of the work of organizing the event."[60]

A vast array of primarily women student volunteers and college staff tackle a multitude of pageant tasks, including shopping for contestants, fundraising for franchise fees and pageant expenses, and advising the queen. They are quite passionate about pageants since they are firmly committed to the educative value they believe to be part of the pageant experience. Leeann Happ, staff director of the Miss Purdue competition, told me that "pageants get into your blood." For some advisors, pageants offer the opportunity to instruct college women in the pedagogies of beautification/makeover/consumption to enhance their beauty, style, and social savvy. Much like the experts on RealityTV makeover shows, they use shame, scolding, maternal mentoring, and friendship to restyle the appearances of contestants and help them to release their inner confident woman. They boast of feminizing tomboys and turning them into well-dressed, gender-conforming ladies as well as helping to transform "shy girls" into confident women. They take contestants shopping to replace their sweat pants, tennis shoes, and t-shirts with high heels, business suits, evening gowns, and pearls that more closely approximate a moneyed and hyper-feminine aesthetic and to camouflage the more visible markers of class location. They use such metaphors as "blossoming," "self-improvement," "empowerment," and "social education" to describe their efforts to groom their charges. Lisa Reeves of Howard University stated that her role as advisor is "like being a second mother."[61] Leann Happ reports that she becomes very "attached to her queen" and enjoys watching her "grow as a woman."[62] She also reports being grateful for the many women friends she has made across the state through her pageant work and feels that pageants have allowed her to become part of a "sisterhood."

Feminism, Post-feminism, and Campus Beauty Pageants

While campus queen aspirants point to a new era of college women's accomplishment that is celebrated through pageantry, campus contests—especially predominantly white pageants—continue to face and deflect opposition from many quarters. Especially since the 1960s, beauty pageant supporters have had to navigate and accommodate feminist fury and protest. Battles over feminist politics have raged on many U.S. campuses, including at Miami University of Ohio, where feminist student groups made repeated attempts throughout the 1960s, 1970s, and 1980s to eliminate the Miss Miami University pageant. After the 1968 Miss America protests, students at Miami were first galvanized to picket their campus pageant. One student protester declared that the pageant was "like presenting your cows, chickens, and canned goods for display."[63] Later, a college women's liberation group took up the cause in 1974, and in 1980, campus feminists again protested but this time they stressed that they were "not condemning the women in the pageant since it gives them a chance to get ahead and we realize this." (This assertion has been continually muted in media accounts of feminist objections to beauty pageants. Instead feminist oppositions have been reduced to catfights between ugly and beautiful women.). Additionally, the protesting students argued that the pageant should not be affiliated with or supported by the university. In 1988, they again critiqued the pageant, noting that pageant profits had been used to fund a trip to Europe for the men's glee club, not to support women. They also challenged date auctions and fraternity pin-up calendars. Despite long and protracted efforts to rid this Ohio campus of beauty competition, the contest was reinstated in 2005 after only a brief hiatus.[64]

Elsewhere, supporters of campus pageants and their critics continue to battle over showcasing beauty. Pat Terrell, a former vice president of student affairs at UK says that she believes that "if Dillard's [a local department store] wants to do them—fine but this kind of meritocracy does not seem consistent with the mission of the university, since scholarships often do not go to those in need, and some of these beauty contestants are rewarded with more resources and visibility than other students."[65] Brenda Bethman, director of the Texas A&M campus women's center, also opposes beauty pageants since, in her view, they promote a "standardized view of beauty" and encourage women to do "dangerous things to achieve this look such as plastic surgery, not eating, work out excessively, and use Botox to achieve pageant bodies."[66] Nonetheless, many students at Texas A&M support beauty pageantry as a professional stepping stone that provides opportunities for enhancing confidence and self-esteem. In 2001, for example, a Student Pageant Association was established at Texas A&M. Gina Ferrer, a founding member of the association, who has appeared as a pageant coach on MTV's Reality TV series *Made* (a self-improvement program that featured an episode in which a teenage girl realized her dream of becoming a beauty queen), explains that its purpose was to "to further young women's interest in beauty pageants, raise money and awareness for our charities and causes, and provide sponsorship for our members' pageants."[67]

Campus beauty pageants were put on trial at Utah Valley State University in a debate sponsored by the college's Center for Ethics. One of the panelists argued that pageants "serve male patriarchy, promote conformity and superficiality"; and that a winner-take-all format creates losers who "feel drab, fat, ugly, and loathsome."[68] The majority of panelists, however, disagreed with such a negative appraisal.

The Miss University of Central Arkansas contest, sponsored by the Alpha Sigma Alpha sorority, was likewise put on trial in 2008. In a letter to the faculty senate, a faculty member wrote:

> It is difficult to believe that today, in 2008, we still have such activities on our campus. . . . It is even more disconcerting, however, that we at UCA offer substantial scholarship dollars for this event. This year, for example, the prize money is over $13,000. I am primarily upset that we still require the bathing suit portion of the competition which requires our students to take off most of their clothes in order to qualify for prize money. . . . Bikinis and pumps are not typical beachwear . . . pumps,

however, do appear with bikinis when the sex appeal of the women is emphasized (such as in girlie magazines and calendars—borderline soft porn).

The author lamented the trafficking of women students but concluded:

> due to the support it [the pageant] gets from very influential individuals, I don't see how we can expect to eliminate this embarrassing activity from our campus. My recommendation is that we demand at least that the bathing suit element be dropped from the proceedings. Under no circumstances should we stand for the display of students' flesh in exchange for money when such display is directly affiliated by name with the university.[69]

The senate committee concurred, stating that the "offering of scholarships on the basis of appearance or academically unrelated talent is an antiquated and sexist practice" and agreed that the "superficial nature of the event has a negative influence on UCA's public image as an institution of higher learning." It concluded, however, that it was beyond the scope of senate authority to remove the university's name from the pageant since the only contribution by the university was the scholarship money and that the Alpha Sigma Alpha sorority had purchased the pageant before the Miss UCA name was trademarked.

Feminist criticism took a surprising turn at Silliman College that prompted a restructuring of the Miss Silliman College Pageant in 2004. In response to charges that the pageant was a gender "dinosaur" that was exploitative of college women, pageant supporters—self-identified as "ardent feminists"—recruited a "feminist" faculty member to serve as the honorary chair of the pageant to help rescue it from "irrelevance."[70] More often, however, pageant supporters and participants simply argue that pageants are not anti-feminist since they promote and empower women.

Donelle Ruwe, a college English professor and veteran of five beauty pageants, has argued that her personal experiences in local and state Miss America competitions helped to shape positive and even "feminist understandings of body, gender performance, and sisterhood."[71] She urges feminist scholars to overcome their fear of "contamination by kitsch," which, she contends, has hijacked the pleasures of watching or participating in pageants. She also suggests that what is performed in beauty contests is a "self-aware gender performance." While contradictorily she reports that she does not really "respect" such performances, she argues nonetheless that they can have positive outcomes, including the development of confidence in one's appearance, skills in public speaking and persuasion, and an enhanced ability "to participate in a process while simultaneously critiquing that process."[73]

Other pageant supporters, however, believe they are directly promoting feminism. Student contestants commonly tell me that beauty pageantry can enhance feminist issues since tiaras, as opposed to picket signs, provide them with golden opportunities to speak out about their platforms (many of which they see as feminist in nature) and to increase their access to those in power. Because of this perceived alliance, an organizer of the Miss Pennsylvania State University Scholarship Pageant told me that she had approached the Penn State Commission on Women about joint projects, believing that they both were "heading in the same direction—empowering women," but was very surprised when the Commission rebuffed her overtures.[74] She also blamed fears of feminist backlash for what she viewed as less than strong support from university officials for her pageant.

Campus beauty contestants, as we have seen, stress the rewards that come with student pageants but minimize the contradictions embedded in them, many of which have been highlighted by feminist critics, including the sexualization and objectification of women. Visual performances of embodied excellence, self-mastery, and appeal on campus catwalks inevitably create only a few winners and a much larger circle of losers, some of whom are candid about the perils and pain of pageantry competition. Elizabeth Jones, a graduate student at Texas A&M, for example, defended pageants by asserting that they "teach poise, presence, and how to communicate" yet confessed that "when you put in all this work and you don't win, it hurts because it's like the judges saying that you're not good enough for the job."[75]

A number of the contestants I have interviewed express at least some degree of body-based shame and apprehension about being judged on their physical appearances. Some have told me apologetically that they were not in "the best physical shape at the moment" and several have described their perceived body flaws and their commitments to intense toning regimes in order to achieve runway-ready bodies before their next pageant competitions. A winner of the University of Northern Alabama contest, a feeder pageant for Miss America, reportedly said that while she was "not critical of the display of bodies, she was critical of her body and therefore was nervous before going on stage." Tamara Esche, a student at the University of Evansville and a veteran of the pageant circuit since she was seven, lamented the surgical-like dissection of body flaws, observing that "there is nothing like having judges pick you apart up there. They evaluate every little thing and point out every imperfection. It's kind of scary."[76]

Despite the qualms some student participants voice about external judgements of their bodies and their internalization of them, disputes over beauty pageants in the U.S. have been relatively restrained and confined largely to debates and student editorials. I have interviewed women's studies directors at universities that sponsor Miss America feeder pageants who report being unaware that such events even take place on their campuses—a gauge of the extent to which faculty and student cultures are often worlds apart.

Outside the U.S., however, the 2008 Miss University London beauty pageant was a noteworthy exception to this gap as both feminist faculty and students organized protest networks and pickets lines to stop the pageant. Incensed by these protests, pageant promoters and contestants attacked the protesters for their rigid interpretations of feminism. They touted the new pleasures and empowerment opportunities of a post-feminst era, including participation in beauty pageants. Their selective appropriations of feminism to refute feminism helps to elucidate further the underpinnings of rationales used by student beauty contestants across the globe. This "catfight" garnered the attention of the media, which, as we shall see, caricatured the protesters in ways that were reminiscent of the reportage on the 1968 Miss America protests. The London pageant conflict exposes the complicated terrain of beauty, choice, consumption, desire, pleasure, sexual objectification, and contemporary feminist politics.

Who and What Makes a Feminist?: Feminist and Post-feminist Battles

Established in 2006, the Miss University London pageant is an extra-mural competition that draws contestants from numerous London universities, including the London School of Economics and the University of London. It is organized by an off-campus, for-profit business, 121 Entertainment, that purportedly raises money for breast cancer research. Promoters accept online applications and send out scouts to student parties to recruit "attractive" contestants.

In 2008, over 400 students participated in the various preliminary qualifying pageants at their universities so they could compete in the Miss University of London pageant before a live audience of over 2,000 people. They faced the wrath, however, of numerous protesters who waved placards such as "SOAS [School of Oriental and African Studies] is here for our education, not your ejaculation" and stormed the stage to disrupt the pageant.[77] An organizer of the protest compared the pageant to "a cattle market." "Contestants," she said, "had to have their waists and breasts measured. I come from a rural area and that's what they do to animals."[78] A women's officer at the London School of Economics said, "We come to the university to be judged on academic ability and not on external characteristics. The LSE is an academic institution and should not have its name tarnished by an event with the single function of the objectification of women."[79]

Initially, students from thirty different colleges collaborated to protest the objectification of women in the Miss University London pageant using Facebook, blogs, and conferences to build their activist networks.[80] In their organizing statement, protesters attacked the exclusionary and commercial nature of the quest for beauty titles.

The notion of beauty attached to the image promoted by beauty pageants is discriminatory according to gender, sexuality, age, race, and disability. In a society where we are bombarded with commercial images, trying to uglify us into buying this notion of beauty, it is almost impossible not to judge oneself and each other according to these ideals. Whether we choose to accept or reject them we are left chasing a mirage of digitally touched up perfection."[81]

One of the protest organizers, Eleanor James, stated that "the pageant is something we cannot ignore because it symbolizes a backlash against feminism that is encroaching onto university territory. . . . Universities (as they have become increasingly corporatized) now have beauty pageants, pole dancing societies, and playboy bunny clubs."[82] She asserted that "we do have bigger battles to face than beauty pageants. But the only way that we can tackle these problems is by uniting against them, not judging each other on a platform." James also helped to organize the Facebook site, Miss-Ogynist.org, to support the battle against the divisiveness and damage caused by beauty spectacles. The students received international media attention for their protests.

In response, pageant supporters utilized post-feminist and girl-power discourses of personal choice and empowerment to defend the pageant, and they constructed its feminist critics as anti-choice and anti-empowerment.[83] Their defense reflects the recent perspective of a number of writers who argue that "personal choice feminism" allows contemporary women freedom from the shackles imposed by outmoded and hypercritical feminists who they see as rabidly anti-beauty as well as intolerant of men, makeup, high heels, bras, and sexual and consumer pleasures. Ellie Levenson, for example, argues that a new "pick-and-mix feminism" that rests on "flexibility" is a needed corrective to the rigidity of lifestyle and thought that, she contends, characterized second-wave feminists.[84] She asserts that "in the past, you had to subscribe to a whole set of beliefs to be a feminist, including how you should look and behave."[85] Furthermore, she argues that picketing and protesting are fossilized modes of achieving women's empowerment. She says she has "no intention of ever throwing myself in front of a horse, very little makes me want to chain myself to the railings at Downing Street, and my longest hunger strike has been about an hour . . . I am a feminist who wears a bra and shaves my armpits. I don't see it as a choice between being feminine and being a feminist."

Also in response to feminist protests, pageant supporters evoked what Bonnie Dow calls the "personalization strategy" of post-feminist rationales that emphasizes contestants' personal agency and empowerment. Dow argues that by the mid-1970s, media discourses had begun to emphasize the "personal agency of beauty contestants, an emphasis that works to refute feminist objections by implying that if women claim that they freely choose to participate in the pageant

and refuse to claim that they are exploited, we should believe them."[86] Writing
about the Miss America pageant, she also observes that by the 1990s, dominant
media discourses had adopted a contradictory stance toward beauty pageants
that wove together elements of liberal and post-feminist empowerment:

> Most media discourse about the pageant adopts a bemused, ironic tone
> towards Miss America, a tone that acknowledges the pageant as an
> anachronism at the same time that it validates it as an empowering voca-
> tion for the women who continue to compete in it. That is, at the same
> time that media discourse shows clear agreement with aspects of femi-
> nist critique of the pageant, it also insists on a kind of liberal, evolution-
> ary narrative in which the pageant has, in some senses, become feminism
> for the contestants.[87]

Christian Emile, the owner of 121 Entertainment, echoed these discourses by
pointing to the personal agency of the Miss University London contestants. He
stated that "feminism is supposed to be about choice for women. They should be
allowed to do whatever they want."[88] In another interview he said, "If you talk to
the contestants, they will tell you it is actually empowering. They get their moment
in the spotlight; it's a bit of fun."[89] In trumpeting the desires of the contestants,
Emile's justifications for the pageant rested upon post-feminist notions that sexualization is freely chosen by strong women subjects. Rosalind Gill has observed
that such post-feminist discourses reflect a shift from "objectification to subjectification" where "women are not straightforwardly objectified but are portrayed as
active, desiring sexual subjects who choose to present themselves in a seemingly
objectified manner because it suits their liberated interests to do so."[90] Similarly,
Susan Douglas has argued that what she has named "enlightened sexism" and
"embedded feminism" champion the idea that it is "through women's calculated
deployment of their faces, bodies, attire, and sexuality that they gain and enjoy
true power that is fun, that men will not resent, and indeed will embrace." In
enlightened sexism, 1970s feminism is rendered as "grim, dowdy, aggrieved, and
passé"—"an impediment to female happiness and fulfillment."[91]

Mainstream media thus characterized the battle over the Miss University London pageant as a conflict between old-style feminists focused on male domination
and post-feminist advocates of personal freedom, choice, and pleasing oneself,
including the option of participating in sexualized and hyper-feminine spectacles
such as beauty pageantry.[92] In a chat room set up by the *Daily Mail*, numerous readers wrote that feminist protesters were limiting the personal freedom of the women
contestants. They also recycled mainstream media characterizations of second-
wave feminist beauty pageant protesters as unnatural, dysfunctional, asexual, and
out of step with the opportunities for the empowerment and pleasures of women
in a post-feminist and girl-power era.[93] Feminist protesters were characterized as

drab and dowdy, unhappy women who were strident, judgmental, puritanical—
women who are out of step and irrelevant in a cultural economy that now offers
women limitless opportunities for power, pleasure, and sexual agency. Lily James,
author of the now-defunct webzine the "Feminist Playground," spoke for many
pageant contestants and supporters when she wrote:

> Post-feminism is a lack of interest in chanting old slogans, waving old
> banners, and crabbing over old injustices. Young women today want to
> exploit and enjoy our freedom, not pout about what freedoms we don't or
> didn't have. If you want to see post-feminism look at the movie *Charlie's
> Angels*, chicks kicking ass in lipstick and short skirts who think of bras as
> a cool way to make your boobs look good, not the shackles of patriarchy.
> Post-feminists want to move on from feminism—that's the simplest way
> of defining it. We're tired of being told if we wear makeup and have fun
> we're betraying our gender and pandering to men.[94]

Although protesters tried primarily to attack the pageant sponsors, it was the
contestants and their responses that received most of the media attention, muting
the protesters' critique of profit-making and reducing the conflict to a catfight
among women. Several of the Miss University London contestants responded to
feminist critiques by promoting their own versions of feminism and empowered
subjectification of women through beauty and hyper-femininity. The 2009 winner of the Miss University London pageant, Susheel Bal, justified her sense of
feminism with a blend of post-feminist personal choice and empowerment justifications while dismissing the feminist politics of the protesters as tyrannical.

> By taking part in the pageant, I did not rescind my equality. I did not
> reject feminism.... There are two versions of feminism that are emerging
> in young women. The first that I subscribe to is that men and women are
> equal. It allows me to win a beauty contest, and gain a degree, and per-
> mits that the complexities of my life should not be reduced to a single act
> of sloganeering or bra burning.... Equality is irrelevant without the free-
> dom to do as we would like. And if the London School of Economics can
> hold a Mr. LSE contest, why can't I enter a similar event for women? The
> protestors are entitled to their opinions. I respect their right to object,
> but they do not reciprocate; they want to limit my freedom to compete in
> the contest which itself is a form of oppression.[95]

Bal also responded by saying she was not "shallow" and that her career ambition to be a lawyer was an indication of her dedication to feminist goals. She criti-
cized feminist protests as "disproportional," since the pageant was a charitable
event. She chastised feminists for not focusing on more serious feminist issues,

such as the imprisonment of a British mother in Dubai for adultery. Bal concluded by saying simply, "I can see where the protesters are coming from, but I think post-feminism is about having a choice."[96] Her understandings of choice are shaped by a grammar of post-feminist individualism that disavows the cultural and market pressures that shape women's choices. Gill has rightfully observed that if women are simply "free agents" who "are just pleasing themselves and following their own autonomously generated desires," how can one account for the fact that "the valued look is so similar?"[97] "Notions of autonomy, choice, and self-improvement," she added, "sit side-by-side with surveillance, discipline, and the vilification of those who make the wrong choices."[98] Even this argument, however, can be turned into a legitimation for pageant participation, as suggested by one of the contestants, who concluded, "I feel that we are all being judged all the time, whenever we walk down the street, so why not just do it for real?"

Other contestants offered a range of post-feminist inspired defenses including definitions of themselves as a new and improved feminist prototype. One said, "I would call myself a feminist. I'm all for women's rights and equality in the workplace but that does not mean we cannot hold competitions like this." Another contender proclaimed that feminism serves a purpose but concluded: "We are now post-feminism. Not so long ago women couldn't receive Firsts at university just because they were women, but we have come a long way since then." Another defended the pleasures of beauty, saying, "I fail to see what is wrong with feeling glamorous for one night. We hardly sold our souls." Finally, one contestant argued that pageants are essential vehicles for reasserting genteel gender and class codes for behavior to counteract the increasing propensity for unruly behaviors among women. She asserted, "I just can't see it as a betrayal of womankind. Young women have a reputation for binge-drinking and loutish behavior. And I think that taking part in an event that celebrates not just beauty but intelligence and elegance too is as necessary to modern women as campaigning for equal rights was when my mum was our age."[99]

The fight over what is feminism continued to rage a year later. Laura King, of Kings College, simultaneously asserted her own feminist sensibilities while repudiating the feminism of the pageant protesters. Feminism, she said, is

> having the freedom to do what they want without fear of being judged. To go out wearing a short skirt, accept drinks from men at a bar, and attend pole dancing lessons, with pride. If women want to take cooking classes or learn how to knit, this is not selling out to the old ways of putting women in the kitchen; it is the essence of feminism—women choosing freely.[100]

In a rejoinder, James countered that the consumer objectification of women "is one of the insidious forms of control that patriarchy has over us. By controlling seemingly free choices to make us feel that we are forging our own identities and our own paths as autonomous individuals, when, in fact, we are following a template set to mold the subordinated female."[101] Indeed, as Brenda Weber has noted about makeover culture, an "economy of sameness" pervades not only valued looks but also the epidemic of personal choice rationales of pageant supporters and contestants.[102]

Manliness and Swagger in Campus Programs and Pageants

Although college men have always been involved as judges and pageant producers, they also have increasingly become contestants in what has been an historically feminized performance site. The question is how and why? In part, the answer lies in the increased emphasis placed on characteristics once assumed to be essentially feminine, such as people skills, emotional literacy, and style, for men in higher education and the workplace.[103] Robert Goldstein has observed that "now, it's not just women who dress to please; everyone is subject to objectification."[104] Along the same lines, Susan Faludi has observed that economic insecurities have produced a "crisis in masculinity" and a "culture of ornament" in which men face increasing social and economic pressures to enhance their appearance and heterosexual allure.[105] Toby Miller likewise notes that although the "burden of beauty remains firmly on women," men too have become subjected to "new forms of governance and commodification" that increase their dissatisfaction with their appearances.[106] Men in greater numbers are featured on television shows where they are encouraged to improve their grooming, image, social skills, and relationships with women. The makeover phenomenon among men has very recently gained a foothold on college campuses.

The emphasis on remaking men has registered in university-sponsored student enhancement programs as well as in student-sponsored programming. College fraternities, for example, have begun to embrace civility and manners makeovers in programs such as Sigma Phi Epsilon's "Balanced Man Program," Sigma Alpha Epsilon's "True Gentlemen," and Beta Theta Pi's "Men of Principle."[107] MIT sponsors an annual charm school that offers its students instruction in "social calculus," including the intricacies of bow-ties, neckties, and business suits as well as table manners, social formalities, the art of small talk, ballroom dancing, online etiquette, and dating.[108]

One of the best examples of the merger of makeover technologies with campus life is the 2009 collegiate enhancement program for African American men, The Come Up Program, developed by the Office of Diversity at Western Kentucky University. It was based on the "curriculum" of MTV's reality TV male makeover show *From G's to Gents*, hosted by Fonzworth Bentley. Bentley is a past winner on Donald Trump's *The Apprentice*, author of the popular hip-hop-centric etiquette guide for African American men *Advance your Swagger: How to Use Manners, Confidence and Style*, and a motivational speaker/entertainer for the BET-sponsored black college tours. Bentley's approach to grooming "gentlemen" shapes the program and replicates the can-do, self-help attitudes expressed by many white women pageant contestants.[109] He has counseled black college men at Sam Houston College to approach life as if they were running a business and tells them "you are the CEO of your purpose. You have to think like a CEO." He emphasizes that students need to evaluate their out-of-class time, warning that if they do not "maximize their downtime, they will limit their lifetime." At the Community College of Philadelphia, Bentley has further expanded upon this approach by telling students to "look at yourself as a brand; dress like a prospect not a suspect; and expand your vision."[110]

The Come Up Program promised to "help men step up their swagga in their looks, talk, grades, finances, and even with the ladies." As in so many campus pageants, a prize of $1,000 was given to the winner. Bentley himself helpsed screen the applicants, each of whom was asked to write an essay and fill out a survey. Survey questions included: "Can you knot a tie? Do men need a manicure? Should man's pants fall below his beltline? Should men wear hats indoors? Have you opened a door for a female?" Participants were promised the opportunities "to become a man and be more mature" and "to make myself a better black man." Students spent each week in workshops, such as "Get Your Game Tight: Etiquette, Dress, and Style" "Breaking the G Code," "Transitioning from Male to Man," "Money, Power, and Respect," and "So Fresh, So Clean," At the graduation ceremony, the emphasis on embodied makeover was apparent in before and after photographs that featured participants shedding hoodies and shades for business suits. Graduates noted that the program had helped them to "learn to apply themselves and understand that they are the masters of their fates."[111]

Men's pageants have paralleled such enhancement programs for remaking collegiate manhood, but makeovers are not the only motive for men who perform on runways or the organizations that sponsor them. Male pageants and contestants cannot simply be understood as replicas of women's pageants, but they share similiarities. Men's pageants, for example, are often organized as charitable events. The University of New Mexico's "Omega Man" pageant, sponsored by the Alpha Chi sorority, raises money for organizations working to prevent domestic violence. Here, ironically, one brawny man is selected as the "Best Chest in the West" based on student voting.[112] Buffed and muscled men at Notre Dame likewise compete for the title of Mr. Notre Dame.

Because of the novelty and popularity of men's pageants, they often have corporate sponsors. Cool Water cologne and *Sports Illustrated on Campus*, for example, sponsored the Mr. Cool Water contest at Notre Dame in 2004 to promote a new cologne. During its evening wear competition, some contestants wore shirtless tuxedos to best display their mannish brawn, and—indicating the comedic level of the occasion—the eight semi-finalists were asked which cartoon super-hero best suited their personality. The winner received a modeling contract and a date with a *Sports Illustrated* swimsuit model.[113] In such contests, the performance of hyper-masculinity echoes the hyper-femininity of sister pageants platformed on predominantly white campuses.

Some schools that do not feature pageants for women hold all-male pageants, including several Ivy League institutions. The 2005 Mr. Harvard University competition, for example, featured a racy display of male muscles and flesh. One contestant wore only see-through tape and rose petal pasties, another did a striptease, and one wore a swim-diaper.[114] Drawing a capacity crowd, Yale University hosted its first male beauty pageant in 2006.

Although male contestants rarely undertake the rigorous preparation and expense that many women devote to pageants, some nonetheless work on honing their stage performances. The annual Mr. University of Kentucky pageant, established in 1999 by the Delta Zeta sorority as a fundraiser for the Lexington Speech and Hearing Center, provides a window for exploring how college men prepare for, and talk about, their pageant experiences. Each contestant gave a pre-pageant interview where he was judged on personality, poise, and conversational fluency. Contestants were required to sell pageant tickets and make personal banners to decorate the stage, but unlike the men's pageants at HBCUs, no service platforms were required.

In 2003, twenty-six men competed for the title of Mr. UK in front of an audience of over 1,000 students that included mostly women. The judging criteria included the following competitions: "Swimsuit to judge personality, poise/appearance, modeling, and stage presence; formal wear to judge personality, poise/appearance, natural good looks, and modeling; and interview to judge personality, poise, speaking skills, and answer content." Each contestant had to write a self-promotion statement for the pageant program, many of which were crafted in hopes of being desirable to women. One contestant wrote: "If you are looking for the man, the myth, and the legend . . . give me a call." Another said sardonically that he had a soft cuddly side since he liked "puppies," while another contestant likewise played up his tender side by noting that he had played the role of the "the cowardly lion in a high school play."[115] Some men characterized themselves as romantics favoring candle-light dinners, dancing, and walks under the stars. By contrast, other contestants emphasized their passions for sports, the stock market, and *Fox News*.

Swimsuit competition has been a regular component of men's pageants on predominantly white campuses and these typically provide comedic moments. At the 2003 Mr. UK pageant, for example, a number of men wore skimpy Speedo suits to display their pelvic protuberances, while others added inflatable beach toys, rubber ducks, or coconut shells to their suits and wiggled their buttocks to add pizzazz to their performances.[116] The "talent" competition also allowed room for humorous antics that would be unlikely in women's pageants. One contestant played "Twinkle Twinkle Little Star" on a trumpet, another performed to the tune of "Mary Had a Little Lamb," and one performed an imitation of a housewife vacuuming that climaxed in a display of gymnastics. Some attempted Michael Jackson–style dancing and one man had his Afro shaved on stage. Although some African American men participated in this mostly white contest, the campy comedy of the swimsuit competition is not typically found in black collegiate pageants such as Mr. HBCU and the Mr. Collegiate African American Pageant.

The evening wear competition in the Mr. UK pageant became more serious as the men strove to be debonair. Sorority women, clad in sleek black gowns, accompanied each contestant dressed in black tuxedoes. After modeling their evening wear, some men kissed their escorts and gave them roses, while still others displayed their brawn by sweeping their escorts off their feet. During the Q&A session, most of the men were clownish in their responses, but a few seemed sincere. One contestant was asked if there were one thing he could change about UK what would it be? He said it would be to reverse the losing streak of the football team. When asked what he would do if he only had one day left on earth, another responded that he would spend time with his family and "cute girls." When one contestant was asked who his role model was, he responded earnestly that it was his mother since she had stood in the welfare line to help support him in his life. The eventual winner of the pageant, an African American man, was asked to describe what he would do on a date "to win his date's heart and soul?" Presenting himself as a tender romantic, he responded that he would "take her to a restaurant or a movie or a park for a long walk and then he would sing her a song at her doorstep and give her a kiss if she let me."[117]

Men's pageants are, generally speaking, less tightly scripted than women's, allowing for comedy and gender parody. While some male contestants do prepare for these contests, the effort required is often minimal. The winner of Mr. UK 2003 told me that all he did was some "intensive working out and pushups trying to get some more muscles" and he fretted about whether to wear silk shorts or a Speedo.[118] He reported that contestants were required to attend three practice sessions to work on the opening dance number but pointed out that each of these sessions provided free chicken wings and pizza to ensure that the men would show up. He was picked up for all of the rehearsals by a sorority escort who also made the required banner for him. His nominating sorority took responsibility for selling enough tickets that he could qualify. Since sorority sisters paid for the rental of tuxedos, there was very little expense for the male contestants.

When I asked him about his overall experience, he told me that he had especially enjoyed opportunities for male bonding and to woo women. He reported a strong sense of "comradeship" among the male contestants, but noted that several men were upset when they did not advance to the second round. He told me that his mother was quite proud of him, but because he got "razzed about his crown" by other men, he stores it in a closet. Unlike women contestants who trumpet their personal and professional growth and transformation, and, as we shall see in the next chapter, contestants in ethnic pageants who identify pageantry participation as a way to promote communal solidarities and counter invisibility, this Mr. UK lamented that since he had "not gotten dates with too many girls," his pageant goals had not been realized. Nonetheless, he viewed his title "as a stepping stone" in that direction. He encouraged other men to participate for the free food, the opportunity to meet men from across campus, and the chance to meet "girls." He said in conclusion that "we had everything handed to us so we just had to show up, have a good time, and not be too vulgar."[119]

In contrast, some pageant organizers use male pageants to critique the world of pageantry itself. Daisy Chain, a Vassar College student organization that traditionally plans events for commencement, established a Mr. Vassar contest to raise money for senior commencement activities. The judges included the dean of students, faculty members, and staff.[120] In 2007, its theme was "King of the Vassar Jungle" and included an opening dance, a talent competition, jungle-wear competition, and a Q&A. Members of the Daisy Chain said that while the "contest could subvert the degrading and sexist institutions of pageants, for the most part, it is just an evening of comic antics and school spirit." Luke Frankson, the 2007 winner, stressed that male pageants are different from women's since men were judged on their "performances," not physical appearances—ironically, a defense that is regularly asserted by pageant women. In a scathing student editorial, however, Tendai Musakwa took issue with the pageant arguing that "turning men into sex objects" does not lessen the "pain of women who live with objectification every day," nor does degrading men achieve gender equality. She argued that the Mr. Vassar pageant perpetuates an "ideal man standard of perfection: the man with a well-defined jaw, a sculpted figure, a huge bulge in his crotch, and a never-ending supply of humor."[121]

In the 1990s, gay men began to compete for the position of homecoming queen to challenge homophobia and the exclusion of LGBT students on college campuses. (Homecoming queens remain highly visible positions on campus both because of their half time appearances at football games and because they often involve campus-wide voting.) In 1999, Aaron Shubert entered the New Mexico State University homecoming queen contest in order to call attention to homophobia on that campus and to protest a decision by the Board of Trustees to deny benefits to domestic partners of university employees. Following his victory, a bill was introduced to the university's senate to mandate that king candidates must be male and queens must be female since the purpose of homecoming was to "promote school spirit and it should not be used to further political beliefs or political ideologies."[122] The bill was passed by a narrow margin.

In the same year, Jason Minter won enough votes to qualify for the homecoming queen contest at Southwest Texas State University. Although expecting backlash from Christian groups and Greek organizations, he competed nonethe-less since his dorm "nominated him as a queen, not king." His platform was to promote the "Out Youth" organization for gay and lesbian teens in Austin, Texas. After his victory, he was presented on the football field wearing a purple gown with a long slit up the leg and a red wig so he "could look like a woman."[123] In 2004, a gay student in drag won a place on the Vanderbilt University's homecom-ing court. He said that an important part of LGBT politics should be directed at challenging exclusionary traditions like homecoming celebrations. He explained:

> When the gay community separates from the mainstream, it's a way of disappearing into the shadows. I really just wanted to put it in everyone's face. I wanted to make alumni and students recognize that on this cam-pus we have gay students, and as much as the administration wants to keep us in the shadows, off to the side and out of the limelight, I am not going to stand for it.[124]

After the election of the first male homecoming queen at St. Cloud State Uni-versity, the mother of an unsuccessful queen candidate circulated a petition to protest the outcome and received over 500 hundred signatures. St. Cloud's presi-dent, Roy Saigo, however, disagreed, noting: "College campuses have long been social catalysts in the work of opening up and creating a fair society. They play a key role in supporting social justice, equality and educational opportunity, even when traditions are challenged."[125] In 2004, students at the University of Wash-ington decided to award its two $1,000 homecoming queen scholarships on a "gender-neutral basis." One of the women who won asserted that she thought "gender-specific titles are becoming obsolete."[126]

The Miss Gay Indiana University pageant is another example of how pageants are sometimes used as oppositional spaces to challenge collegiate heteronorma-tivity. Since 1989, the Miss Gay IU pageant, hosted by OUT, the gay, lesbian, bisexual, and trans-gendered student union, has drawn over 1,000 people each year in America's heartland. The faculty advisor and veteran judge describes the pageant as "a great way to end the year and educate students about drag, which has been around for 2,000 years as an art form."[127] More recently, a gay drag queen won the title of Miss George Mason University. A university spokesperson said that the university is "very comfortable with it since it does not require partici-pants in the Mr. and Ms. Mason pageant to compete along precise gender lines." However, a student ambassador for the admissions office felt shamed, saying, "The game was on TV. Everyone was there. All eyes were on us and we had to do some-thing like this?"[128]

Just as in the 1970s, when men entered campus homecoming queen pageants to express a variety of motives from the comedic to the political, pageants today give rise to conflicts over gendered boundaries when women attempt to compete in male pageants. Meaghan Ford, for instance, was barred from entering a pageant sponsored by the College Republicans at the University of Mary Washington. John Kelly, the club's vice president, said that having women compete would "ruin the masculinity of the competition." After researching federal law, he concluded that beauty pageants were exempt from sexual discrimination laws.[129]

In contrast to white men, who lack a network of national pageants, African American men often enter black-only local and national collegiate pageants with racially specific missions. Unlike the men's contests at predominantly white campuses, there are no coconut shells and pasties on stage. Instead, the tone is more serious, a validation of exceptional black manhood, a counter to the criminality and deviance imputed to black men in general. The Mr. Collegiate African American Pageant, for example, was created "to empower black college men and to counteract the negative imagery of them . . . using the principles of character, self-esteem, positive role-modeling, and services." Its "goal is to dispel the myth that one has to be a product of a negative environment."[130] A second national pageant for black college men, Mr. Historically Black College and University (Mr. HBCU), was established in 2004. Its mission statement more closely resembles pageants for women in its emphasis on personal development and skill building. However, unlike white women's pageantry, advancement is rooted in notions of communal race responsibilities.

> To help black men with role modeling, character education, value clarifica-
> tion, and to handle every opportunity in a proper manner, . . . students
> should participate in the pageant to develop the spirit of competition, . . .
> personal and professional development, self-esteem, and confidence build-
> ing, enhancement of leadership skills, and developing a sense of responsibil-
> ity to help the race.[131]

Unlike most white male pageants, the Mr. HBCU contest requires its contestants to have platforms and its contestants must attend a leadership and personal growth workshop prior to the national competition.[132] Despite such requirements and its more serious demeanor, there are significant overlaps with white men's pageants nonetheless. To qualify for its 2008 pageant, contestants were asked to provide the following information: their ultimate dream cars, the four guests they would include at a fantasy dinner party, and the best advice they had received from their parents as well as a list of their favorite singers, actors, authors, actresses, TV shows, and black male role models. The judging criteria also overlap with traditional pageants by including "elocution, ease of manner, projection, talent, and professional demeanor."[133]

Antwan Suttle, Mr. Tennessee State University 2004, reports having prepared for the Mr. 2006 HBCU pageant much as a woman pageant contender would do; taking lessons from personal advisors to hone his "poise, speech, etiquette, and runway presence."[134] Suttle reportedly hoped to offer seminars for other black men on how to interview and dress professionally. One student, however, observed that the pageant "seems a little feminine."[135] Possibly in response to such an observation and to avoid anything that could be read as feminine, James Alderman, the recently crowned 2009–10 Mr. HBCU, adopted a hyper-masculine persona in his competition for the throne including his talent, a short movie he produced, "I Am King," inspired in part by James Bond.

The staging of men's pageants and performances also attempts to deflect concerns about feminization, sexualities, homophobia, and, especially for black men, the appearance of being ghetto/working-class/gangsta. Many black campuses have recently enacted new codes of conduct and dress. In 2010, for example, a new "Appropriate Attire Policy" was introduced at Morehouse College along with President Robert Franklin's "Five Wells" strategy for cultivating male students who are "well-read, well-spoken, well-traveled, well-dressed, and well-balanced." Mostly a response to cross-dressing among its male students, Morehouse banned not only any clothing associated with women's garb (wigs, pumps, purses, etc.) but also hoods, sagging pants, grillz teeth, do-rags, and sunglasses, etc.[136] Black college kings are expected to uphold such racialized expectations and as a result their pageant outfits are newsworthy. The winner of the 2003 Mr. Black University of Connecticut pageant was reported to have worn a "dashing lavender tuxedo, with a dark purple shirt, and black and lavender gator shoes."[137] Men, however, are nonetheless allowed more leeway in terms of their pageant performances and persona. At the 2009 Berea College Black Student Union Scholarship Pageant I attended, black male contestants struck a variety of masculine poses including stylish hip-hop, urban sophisticate, professional-business suave, metrosexual, and muscular athlete. Although women are typically given a more restrictive range of expression in pageants, this particular competition was noteworthy in that one woman contestant wore a pantsuit throughout the entire pageant including in the evening wear competition. Despite her unconventional choice of dress, she was crowned a runner-up.

As we have seen, many white heterosexual women contestants talk about their pageant experiences as opportunities to perfect their life skills, increase their personal potency, promote their platforms, win money, and enjoy campus celebrity. The winners tend to use a variety of vocabularies of motive to defend and justify campus pageantry, including self-enterprise and self-promotion, the acquisition of social savvy and social capital, social benevolence, liberal and post-feminist discourses of personal choice and empowerment, and career opportunities. Many use the grammars of individualism, personal empowerment, and self-advancement to quell both pageant critics and, at times, their own disquiet about how best to reconcile academics and embodied distinction. Men are less invested than women in campus pageants as professional passageways and they less embroiled in the whirlpools of dissent that have characterized pageants for women.

While white women's pageants have struggled for academic relevance in the new millennium, as we shall see in the next chapter, they have not had to shoulder the weight of responsibilities carried by black queens and kings, which is often rooted in a sense of history, legacy, and collective solidarities. Black queens frequently aspire to the campus throne as a strategy to challenge exclusivity and invisibility, to repair the damaging legacies of racism, and to advance a range of communal responsibilities and activist agendas, as well as to affirm racial solidarities, not the individualized theme of self-advancement that so often is asserted by white campus queens. Possibilities for subversive confusion and resignification of pageants by black women are the focus of the next chapter.

"We Are Here"

Pageants as Racial "Homeplaces" and Ethnic Combat Zones

It's not about me. It's about us.

—Miss Florida A&M University[1]

I think the pageant [Miss Native American University of Arizona] helps to create a safe space. When I go to this pageant, I at least saw that there were people who were proud of who we were.

—2009 Miss Native American, University of Arizona[2]

Silliman University is a large Christian university in the Philippines. Its 2004 campus queen, Stacy Danika Alcantara, is a proponent of campus pageants. She believes that pageants can be remade to become a "significant force for local socio-civic concerns."[3] While she knows that many people believe that beauty pageants are "inherently exploitative, given the context of beauty pageants that most of us may be more familiar with . . . mere parades of female flesh," she nonetheless believes that "the concept of subversion will actually make the pageant structure bear the burden of our social concerns."[4]

The proliferation of racial and ethnic pageants on predominantly white campuses, the greater number of women of color entering white campus contests, and the ever-increasing veneration of queens on historically black campuses all raise thorny questions about normativity and subversion. Can black college pageants indeed be subversive, as Miss Silliman hopes, or do they largely reinscribe the normative and the exceptional? What does it mean to challenge racism or ethnic marginalization in pageants if the pageant form itself implicitly reaffirms normative class, gender, and heterosexual assumptions? What is being subverted when aspirations for racial pride and embodied distinction are combined on the college catwalk?

Vast differences and contradictions in meanings and aesthetics exist within and among ethnic pageants and among the strategies of signification that student contestants use to frame and narrate their pageant experiences. On one level, black pageant contestants often provide a sharp contrast to the white queens profiled in chapter 4. As we have seen, they primarily emphasize pageantry's contributions to the enhancement of personal pride and self-confidence, public presentation skills, poise, careerism, and self-advancement. In contrast, contestants in ethnic pageants are more likely to claim pageants as public platforms to advance positive racial representations and identities, honor legacies, and build community.[5] On another level, however, they generate important scholarly debate over the degree to which they emphasize resistance or accommodation.[6] This tension is no less present in college-based racial and ethnic pageants.

College pageants are important venues that reveal the shifting and contradictory impacts of gender, race, ethnicity, class, and institutional mission on student cultures. They can be differentiated as racially marked "comfort," "contact," or "combat zones" that reflect historically racialized legacies and ongoing patterns of assimilation, affiliation, community, and separatism. This chapter examines some of the perplexing racial and ethnic questions embedded in campus pageants by exploring the collective, strategic, and occasionally emancipatory aspects of academic pageantry along with their damaging, disciplinary, and regulatory effects.

Thus in this chapter, in addition to probing the palliative effects that many participants experience in ethnic pageants, I also explore how these campus pageants can re-authorize and prolong longstanding lacerations and discontents that inevitably accompany the public appraisal of college women's bodies, behaviors, and aspirations, whatever their social location. In addressing how race and ethnicity are mediated in pageant pursuits, I use notions of "wounding," "restoration," and "preservation" to emphasize the interplay of visceral tensions, history, and gratifications that circulate through pageant spectacles, narratives, and agendas. For many African American contestants in particular, pageantry provides openings for mending the festering wounds of the racist disparagement of black women's bodies and for celebrating black pride, cultural history, and life-worlds. When these positive elements are brought into play, black pageants can serve as restorative and safe "homeplaces" to counter racial exclusion and isolation. Especially at historically black colleges, queens identify communal attachment, lineage, and the promotion of black excellence and the black college experience itself to explain the prominent place of student royalty on black campuses. Unlike traditional white pageants, black pageants on historically black campuses have rarely been targeted by student protest and mockery, or dismissed as sexist and trivial.

Pomp and Pride

For starters, black and white campuses differ in what is expected of their queens during their reigns. Especially on HBCU campuses, queens are typically integral to campus life and well-known to university officials. Pageant queens tend to be given greater official campus responsibilities and play more active parts in official university events on these campuses than on predominantly white campuses. For example, Morehouse College queens are centrally involved in the college orientation of first-year students, greeting them as the first ladies of the college. A former Miss Maroon and White described this event to me as "so much deeper than giving you a class schedule and an advisor. It is where you become part of the brotherhood, sisterhood, where they instill in you school pride, the school song. Part of this school pride is the queen and how you revere her."[7] She continued by noting that since white popular culture tends to portray black colleges as merely "fraternities, step shows, and marching bands," African American queens must be "vocal and mobile" in speaking out about the academic strength of black colleges since they can reach a large audience as ambassadors for their campuses.[8]

Consequently, queen coronations on black colleges are often elaborate and expensive productions with pomp, debutante-style presentations, and celebrity performances, despite the financial struggles of many black colleges to remain open. Academic queen coronations on these campuses involve lavish gift-giving and extensive planning, much like wedding ceremonies. In 2004, I attended the National Black Queens Leadership Conference, which included a workshop, "Making It a Night to Remember: The Perfect Coronation." This workshop was designed to help newly elected HBCU queens select their coronation themes, gowns, and crowns and to be "creative and classy."[9] Here, they were urged to "think drama, production, and originality" when designing their coronations and to consider using "decorative enhancements" such as arriving in horse-drawn carriages, being lowered onto the stage from the ceiling, or being carried on a dais by an entourage of male students dressed in loincloths, for their grand entrances. They were coached to think about using theatrical staging and special effects such as dry ice and smoke.[10] Conference organizer Dale Williams suggested a range of themes including "Angelic (Heaven, Pearly Gates, and Angels), Cinderella, Cotton Club, African, Broadway (popular plays such as the *Lion King* and *Chicago*), and Oriental"; however, she warned the queens that they must research their "Oriental countries" so as to not offend others.[11] The same conference featured a fashion show sponsored by a pageant gown boutique and bridal salon in which former campus queens modeled sparkling crowns and iridescent gowns befitting just such coronation ceremonies. The fashion show narrator peppered his remarks with reminders that "beauty comes in all sizes" and that certain gowns are designed to "tame your bountiful blessings" and urged the queens to order their gowns in advance especially if wearing a "wedding or bridesmaid gown." Already we can see the styling of race and ethnicity into class-laden displays of glamour, sophistication, and body management.

Drawing large crowds of students and staff, HBCU coronations—whether with generic themes such as "Princess Diana" and "Unveiling a True Star" or racialized ones that evoke Diaspora and African roots such as "A Long Journey Home" and "Elegance through the Ages: Returning to the Source"—are both expensive and time-consuming to stage. A recent KSU coronation had to be moved to the city civic center to accommodate the entrance of the queen in a horse-drawn carriage. Egyptian-themed coronations are especially popular, and both KSU and Morris Brown College have featured queens reclining on divans or sitting on thrones decorated with palm trees and carried on stage by well-muscled, bare-chested men dressed in Egyptian garb representing Pharaohs.[12]

The 2002 coronation of Mr. and Miss Kentucky State University was an especially extravagant occasion. That year's coronation theme was "The Essence of a Harlem Night: The Renaissance of a Soulful Past to Revive our Present and Ignite Our Future." Hundreds of students, alumni, and staff attended the crowning. A lengthy processional preceded the entrance of the king and queen that included the university president, relatives of the king and queen, eight lords and ladies of the Regalia bearing imperial accoutrements including robes, sashes, golden scepters, and medallions. Over thirty organizational queens and kings, four class queens, three ladies-in-waiting, and finally two young elementary school children, Little Mr. and Miss KSU, were also present on stage. After the king had made his way to center stage, the audience was told to "Rise all thee subjects for your Royal Highness." With smoke billowing throughout the campus auditorium, the queen was then lowered from a balcony on a forklift. Dressed in robes and crowns, the king and queen were serenaded and the queen received a kiss from the president. After their speeches, the queen anointed the heads of award-winning athletes who were bowed down before her, and then both the king and queen ascended a stairway to their thrones. Representatives of campus organizations and numerous campus officials, including the university president, the general legal counsel, and several vice presidents, each laid gifts at their feet. [13]

Such heights of reverence, pomp, and adoration are rarely seen on predominantly white campuses. At best, the post-pageant experiences of white academic royals are ephemeral, often amounting to little more than brief appearances at homecoming football games and rallies. The 2001 homecoming queen at UK, Courtney Reynolds, observed that "my only job was to be in the parade and maybe do something at the pep rally." She concluded, "It's fun and that's all it is. I'm not sentimental about it. It's something funny to put on my resume when I apply to med school."[14] Black queens competing in historically black contests rarely describe their reigns as fun, but rather emphasize their responsibilities to serve their racial communities and to uphold legacies. Black queens in historically white pageants on the other hand, as we shall see, often equate their pageant experiences with being in a racial combat zone.

Collegiate black pageants are also more likely than white pageants to feed into national and even international competitions. The Alpha Phi Alpha fraternity's Miss Black and Gold pageants are held on many campuses and have been scaled up to include state and national level competitions. The National Black College Alumni Hall of Fame Foundation established a national campus queen pageant in

1985 for historically black colleges and universities that continues today. According to its 2008 pageant guidelines, this national competition plays "a pivotal role in supporting the Hall of Fame mission to be a catalyst and partner for ensuring the stability, strength, and excellence of the nation's historically black colleges and universities."[15] Paradoxically, while candidates must prepare an oration on "HBCUs: Bringing Dreams to Reality," they were also asked to report their bust, waist, and hip sizes.[16] Indeed, the Alumni Hall of Fame competition both overlaps with and diverges from traditional pageant protocols in interesting ways. For example, its contestants are asked how they would intervene in structural inequalities facing African Americans, such as single-parent families, teen violence, drugs, and homelessness, and how they would work to strengthen black collectivities. Yet they are also asked to answer typically mundane pageant questions, such as what they would put in a time capsule or how they define beauty. Scoring guidelines recycle conventional pageant norms including "confidence in presentation and appearance, poise, grace, elegance, personality, and deportment."[17]

On the international stage, the Thurgood Marshall Fund and United Negro Fund select U.S. black campus queens to compete in the International Miss Malaika competition. Designed "to celebrate and unite African culture and its Diaspora through beauty," contestants are judged on interviews, tropical wear, traditional dress, and formal wear.[18] Organizers acknowledge that although the pageant has similarities to the Miss World and Miss Universe pageants, it is distinct from these since there is no swimsuit competition, surgical implants are banned, and the judging of contestants is based on non-Western standards of beauty.[19]

Expensive and elaborate as they are to stage, black college pageants are far more likely than white contests to be sponsored by corporations including Gillette, Delta and American Airlines, and Coca-Cola and to receive media attention. In 2007, Fashion Fair Cosmetics and the Tom Joyner Foundation established their own region-wide black college queen pageant, the Miss Mid-Eastern Athletic Conference. National media outlets such as *Ebony* have for many decades showcased black college queens, an indication of how important these pageants are believed to be. *Ebony's* managing editor, Lynn Norment, observed that "for so many years, black college queens did not get the recognition they have deserved. We feel it is important to share with our readers these academically exceptional black women who represent their various college campuses."[20]

Black College Queens: Lineage and Mission

Black queens carry a strong sense of history, lineage, duty, and mission into campus pageants, and they explicitly differentiate their pageants from white ones. A Miss Morris Brown College, for example, said that African Americans "must commit ourselves to the excellence of self so that no one else can define us" and that pageants provide an important platform for achieving this goal.[21] A More-house College Miss Maroon and White declared that "white women haven't had to prove they are beautiful so there is not any political backbone to a white pageant. There isn't the sense of racial pride and upward mobility that we have." [22] Shirley Massey, wife of the president of Morehouse College, concurs that royalty traditions are vital "since we have been uprooted." "Tradition," she adds, "is very important because it keeps us attached."[23] Freda Mask Jackson, a former attendant to a Miss Maroon and White, agrees that black royalty traditions have "always been about culture, not just the queens. It's the pageantry of it, the recognition by your peers and an expression of sexuality. It never diminished us intellectually or meant we were less intelligent females. It is about black men seeing us as queens, and that's how all black women should be treated."[24]

Black queens from HBCUs emphasize history, healing, and renewal to convey the significance of queen rituals on black campuses. The post-pageant narratives offered by some of these black queens indicate a significant degree of politicization and a strong sense of communal mission. In 1974, the National Miss Collegiate African American pageant, a star-studded, nationally televised pageant, was established and held in Hollywood.[25] A recent winner reports that being a queen helped to strengthen her political commitments to saving black colleges and her connections to Africa as well as enriching her sense of community and black culture. She also reports having met with four state governors to advocate additional funding for HBCUs. After making official visits as a campus queen to several African countries, she experienced an awakening after she got a "taste of home." She told a reporter that "seeing the beauty of our African history and culture, I decided that when I come back to campus that part of my message to students at black universities would be to rededicate ourselves to our institutions and to the history of Africa."[26] Her mission was to promote "education and the infusion of an Afro-centric curriculum, particularly Afro-centric values, like collectivity and spirituality."[27]

Sarah Poole, the student director of Berea College's black pageant, likewise affirms the importance of acknowledging African roots and heritage.

> This year's theme is "African Pride: Reclaiming our Heritage." The focus is on expressing African culture through African beats, attire, music, dance, and more. . . . The pageant symbol is Sankofa—of a symbol of learning from the past. Sankofa is an Akan (southern Ghana) word that means we must go back and reclaim the past so we can move forward; so we can understand why and how we came to be who we are today.[28]

Ali'yah Arnold, Miss Albany State University 2010, pointed out that HBCU royalty has its roots in Africa because such traditions "go back to our heritage and where we come from. In Africa, we had kings and queens of our villages" and campus royalty represent "where you come from historically."[29]

The survival of black colleges is a key concern for many black queens of academe. I learned much about this from a recent Morehouse College Miss Maroon and White, whom I refer to as Tanya (a pseudonym). More than any other informant, Tanya helped me understand the commitments and motivations of HBCU queens. She stressed, for example, that black colleges have had to navigate racialized barriers that white higher education institutions do not face. The survival of black colleges is precarious, and queens, she believes, play important roles in promoting them.

> White colleges have never had to do much self-promotion. They never had to go out and defend themselves. Your white colleges do not have to do much work. You have authentic institutions for higher learning. It is not the same for black colleges. They have to work to validate themselves in everyone's eyes. They literally had to pull themselves out of church basements. A decent building might take over twenty-five years to build because of fundraising difficulties. Black colleges have had to work to promote themselves, they need to say here is our best and brightest. Here are the alumni we produce.[30]

These themes of preservation and promotion, as well as the need to counter deeply entrenched racist legacies, are indeed major catalyses for black campus pageantry. A speaker at the 2004 National Black Queen's Conference, Dr. Tonea Steward, told the newly crowned queens gathered there that as campus royalty, they played significant roles in the ongoing struggles to counter racial exclusion and the white disparagement of black womanhood. She exhorted the queens to remember the legacy of disfigurement and violence wrought by white slavery on black womanhood during their reigns.

> You are a legacy and your job is to keep the image and flame of black females alive . . . you will represent every black female on campus. You are the epitome of womanhood, strength, and power. You will let them know that out of the dust of slavery, we have risen. You represent the broken shackles of slavery, you represent scrubbing floors in someone else's house, and you represent cotton sacks on our backs. You represent what we have achieved as black women.[31]

Both legacy and collective well-being are predominant themes for many black queens and they are expected to be activists by many students. After reciting the statistics on the state of Black America including the number of black men in prison, the increasing displacement of poor blacks in cities, and HIV/AIDS in the black community, Jamie Jenkins, a student columnist at Clark Atlantic University, reminded a newly crowned queen that there are major differences between Miss America and the queen of a HBCU. A black queen, she said, "should be more politically conscious and involved" given the rampant racial inequality in the U.S. She urged black queens "to be about the business of queen-ship, not the beauty of it. Simple platforms may have been sufficient for her reign in the past, but how can that suffice any longer with the state of Black America as it is today?"[32]

Other queens have echoed the importance of communal survival and the urgency of cultivating a robust racial community in light of rampant racism. Morehouse College's Tanya told me that it is important to understand both history and the current racial climate in order to appreciate the curative effects of black pageants.

> Black pageants are part of a history of what black people have done to survive and be proud of ourselves. It keeps us sane in an insane country. It is so easy not to love being black. Because so many people question why would one be proud to be black. Everything in this country says that black is the bottom. So they say, why do you think black is beautiful? Why would you want to attach yourself to Africa with its diseases and plagues? But in the face of all this we have our cultures that love being black all day long. We set our own standards of what black excellence is and what black beauty is.[33]

In contrast to such passionate commitments to political change through pageantry, the only white speaker at the black queen conference, a pageant coach for the "Boot Camp for Beauty Queens," horrified the black queens when she told them that she had changed her platform, much as one changes her clothes, because she decided another social problem was more palatable.[34]

In addition to collective history and political activism, communal connection, sanity, and love are said to motivate black pageants and homecoming rituals. Tanya asserts that because of racism, black homecomings are safe and loving homeplaces that promote restorative effects for students and alumni.

> The legacies of black campus homecomings are all about reinvesting your love in that school. They are not pagan celebrations like the ones at say Dartmouth College where they built a bonfire and ran around it. There was absolutely nothing about the love for the community there. Everything was about the game. At black college homecomings, however, we say to hell with the game. We came because we wanted to be with each other. We came because we love this place. All these tokens, the bands, queens, and pom squads represent love for black colleges and black people.[35]

Community, connection, and the healing effects of homecoming draw black alumni to campus in large numbers. She explained that black college graduates need a homeplace and a buffer zone to recover from the assaults of daily racism they experience. She observed further that black alumni "get lonely in that world and coming back to homecoming becomes therapy. I have to get back to people who understand me. I have to get back to people whom I do not have to explain everything to."[36]

Many of the contestants and organizers of racial/ethnic campus pageants argue that their pageants are thus quite distinct from traditional white contests. They are quick to point to unique characteristics and missions that distinguish their pageants from the conventionality and whiteness that permeate the archetypal Miss America contest. Miss Maroon and White emphatically assured me that she would not participate in the historically white Miss Georgia pageant, part of the Miss America system, since "converting the culture of what it takes to represent a black school into what it takes to be in a white pageant is like converting oil to water. What we value in one as our black college queen has little to do with what is valued at the Miss Kentucky, Miss Georgia, and Miss Virginia pageants."[37] She also pointed out that although some black queens, such as Miss Hampton University, regularly compete in Miss Virginia, a Miss America feeder pageant, she believes that such traditions compromise the principles of black pageants and black women's bodies.

> If you give girls the idea that they have to compete in Miss Virginia, you are only going to get a certain kind of girl to go out for Miss Hampton University, which totally undoes the whole process. You are going to get mostly black pageant girls who might not represent the student body. Black pageant girls are such a minority. They also have this body stuff in Miss America. Black pageant girls must have this moderated white woman's body. So they are not going to be my size at all. I mean I would be too big for a white pageant. Their hair, makeup, and everything else is going to reflect that cultural expectation and nothing of the black experience. I do not want to hear Whitney Houston songs over and over again. I do not want to alter my body to be in those pageants. . . . You have to put Vaseline on your teeth. I'm not doing it.[38]

Tanya concluded by evoking the wounds of slavery, asserting that "white pageants were created to celebrate the mythology of white chastity, white beauty, and a very narrow perception of white beauty at that. I mean you might as well put me on the auction block. It would be less humiliating." [39]

Tanya is not the only black queen to contend that black pageants have both distinct body politics and meanings for their participants and audiences. The 2001 winner of the Mr. Black UK pageant, William Wright, celebrated the embrace of big bodies in black pageants. He said, "Generally you do not find overweight people who are willing to participate in pageants. However, both Ms. Black UK and I are nice-sized people. It is rare because people who are overweight have insecurities, yet both of us are outgoing people with good stage presence. We both think we are nice looking and we feel like we broke a few stereotypes."[40] A contestant for the 2002 Ms. Black UK pageant did a monologue on how her weight had eliminated her from white student dance teams and campus pageants. She told the audience proudly, "I am a big-boned black woman whose intellect is wider than my body."[41] As we shall see, not all ethnic pageant organizers and contestants share such fervor for marking difference and opposition from white contests, nor do all black contestants share the same racial politics and beauty aesthetics. As Craig has observed, "standards of beauty within non-white communities have been neither monolithic nor identical with dominant standards."[42]

In 1990, Leslie Thomas, the white director of student life at historically black KSU, initiated the Miss Pride pageant (a feeder pageant for Miss America) despite resistance she encountered from those who believed it would detract attention and resources from the Miss Kentucky State University pageant, the traditional homecoming pageant. Although she believed that both pageants were equally important, rather than amplify the racialized mission that characterizes many black college homecoming pageants, Thomas stressed that black women need remedial coaching and practice to perform competitively in the traditionally white, middle-class Miss America system. She believed that there is an experiential difference between black and white contestants and their pageant performances.

> Historically, not many African American women have been involved in pageants whereas many white women, "Jon Benet types," have competed since they were little. Therefore, white women do not have to be trained on how to walk, smile, or fix their hair and makeup because they have been doing it since they were young girls when their mothers put mascara on them. If white women have a talent and good interviewing skills, they have an advantage since my ladies usually do not have any experience, and they have never walked on a pageant stage. Although there are many black pageants, this lack of experience is especially apparent in the Miss America system. However, the increased number of African Americans in Miss America, such as Vanessa Williams as well as two recent biracial and one African American Miss Kentucky winners, means that they now have those images and experiences.[43]

Despite desires for communal restoration and the disruption of racialized hierarchies and exclusions, the reliance on conventional pageant formatting—especially evening gown, swimsuit, and talent segments—dilutes and tames ethnic pageants by heightening their resemblance to prototypical whitened pageant performances. Furthermore, the competitiveness and public appraisal of beauty and bodies in ethnic pageants may serve to adulterate political and cultural claims of difference. Black contestants sometimes modify, reinvent, and/or overlook problematic pageant components. Although some queens reinvent and stretch pageant customs, their participation nonetheless helps to ensure the survival of the traditional pageant competition to determine gendered merit on college campuses.

Tanya, a recent Miss Maroon and White, for example, admitted that in addition to losing the pageant, contestants face other risks. She explains that, in her case, she had to be screened and judged by twenty Morehouse men even to qualify to compete in the pageant. Once she successfully passed the screening interview, she and the other survivors of this preliminary interview advanced to the pageant stage, where their performances were cheered or jeered by hundreds of Morehouse men. She explains that contestants whose stage performances failed to ignite Morehouse men are "talked about for years," so contestants work hard to earn the approval of their largely male audience. She also admits that she agonized over what to do for her pageant talent to avoid such ignominy.

In her case, Tanya was able to stretch the tightly corseted pageant format to allow her to politicize her mission. After much consternation, she decided that since she was a writer, and had written some very pointed pieces on class politics and homophobia at Morehouse in the past, she would perform a political monologue about black colleges while she had the attention of hundreds of black college students. Her monologue urged the audience to fight for black colleges in Atlanta such as Morris Brown College, which, unlike neighboring Spelman College and Morehouse College, was facing severe financial crisis. Situating her piece in the national context of the closure of many black schools, and using the imagery of archeological ruins, she asked her audience to imagine in the future that two white Emory University students were digging through the dirt only to find a bounced check where Morris Brown College once stood.

Despite valiant efforts by black queens like Tanya to invest pageants with political significance, pageant orthodoxies prevail. The disabling effects of class are unrecognized in most black pageants. Evening gown competitions and the showcasing and evaluations of classed feminine allure often seem to supersede the counter-hegemonic pageant aspirations at black colleges. In 2005, I attended Morehouse College's Miss Maroon and White pageant. The publicity for the pageant featured seven slender contestants wearing low-cut, strapless, or spaghetti-strap black dresses. A former Miss Maroon and White told me that it was typical that no "contestants with big bodies" had made it past the initial screening by a committee of Morehouse men to advance as finalists.[44]

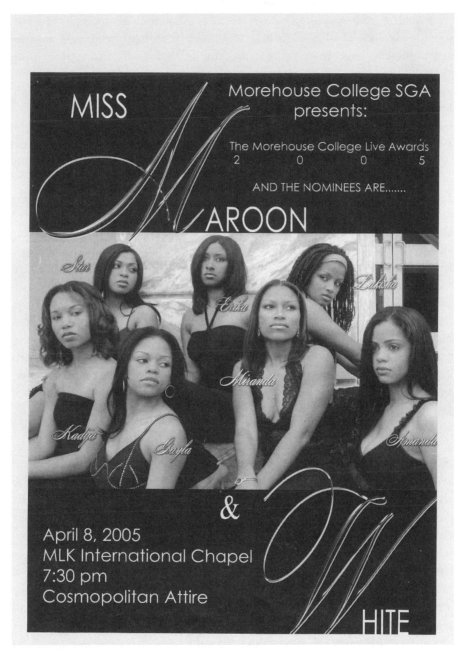

Figure 5.1 2005 Miss Maroon and White pageant contestants platforming normative beauty and bodies. Courtesy of Morehouse College Student Government Association, 2005.

Annually, the *Morehouse Quarterly* features glamorous photographs and bio-graphic sketches of each contestant. Although academic credentials are pre-sented, descriptions are very similar to those of 1950s, with their emphasis on desirability to men. One contestant was described as being "magnificent, capti-vating in coral. This vivacious candidate transcends beauty. This Georgia Peach, best known for her sweet southern hospitality, is a junior biology major at Spelman College with professional plans to enter the dynamic medical field of cosmetic surgery."[45] A student majoring in women's studies was described as an "original distraction, stopper of any show and [one who] can truly compete with the beauty of the rainbow. She is the vision of which all men dream."[46]

Morehouse pageants are major productions, perpetuating a tradition started in 1977 when student director George Folks, along with Spike Lee (who directed the pageant in 1979), revitalized the pageant to resemble a fast-paced variety show. An invitation-only buffet sponsored by the Office of Student Services and the Student Government Association preceded the 2005 pageant I attended. In front of a mainly male audience, while fog billowed on stage and bass music pul-sated in the background, seven finalists took to the stage to compete for the crown. Wearing heels, mini-skirts, and evening gowns, some danced, others played piano, and a few recited monologues to woo the Morehouse men's vote. Each con-testant chose her own outfit to wear during the Q&A. Several wore skimpy outfits as they responded to questions such as "What is the most divisive issue at More-house? What is your definition of peace? Are blacks guilty of stereotyping whites? Do you think the Bible is a sexually oppressive book?"

After the Q&A, while each candidate modeled her evening gown on stage, a short synopsis of her career ambitions, major, student activities, and favorite motto was read to the audience. Although there was no swimsuit competition, it seemed obvious to me that the contestants who garnered the most applause throughout the pageant were those who gave the most sexualized performances. Amid sexualized performances and scanty clothing, the loud appraisals of female desirability made by the male student body, and the disappointed faces of women who lost the competition, I found it hard to find counter-hegemonic moments in the pageant. While racial wounds and afflictions, the legacy of a long history of racism, and the degradation of black women were often referenced during the competition, gendered hetero-normativity, stylishness, and class savvy seemed to reign supreme on the stage of the Morehouse chapel that evening.

Although Morehouse College does not conduct a swimsuit competition, other HBCUs do. Since 1968, Grambling State University has held the annual Miss Cover Girl and Calendar Girl Pageant. It is co-sponsored by American Airlines and the Division of Student Affairs. Stephan Fontenot, Grambling's director of student affairs, has stated: "It is a great opportunity for young ladies at our institu-tion not only for exposure to pageantry, but for scholarship opportunities."[47] The thirteen winners are pictured in their swimsuits in both the student yearbook and in an official and widely circulated school calendar listing a variety of campus events. In 2004, Grambling State University's president, Horace Judson, issued greetings to new students on the cover of the GSU academic/swimsuit calendar and offered his congratulations to the women "whose beauty enhances these pages."[48] Each month displays a page of photographs of each "calendar girl" in her swimsuit and evening gown. Twenty-two contestants competed in the 2008–9 Miss Cover Girl Pageant when four special awards were given to Miss Academic Excellence, Miss Beauty, Miss Self-Expression, and Miss Sense of Style. In addition to these official swimsuit competitions, GSU students also participate in an annual "Best Bodies in Town—A Shapely Campus Contest" and the annual Black and Gold pageant, which also features a swimsuit competition. The Miss Grambling State University pageant does not require a swimsuit competition, but many of its contestants boast extensive pageant credentials and have competed in bathing suits in other venues, including the Miss Cover and Calendar Girl pageant.

Black pageants at Morehouse, Grambling, and elsewhere each showcase and perpetuate variant degrees of pageant conventionality, middle-class sensibilities, and gendered normativity. At the same time, some also seek to unsettle public meanings of black bodies by showcasing embodied excellence, providing alternative rituals and recognition for black women, and fostering oppositional politics. These tensions between format and content sometimes escalate when ethnic women establish separate racial/ethnic pageants or compete in historically white contests. Here, they must confront not only the inherent contradictions deeply embedded in pageantry itself but also stiff white resistance.

Pageants as Contact and Combat Zones

Inheriting a tradition extending back to the early decades of the twentieth century, some women of color and ethnic organizations continue to use campus pageants as symbolic venues from which to stake claims for recognition and visibility. Entering historically white beauty pageants, especially homecoming pageants, has been one strategy used by students to challenge racial and ethnic invisibility and exclusion on predominantly white college campuses. Valerie Felita Kinloch has deftly explored the issue of racial empowerment and inclusion of African Americans in non-collegiate white pageants, such as Miss America, asking whether and to what extent the resignification of historically white pageants is possible. She concludes that "Miss America is not a space where black women can engage in acts of individual and collective self-healing or cultural affirmation for the pageant has never been and probably will never become, to use bell hooks's terminology, a *homeplace*, a place of safety. For black women, it has always been, to use Mary Louise Pratt's phrase, a *contact zone*, a space of asymmetrical power relations."[49]

Figure 5.2 Grambling State University students competing in campus best bodies contest. Grambling State University *Tiger Yearbook*. Courtesy of the A. C. Lewis Memorial Library, Grambling State University, 1992.

For at least ten years, the University of North Carolina at Chapel Hill has been one such racial contact zone. In 1994, *Jet* magazine reported that racial tensions had once again erupted in Chapel Hill over the election of the sixth African American University of North Carolina homecoming queen. In a series of interviews, former black queens at the university reported numerous instances of racial harassment, including one queen who had her tires slashed and another who had a note on her car windshield that read "We will not have another 'N' queen." Cheri Gibson, the 1991 homecoming queen, told *Jet* that her win was the "worst week of her life." The student newspaper portrayed her "as a person who cried racism at the drop of a hat as well as somebody who would do anything to get the crown. I was seen as someone completely opposite myself. The problem is simple. White students and alumni resent that blacks are winning."[50] The 1992 queen, Tywanda Ellison, reported that people refused to applaud at her crowning ceremony, and many people told her that "she did not represent this university."[51] With only 1,800 black students on a campus of 22,000, Ellison said, "Being a homecoming queen is a *way for us to say we are here* [emphasis added]. We want to be recognized. We have to demand representation because we are outnumbered." Finally, the 1993 queen lamented that because the student newspaper did not mention her qualifications, other contestants appeared more qualified. Despite these barriers, vice-chancellor Harold Wallace said that "black students have learned how politics work—they pool their votes and that's why they are successful."[52]

Four years later, the conflict still raged. The president of the university's Black Student Movement, Tamara Brown, said that "we are at a university where everyone gets in an uproar when a minority is crowned." She said that during the 1998 halftime crowning, "ninety-five percent of the people were not standing up in honor of the people we just crowned. Hardly anyone else (besides the black population) was applauding the queen."[53] A white king nominee, Lester Crafton, a member of the university's marketing club, observed that the Black Student Movement vote was a significant factor but added, "Often, they are the most qualified candidates." Nonetheless, he complained: "It's kind of ridiculous that for nine years, black students have won. It's not representative of the entire campus."[54] Student president Reyna Walters, on the other hand, said, "I think it is ridiculous that people get upset because there has been a black homecoming queen for the last nine years. I mean, think about how many years there wasn't a black homecoming queen."[55]

Supporters of campus cultural centers elsewhere often contend that campus administrators do not take strong enough steps to validate their campus presence, a concern that often surfaces around campus queen pageants.[56] In the 1990s, both Duke University and the University of South Carolina stopped selecting homecoming queens, in part because of the racial turmoil that ensued when African American women were selected.[57]

Although pageant traditions pose formidable obstacles to change, contestant testimonies reveal the ongoing political importance they attach to entering historically white pageants. These women assert that their pageant victories can help to crumble racial boundaries, counter exclusion and invisibility, and offer learning opportunities for white students to understand different cultural traditions. An African American member of the UK homecoming royalty court urged other African American students to "consider running not just to represent themselves but to make a statement that we are here."[58] The 2008 University of Alabama homecoming queen asserted that she sought the crown so she could "set a good example" and encourage others to be "accepting of a more modern social situation like having a black queen."[59]

One of my former African American students recently entered the Miss Kentucky Derby Princess pageant with a similar agenda. She received cautionary advice from a former black Derby Princess contestant, her mother, and from me when she asked me for a letter of recommendation that was required for pageant entry. She, like many others, was buoyed by a sense of racial mission, especially since, as she put it, "it does not happen every year—just every now and then that they [the white women sponsors] decide to throw one [an African American woman] into the competition."[60] Her sense of duty is a cornerstone of many black contestants' narratives and a catalyst for entering these racialized combat zones.

Students representing other ethnic constituencies also voice similar ambitions. Tania Rivera, the first Latina homecoming queen at the University of Connecticut, described both her pre-pageant nervousness and her ultimate victory as advancing the collective good of Latinas on campus.

> The night before I kept thinking what if I fall in front of these people? What if I don't win? I'll disappoint all of my friends and the Puerto Rican Latin American Cultural Center. How I got into the running was by chance, but the most important reason why my journey began was to show the University of Connecticut the beauty of being Latina. I wanted them to see the different faces we are. Latinas are of different shades, sizes, and personalities. From every walk of life, we are still Latina. However, our common link, which is truly beautiful, is the home we come from; a festive, rich culture that thrives within us.[61]

A UK Black Student Union nominee for homecoming queen told me that she "was not seeking the crown or the hype that comes with being a queen," nor did she want to win "just because I thought it was time for a woman of color to win, but because I think I am an excellent representative of many different groups including women, black people, and the people of Appalachia." She aspired to reduce the partitioning of the student body by participating in the homecoming queen pageant.

I hoped that this would be another line that we could erase because this is a campus community and we pass each other every day often without looking at each others' faces and that has to change. This all could begin with one person and if that could be me that would be great. We have to intertwine if we are ever going to be a true community. Lots of folks on both sides do not agree with this but we have a choice about being here. UK is not a perfect place but no college is and there is room for change.[62]

Not only do ethnic women enter and, in some cases, win traditionally white contests, but recently a few white women have entered and won key positions as queens of historically black colleges and universities. In 2009, Elisabeth Martin, a white woman attending KSU, embarked upon a well-lubricated campaign to become Miss Kentucky State University with the help of seventy-five volunteers. Unlike most white students attending HBCUs, Martin lived in the dorms and asserted "I love diversity."[63] Despite her mother's worry that "people would think she was trying to usurp their authority or run for Miss KSU just to be the first white title holder," Martin threw herself into the campaign for student votes as well as preparing for the pageant competition itself.[64] Although she spent less than her opponents, she flooded the campus with postcards, bookmarks, and banners written in five different languages, baked brownies for Men's Appreciation Day, held a luncheon for off-campus students, and staged a movie night for international students. She also offered a "true beauty" seminar that included a talk by the campus minister on inner beauty as well as information on how to "dress to impress." Participants in the seminar received free gifts including manicures and "girly stuff" that she had purchased at Big Lots. After Martin was crowned the first white queen of an HBCU, she told me that she "did not run to be the first white queen of an HBCU but rather to serve the university."[65] Anticipating possible fallout from her victory, the president of KSU said, "People forgot that 40% of our students are other than African Americans. She could not win without the support of all of the students."[66] Not everyone was supportive, however. Martin told me she felt some tensions including negative student comments on Facebook and from staff who felt that she could not represent and relate to black women. One staff person even told Martin that she was a "disgrace to the university."[67] She defended herself by saying, "as a woman, I know what other women go through." Despite the media frenzy surrounding her win, she felt that she was "not promoted as much as former queens had been by the university" since she was white. For example, she had hoped to compete in the National Black College Alumni Hall of Fame pageant but she did not receive permission either from KSU or the pageant organizing committee to do so. Although Martin's coronation included a much larger than usual white audience and its theme, "A Royal Affair," did not reference racial heritage, the event was not marred by walkouts or protest.

The crowning of the first white woman as queen at Hampton University in 2009, however, did produce strife. Competing against nine black women, Nikole Churchill, a white woman from Hawaii who attended a branch campus of Hampton University in Virginia Beach, was selected by five judges as Miss Hampton University. She performed a Hawaiian hula in a swimsuit and spoke about the importance of mentoring girls on self-esteem and body image. After her victory, numerous students walked out of the pageant and the following day she was heckled at a football game. Subsequently, Churchill, pejoratively nicknamed "Lil Obama," wrote to the president and invited him to speak about racial tolerance because she felt that he would relate to her situation. She hoped that he would come to Hampton so students would "stop focusing so much on the color of my skin and doubting my abilities to represent, but rather to be proud of the changes our nation is making towards celebrating diversity."[68] She was subsequently summoned by the president of the student body to explain her hasty actions in writing President Obama. The lack of support for Churchill by some black students inspired numerous blog postings chastising black students and accusing them of racism against white women.[69]

In addition to the border crossings at historically white and black pageants that disrupt racialized boundaries, the growth of separate, and to some degree distinctive, racial/ethnic contests pageants on predominantly white campuses suggest that multiple desires are operative including making homeplaces and educating white students. Many black women are choosing to enter these ethnic pageants rather than competing in predominantly white contests. They do so with high hopes of affirming communal connections and cultural preservation and furthering cultural understandings. When asked if it is important to hold separate black pageants, a contestant in the 2002 Ms. Black University of Kentucky pageant responded to my question with a resounding yes, asserting that it is important to "show other races that we have positive characteristics and to showcase our talents." Another Ms. Black UK pageant contestant emphasized the importance of nourishing racial community, saying simply that black pageants on white campuses foster "community among black college women."[70] One African American woman told me that she participated in black pageants because, at the predominantly white UK "you don't get to do as many things with your own people."[71] Tutan Smith, secretary of the Ohio State chapter of the APA fraternity, described his university's Miss Black and Gold pageant as "a way to get our best and brightest faces out there. It boosts the morale of minorities on campus."[72]

Other ethnic groups express similar motivations. Ten Asian Pacific student clubs established a pageant at the University of Illinois-Chicago in 2003 as part of Asian American history month. Organizers and participants from the various clubs declared that the pageant was not merely a "venue for entertainment" but an opportunity to "showcase our diversity and to promote our culture."[73] This pageant, they contend, also "helps people stay connected with their culture when they are away from home. For many overseas students, this helps them meet new friends and continue to observe traditional habits. It also helps to bring Asian awareness to campus. It has a huge impact; . . . we show everyone that we have pride in our culture."[74] The Miss Asian America University of Washington Scholarship program is similarly designed to showcase "unique/special, goal-oriented, directed, ambitious" Asian women. In recruiting for the pageant, "personal enhancement" was the overarching theme, but pageant contestants here were assured that this Asian pageant was distinctive from other beauty pageants. They were told that "this pageant is organized for women by women, unlike the pageants on campus that are run by fraternity men. Not interested in becoming a tiara-wearing beauty queen who cuts ribbons? Good! We're not looking for one; we want girls who want to make a difference in their communities."[75] Nonetheless, the pageant's primary emphasis on individual enhancement and advancement, including "winning monetary grants, developing public speaking skills, self-confidence, poise, persistence, assertiveness, and increasing influential contacts that will be essential in professional and personal encounters for the rest of your life," affirms the proverbial narrative of personal empowerment through middle-class dispositions that circulates throughout mainstream white pageant rationales.[76]

Another persistent contradiction of ethnic pageants arises from the performance of ethnicity itself, since it is often done in truncated, individualized styles that reduce difference to a matter of costume and dance.[77] As a result of the momentum to renew connections to Africa, many campus pageants for AfricanAmerican and African women have redesigned competitions to include cultural lessons and fashions from Africa—small bits of ethnic piquancy.[78]

In this genre of pageantry, contestants explicitly stage cultural education by wearing African-inspired dress to showcase cultural pride and knowledge. Clemson University's Alpha Phi Alpha fraternity asserts that the most distinctive element of its Miss Black and Gold pageant is its African fashion competition, described as "vital since it allows others to view firsthand the clothing they may not have seen in person. This exposure permits some to view an aspect of one of the most important ingredients in America's melting pot."[79] Showcasing African clothes is a common part of the performances at such pageants. The 1997 Miss Black Pennsylvania State University Pageant required each contestant to wear a traditional African dress of purple and gold on stage that "signified the wealth and royalty in Africa. The clothing had to be made by the contestant or brought to her from Africa."[80]

Likewise, the 2003 UK Mr. and Ms. Black pageant featured a stage decorated with a golden gate, red flowers, and smoke that billowed from behind closed curtains. After the pageant opened with the singing of the Black National Anthem, a dance troupe performed an African dance to drum music. Next, each contestant represented an African nation by dressing in ethnic garb and giving a three minute "tour" of his or her chosen African nation, including its location, major resources, and population figures.[81]

Ms. Collegiate African American

"Don't be afraid of trying anything new and don't let anyone stop you from achieving it."

Tiffany Williams had that piece of advice after capuring the Miss Collegiate African American crown for 1990-91.

The sixth annual pageant was televised nationally from Los Angeles.

Her reign began with a two-and-a-half week visit to Africa where the 22-year-old beauty met with various ministers of ourism and foreign affairs, attended seminars and conferences and even performed.

Tiffany also took part in a two-week tour of selected black colleges and universities and was featured in numerous promotions and advertisements.

"The pageant experience has molded me to become more Afrocentric," she explained.

During the beauty contest, the candidates attended seminars and held discussions on their roles as black leaders and the evelopment of black pride and heritage appreciation.

Also, they had naming ceremonies. "We had to go through rituals to recive African names," Tiffany noted. She was named geri which means annointed.

Miss Collegiate African American 1991-92--Tiffany Williams.

Royalty/81

Figure 5.3 Winner of the Ms. Collegiate African American national pageant performing Afro-centric elegance. Grambling State University *Tiger Yearbook*. Courtesy of the A. C. Lewis Memorial Library, Grambling State University, 1992.

But pageant presentations such as these are contradictory events. Performances of ethnicity often express hybrid and individualized styles, reducing cultural complexity to appearance, costume, music, and dance. While positive gestures are made toward cultural pride, few learning demands were placed on contestants or audiences. Indeed, such performances often resemble little more than the brief culture and language lessons packaged with international Barbie dolls that Ann Ducille has termed "reductive ethnographies."[82]

Additionally, since most ethnic pageants, like their white counterparts, also include formal-wear competitions and, in some cases, swimsuit competitions, their display of sexuality and class-based elegance further undermines and displaces intended ethnic and cultural agendas. Consequently, differences from traditionally structured, white pageants that likewise trumpet conventional class and gender codes are, at least in part, effaced. This displacement was especially apparent at the 2003 state wide Miss Black and Gold Kentucky pageant designed, to "uplift the collegiate African American woman by giving her the opportunity to showcase her intelligence, talent, beauty, and poise in front of an audience of her peers."[83] Other than the black audience and contestants, the pageant itself made no nods to cultural distinctiveness. The fraternity men who moderated the pageant began by asserting "It is no longer a man's world. Women are stepping out." Indeed, the contestants did step out—in swimsuits, evening gowns, and debutante-style presentations. Contestants in the evening gown competition were escorted by men in tuxedos to be presented on stage while a male moderator described the gown and "charms" of each contestant. (He described one contestant's gown as "hugging every curve but thank God leaving a few details to the imagination.")[84] Contestants were then asked such questions as "Should women be represented as sex objects in rap? What does being an independent woman mean to you? Name an African American woman who has been a positive influence on your life." In the final viewing of contestants before the winner was announced, participating women promenaded across the stage in their finery and gave the royal wave of queens to the tune of "Golden Lady."

At the 2003 Mr. and Ms. Black University of Connecticut pageant's tribute to Black History Month, the problematics of stretching the girdle of beauty pageantry from sexualized spectacle to a forum for oppositional politics was particularly evident. A contestant who read the poem "The Black Girl Misunderstood" to protest racism in the U.S. was followed on stage by another contestant wearing four-inch stiletto heels described by an audience member as *"Sex in the City* shoes."[85] Such contradictions are often evident as contestants comply with the various categories for pageant competition. Ms. Indian Arizona State University 2007 reports that she wrote an essay for the pageant, "Honoring the Past by Preparing for the Future." As well as packing "her tribal regalia," she "purchased an evening gown and practiced walking in high heels." Presented with the option of either performing a traditional or contemporary talent, she chose to sing "Angel Baby" during the competition.[86]

The Miss Native American University of Arizona pageant is one of a few ethnic campus pageants without a formal evening gown performance. Instead, the pageant is based on an essay competition, Q&A, traditional Native American talent, contemporary talent, and traditional attire in order to crown a woman who "is able to live in two worlds, by practicing traditional values and incorporating them into the contemporary society in which we live."[87] Cheryl Yazzie, a Miss Native American University of Arizona back in the late 1990s, narrated the clan tradition in Navajo culture for her contemporary talent and explained the significance of cradle boards in Navajo culture for her traditional talent.[88]

Efforts to promote positive images of ethnicity and culture on predominantly white campuses are also hampered by the fact that audiences tend to be mainly ethnic students themselves since white students often resist and avoid them. Shonda Canada was angered when racist remarks appeared on a poster announcing a Mr. and Ms. Black University of Kentucky pageant. She wrote that "next time you are in class, count how many black students there are. Don't be surprised to find five or less. Maybe NONE. There are not simply enough minority students here to elect a Homecoming candidate into the winning position."[89] Another Ms. Black UK said that student sponsors had made a concerted effort to invite various predominantly white student organizations since "it's important for white students to understand this event is held to recognize the accomplishments of black students. People want to know why we can't just run for Homecoming Queen and King. . . . They don't understand we are a minority in numbers. We don't have the same chance as white students do to win the homecoming race."[90]

The 2002 Miss UK Black and Gold winner told me she was disappointed when the student newspaper did not adequately cover this black pageant since, if they had, white students would learn that it "was a reputable pageant," not a racialized working-class or uncultured spectacle. She said:

> Often, people think it [the UK Black and Gold pageant] will be ghetto and it is not going to be run properly. You do not have to be African American to enter the Miss Black and Gold since it has nothing to do with race but because the fraternity is majority black and mostly black women enter, you are not going to see too many white females do anything that is associated primarily with black people. This university is a very segregated place.[91]

Despite hopes on the part of participants and sponsors that black pageants will be educative vehicles, African American pageants on white campuses typically receive much less media attention than white royalty and, indeed, are often subjected to media black outs. Students at a variety of campuses have protested that African American royalty winners do not enjoy the same media coverage as white homecoming queens and kings.[92] Despite hopes of breaking boundaries, ethnic homecoming queen contestants more commonly encounter a contact zone of deeply embedded hegemonic racial, ethnic, and gender barriers.

Historically white pageants and the black-only pageants on both black and white campuses have thus been regulated by the obdurate forms of pageantry itself—competition, bodily display, runways and swimsuits, evening gowns and crowns, and platforms and platitudes. These forms both promote homogenization and permit a modicum of difference. Pageants may provide forums for alternative identity politics, yet they also reinforce hegemonic social relations and classed hierarchies of distinction while subverting and taming potentially oppositional racial agendas, even in black-only and ethnic contests. While the corset of beauty pageantry can be stretched, hopes for the expression and validation of difference are too often adulterated by the internal contradictions of pageants as well as their reliance on competition and appraisals of gendered merit to build community and showcase ethnic pride. The passion and depth of many contestants' and organizers' hopes and motives, especially those of contestants' intent on healing racialized wounds and presenting cultural complexity, are muted by pageant performances that parade sleek women in shimmering evening gowns and, often, swimsuits. The Westernized pageant template often proves to be as durable as the duct tape that contestants use to bind and shape their bodies.

Although ethnic queen rituals have been likened to restorative homeplaces that affirm racial solidarities, belonging, and tradition, these are not rest homes. As we shall see, there is often not only little respite from pressures to challenge white racism but also much pressure to conform to communal expectations for middle-class proficiencies and refined and/or glamorous femininities. Communal policing, shaming, and, for some, boot camp training for upgrading class-coded proficiencies are ongoing parts of their reigns. Demands for class assimilation and respectability, as well as contemporary neo-liberal technologies for personal transformation, animate and tightly constrain whatever oppositional possibilities may seem to exist for campus pageants and their participants.

6

Class Acts and Class Work

Poise and the Polishing of Campus Queens

Do not be deceived. Everyone, including your student body, administrators, faculty, and the outside community, wants the queen of their university to represent them with class, dignity, and grace, anything less weakens the image of the university.

—"College Queens Striving for Excellence"[1]

Whether you believe it or not, everyone wants a lady to represent their college.

—Dale Williams[2]

Being a campus queen contestant requires an ensemble of class-coded performances and competencies that I have termed "platformed" femininity. Once crowned, campus queens are expected continually to present and "platform" themselves as accomplished "scholar-ladies" who can confidently manage the everyday pressures of performing and upholding middle-class aesthetic and moralized norms for image, aspiration, academic knowledge, lifestyle, and taste throughout their reigns and to erase any stigmatizing markers of class disadvantage. They are expected to be self-assured in their etiquette, conduct, and fashion and proficient in casual conversations about food, wine, travel, fashion, academics, shopping, and cultural events as they attend alumni dinners, campus recruitment drives, and fundraising events. Reflecting the rationalities of a cultural economy emphasizing self-responsibility, personal packaging, and transformation as strategies to achieve class mobility, campus queens are expected to be connoisseurs of self-improvement, resulting in virtuoso performances of class-coded emotional, behavioral, and bodily savvy. Queens are expected to work hard on pulling themselves up by their bras and boot straps.

The 2009 Miss Kentucky State University, Elisabeth Martin, wistfully reported that being the campus queen "is intimidating since you are looked at every second. There is a great deal of pressure to dress nicely and put on makeup."[3] For many queens, the daily scrutiny of their behavior and bodies is fraught with uncertainty and strain. They are embroiled in a latticework of communal and class allegiances, desires for social mobility, and doubts over the ability to sustain the ongoing project of self-mastery. Coletta Reid, for example, poignantly recounted the concealments and accommodations she enacted to survive as a working-class scholarship college student.

> There, I began a long apprenticeship in the art of appearing middle-class. I improved my grammar, increased my vocabulary, learned about classical music. College initiated me into an alien culture that I knew I had to master to go anywhere. From the first week on I stood demurely chatting and sipping tea, took showers and acted like I felt right at home in long-winded academic discussions. I found out that there were hundreds of books everyone else could discuss that I hadn't even heard of. I went to college so I wouldn't always be a waitress or nurse's aid, getting the smallest salary for the heaviest work in the place. But I found that college doesn't just prepare you for an easier, better paying job; it ensures that you dress, talk, and think like a member of the professional class—that includes thinking you're better than working-class people and their culture.[4]

Helen Lynd notes the constant risk of failure and shame for all women who struggle to perform middle-class protocols, aspiration, and knowledge.

> It is the very triviality of the cause—an awkward gesture, a gaucherie in dress or table manners, "an untimely joke," always "a source of bitter regret," a gift or witticism that falls flat, an expressed naiveté in taste, a mispronounced word, ignorance of some unimportant detail that everyone else surprisingly knows—that helps give shame its unbearable character.[5]

The expectation that campus queens publicly represent their academic institutions with "class, dignity, and grace" multiplies the opportunities for such class ineptitude and shame. Ruth Felski notes that "opportunities for shame increase dramatically with geographic and social mobility, which provide an array of chances for failure, for betraying by word or gestures that one does not belong in the new environment."[6] Campus queens must be especially sensitive to middle-class codes for self-presentation as campus figureheads who are constantly inspected on what they wear, say, and do. This class work can be a challenge since it entails ongoing translations and performances of class codes that require considerable deftness. Since campus queens are continually subjected to class assessments, they can not rest on their laurels. As we shall see, an army of self-help and makeover industries; reality TV shows; etiquette, image, and pageant trainers; beauty academies; and charm schools stand ready to help upgrade the appearances, lifestyles, and manners of campus queens.

This chapter explores the contours of class instructions for platforming the behaviors and bodies of campus queens and contestants. I first examine the neo-liberal and meritocratic logics behind contemporary forms of makeover education and life long training that help to produce a cultural economy where class is represented as a matter of self-production, not social location, and where inequality is understood to result from improper subjectivities and cultural deficits. In order to dissect the micro-politics of racialized class training, I examine a training conference on image enhancement, makeover, and etiquette designed to help "platform" the newly crowned queens and kings of historically black colleges. I also analyze the materialization of class proficiencies expected of college women participating in two state wide, historically white pageants for college women in Kentucky, the Kentucky Derby Princess Festival and the Kentucky Mountain Laurel Festival. Through interviews with both black and white contestants, I highlight the continuing import of race for platforming class in college pageantry.

Poise and Performativity

To be successful, queen contestants are expected to radiate poise, an amalgam of class-coded behaviors, aspirations, and appearances—on and off the runway. Poise has always played a prominent role in pageant parlance, training, and competition and is a euphemism for class. In 1971, Frank Deford noted that poise is the "singular ingredient that every Miss America judge at every level is searching for."[7] Poise, he said, encompasses a variety of behaviors and bodily dispositions including

> evidence of good breeding; the way a girl takes care of herself and her appearance; femininity, with character; you can see it when you look in her eyes; the ability to handle any situation in good taste; carriage, that's all, really; style and grace, with just the right amount of confidence; something you are born with that can't be described, but you can see it; etc.[8]

Even earlier, Ophelia DeVore, owner of the Ophelia DeVore School of Charm for African American women, had noted that while difficult to define, poise and charm are foundational to social success and survival. According to Devore, charm "is the sort of bloom on a woman. If you have it, you don't need anything else; and if you don't, it doesn't much matter what else you have."[9]

Despite the lack of precise consensus on the meanings of feminine poise, charm, and bloom, these class-laden virtues have not fallen out of favor. They continue to form the core of collegiate pageant competition indexed as good taste, self-assurance, style, and manners. Contemporary campus pageants validate those contestants who can perform normative iterations of "class" understood as an ensemble of aesthetic and moralized codes for performances of self and the body. Consequently, many pageant contestants and winners work hard to enhance their class appeal through etiquette and image training—practices that contest earlier notions that poise is something you are born with.

While many college students face pressure to camouflage their working-class backgrounds and modify class markers, doing so is especially necessary for queen hopefuls.[10] To be competitive in campus contests, they must be convincing in their performances of middle-class codes of attractiveness, lifestyle, self-management, psychic and corporeal prudence, and self-presentation. Pageant selection procedures ferret out contestants who can persuasively present normative codes of middle-class taste and expression from those who lack such panache. In order to compete in a campus homecoming contest, a very enterprising working-class single mother, Stella (a pseudonym), who lived in subsidized housing and attended a community college, told me how she had successfully performed and passed as middle-class throughout the competition. When applying to compete in the homecoming competition, Stella had to complete an application that asked her to list her hobbies. Initially, she could think of nothing that would pass as a middle-class leisure pursuit. After noticing several dead house plants in her apartment, however, she decided that a claim to gardening could be read as an appropriate middle-class hobby.[11]

Stella won the competition but encountered further demands for convincing performances of middle-class status. The crowning ceremony required that she wear a tailored, suit which she neither owned nor could afford. Nevertheless, she went to a fancy department store and bought an expensive suit. After sewing the price tags in the sleeves and collar so they would be hidden from view, she made her debut on the college football field and was crowned homecoming queen in front of 30,000 spectators. She promptly returned the suit the next day so she could get her money back. Despite her lack of cash, her enterprising spirit and performance skills allowed her to win the coveted tiara. Stella's knowledge of middle-class display, along with her ingenuity in self-packaging, concealed her lack of middle-class pecuniary assets and her working-class life-world, allowing her to pass as middle-class throughout the competition. After her appearance on the football field, Stella did not have to engage in an ongoing series of class performances, displaying ease and confidence in the world of buffets and teas, alumni relations, campus marketing, and recruitment efforts as many other queens, especially on black campuses, are required to do. Hers was a one-time, albeit very visible performance on a football field. As a working-class student, however, the demands for class competence did not end when Stella stepped off the football field. For many working-class students, educational mobility requires an ongoing process of border crossings and code-switching, as well as negotiation of competing identities and allegiances. As Lucey, Melody, and Walkerdine note, for working-class students the process of educational achievement involves "uneasy hybrid subjectivities" since higher education often means differentiating themselves from family, peers, and home communities. They argue further that higher education requires both an "internal and external makeover," demanding "constant policing of internal and external boundaries, where competing and conflictual people, behavior, identifications, and ideas must be kept apart."[12]

Gwendolyn Foster has noted the paradoxical set of maneuvers, that is, etiquette, that are required to perform class in everyday life, noting that "one must seem natural in society, lacking obvious performative gestures, yet one must simultaneously be continually conscious of rules and standards that oppressively mandate everyday social commerce. Thus, one is always on display, always striving for the real in the world of the artificial."[13] John Kasson notes that etiquette requires "deep acting" achieved through "habitual emotional management to achieve polished social performances" and T. O. Beidelman notes that it requires conformity and restraint since "etiquette creates culture through bodily discipline, through modulation and repression of our impulses."[14]

The benefits of beauty pageant training in bodily and emotional regulation as a salve for structural/material inequalities and as a promised superhighway to social mobility and celebrity are evident in the laudatory narratives of beauty queens. Radhika Parameswaran has observed the global popularity of "tales of ascent and feminine triumph" in which beauty queens are valorized as ambitious and tenacious professionals who work hard to "subdue the wayward impulses" of their unruly bodies and behaviors and the traces of their working-class origins. Pageant trainers for Miss World and Miss Universe praise contestants for their warrior-like attributes including "tolerance for exhaustion, burning ambition, ability to take a beating, and soldier-like fortitude."[15]

These attributes of determination and self-makeover are embedded in the quest for the collegiate throne. Etiquette, self-enterprise, emotional management, social skills, and body regulation are key class proficiencies for achieving pageant success. Pageant contestants and queens are expected to exude or at least mimic the appearance, conduct, and tastes of the middle-class as well as the sophistication and cosmopolitanism of the elite. Pageant advisors promise that cultivating normative standards for self-presentation, comportment, and hyper-femininity will yield financial gain, self-assurance, social distinction, mobility, and, of course, the coveted crown.

Once crowned, campus queens continue to encounter a barrage of class-coded and racialized lesson plans for enhancing and enacting middle-class proprieties. As campus icons, their appearances, attitudes, and aspirations are continually scrutinized and tested. They must be tastefully groomed, poised, well-mannered, and at ease in a variety of social occasions with alumni, students, and university officials. Some queens are assigned faculty and staff as advisors and others attend special post-pageant training conferences to enhance their manners, image, and style. In return, some campus queens offer etiquette/style workshops on campus to other students as part of their service projects. Many former queens credit the instruction in etiquette and charm they received as campus queens as integral parts of their education. Alicia Reece, Vice Mayor of Cincinnati and a former Miss Grambling State University, asserts that her campus queen experiences allowed her "to develop the woman inside of me and taught me about grace and class. It completed me as a woman and as a leader."[16]

Many campus queen aspirants have had extensive pageant experiences and they have been thoroughly coached in etiquette, fashion, self-presentation, and style in order to outclass their competition. Rebekah Rotton, winner of the Miss Georgia Southern University pageant and a pageant veteran, was well schooled in the art of platforming herself since she had been, as she described it, "on the pageant circuit," which meant that "you just get your bag of tricks together" and "take your show on the road."[17] Steely determination and confidence, as well as familiarity with pageant tricks, can enable convincing performances of middle-class appearance, attitudes, and adornment that are essential for success in collegiate competitions. Not all aspirants to the throne, however, are products of the "pageant circuit," nor are they all equally comfortable and experienced with the performances of class-coded competencies that are valorized and tested in campus contests. Nonetheless, many working-class girls and women understand beauty pageants as vehicles for moving up the social ladder. In describing her own pageant participation, feminist Gloria Steinem, for example, once observed that:

> Beauty contests are ways that if you live in a poor neighborhood, you can imagine getting ahead because it is a way up. It is a way to a scholarship, to attention, and it's one of the few things you see out there as a popular symbol.... I thought I would get money for college. And it seemed glamorous. It seemed to me in high school like a way out of a not too great life in a pretty poor neighborhood.[18]

The lure of both material and symbolic rewards, including celebrity, validation, and scholarship money, propels many young women toward beauty pageantry, yet pageant success often demands intensive training as well as major investments of time and money. Harriet Levey reports that one working-class mother told her that she knew "people who had spent so much on pageants that they lost their trailers."[19]

Neo-liberal Pedagogies of Conduct and Charm

Etiquette training and social correction for and by women have had a very long history. The importance of training and mastery of the body and social amenities, however, has undergone numerous revivals that correlate with shifts in political and economic structures and sensibilities throughout the twentieth century.[20] Anxieties today about gender and race relations appear to be fueling a renewed interest in etiquette as a means of social governance. Increasingly revered as a stabilizing panacea for the vicissitudes of contemporary life and work, manners are being called upon once again to meet the demands of a deregulated and unstable economy that promises to reward self-branding and entrepreneurship.

As a nexus of purportedly neutral technologies for fostering decency and civility by corseting behaviors and bodily dispositions, etiquette is deeply imbricated with race, class, and gendered hierarchies. Bound by normative mechanisms for assigning distinction, belonging, and social trespass, etiquette structures bodies, conduct, and social relations. Numerous scholars point to the concealed interests, exclusions, othering, and power hierarchies promoted in mainstream etiquette advice and training. John Harrigan, for example, notes that etiquette is a critical part of class identity formation. He argues:

> Etiquette is a mode of naturalizing social classifications, schemes, and hierarchies, making their importance tangible through a series of restrictions on what can be said or done and linking transgressions of these prohibitions to the viability of the social order.[21]

Harrigan also observes that "social hierarchies rest on the perception that unshakable rules for behavior both derive from and support a 'natural order' of relations." John Kasson likewise argues that codes of etiquette are not merely superficial formalities but rather serve "in support of special interests, institutions of privilege, and structures of domination."[22] He concludes that "if class is a dirty secret in American life, manners is a way we launder it."[23] I would add that campus pageants, as class-laden and gendered spectacles of manners, bodies, and behaviors, are important venues for its display. Through their roles as campus figureheads and paragons of gendered conventionality, campus queens help to fortify hierarchical class-based standards for collegiate distinction.

Some scholars, I believe, rightfully interpret the proliferation of makeover technologies that celebrate personal empowerment and self-enhancement as closely tethered to neo-liberal rationalities. Nikolas Rose astutely notes that neo-liberalism has spawned a proliferation of "devices for governing conduct" that "implant in citizens the aspiration to pursue their own civility, well-being, and advancement," thereby promoting "individual and national well-being by their responsibility."[24] Individuals are encouraged to "capitalize themselves, to invest in the management, presentation, promotion, and enhancement of their own economic capital as a capacity of their selves and as a lifelong project."[25] Michael Apple likewise observes that neo-liberalism requires the "constant production of evidence that one is in fact making an enterprise of oneself."[26] Rosalind Gill notes the parallels between the post-feminist sensibilities promoted in media culture and neo-liberalism, both of which tout responsible individualism, taking control of one's life, discipline and self-surveillance, consumerism, the privatization of social and political issues, and a preoccupation with the body.[27] Instruction in etiquette, image-making, fashion, and self-branding play a pivotal part of this escalation of new, lifelong learning technologies for the ongoing project of capitalizing on and upgrading oneself. Etiquette mediates gendered and classed normativity and uses both shame and promises to rehabilitate those perceived as irresponsible or dissolute.

Neo-liberalism champions regulatory vocabularies of individual enterprise, choice, willpower, and self-control to regulate behavior and generate numerous personal strategies for improving and branding oneself to achieve success. Again, according to Nikolas Rose, the governance of subjectivity in neo-liberalism is achieved through "lifestyle maximization" and "through the regulated choices of individual citizens, now constructed as subjects of choices and aspirations to self-actualization and self-fulfillment."[28] Rose argues that the "enterprising self will make an enterprise of its life, seek to maximize its own human capital, project itself a future, and seek to shape itself in order to become that which it wishes to be. The enterprising self is thus both an active self and a calculating self."[29] Valerie Walkerdine has observed that today's demands for self-transformation are based on middle-class aesthetics and models of femininity. She argues:

> It is the qualities ascribed to femininity which are understood as the central carriers of the new middle-class individuality, building upon the long-standing incitement to women to become producers of themselves as objects of the gaze. They are to look the part, sound the part, and, moreover, they can make themselves and their homes over to conform to this middle-class aesthetic.[30]

Neo-liberal discourses of "free markets," competitiveness, and commodity consumption thus help to normalize an ethos of self-enterprise and enhancement including the importance of being what Paul Du Gay has termed the "entrepreneur of self" for maximizing opportunities.[31] Heidi Rimke characterizes our entire political era as one that champions "hyper-individual responsibility" but conceals social relations of power.[32] In such a cultural climate, Lisa Atkins and Beverley Skeggs note that the failure to participate in "middle-class taste culture" is read as an "individualized moral fault, a pathology, a problem of bad-choice, bad culture, a failure to be enterprising or to be reflexive . . . a failure of self to know, play, do, think, and/or repeat itself in a proper way."[33] The failure to thrive is attributed to the lack of willpower, accountability, and poor life choices, not to inequitable social relations. L. S. Kim notes the racialized dimensions of this fusion of self-transformation and propriety with class mobility and assimilation.

Personal transformation—whether from ugly ducking to "swan" or from poor country-bumpkin to rich, sophisticated entrepreneur—is integral to the grand American myths of race. It lies at the heart of how immigrants and their children are expected to assimilate. It also animates the expectations of those who believe in a colorblind approach to racial minorities.[34]

The lack of jobs, housing, schooling opportunities, racism, and poverty are assumed to be irrelevant to the neo-liberal logics of access and ascension. Disparities and exclusions are to be reversed and superseded by willpower and constant self-reinvention through education, life long learning, and self-help.

Under the rubric of makeover, post-feminism, personal empowerment, and self-responsibility—and drawing from multiple ideological rationales, but especially neo-liberalism—instruction in etiquette, social refinement, and self-promotion is flourishing. Valerie Walkerdine notes the importance of continuously bettering, maximizing, and marketing the self since "it is the flexible and autonomous subject who negotiates, chooses, and succeeds in the array of educational and retraining forms that fashion 'lifelong learning' and 'multiple career trajectories' that have replaced the linear hierarchies of the educational systems of the past and the jobs for life of the old economy."[35] Writing in a popular vein and uncritically, Judith Martin (Miss Manners), author of *Star-Spangled Manners: In Which Miss Manners Defends American Etiquette for a Change*, argues that self-promotion and performativity are indispensible for success. Equating etiquette with theater, since both rely upon "knowledge of how to use outward manifestations to the best effect," Martin counsels readers that

> they should have ambition to go after whatever roles they want to play, willing to keep rewriting in the determination to achieve the desired effect, confident that talent and work will succeed (although knowing the right people never hurts). They should know how to use design and gesture to capture attention and dramatize a message. They should be able to participate in dazzling displays that produce a sense of identity and delight. They need to realize that selling the project is part of the job.[36]

The escalation of interest and investment in cultivating cultured women and urbane business men has led to an explosion of etiquette merchants and manuals.[37] In the first decade of the new millennium, numerous etiquette and conduct books have flooded the publishing market including Candace Simpson Giles's 2005 *How to Be a Lady: A Contemporary Guide to Common Courtesy*, Noelle Cleary's 2001 *The Art and Power of Being a Lady*, and Jordan Christy's 2009 *How to be a Hepburn in a Hilton World: The Art of Living with Style, Class, and Grace*. Niche market etiquette guides, including Fonzworth Bentley's hip-hop-centric guide for

African American men, *Advance Your Swagger: How to Use Manners, Confidence and Style,* Alex Ellis's *Restoring the Male Image: A Look from the Inside Out,* and Karen Grigsby Bate's 2006 *The New Basic Black: Home Training for Modern Times* are also widely available.

Charm Schools and Boot Camps

Prescriptive gendered makeover pedagogies for self-advancement and beautification are flourishing in the U.S. and spreading rapidly via the widespread diffusion of popular culture, especially in reality TV programming, across global cultural economies. Reality TV makeover shows and lifestyle TV have emerged as significant conveyers of neo-liberal self-governance, imparting lifestyle, citizenship, taste hierarchies, and risk-avoidance instruction designed to regulate and normalize personal responsibility, accountability, and self-investment.[38] Working-class women are prime targets for TV transformations. As Skeggs points out, makeover TV "is often structured through class relations, whereby one group's standards are found lacking and in need of improvement," a matter not just of "deficient culture but also deficient subjectivity."[39] Martin Roberts notes that televised forms of improvement stress self-making and consumerism since "they have to do more with understanding wines, where to go on holiday, or the right way to shave rather than political participation. They are about the self and the achievement of social distinction through consumption."[40]

Since 2000, under the banner of transformation, personal empowerment, and self-responsibility—language echoing the 1996 welfare "reform" legislation that was titled the "Personal Responsibility and Work Reconciliation Act"—a surge of Reality TV transformation shows has promised prosperity, empowerment, and self-confidence to those who would trim and tone their sagging bodies and refine and re-energize their sluggish spirits through surgery, weight loss, fashion, lifestyle, and etiquette makeovers. Reality TV makeover shows that promise to help tame and refine the tastes, tempers, and manners of people perceived to be deficient in cultural capital through etiquette training have vastly increased in popularity. Shows in the U.S. and Britain that utilize the *Pygmalion, My Fair Lady,* and *Cinderella* narrative templates of gendered transformation and class metamorphosis to transform multi-ethnic and working-class women into beauty queens and ladies and men into responsible partners, fathers, and gentlemen include *Ladette to Lady, Asbo Teen to Beauty Queen, My Bare Ladies, The Girls of Hedsor Hall, Flavor of Love Girls: Charm School, Rock of Love: Charm School, American Princess, From G's to Gents, Dad Camp,* and *Tool Academy.* Some of these makeover shows culminate by bestowing a tiara on those contestants who best embody the transformation from coarse and improper women to chaste ladies and elegant beauties. Lest it be discounted as merely cheap and non-consequential programming, transformational

Reality TV programming for etiquette and refinement has very long tentacles that reach into higher education. In 2009, Veleashia Smith, director of student development for the Office of Diversity Programs at Western Kentucky University, for example, adopted the etiquette curriculum from VH1's reality TV series *Flavor of Love Girls: Charm School* and MTV's *From G's to Gents* as the basis for a semester-long "enhancement" training for African American students. Smith, herself a first-generation college student, established the program in order to assist other first-generation college students.[41] The women's enhancement program "Project Class" (Creating Leaders and Shaping Sisters) included workshops such as "Diva Dress," "Act like a Lady," and "Upgrade You."[42]

Accompanying the Reality TV makeover craze is a new circuitry of celebrity etiquette instructors, pageant coaches, and image entrepreneurs/educators including Sharon Osbourne, Mo'Nique, Princess Di's butler, and numerous beauty queens. They, like etiquette writers, proffer strategies for self-help, personal transformation, and social mobility. They are helping to engineer a contradictory blend of pedagogies that fuse shame, boot camp instruction, individualization, and willpower as pathways to middle-class lifestyles, social savvy, celebrity, glamour, and cultural belonging. (Not incidentally, they relegate problems such as poverty and racism to positions of minimal importance.) Their tutorials include an array of gendered, racialized, and class-coded instruction for maximizing cultural and embodied capital and marketability through manners, image, and lifestyle. In doing so, they help to enable and enlarge moral value attributions that mark some people as productive and proactive and others as abject by virtue of their failures to invest in improving themselves.

The global diffusion of makeover and polishing technologies extends to young girls as well. Charm schools that teach the arts of glamour, social graces, and pageant preparation to girls aspiring to beauty titles and class mobility are thriving worldwide. At the World of Disney store in New York City, young girls sip tea and learn manners in Cinderella's Princess Court and the American Girl Place.[43] Many go for makeovers at Club Libby Lu's "Sparkle Spa" for tiaras, hair extensions, or Britney Spears hair styling.[44]

Outside the U.S., over two thousand preteen girls enroll each year in Giselle's Beauty Academy in Venezuela for four months of training in modeling social presentation and etiquette, where they learn strategies for beauty pageant success.[45] Its owner, Giselle Reyes, a former beauty queen, asserts that social advancement for girls "takes class and that means learning how to apply the right amount of makeup, pose for a photo-op, and choose the right clothes."[46] She contends that beauty academies such as hers "give self-esteem, teaching girls how to talk like an adult, how to have personality. The idea is to instill in them the desire to be different from other girls."[47] Beauty grooming schools are also popular in other parts of the world, including India where numerous low-cost finishing schools are grooming young Indians to take part in the global economy.[48] Interviewing one of the owners of a school in New Delhi, Ahmed-Ghosh reported that the mission of the school was to "create well-groomed individuals who could achieve their full potential in the changing culture of India; . . . these days you have to look good, talk well, and present your best side to succeed in life." Amed-Gosh observed that this meant "walking tall and confidently, speaking English with a proper accent, using proper table manners, dressing sharply, especially in Western clothes, and having good conversational skills."[49]

Here is the U.S., in addition to charm schools, lavish coming-of-age rituals such as cotillions, quinceaneras, and proms have also regained popularity, elevating elite life-styling, hyper-femininity, and consumption.[50] Numerous black sororities sponsor cotillion presentation balls and offer training programs in etiquette and dance as well as tours of elite colleges. Five hundred people attended the 2004 Delta Sigma Theta Sorority debutante ball in Lexington, Kentucky to watch twenty African American high school women who had completed months of training in beauty, image, and etiquette make their debut.[51]

Building upon long-standing traditions of faith in old-time virtues for gendered collegiate success, many college campuses now offer charm schools, publish online decorum and dress manuals, and hire etiquette entrepreneurs as campus consultants. Indeed, an explosion of collegiate etiquette experts is instructing students on how to handle a wide range of social and culinary occasions with elegance and confidence. Marist College, for instance, offers a dining etiquette seminar titled "Goofs, Goblets, and Getting the Edge."[52] Ann Marie Sabath has given numerous workshops such as "Put Your Best Fork Forward" at Duke, Pennsylvania State, Cornell, and Clemson universities. After observing a Chinese student trying to eat a burrito, Tom Koziciki, director of the career center at University of California at Irvine, hired Sabath to give campus workshops on manners because he believed that "EQ (etiquette) is as important as IQ."[53] Campus etiquette modules typically include personal style tips and formal dining skills, such as how to contend with inedible foods such as olive pits and fish bones, potentially disruptive foods like cherry tomatoes and peas, and foods with high splash and drip potential like spaghetti, while engaging in edifying dinner conversations.

Style shows are also enjoying new popularity. Wellesley College, for example, offered fashion and shopping advice to its students at a style show I attended in 2008 entitled "Ladies Who Will," sponsored by Bloomingdales, The Gap, Banana Republic, and the Office of Student Life. Outfits appropriate for various postgraduate opportunities such as Fulbright, medical and law school interviews, public relations positions, and more "casual" government jobs such as Teach for America, along with cocktail and evening wear, were modeled on a makeshift runway. Short skirts, spike heels, and plunging necklines were touted as very appropriate since, as the emcee put it, "sometimes it is nice to point out that you are a woman."[54]

On the other hand, Bennett College, a historically black women's college, takes a more prudent approach to student fashion. It offers a "cultural enrichment program" that is designed to enhance the "presentation skills, social behavior, and etiquette" of its women students and imposes a strict dress code that includes a long litany of "inappropriate and offensive attire" including "skirts higher than three inches above the knee, tight blouses, sagging bottom wear, and showing cleavage." The dress code also states that "we bathe/shower daily, comb our hair, fix our faces, and select appropriate clothing because we may meet someone who can make a change in our lives or just because we want to feel good. 'A little powder and a little paint can make us feel like what we ain't.'" [55]

Campus-based instruction in personal packaging and image-making reflects the differing demographics of student bodies on various campuses but regardless of racialized and class differences, such training is helping to produce new narratives of gendered meritocracy and collegiate refinement. Academic ardor for image and manners further heightens expectations for campus queens to be accomplished in style, grace, and decorum. In order to more fully flesh out the parameters for understanding the often differing legacies, investments, and meanings of etiquette and body regulation by African American and white campus queen contestants, I will explore both extra-mural campus beauty contests that attract mostly white participants and an etiquette boot camp for black campus queens. I attended and interviewed participants and sponsors at the annual HBCU Leadership Conference for Kings and Queens in 2004 as well as the Kentucky Mountain Laurel Festival, a predominantly white state wide competition for college women in Kentucky. I also interviewed contestants in the Kentucky Derby Princess Festival, another state-wide collegiate competition for college women in Kentucky. What follows is my sense of how class is mobilized, taught, performed, and racialized in these differing contexts.

Elevation, Enhancement, and Black College Queens

If you would like to change your image from nose to toes, let's start with perfecting your look from the head down. . . . Whether you would like makeup or a makeover, . . . we all can be enhanced.

—Debi Dozier[56]

When you look a mess, it says you don't care—so how can you care about me; When you sound a mess it says you are not intelligent—so why should I take you seriously; When you speak without thinking it says you are rash (fool)—so why should I listen to you.

—Dale Williams[57]

In 2001, Dale Williams, then coordinator of student affairs at Tennessee State University and a beauty queen herself, founded the Leadership Conference for

Historically Black College and University Queens. (Williams had been a high school queen, the 1992 Miss Tennessee State University, and a contestant in the 1993 Miss African American Collegiate pageant.) She told me that she had felt "overwhelmed" as a college queen since she believed that she had not been given adequate preparation to "work the crowd," "be in the spotlight," and help in the communal project of "breaking down stereotypes."[58] She noted that "young ladies who find themselves in the position as queens of a higher education institution are not always ready for the tasks and activities ahead of them including representing their college or university at banquets, receptions, and speaking engagements" and that "typically black queens have not been taught the graces or skills needed for these assignments."[59] For Williams, a remedial education of class-coded skills is needed to properly groom new queens for their reigns, many of whom are first-generation middle-class or working-class women.

Since most universities provide no specialized image training to their queens prior to their reigns, Williams established the national HBCU Leadership Conference for Kings and Queens, which brings together image, motivational, and etiquette coaches as well as ministers, TV celebrities, fashion models, and former campus queens to provide newly crowned black queens "with the proper tools and training to reign well." The 2009 conference speakers, for example, included Lecia J. Rivers, author of *Get Up and Be Somebody* and *Wisdom and Inspiration for Campus Superstars*, and Tanya Hutchinson, former beauty queen and winner of the reality TV show *She's Got the Look* and author of *PhenomenalBeauty*.[60] The training included the art of makeup, self-presentation, stage presence, public speaking, personal style, social etiquette, and the cultivation of spiritual/inner beauty. William's mantra that "excellence is a choice" is a continual theme in the training conferences.

In 2004, black college kings were invited to this royal boot camp for the first time, and they have become a regular part of the training conference ever since, with specialized workshops, such as "Manhood 101" and "Inside Your King's Court: Tyrants, Warriors, and Jesters." Alex Ellis, author of *Restoring the Male Image* and owner of *Simply Ellis* (a clothing business that sells custom tailored suits, Italian neckwear, and cufflinks), is a regular speaker at the conference. To help "restore the pride of men" and "develop wholesome sophistication," Ellis evokes both theology and the legacy of the Harlem Renaissance to revive men's interest in their personal appearance, self-presentation, relationships, and spiritual growth. Ellis's motto is "We are always in a process of refinement, especially in the school of life."[61]

In 2004, I attended this three-day training conference for black kings and queens and observed the etiquette and image enhancement training given to the newly crowned campus queens. Dale Williams told the queens that because of their pivotal role in representing and recruiting for their universities, they could choose whether or not to be "the best or worst marketing tool for their university or college."[62] Beverley Skeggs has noted that "being, becoming, practicing, and doing femininity are various different things for women of different classes, races, ages, and nations."[63] Indeed, U.S. campus queens, black and white but especially black, are expected to be "classy" and ladylike in their self-presentations as well as vigilant role models. Lending their faces, bodies, and biographies to their campuses, they are asked to navigate numerous formal and "upper crust" events with charm and grace, including social occasions with alumni, corporate supporters, and university officials. Such events demand considerable knowledge and skill.

Not surprisingly, campus queens claim they benefit from the performance-enhancing training given at the black queen leadership conferences, especially in light of their representational responsibilities. The training of black campus royalty is deeply tethered to racialized and classed histories of representation, communal duty, and uplift. Patricia Williams has noted the significance of "generational bodies" for black women:

> I, like so many blacks, have been trying to pin myself down in history, place myself in the stream of time as significant, evolved, present, in the past, continuing into the future. To be without documentation is too unsustaining, too spontaneously ahistorical, too dangerously malleable in the hands of those who would rewrite not merely my past but my future as well.[64]

Her sentiments are echoed by many black queens including Tanya (pseudonym), who told me that she understood her reign to be a link in the progression of black education from its roots in the literacy training of slaves and sharecroppers to the creation of black colleges and the rise of the black middle class. She believes that black college queens "represent the best of blackness. They show how far our campuses have come and where we are going. They represent for us a vision of the future."[65] She also asserts that etiquette, in particular, has had a distinctive history in the lives of African American college women that must be contextualized in light of past and ongoing white racism. She believes that black colleges perceive etiquette training as a "responsibility."

> Black colleges have to even the playing field. You can not assume that girls have had this kind of training. Lots of black children did not. Black colleges cannot send one out into the world, representing your people, your school, yourself, and your family and not give you the skills. If you want to use them or not, it's your choice. But they can not send you out there and not give you the savvy.[66]

Dale Williams echoes these themes of responsibility and lineage when she points out that black campus queens must have the savvy and commitment to "uphold the traditions of the university that keep alumni coming back, by loving their university, and by respecting the royal lineage they are now part of."[67]

Serving as human campus billboards representing black colleges is not for the fainthearted. The historical, collective, and symbolic weight of representing black middle-class ladyhood falls squarely on the shoulders of black campus queens. Unlike white queens, black queens attach distinctly racialized meanings to their class work in beauty, etiquette, style, and grooming. Their special duty to maintain appearances and manners, improve self, and embody "finer womanhood" and "savvy" is freighted with longstanding racial and classist baggage that requires distinctive maneuvering to counter the stereotypical stock images of black women as loud-mouthed, aggressive, working-class Sapphires, oversexed Jezebels, welfare queens, and masculine matriarchs.[68] Patricia Hill Collins notes how such cultural representations of black women are imbricated with class. She observes that middle-class professional black women must not only challenge longstanding images of unbridled sexuality and aggression attributed to working-class black women but also present a carefully balanced "level of ambition and aggressiveness" essential for success in middle-class employment.[69] Indeed, black college queens are expected to defy tenacious legacies of white disparagement of both working-class and middle-class black women as well as to improve the entire student body by inspiring it through their composure and poise.

Dr. Tonea Steward, a former Miss Jackson State University, reminded the newly crowned HBCU campus queens at the 2004 leadership conference that they have a social responsibility to elevate their communities as the exemplars of black collegiate womanhood. She told the queens:

> You embody everything about the university, womanhood, marriage, professionalism, power, and potentiality. . . . You are the mothers of today and tomorrow. You are the leaders of today and tomorrow. You are the representatives of all the female students on campus. You are the elevator for all of the male students. You tell the world who you are by the way you walk, by the way you talk, by the way you think, by the way you act, by the way you dress yourself.[70]

Throughout the conference, queens were continually referred to as "hope dealers," "elevators," and "civilizers" who must inspire their student communities and promote their campuses with savvy and grace. Dale Williams asserted that black queens have special demands "since African American women and men need role models. They're not just role model beauties; they are promoting college education and professionalism."[71]

Because of the responsibility to counter white stereotypes and inspire students, Williams argues that black queens cannot "just take the crown and walk away from it. It has a life of its own." She counsels newly crowned queens that numerous restrictions are attached to their "fame" since they will be expected to represent their campuses "24/7" and that their behavior and bodies will be constantly scrutinized. She concluded if they "do not want to be judged publicly," they should not be in a public position. Queens themselves confirmed the obligations they incur on black campuses. A Morehouse College queen summed up her queenly duties as being "on speed dial to the university," while a Miss Black Alumni Hall of Fame winner described her reign, less benignly, as "a life sentence."

Conference speakers continually reminded black royalty that their special responsibilities to represent their race and their universities demanded sacrifice and hard work. As emissaries of the student body, their conduct, clothing, accessories, hair, and social activities would be closely and continuously monitored. Dale Williams repeatedly stressed the importance of image and the unrelenting public inspections of black queens on and off campus. She warned the queens that they "should not be misled—understand this walk—your reign will be 70% visual. Either you rise to the occasion or fall."[72] She told them that "every time you step out—you are your university" and that there would be "some things you just cannot do anymore, wear anymore, say anymore, be anymore, and, unfortunately, date anymore, for a queen's reputation counts twice." She declared that queens must be especially vigilant about their appearance, since "people are constantly watching and talking about YOU. . . . Image is everything."[73] Another conference speaker, Benecia Williams, assistant director of student affairs at Lincoln University (Missouri), agreed that black queens face ongoing surveillance of their behaviors and bodies, but she urged them to use this as an opportunity for role-modeling and racial elevation. She stated that "a queen's reign is a performance—you are constantly on a stage and under a microscope. . . . People are watching you, but the beauty of it all is your example could change their lives."[74]

The black queens at the conference whom I interviewed noted the numerous prohibitions they have encountered and the repercussions that had ensued when they failed to live up to class-specific expectations. One queen told me that "boisterousness and shoveling food and all of that kind of stuff" was now prohibited since she had become a public symbol of tastefulness and grace. Another HBCU queen related to me the turmoil that ensued when she wore shorts and flip flops to her first official appearance at a campus football game.

> You would have thought hell broke loose. Parents and alumni were really disappointed because to them, I did not get it that I wasn't representing myself, that I was representing them and the school. That was my first wakeup call that I got that I had done something much greater than me. Not only do you never know who is watching you but the way black communities and colleges work, everyone talks to each other. So it is nothing for the dean to be in the grocery store talking to alumni who say "I went

to the game and saw the new queen and she had the nerve to dress like that. Don't you tell her what to wear and doesn't she have a clothing budget?" Then it trickles down to me, and I now wear a suit.[75]

Many scholars, as we have seen, have pointed out that shame is a potent force in the patrolling of the behavior of individuals and communities that "responsibilizes" people.[76] Unlike middle-class white queens, black campus queens must shoulder the wounds and legacies of hostile white gazes. Thus they are repeatedly warned that they must avoid shaming both their educational and racial communities by cultivating proper self-control throughout their reigns. Williams sternly reminds queens at her national training conferences about the dishonor and disgrace that some non-disciplined black queens have caused by drinking, fighting, or getting pregnant during their reigns. Black campus queens, in sum, are expected to work hard at being class acts.

Because of the pressures for queens to represent their campuses with finesse and prudence, cultivating the right look and dress were the foci of the conference. Many conference speakers, including Tonea Steward, argued that queens should be supported and clad by their universities since they play a vital role in the promotion and representation of their campuses. Steward had harsh criticism for those educational administrators who do not adequately pay to properly dress their campus queens for their class performances.

> What's happening to our people? Are they forgetting poor girls? I could never have been a queen if I had to pay something. . . . And I want to say to folks, "So what is your problem, Mr. President?" We're talking about the queen, the examples of your own mama. We're talking an opportunity for a young woman to be lifted up to represent the finest womanhood for this campus. *We're not talking about a beauty pageant. We're talking about assuring that our women are sophisticated and classy;* that they have an attitude about their outward look and that they are aware of how to be politically astute when news reporters want to talk to them about a crisis that might be happening. They are the ones who are going to save your job, Mr. President, because when the board comes they will have a prepared speech that someone hopefully has rehearsed with them so they can sound articulate and give the impression that they are the kind of students that you are generating thousands of each year [emphasis added].[77]

To supplement their limited campus budgets, Steward urged queens to engage in fundraising, suggesting that they might approach alumni chapters and local churches to ask them to support "finer womanhood." Additionally, to further lure people into contributing to the royal wardrobe, she reminded the queens that donors could be told that they would receive favorable campus publicity as a result.[78]

Under the conference mantra of "maximizing their reigns," conference speakers concentrated on image, attitude, and etiquette. Queens were told that since "most public figures, especially corporate America executives, spend numerous dollars and time on image consulting, business etiquette, speech trainers, and workshops on business professionalism . . . as well as personal shoppers and hairdressers," they must also make similar investments in their appearances.[79] Conference speakers also touted a variety of techniques to enhance the charm and charisma of black campus queens, to moderate their bodies, and to eliminate any residual working-class behaviors. Hegemonic discourses of class and femininity champion temperance, composure, and the avoidance of a multitude of embodied and behavioral excesses long thought to be associated with working-class life. Hefty bodies, bleached hair, flashy and tight clothes, tawdry jewelry, sloppiness, and strong emotions all signify working-class and ethnic negligence to middle-class and corporate gatekeepers. Loudness, brashness, crassness, anger, and cursing also mark women as not middle-class. For conference speakers, however, class is malleable, performative, and transformable. Gwendolyn Foster has aptly observed that etiquette and conduct trainings "necessitate transforming the performing self, and the grotesque desires of the body, into an aestheticized version of the 'natural' self, a gilded body at times indistinguishable from a decorated home."[80] Conference speakers imparted numerous techniques for gilding the bodies and behaviors of black queens.

As I have already stressed, the idea that bodies and psyches can be enhanced without challenging systemic inequalities is a central presupposition of a neo-liberal cultural economy of self-enterprise and makeover technologies. Helen Wood and Beverley Skeggs argue that contemporary reformulations of gender and class offer "particular forms of selfhood" and a "grammar of conduct" for "making a more aesthetically appealing and thus competent femininity," as strategies to transcend one's class origins and eclipse hierarchical social structures in a presumed meritocratic society.[81] The proliferation of "improvement discourses" based on "generating, accruing and/or displaying cultural capital by improving their appearance; their bodies; their minds; their flats/houses; their relationships; their future" are integral parts of achieving middle-class appearances and lives.[82] These ideas were fully evident at the queens' conference as presenters promised that gendered and class transmutation would yield success since class was understood not as a rigid location in social structure but rather a malleable identity that could be modified by improving one's corporeal, moral, and psychic dispositions. The self-enhancement and racial advancement discourses promulgated at the conference constructed queens' bodies and selves as investments beholden to ongoing training programs. The pedagogies promulgated were upbeat, championing the idea that the appearance, conduct, and resultant privileges of middle-class lifestyles could be achieved, with effort, through the ministrations of image and etiquette experts.

Corporeal restraint and poise were key components of the platformed femininity valorized at the black queens' leadership conference. Queens were schooled to be prudent for the greater good of their campuses, and they were given a variety of commandments for enhancing their class appeal. Dale Williams enumerated a lengthy laundry list of tips to ensure emotional moderation and social acceptability including: "Be humble, grateful, kind, pleasant, professional, confident, respectable, and professional as well as maintain composure at all times." Queens were urged to monitor their appearances and manners. They were told: "To love their school, practice good etiquette, know that people were watching them, have a plan for after graduation, send thank you cards, learn to smile, have a good handshake, look presentable at all times, have a good first impression, and always leave a good lasting impression."[83] They were also given a lengthy list of conduct prohibitions: "Do not chew gum, complain in public, curse, lose your faith, lose your temper, be arrogant or ghetto, criticize your university or its officials, as well as underestimate your position and students' expectations of your role." Queens were also advised to drink only clear liquids when in public to avoid staining their clothes and avoid wearing big bold hats since they evoke the "sanctified church look," which was not considered an appropriate class image for black college queens. Williams also counseled them to be prepared at all times by having safety pins, breath mints, lipstick, and "tissues and powder to take the shine off your t-zone in case you have to take a picture."[84] Always in the limelight, campus queens' bodies, clothes, makeup, dress, diction, manners, and taste must visibly denote them as refined and restrained, that is, properly middle-classed.

Body management is pivotal to the project of producing successful black campus royalty. Beverley Skeggs has rightly noted, in general, that "bodies are the physical sites where the relations of class, gender, race, sexuality, and age come together and are embodied and practiced. . . . Class is always coded through bodily dispositions: the body is the most ubiquitous signifier of class."[85] Sloth and indifference to the body are portentous signs that one has deserted the quest for regal sophistication and grace. Regardless of whether or not women students aspire to campus queen status, Jocey Quinn has observed that for many women college students "the recurring theme was femininity and the efforts taken to produce and maintain the culturally ascribed body. Interspersed with days of study were days of body regulation: an equally time-consuming process to gaining a degree." She concludes that "becoming the right kind of student and female body can not be separated."[86] For those seeking campus queen titles, the pressures for body regulation, self-transformation, and optimizing class proficiencies are all the more intensified.

Class-coded corporeal expectations are a recurring theme at the black queens' conferences. Queens are reminded that all of aspects of their body signify character and class, and they are told that their "attire, shoes, hair, nails, and speech auto-matically categorize them into an economic background." Consequently, they must be vigilant about the ongoing public appraisals of their bodies. Well-tended and mannered bodies signify strong interiors and spirits, whereas neglect of the hegemonic body codes women as coarse and languorous.

Middle-class proprieties for self-presentation were thus a major theme through-out the conference I attended, and queens were given an extensive range of image tutorials in the spirit of the widely popular *What Not to Wear* reality TV series. Linda Porter, a former Miss Cover Girl at Grambling State University, conducted a workshop in 2004 titled "What Should I Wear? Learning to Dress for Any Occasion." Porter told the queens that from then on they must shed their "distinctive fashion identities." She warned them that their "college presidents do not care if they were PMS or not," that they must be sure that their hair is combed and their clothes are ironed whenever they leave their dorm rooms. They must never wear shorts, cutoff tops, or outfits that made them look "trampish" or "ghetto." Instead, they were urged to revamp their wardrobes and to invest in a pearl necklace. They were even instructed in how to shop for proper foundation garments. One queen likened this fashion instruction to what Pat Hill Collins has termed "other-mothering."

> Although this can seem silly, bra shopping was one of the things that Black women used to do with each other. If your mother did not have time to take you, black women from the community did. It was like "other-mothering." So when you have black women on campus that did not necessarily grow up in communities where people had the means to do this, it is important to teach them how their clothes are supposed to fit. There is a level of love to this and I appreciate the level of responsibil-ity that makes some black college staff believe that that they must teach you this. This is what segregated schools used to be for black children. It was an extension of the home.[87]

Debbie Dozier, another conference trainer, is the associate director of student activities at Bowie State University and owner of *Total Images Concepts*, a com-pany "dedicated to teaching and promoting civility, courtesy, and carriage for individuals, colleges, and corporations who want to outclass the competition by reaching the pinnacle of refinement from the inside out and from head to toe." Dozier offers a seminar, "The Power of Image," designed to help women "develop your image and sense of style, empowering you as an individual and enriching your personal, social, and business life. Be it your appearance, how you dress, your voice or your body language, *find out how to improve your image and revamp your style* [emphasis in original]."[88] I attended her 2004 workshop for black queens, "Promoting a Poised, Polished, Professional You!" It started with a warning that queens "don't get a second chance to make a first impression." It is imperative that they prepare themselves much as a warrior would "by developing grace under fire and poise under pressure." In order to motivate campus queens to revamp their style, Dozier told them that they were a "walking image advertisement" and that how they "visually present" themselves to the outside accounts for 93 percent of first impressions. She scolded queens who neglected their appearance by asserting that their "advertisement to the world indicates that you're probably incapable of making any effort in general, or that you don't value yourself highly enough to take pride in your appearance. *And if you don't value yourself, who else will?* [emphasis in original]."

Dozier's fashion instruction included what to wear to flatter wedge, pear, hour-glass, or diamond body shapes. She advised queens to be restrained and muted in their fashion choices and recommended "solid colors, conservative dress, nude hose, and conservative jewelry." She urged queens to keep their "makeup light and natural and their hair combed." Conversely, she told them to avoid big flashy earrings, jewelry that jingled, bright colors, too much perfume, and open toe shoes, which mark one as déclassé. According to Dozier, "discreet elegance" should be the goal for every black college queen.

Dozier concluded her workshop by promoting a variety of special services she offers, including image clinics, pampering parties, contextual dressing, wardrobe analysis, closet audits, lifestyle assessment, digital wardrobe coordination, and personal shopping, to further help queens refurbish their style. She also promoted several training packages she offers, including "Your Ideal Silhouette," where one's body measurements are fed into a computer and out pops a forty-page port-folio for how best to dress one's unique body shape.

In addition to dressing and accessorizing in ways befitting their roles as college emissaries, black queens were given instruction in how to improve their comport-ment. Etiquette coach Denise Marcia, a former gospel music executive, established "Essentials!: The Personal Development Company" and offers workshops on "eti-quette and self-promotion to enhance your social IQ."[89] She contends that "excel-ling in life not only requires an exceptional education, but also rests heavily upon one's social skills." According to Marcia, the "necessary nuances of life" are not necessarily being taught in higher education and this failure compromises career advancement and personal effectiveness. The purpose of her company is to be "a link in the chain of preparing students for total achievement in life situations at HBCUs."[90] Harriet Roland, of South Carolina State University, has observed that not only does Marcia help to "mold a professional persona," she also "polishes our diamonds in the rough," a popular metaphor for charm schools. Marcia also teaches at the Children's Entrepreneurial Opportunities Academy, Inc, which offers a variety of programs to train middle school age children in spiritually-based entrepreneurship including a program, "Millionaires in the Making," which helps students to understand the "biblical principles relating to character, stewardship, and self-sufficiency." As we shall see in the next chapter, many campus queens, like many beauty entrepreneurs, merge evangelical Christianity, beautification, body stewardship, and etiquette as well as embracing beauty pageants as divine opportunities for professing faith and bringing holiness to higher education.

Marcia's dining workshop was held after the queens had been treated to a free massage and were then told to retire to their rooms and to dress as if they were going to a formal banquet. Decked out in their finery, the twenty-some excited queens lined up in the hotel lobby, uncertain how the night would unfold. After a group photograph, they were delighted to find stretch limousines idling outside of the hotel lobby ready to chauffeur them to their dining destination. I followed in a van with their campus advisors to the very upscale Stockyards Restaurant in Nashville, Tennessee. Once they arrived at the restaurant, they were seated in private banquet room set up with tables for eight. Each table was draped in white linen table cloths displaying a dazzling array of formal silverware, china, and glassware.

In conjunction with the head waiter, Marcia conducted a highly theatrical session on the dos and don'ts of fine dining. She told the queens that "manners open doors that position, power, and money cannot." She walked attendees through the many dilemmas of dining including how to eat Continental style, the proper use and placement of glassware, silverware, and napkins, and other dining proprieties. While engaging in intricate food maneuvers, attendees were expected to engage in edifying conversations with their neighbors at the table. Four courses provided many opportunities for food faux pas. Anxiety levels were high as participants struggled to land their food safely in their mouths. Many, including me, did so slowly and awkwardly, fearing public embarrassment. Finally, Marcia told the queens that it ultimately would be best to eat before going to business meals and banquets in order to avoid the risk of offending others by incorrectly stabbing and chewing one's food.

In addition to workshops designed to polish the queens, the queens' advisors and chaperones who attended the 2004 conference had the opportunity to meet separately from their queens to discuss the many challenges of advising and grooming their charges. Mary Terry Wiley, a playwright and motivational speaker, began the workshop by stating that "it takes a queen to make a queen." She argued that the effective advising of campus queens involves "spiritual transference." Wiley noted that being an advisor is especially difficult today since many queens "have had a different upbringing that makes it difficult to groom the girls." Some advisors lamented that they have had to coach queens who were "witches" and "crazies," but hoped their current charges would be receptive to their ministrations. Concerns were raised over queens with tattoos, "plus sized" queens, and queens with cornrows, which some of the advisors described as "lazy hairdos worn by women with lots of children." Other issues involved how to prepare campus queens for competition in the Miss Black Alumni Hall of Fame contest, how to ensure that queens uphold their school traditions, what to do if queens refused to wear school colors at public events and thereby angered alumni, and how to select coronation gowns that would help slenderize "full-figured" queens. The conference ended with a bus trip to the local mall so the queens could begin to revamp their wardrobes in light of the fashion advice they had received over the course of the conference.

Most of the workshop leaders believed in the powers of self-transformation, etiquette, and positive thinking to foster racial advancement. As successful ex–beauty queens and entrepreneurs, the conference trainers embraced hegemonic values and self-improvement strategies for unlocking the doors of opportunity and prevailing over racism. Modeling the successes they have enjoyed in higher education, beauty pageants, and their business endeavors, they peddled poise, self-promotion, image, social savvy, faith, and determination. Impeccable manners, hard work, and a string of pearls were promoted as necessary ingredients for imperial and life success. One queen, Carla Stitt, Miss Tennessee State University, said she found the fashion and style training modules in 2003 particularly useful for enhancing her fashion knowledge since they had provided "insights on how to exude class and style in my everyday attire," aptly noting the importance of appearance for the performance of middle-classiness.[91] In a cultural context that celebrates makeovers, self-responsibility, personal transformation, and cultural/personal explanations for failure, the lessons in grace, grit, aspiration, etiquette, and image resonated deeply with hegemonic values for the pursuit of fame and fortune.

Although there are no national training camps for white campus queens, class-coded etiquette and corporeal technologies are nonetheless vital in historically white campus contests as well. The practice of sending campus queens to represent their universities in off-campus pageants provides another close-up view of the oscillations of race, class, gender signification, and commerce in extra-mural campus pageants.

Historically White Extra-mural Collegiate Pageants

Throughout the twentieth century, as we have seen, campus queens have been called upon to represent their universities and colleges at sporting events, trade shows, state and national beauty/scholarship pageants, and community festivals sponsored by various businesses and local elites to enhance trade and tourism. Unlike the fate of commodity beauty pageants like Lexington, Kentucky's Tobacco Carnival that caused so much controversy among campus deans in the 1930s, two annual state wide collegiate pageants in Kentucky, the Miss Kentucky Derby Princess Festival and the Kentucky Mountain Laurel Festival, have successfully managed to merge gendered and class respectability with commerce and tourism. Both of these competitions have enjoyed a long and illustrious pedigree in Kentucky history, and almost all universities and colleges in the state still select contestants to participate in each. Both contests include debutante-style presentation balls and aristocratic and courtly rituals. Both pageants have elite sponsorship and help to promote nostalgia for the gendered traditions of the Old South. Although a few African American women have recently participated in both contests, they remain overwhelmingly white events. Within both contests, there is a presumption that contestants have successfully mastered class competencies since their relationship with judges and elite sponsors spans a significant amount of time. The five college women selected to be on the princess court for the Kentucky Derby Festival spend almost four months attending social events with their elite sponsors and the Kentucky Mountain Laurel Festival selection process requires contestants to spent three days being evaluated by secret judges while they are resident in that community.

The Miss Kentucky Derby Festival Princess Program was established in 1959 by the Fillies Club, a volunteer service organization of elite white women in Louisville, Kentucky.[92] To qualify as a Filly, one must have the time and resources to work to "further the fame of Kentucky." According to the 1996 Derby queen (who is one of the few African American women to have won the title), being merely "middle class" is not enough to ensure membership in the Fillies. She told me that one has to have "old money," "be married well," have "social register distinction," as well as the time and ability to fundraise for the Fillies organization.[93] The Fillies nomination form requires one to state one's spouse's occupation and list any friends or family who have been members of the Fillies. Fillies work all year to plan for the Kentucky Derby Festival, which includes over a hundred events that begin in March and culminate in the running of the famed Kentucky Derby. In addition to overseeing and coaching the Derby Princesses, the Fillies host a Derby Ball and Queen's Coronation, decorate the queen's float for the city's Pegasus Parade, and publish the Festival's official program. Incorporated as a nonprofit organization in 1971, Fillies, Inc., now boasts over 250 members.

In order to be selected as one of the five Derby Princesses, contestants originally had to be nominated by a Filly member, ensuring that traditional class and racial borders were maintained within the organization. The rules were changed in the 1990s so that any interested Kentucky college woman could compete for a princess slot without Filly sponsorship. The selection process is laden with class evaluations. In the 1990s, an African American student at KSU was urged to represent her campus in the competition by the vice-president of student affairs. After submitting her initial application and essay, she received an invitation to come to a fancy Louisville hotel for her first interview before four white judges. Michelle (a pseudonym) told me that she faltered when asked to name her favorite Derby festival event since she had never attended a Derby event nor did she live in Louisville. She finally remembered hearing on the news about a Tiger Woods golf tournament to benefit children so she named that event. At the end of her screening interview, she learned that she had made the cut and was chosen as one of five princesses who would vie for the coveted position of Derby Queen, an honor to be determined by the spin of a dial at the Derby Ball.[94] Although she was eventually crowned queen, she told me that she had to navigate formidable obstacles posed by race and class differences throughout the months that she was a Derby princess.

After seeing a poster in her dorm, a former African American student of mine, Keisha (a pseudonym) decided to compete in the Derby Princess Festival. Over one hundred other college women also competed for one of the five princess slots, which came with a prize package that included a $1,000 scholarship, six outfits including earrings and shoes picked out by a personal shopper, and free passes to all Kentucky Derby activities. She, too, faced a series of interviews with members of the Fillies to ensure that the contestants possessed the basic class prerequisites for participation in the Derby pageant. Keisha told me that she wanted to compete since the "competition should be open to everyone, not just the young women they want or those that fit a narrow profile." She added, "Organizations that make it difficult for minorities to apply and/or win (other than as tokens) make me mad. . . . Why shouldn't everyone have a fair shake?" She said that her purpose "was to open the door for other girls and see if the world is really like others say it is—how much has changed?—how far have we come?—what more needs to be done?"[95] Despite the objections of her mother, Keisha entered the contest and was chosen as one of the five princesses. Her subsequent experiences with one of the Fillies were so tense that she kept a record of the daily insults and exclusions she experienced and planned to go to the Derby festival board and the local newspaper to air her complaints.

Following an unsuccessful try the previous year, Keisha told me that she had "learned the art of polishing her answers." In order to better platform herself, she told me that she had studied the Filly website to learn as much as possible about the organization. At her interview, the judges asked her opinion on the war in Iraq and how to address the gender pay gap. She was also asked to tell a joke or do an impression of a celebrity. She stated that she chose to impersonate Clinton "because probably most of them were Republicans, so they probably would get a kick of out me doing him." She also speculated that since "my hair was straightened, I am not extremely dark, and I talk in a certain way, I made them comfortable. They definitely pick women who fit the mold or that appear to fit their mold. They don't want you to have political opinions. It is a pageant so you know you have to put on a show."[96] She told me that the pageant remained a "closed class society," since many of the princesses were related or known to members of the Fillies. Furthermore, she reported that most of the princesses "stuck together because they had the same background. They were all in the same sororities and knew many of the same people."[97]

Derby princesses are selected in January. During the four months before the Derby, they participate in a constant whirl of appearances, luncheons, and speeches at schools, charity events, and businesses. They attend more than seventy pre-Derby

events, including media events such as NBC's *Today Show*, the governor's luncheon, the Derby Festival Celebrity luncheon, fashion shows, hot air balloon races,
the Easter and Pegasus parades, sporting events and car tournaments, fireworks
displays, a Great Steamboat Race, and finally the Derby Ball. Alongside celebrities,
the princesses watch the race from box seats at Churchill Downs. The five-pack of
princesses are always expected to be temperate and tasteful. To ensure that their
behavior is genteel, they are chauffeured to events by an "executive protection spe-
cialist." Keisha, who was attending a predominantly white state university, admitted to me that her grades suffered as a result of the Derby whirl, but the tug of the
limelight spurs many women to compete. When this princess told one of the Fillies
that she was missing too many classes, the woman responded by saying, "Wow! I
cannot believe that your professors are not making an exception for you." Michelle,
a queen who had represented an HBCU, said her two weeks of absences did not
create a problem since faculty understood that she was representing "them." She
also pointed out that participating "provided an excellent learning opportunity to
improve my communication skills and interpersonal skills."[98]

Throughout the months leading up to the Derby ball and parade, both Kesiha
and Michelle reported experiencing numerous racist and classist encounters.
Kesiha recounted how she had to model fur coats at a luncheon for the Fillies.
She said it "made her uncomfortable. I felt like one of those cigarette girls. I'm
thinking who eats lunch while other people model fur. Is that something normal?" She also said that she was constantly fatigued by trying to battle racial
stereotypes.

> I had to constantly smile. It was so draining because I had to constantly
> watch myself to make sure I was not giving them ammunition. They were
> constantly watching me and it was so stressful. I would not even say that
> the chicken is good because of racial overtones. Sometime you just want
> to be like everyone else but I felt singled out because I am black which is
> okay, but sometimes you get so tired. I feel like I have to live in two differ-
> ent worlds.[99]

Keisha never mentioned class as a source of her discomfort. However, Michelle
was quite explicit that class mattered as well as race. She reported that the Fillies
had quizzed her about what type of house her family lived in. She also noted that
another princess who was white was subjected to disparaging comments from the
Fillies since her mother worked in a "bra store" and she lived on "the other side of
town." She said that she was praised by one Filly for not having "her hair plastered
to her head" and for not projecting an overtly racialized appearance.[100] She also
overheard a conversation where one Filly conveyed to another her astonishment
that she was "so smart and articulate." She told me that she "got a bit snappish with
the Fillies partly out of fatigue but mostly because of their snide comments."

Each year, on the day of the Derby ball, the five princesses, along with over 200 Fillies, gather in a hotel banquet room packed with beauty and hair specialists. Each princess has her hair, nails, and makeup done professionally to ready her for the ball. At the ball, each princess takes her turn sashaying down a red-carpeted runway wearing a white bell-shaped ball gown and carrying a ruffled white parasol, reminiscent of the Plantation Old South, while a biographic summary of her achievements is read to the audience. On stage, the mood shifts from Old South to game show competition as each princess awaits the results of a spin of a large wheel by the president of the Fillies to determine which one of them will be crowned the queen of the Derby. The winner is then swathed in a red velvet robe and bedecked with a crown of emeralds and pearls. Wielding the royal scepter featuring the corporate logo of the Derby festival and the Fillies crest, and wearing a Pegasus crown, the first official act of the queen is to induct selected individuals as dames and knights into the Derby Festival Court of Pegasus, a hall of fame for elites.

Michelle told me that, her family members besides the waiters, were the only African Americans present at the Derby ball. The theme of the ball was "Southern Belles" and she described the stage setting as an Old South "plantation house." Invited back the following year to help screen candidates, she noted that the Fillies forgot to include her in the luncheon. She also recounted that two years later she ran into the president of the Derby festival at a black community event. She said "It was humbling. It was like I never was the Derby Queen—just another black face." Nonetheless, she would still urge African American women to compete in the festival, in part, because they get a $1,000 worth of clothing and scholarships, have the opportunity to attend Derby events, and—most important, —it is "for the black community." But her bottom line is "They will have to be strong to do it."[101]

Keisha was more equivocal about her princess experiences, identifying such benefits as visiting mansions, meeting celebrities, and learning how to handle difficult situations but also noting the ephemeral nature of these opportunities. She stated:

> I got to meet lots of people. The title carries lots of weight in Kentucky— like you graduated from Harvard. I mean there is definitely a lot of old money, a lot of old white people who hold power and stereotypes about blacks. Sometimes it is obvious and sometimes it is more subtle. But as far as you actually meeting people and being able to go back and benefit from it, I don't know. But I would suggest another black woman do it for the experience. I had to learn how to handle myself in many difficult situations which will probably come up again. I got to learn different things that I would never have gotten to, like, going to the Derby, going to a mansion, and meeting celebrities. We got to go first-class everywhere. I will never be able to do that again.[102]

Despite getting a taste of elite lifestyles and celebrity, she nonetheless concluded, "It was like a job that did not pay too well."

There are other opportunities for college women to win a tiara since the Kentucky Derby Festival is not the only state wide queen's festival. Not to be outclassed by the urbane city of Louisville, the Kentucky Mountain Laurel Festival in Eastern Kentucky also makes use of college women's bodies, hyper-femininity, and middle-class comportment to showcase its own version of class, heritage, commerce, and Appalachian civic pride.

The Kentucky Mountain Laurel Festival

Pineville is a small town in the heart of what once was the feuding country in Southeastern Kentucky. Public-spirited citizens started the festival in 1931 to counteract the false impression strangers had of that region and partly to give their local pride a boost.

—William Stucky[103]

The Kentucky Mountain Laurel Queen Festival is needed to show the rest of Kentucky that everything here [is] not moonshine and chewing tobacco.
—"Festival Draws Thousands to Celebrate the Blooming of Mountain Laurel"[104]

Supported by ideologies of middle-class enterprise, civic pride, and self-and community advancement, pageants celebrating idealized collegiate femininity in Appalachian mountain communities have been significant sites for consolidating the meanings of place, tradition, local enterprise and coal, gendered value and virtue, and social hierarchies. They also perpetuate longstanding patterns of racialized and class inclusion and exclusion. Despite narrow models of embodied excellence and visual meritocracy, a wide range of pageant promoters and supporters applaud the opportunities for entrepreneurship and positive promotional representations of their mountain communities by staging beauty pageants.

The Kentucky Mountain Laurel Festival (KMLF), an annual statewide beauty festival that brings together queens representing most of Kentucky's colleges and universities, is one of the oldest continuing community beauty pageants in the southern Appalachian mountains. It was established in 1931 in Pineville, Kentucky, by local elites as a way to reinvigorate the local economy, promote tourism, counter longstanding popular images of mountain people as uncultured and uncivilized, and refine the area's reputation when national attention was riveted on Bell and neighboring Harlan County's protracted coal strikes and the violent suppression of union and Communist Party organizing efforts. One of the KMLF's principal organizers, Bell County attorney Walter Smith, played a key role in suppressing union activity in the area. Smith banned public meetings, turned away trucks bringing food to striking miners at the county line, and is said to have encouraged mob violence and the intimidation of writers such as Theodore Dreiser and John Dos Passos, who were there to bring national attention to the miners' plight.[105] Smith helped to establish the KMLF festival in 1931, and he served as its first president.

Annie Walker Burns of Harlan County also played a pivotal part in establishing the KMLF. An avid genealogist, she published a book, *Dr. Thomas D. Walker: First White Man of Any Distinction to Explore Kentucky.* While working in the governor's office, she convinced Governor Flem B. Sampson to honor the pioneer explorer. Sampson noted that "since beauty pageants were becoming the norm nationwide," he thought it appropriate to invite the commonwealth's colleges and universities to send a representative to compete in the KMLF.[106] Dr. H. L. Donovan, president of Eastern State Teachers College and president of UK, served as president of the KMLF for six years and helped to legitimate the relationship between Kentucky universities and this Eastern Kentucky pageant.

According to James O. Roan, a longtime member of the festival board, the KMLF was conceived to honor Walker and the spring-time blooming of the mountain laurel as well as to show the world that the people of southeastern Kentucky had "culture" and pride by showcasing wholesome and attractive Kentucky college women and high school girls.[107] Today, board members tend to come from elite mountain and bluegrass families, including Lexington's Marylou Whitney (an heir to the Vanderbilt fortune), numerous Kentucky governors, district judges, and local business and political elites. Festival sponsors, judges, host families, and contestants are predominantly white, middle-class, and members of the professional and business local elite.

Although the KMLF has mercantile interests, the festival seeks to construct an alternative image for its queens and princesses—not the sexualized, commercialized display of women's bodies but a debutante-style presentation of wholesome and classy womanhood—in my terms, "platformed femininity." The KMLF's operating rules are based on the rules for the Miss America pageant. All candidates chosen by their schools to represent them at the KMLF must never have been pregnant or married. In the 1990s, two campus queens were barred from representing their universities at the KMLF because they were single mothers. One of them, the first UK homecoming queen from UK's community college system, hired an attorney and held a press conference in order to fight, unsuccessfully, the ban on mothers. Similar battles have occurred on other campuses. For example, in 2011 a divorced single mother spearheaded a campus movement at Utah Valley University to create a new campus pageant after being disqualified from the Miss UVU pageant, saying that she "didn't know I'd be judged on the status of my uterus."[108]

Since its inception, the pageant coronation has mimicked British royalty traditions (there is a curtsy competition) and images of the Plantation South by parading forty-eight young girls in long pink frocks, two jesters wearing silver bells over purple tights, ten couriers, and sixteen ladies-in-waiting attending the queen, who is clad in a white bell-shaped ball gown and long white gloves in the coronation ceremony. Contestants must each enact a regionalized and whitened mixture of middle-class femininity as well as Old South rituals. Since the contestants' dress, poise, conversational skills, and social savvy are scrutinized by a secret panel of judges, over an extended period of time, this pageant requires deep knowledge and the successful performance of regionalized gendered and racialized class codes.

Today, the KMLF continues to showcase community business, tourism, Appalachian cultural heritage, coal, and college women's beauty and poise. Amy Redmon, a contestant in 2008, concluded, "It's your old Southern beauty pageant. There are no score sheets, no talent show. It's just for fun," unlike the working-class or African American contestants I interviewed, who talk about fatigue, given the juggling acts of suppression and negotiation they engage in.[109] The KMLF features three pageants including the "Little Miss KMLF" for girls from three months to eleven years old, a princess pageant for high school girls, and the queen competition for college women. In addition to these pageants, the festival sponsors mine rescue competitions, gospel singing, antique and low-rider car shows, Elvis impersonations, a golf classic, the governor's luncheon, and finally the queen's coronation and grand ball. It also features a parade with each campus queen riding on the back of a convertible displaying the name of her university or college. Events are planned to allow visitors and contestants to attend Sunday morning worship opportunities at local Protestant and Catholic churches. (Presumably the assumption is that these two options provide adequate worship choice.) Area church services are listed in the KMLF program and to ensure that queen contestants attend, they are explicitly told in their orientation letters that "everyone is expected to attend mass or the community worship."[110]

The local newspaper runs endorsements from businesses, including Kentucky Fried Chicken, Pic-Pac supermarket, Kentucky Farm Bureau Insurance, funeral homes, a tire company, a drug store, a trucking company, and local professionals. Still a major tourist event after seventy-five years, the KMLF attracts as many as 20,000 visitors annually. Many people in attendance who have moved away from Pineville travel back long distances each year to attend the festival and reunite with the local community.

There are no runway performances from which to appraise the talent, evening gown, or swimsuit prowess of the contestants nor are there community service or platforms in the KMLF. Instead, five undercover judges "observe the candidates' appearance, personality, manners, poise, and cooperativeness throughout all festival events."[111] Many contestants believe that because of this judging process, the KMLF is "classy" and thus quite unlike the tawdry and demeaning pageants that showcase women in swimsuits. A recent winner, a UK cheerleader, described the festival as "unique and better" than other pageants since the judges get to "know you personally" and allow you to interact with members of the local business and professional elites in their homes. The 1997 queen, Brittany Lea

Johnson, agreed, adding that there are no "superficial" interviews or swimsuit competitions at KMLF.[112] Such assertions, however, overlook the overlaps between the KMLF and other beauty pageants such as Miss America in normalizing the importance of body-centered gendered distinction and middle-class proprieties and tastes.

Successful contestants must display middle-class competencies and aspirations and espouse values consistent with those of their elite sponsors. Although there is no swimsuit competition, the scrutiny of bodies and social etiquette is nonetheless a major part of the competition. Contestants are told that "there are many events in which appearance is the feature." A winning style is expensive at the KMLF since contestants are expected to be properly dressed for all aspects of the competition. They are told that they will need to bring a casual sundress, sports clothes, a cocktail dress, a casual suit, and a floor-length white ball gown that will allow them the range of motion to curtsy to the governor. At the same time, their male escorts are required to bring a white dinner jacket, black trousers, and bow tie. Although the requirements for dress and appearance are made explicit, contestants are expected to have already internalized other markers of middle-class taste and dispositions including etiquette, makeup, comportment, personal enterprise, small talk, and table manners as they dine and socialize in the homes of the local elite. They are expected to be genteel, socially savvy, and artful in their performances.

After seventy-five years, the traditions of white faces, southern ladyhood, purity, charm, and heritage continue to prevail. When I attended the festival in 2000, nineteen white university students competed for the crown of mountain laurel and a $3,000 scholarship. The curtsy competition and coronation ceremony were held at the Pine Mountain State Park, out of sight of underground and mountain top removal coal mining. In addition to the selection of the KMLF queen and princess, a Miss Congeniality, Miss Photogenic, and Best Escort were chosen. The audience was treated to a lengthy processional of queen contestants clad in long white bell-shaped gowns and over-the-elbow white gloves. They were accompanied by a "miniature court" consisting of scores of elementary school-age children, all dressed in white and carrying small bouquets of mountain laurel wrapped in white doilies, the nineteen princess candidates, and the queen's escorts. In 2000, Kentucky governor Paul Patton presided over the coronation ceremony. After a flag-raising ceremony, the recitation of the Lord's Prayer, and the singing of "My Old Kentucky Home," each campus queen contestant came forward to the edge of a reflecting pool and performed a formal curtsy reminiscent of English court and May Day rituals.[113]

Sarah Hargis, the 2007 KMLF queen who represented Centre College in Danville, Kentucky, pointed out that the contestants must not only know how to curtsy but must also impress the judges with their "poise" and "substance." She described the contest as follows:

Figure 6.1 Elaborate coronation of the 2005 Kentucky Mountain Laurel queen evoking legacies of the old plantation South. Pineville, Kentucky. Photograph by Karen W. Tice, 2000.

Over the course of three days all the girls attend luncheons and dinner parties, mingling with prominent figures of Pineville. A panel of secret judges observes each girl's manners, poise, character, and personality. Then, on the final day, the girls dress in white wedding dresses and long white gloves to perform a creative yet elegant curtsy to the governor of Kentucky. After observing the substance of the girls throughout the week, this curtsy becomes the deciding factor of who becomes queen.[114]

Significantly, Hargis's mother is from Honduras, making her the first woman of color to win the KMLF tiara. All previous KMLF queens, however, have been white women with extensive family roots in Kentucky, suggesting the importance of sponsorship and class connections.[115]

In recent years, festival organizers have actively sought the participation of black women from KSU. However, when one of the African American campus queens attempted to breach some of the class and racial fortifications that have been operative since the KMLF's inception, she found the experience deeply distressing:

There were only two black families in all of Pineville and I stayed in the home of elderly white folks. . . . I spent time with the black family who was hosting my black escort. I felt comfortable there since I was with black folks. The pageant was all about being a lady. You don't even know what they are judging on. The girl who won had a sister who won a few years prior. I do not know if that factored into her winning. You know you had to curtsy to the governor; you had to wear white including your gloves. The purity thing is what they want with that association. An uncomfortable experience. They are constantly watching you.[116]

Although she had crossed the KMLF color line, the "tradition" of showcasing white middle-class college women as signifiers of Appalachian culture and excellence remained intact.

The KMLF raises deeply troubling questions about body-based gendered distinction: the commercialization of college women's bodies to sell products, communities, and Appalachian culture; and dynamics of belonging, exclusion, and difference in the region. It also offers a truncated version of heritage and local culture, selecting and revering certain elements of imagined tradition, while suppressing many others including a history of violent labor and class conflict. Despite the efforts to challenge stereotypes, in the main, Appalachian beauty pageantry, including KMLF, perpetuates restrictive and exclusionary patterns of culture, heritage, memory, belonging, normativity, and exceptionality throughout the region.

Demands for the proper enactment of aesthetic and moralized class norms bind the Derby Princess Festival and the KMLF to the HBCU campus queen training. Both of the festivals as well as the HBCU conference are invested in class-coded notions of beauty, virtue, character, poise, and fortitude. However, in the KMLF as well as in the HBCU queens' training, both cultural and divine capital helps to pave the way to the throne. As noted, contestants in the KMLF are required to attend church services, and prayers are an integral part of the coronation ceremony and social events. Many of the speakers at the national leadership conference for black kings and queens run ministries and use scripture to motivate corporeal and psychic conversions. Indeed—in addition to evening gowns, swimsuits, gels, and lipstick—Bibles and psalms have become important components of pageant fare. Increasingly, religious justifications have been used not only to cloak beauty pageantry with wholesomeness, class, and respectability, but to imbue it with divine purpose. The seesawing of flesh and spirit and inner and outer beauty in campus pageants is the focus of the next chapter.

Flesh and Spirit

Bibles, Beauty, and Bikinis

God can even use pageant girls. He can use somebody besides a pastor or a missionary.

—Tara Dawn Holland Christensen, 1997 Miss America[1]

We have been made in the image of the most beautiful One ever. We are drawn to, nourished by, and stimulated by beauty. We should not dismiss it from our lives.

—Nancy Stafford, Miss Florida[2]

We need Christians everywhere—we need believers in the workplace, the government, and Hollywood so that we can be the salt and light to the world around us. But that doesn't mean we should become strippers for the sake of reaching other strippers. The Miss America pageant is not nearly that extreme, but it is a point worth considering. Is it possible for a Christian woman to participate in a competition that compares her with others on the basis of her looks, shed their modesty as they stand before millions in a tiny bikini, and still be uncompromisingly faithful to God?

—"Should Christians Participate in Beauty Pageants?"[3]

Throughout much of the twentieth century, Bibles, bodies, and beauty pageantry have had a volatile relationship. The popularity of beauty pageants in the early 1920s ignited religious revulsion at the display of women's bodies. Many churches condemned beauty pageants as tawdry exhibits of flesh-peddling, sin, and crass commercial interests. In 1929, for example, Bishop Christopher Brye warned the reigning Miss Europe about the dangers of participating in a Galveston, Texas, bathing beauty contest. The bishop described the pageant as

an uncouth and vulgar display for the purpose of advertising. No lady enters it. Many frown on it. When you come here, you will be asked to parade only in a bathing suit before a motley crowd, who will view you at close range as they might a beautiful animal. I cannot see how any self-respecting modest young woman will enter such a contest.[4]

Over time, beauty pageantry has become increasingly freighted with religious significance, and many contestants are now imbuing campus catwalks with divine purposes. Conjoining faith, evangelism, self-maximization, worldly prosperity and empowerment, spiritual stamina, inner beauty, and community servant-hood, campus royalty use their personal religious commitments as a basis for demonstrating both their pageant competitiveness and spiritual worthiness. Jean Comaroff argues that the unsettling effects of changing social and market relations of neo-liberal economies and religion have helped to promote a Christian revitalization in which "[c]ommerce, government, education, media, and popular arts—nothing seems too trivial or debased to offer grist to the spiritual mill. The task according to Ted Haggard, the former president of the National Association of Evangelicals, is to put "'God in everything,' so anything-can-be-holy."[5]

There are numerous signs of religious revival on campus.[6] Christian guide books for college students are popular, including J. Budzisezenski's *How to Stay Christian in College* (2004); Jonathan Morrow's *Welcome to College: A Christ Followers Guide for the Journey* (2008); Tony Campulo's *Survival Guide for Christians on Campus: How to Be Students and Disciples at the Same Time* (2002); and Abbie Smith's *Can you Keep the Faith in College: Students from 50 Campuses Tell You How and Why* (2006). At MIT, there are over fifteen different student evangelical groups, some of which are affiliated with national evangelical organizations including Intervarsity Christian Fellowship and the Campus Crusade for Christ (CCC), one of the largest student Christian organizations with a foothold on over 1,000 campuses. Using its globally distributed feature-length film *Jesus*, as well as two websites, godsquad.com and everystudent.com, CCC furthers its mission to "turn lost students into Christ-centered laborers," and to "take the initiative to share our faith so that every student can hear the gospel in an *attractive and meaningful way* [emphasis added]." The CCC has also used campus queens and athletes in their publications to actively counter images of the dour and anemic Christian fundamentalist.[7] Campus royalty, using worldly class-specific currencies of image, beauty, style, and self-investment as well as psycho-spiritual discourses have contributed to this project of Christianizing college campuses.

Campus queens and kings are a highly visible part of God's campus labor force, and they serve as attractive disciples promoting the beauty of the Bible while wearing their crowns of glory. Campus religious student organizations including such groups as the Baptist Student Ministry regularly select women to serve as figureheads for their organizations. Women students have received such titles as Miss Religion, Miss Christian Student Union, Miss Gospel Ensemble, and Miss Ministries. Many of the contestants in Georgetown College's Belle of the Blue pageant sang gospel

songs for their talent portion and one contestant used the Q&A competition to tes-
tify that "Jesus, my personal Savior, helped me to get up each morning and do the
Lord's work," which included competing in the Belle of the Blue.[8] In 2007, Whitney
McClain said that she was blessed to be able to be the queen of Georgetown College,
stating that "Ever since I was a little girl, creative ministries have been my passion. I
wanted to do more than just a performance; I wanted to show who I was." She concluded that for her, the pageant meant "coming together to exhibit more than just
beauty, but true inner beauty."[9] McClain, like many other campus queens, claims
that pageants are a "creative" pulpit giving voice to religiously-identified women.

Many Christian queens contend that pageants offer opportunities to increase
their cultural, embodied, and divine capital. The body is resurrected as part of a
divine arsenal for doing God's work and showcasing inner spiritual beauty. However, the contradictions of using pageant performances of disciplined bodies to
signify inner spiritual beauty and worthiness requires deft maneuvering. Many
contestants groom and display their staged bodies only to ultimately repudiate
the relative importance of doing so. In 2007, Emily Wasonga, an Andersen University student, for example, straddled the contradictions of flesh and spirit when
she established a Christian campus pageant that showcased the "beauty of love
and service." Wasonga testified that "God had prompted her to create a pageant—
one that wasn't just about outward looks, but inner worth and innate beauty
reflected in Christian love and servant-hood," acknowledging that physical
appearance matters as a gateway to the soul but ultimately one transcends it.[10]
Wasonga also justified the pageant in terms of Christian ministry, noting that it
would be used to fund a "program that would build that brother-and-sister-in-
Christ relationship so we can connect with those children [in Kenya] to give them
another resource and support person in their life."[11]

Contestants at both Christian and secular U.S. universities and colleges regularly assert their religious convictions and inner spiritual beauty at campus pageants, but platforming God is not limited to Christians. A noteworthy example
occurred in 2005 when Anisah Rasheed, a practicing Muslim, was crowned Miss
North Carolina A&T State University. Rasheed said she was at peace with her
decision to participate in the pageant since "at the end of the day, it is between me
and God; . . . I know I'm doing what God intends me to do." She also argued, as do
many Christian queens, that the pageant was not about "outer beauty but brains
and intellect."[12] Lelia Ahmed, a professor of women's studies and religion, has
said, "On the face of it, I don't know why her faith should interfere with her. There
is nothing that she is doing that is degrading. Why do women who wear the hajib
also put on makeup and tight jeans? It is true that Muslims require modesty and
you shouldn't be flaunting yourself sexually. But isn't that also true for people who
are of the Christian and Jewish faiths?"[13]

Religious biographies and proverbs have become a common component of pageant platforming. In 2008, the Howard University website profiled its campus king
and queen by noting their strong religious convictions to faith and fellowship as well

as their commitments to a Christianized class-laden grammar of individualized spiritual empowerment and self-maximization. Brittany Brooks, the queen, was described as a "devout Christian" who understandsood the "value of unconditional love, community service, and fellowship." Striking a more muscular tone, Edward Williams, Mr. Howard University, asserted the power of God for self-maximization. Evoking by far the most popular pageant proverb used by both black and white pageant campus contestants, Williams described himself as a "true believer" who "can do all things through Christ who strengthens him" (Philippians 4:13).[14] Affirming God's power to strengthen personal productivity and assist devout college women and men in their quest for success and achievement is an essential part of the narrative architecture that contestants use in their rationales for pageant participation and religious platforming. Such sentiments have much in common with neo-liberal discourses of enterprising self-hood.

The 2009 KSU pageant program, like that of Howard University, detailed the deep religious commitments of its royalty and illuminates how contestants package spirituality for campus pageants. Mr. KSU 2009 shared his spiritual biography, which noted that he had "accepted Christ and was baptized at the age of nine at the New Testament Baptist church. . . . Growing up in the Body of Christ, he has participated in a myriad of ministries and organizations to advance God's Kingdom" and he "gives God the highest praise because he realizes that God wants to transform him into a vessel of honor."[15]

The 2009 KSU queen, Elisabeth Martin, who had previously won the title of Miss Baptist Campus Ministries, also trumpeted her Christian upbringing, which had taught her to "lean on Christ." She chose the scriptural passage "Who knows but that you have come to royal position for such a time as this" (Esther 4:14) as the guiding proverb for her reign.[16] In an interview, she told me that Christianity helped to pave the way to the throne since "it is helpful to be a Christian and have good morals when running for campus queen since people do not want a floozy as their queen."[17] When she was asked, as the first white queen of an HBCU, what she would do if someone made negative comments about the racial politics of her win, she replied: "First and foremost I'm a Christian, and when I see someone who doesn't understand or is just not open to that at first, I feel like I just need to love them like Jesus would."[18]

Not only did Martin's Christian beliefs help her to navigate the minefields of campus race politics, but were foundational to her campus mission of helping students groom their bodies to achieve empowered Christian subjectivities. She established a variety of campus programs that fused beauty, faith, and the styling of the body. Among these was a "True Beauty" seminar (a common way to spiritualize the project of feminine body transformation and beautification) for women students that combined talks by a campus minister as well as style experts on "how to dress to impress." She also organized a conference, "Behind the Mask: Revealing the Soul Within," that included representatives from the Elite Makeover Tour and the winner of the Mrs. Wyoming pageant, each of whom provided guidance on makeup, body fitness, and spiritual strength. In such a world, disciplining and dressing the outer body is deemed essential both for the project of saving souls and for enhancing one's spiritual interiority.

Numerous beauty contestants in both campus and national pageants routinely and unabashedly display zeal for Jesus and assertively use their tiaras and titles to embody and spread evangelical Christian convictions, body theologies, and self-enhancement homilies while combining them with secularized grammars of class and body makeovers. The conversion of campus pageantry into showcases for public affirmations of faith can first be understood by exploring the increasing spiritualization of the Miss America pageant in its holy war with religious critics throughout the twentieth century. As a consequence of this spiritualization, as well as the emergence of neo-liberal rationalities and market theologies for self-hood and makeover, many beauty contestants comfortably deploy discourses of self-maximization, body stewardship, life makeover, witnessing and testimony, inner beauty, and God's design as the catalysts for their beauty pageant participation. Always the pageant pacesetter, Miss America has been on the frontlines of fusing the biblical and the beautiful.

Beauty and the Bible: The National Context

In response to widespread religious critique in the 1920s, the Miss America pageant began to champion the piety and wholesomeness of its pageant winners. The 1924 winner, Ruth Malcolmson, was touted for her membership in a church choir and Lois Delander, Miss America 1927, was praised for having won a medal for knowing the most Bible verses.[19] Anticipating many of the contemporary contortions that pageant organizers would later undertake to promote virtue and sexuality simultaneously, especially in those contests where contestants promenade on stage in bathing suits, Miss America organizers asked contestants to wear their most revealing bathing suits only during a private showing with judges and news reporters and their less scanty swimwear for the general public. In 1935, Lenore Slaughter was hired as pageant director. For over thirty years, Slaughter was described as having "a crusader's impulse to drag Miss America into respectability" and purge it of its prurient past.[20] A Southern Baptist, Slaughter "picked the pageant up by its bathing suit straps and put in an evening gown," in part by actively recruiting Christian women from the South and West as contestants in the Miss America pageant during the 1950s and 1960s.[21] While unwilling to eliminate the swimsuit, Slaughter regulated the wardrobes for pageant competition, including a prohibition on mini-skirts because they were "ungodly."[22]

While a good many Miss Americas have been religious, 1965 was a watershed year for women who sought to position themselves as highly visible promoters of Christianity. Vonda Kay Van Dyke, that year's winner, proclaimed her Christian faith during the pageant competition. She told emcee Bert Parks that she always carried her Bible with her since it was "the most important book she owned."[23] She later declared, "I wanted to be Miss America for one reason—I wanted to tell people about the Christ I love and try to serve."[24] Church groups flooded the Miss America organization with requests to have Van Dyke speak to their congregations. Like many subsequent born-again beauty queens, Van Dyke used her post-pageant fame to evangelize by publishing a faith-based advice book that counseled teen girls that "each step to beauty will be hard to mount alone in the dark, but with God's light and His guiding hand, you will find your way to new heights of beauty" and "that inner sparkle that only Christ can give."[25]

In response to favorable reactions to Van Dyke's religiosity, the Miss America pageant dropped its ban against public expressions of religious convictions by contestants, paving the way for subsequent Christian beauty queens to use their thrones for public evangelization. By allowing public affirmations of Christian faith on stage, the longstanding rupture between Bibles and bathing suits was moderated and many evangelical Christian women, in particular, increasingly began to mediate the crosscurrents of glamour, glitter, and godliness in secular beauty pageants.

With the election of Jimmy Carter and political organizing by religious right leaders such as Jerry Falwell, *Newsweek* declared 1976 to be "the year of the evangelical." Although historically excluded from formal church leadership and marginalized by discourses of women's submissiveness and domesticity, evangelical women found increased opportunities for leadership and outreach through publishing devotional and self-help books, establishing special women's ministries, participating in Bible conferences, Christian education, and missionary work; some chose beauty pageantry. beauty pageantry.[26] In the 1970s, evangelical Christian women gravitated to beauty pageantry, as an additional gateway for faith-based leadership.

Coinciding and colliding with second-wave feminism and the 1970s drive to ratify the ERA, numerous Christian women, including beauty queens, championed traditional femininities and family values predicated on notions of essentialist but "complementary" roles for women and men and a purported balance between women's submission and familial influence and responsibility. They published numerous bestselling books on proper Christian womanhood that offered faith-based advice on marriage, beauty, weight loss, and self-improvement including Mabel Morgan's (1973) bestseller *The Total Women*; beauty queen Anita Bryant's (1972) *Bless This House* and (1977) *The Anita Bryant Story: The Survival of Our Nation's Families and the Threat of Militant Homosexuality*; Phyllis Schlafly's (1977) *The Power of Positive Women*; Joan Cavanaugh's (1976) *More of Jesus, Less of Me* (a weight-loss book); and Patricia Krenml's (1978) *Slim for Him*.[27] These books were important precursors to the devotional beauty/life makeover books that have occupied an important niche in contemporary Christian women's self-help literature and ministries, many of which are spearheaded by former beauty queens.

Fervent born-again women increasingly used the Miss America pageant stage as a pulpit. (Indeed, like Sunday schools and overseas missions, beauty pageants have provided evangelical platforms for members of conservative Protestant denominations that prohibit women from ordination.) Terry Meeuwsen, who won the title of Miss America in 1973, was especially successful in navigating the tensions between commercialized displays of pulchritude and the pulpit by making effective use of her post-pageant fame to evangelize for Jesus. On the eve of her Miss America pageant, Meeuwsen acknowledged the labors she undertook to discipline her flesh in striving for the crown, saying that she "felt like a racehorse that had been exercised, fed, and groomed for a year. I was ready to go."[28] Like many evangelical queens, Meeuwsen justified her pageant participation and fixation on fine-tuning her body as rooted in a Christian mission, claiming that Miss America was "a great vehicle" for doing the work of the Lord.[29] After her reign, Meeuwsen became a popular televangelist and since 1993, she has co-hosted *The 700 Club*, a weekly TV evangelical Christian ministry with Pat Robertson. She also co-hosts the Christian Broadcast Network's *Living the Life*, and she has published four devotional books for women.

Cheryl Prewitt-Salem, Miss America 1980, is another noteworthy example of a Miss America who has successfully merged pageants and preaching. Like many other contestants in national beauty pageants, Prewitt-Salem first graced a campus runway. In her autobiography, she described her decision to compete for the campus title at Mississippi State University as follows: "If only I could combine my love for pageants and for my school and somehow win the title of Miss MSU. . . . What better way to spend my senior year? Still, to return to the pageant for the third time would be embarrassing. And, what if, for all my efforts, I was again to lose?"[30] Despite her worries, she was crowned Miss MSU and thereby qualified to compete in the state and national Miss America contests. Crowned Miss America in 1980, Prewitt-Salem has since engaged in a wide variety of post-pageant, faith-based endeavors including the publication of her autobiography, *A Bright Shining Place: The Story of a Miracle*. Here she recounts her devotion to beauty pageantry as a forum to showcase God's healing miracles, deploying the themes of suffering, surrender to God, and personal healing/salvation to anchor her narrative. After a car accident that preceded her pageant career, Prewitt-Salem had been told that she would never walk again since one of her legs was two inches shorter than the other. She later attended a revival meeting and after a Pentecostal minister laid his hands on her legs, she claimed to have felt like she was immersed in a hot tub and then was whisked away to "some faraway bright-shining place—a private place inhabited only by me and Jesus."[31] Subsequently, she testified that her leg grew two inches instantaneously.

According to Prewitt-Salem, this body "miracle" was a sign of God's power and love. As a result, she had a burning desire to connect people to Christianity. She wondered if "trying for the title of Miss America could be what God wanted me to do with my life; that is, if my purpose was to use the position as a means of witnessing for Him on a world-wide scale? The more I thought and prayed about it, the more certain I became that it was."[32] During the swimsuit competition, she exclaimed: "Anyone who had any doubts about my story, just look at these legs. Look at them! They're great. They're perfect. They are living proof that God, in his love and power, can take the most crippled legs and transform them into something beautiful."[33]Facing her first national press conference as Miss America, Prewitt-Salem stated that she had hoped that the press "might ignore the story of her healing and stick to questions about women's rights and the like. I could save my Christian testimony for the churches," since as "Miss America, I was sure to be appearing in a lot of them."[34] Yet after much soul searching, she turned to scripture for guidance, noting that "hadn't Jesus commanded believers to 'Go into the world and preach the gospel' (Mark 16:15), 'not to hide our light under a bushel' (Matthew 5:15), ... and moreover 'not be ashamed of Him and His words' (Mark 8:38)?"[35] Consequently, she highlighted her tale of faith healing for the national press.

Prewitt-Salem, in her words, used her Miss America title as a "springboard to launch the Gospel of Jesus Christ into churches, schools, women's retreats, and on television."[36] Along with her husband, Robert Salem, she is deeply involved in the Salem Family Ministries. Prewitt-Salem's healing ministry has spanned Christian television, numerous gospel CDs including *I'm a Miracle*, a spiritual health/ fitness video *"Take Charge of Your Life with Cheryl and Friends"* designed to develop "a winning attitude and the desire to be the best," and a book (*Choose to Be Happy*), all of which blend normative class prescriptions for mobility and plenitude with divinity. As we shall see, Prewitt-Salem also markets beauty pageant competition products, including swimwear. Charles Reagan Wilson notes the confluence of outer and inner beauty for Christian queens such as Prewitt-Salem.

> In Prewitt's persona, the beauty queen has become an icon of religious edification. ... The beauty queen represents a conspicuous display of corporeality, in one sense, but in another sense the display is within clearly regimented and restricted codes. The beauty queen represents purity. She is also a triumphant contestant, who wins by embodying—in the evangelical view—not just outward beauty but inner beauty. She represents values and retains her virtue.[37]

Following the crowning of Meeuwsen and Prewitt-Salem, increasing numbers of other born-again beauties have chosen the pageant stage to showcase both their flesh and their devotion to Jesus. Since 1980, more than half of the Miss America winners have identified as evangelical Christians.[38]

Religion was also used to rescue the pageant in 1984 when Vanessa Williams, the first African American woman to win the Miss America title, was dethroned after it was revealed that she had previously posed in the nude. With the sanctity of the crown violated, the selection of a pious queen was needed to purify the pageant. Thus, the following year, Sharlene Wells, a Mormon, was crowned Miss America. Wells attributed her win in part to the fact that the pageant needed an especially "conservative" and virtuous queen. White, blonde, patriotic, and religious, Wells proclaimed: "I am very proud of my Mormon background. I live my values seven days a week. I believe very strongly in God and country. I follow the flag with my whole body."[39] A supporter of then-president Ronald Reagan and a foe of abortion, pre-martial sex, and the proposed equal rights amendment, Wells's embodiment of God, nation, and chaste womanhood helped to sanitize the reputation of the Miss America pageant and whiten the stains left by the imputed debauchery of Vanessa Williams. In 1989, Miss America bestowed the crown on Debbye Turner, another born-again Christian. Turner received media attention not only for being black but for her willingness to publicly identify as a queen "whose Bible was her constant companion."[40]

The Christianization of Miss America was further solidified in 2003 with the crowning of Erika Harold,who was described by one of her fellow beauty contestants as "just on fire for the Lord." Harold observed that "God has creative ways of using people to make a difference. We should never limit Him to the traditional ways we conceive of ministry."[41] Harold vehemently defended her religious convictions on sexual abstinence throughout her beauty reign, despite the fiery tempest that her chastity platform unleashed within the Miss America organization. Harold's pastor, Gary Grogan, recognized the effectiveness of Harold's merger of beauty pageantry and religious zeal, boasting that although "she has been through the wringer, the Lord has vindicated her. It's one thing to be bold in church; it's another thing in the public arena. She's reaching more lost people in a year that the average preacher will in a lifetime."[42] Harold spoke at the 2004 Republican National Convention and, not unlike a later beauty queen of note, Sarah Palin, stated that she has aspirations to run for president of the U.S.

In addition to Harold, other Miss America winners view beauty pageantry as an outlet for women's ministry and empowerment. Miss America 1997, Tara Dawn Holland Christensen, testified that "God called her to do quite a strange ministry; ... He wanted her to do beauty pageants in the name of the Lord and to give Him the glory and the praise."[43] Like Harold, Christensen trumpeted the divine opportunities that Miss America offered evangelical women by noting that the "winner is watched not only for a year but for a lifetime. No other program gives such a voice to women. When I was at the pageant I cared nothing about the crown, the money, the glitz, or the glamour. I realized this was my opportunity to make a difference for everything from literacy to abstinence. There is something about a crown that makes people listen to what you say."[44] Tangra Riggle, a former Miss Indiana, likewise celebrates the virtues of secular pageants as a showcase, a power base, and a source of authority for evangelical women. She claims that "because of the state crown I now have a microphone. Miss Indiana is a platform to effectively minister to many."[45]

These evangelical women have embraced beauty pageantry as a strategy for doing God's work and promoting themselves as public evangelists. Charles Reagan Wilson has aptly observed that "all aspects of life can provide religious illumination when believers see them in a sacred perspective."[46] Beauty pageantry is no exception. The Westernized beauty contest of individuated competition itself is somewhat pliable and has been altered to serve a variety of personal and political convictions, including sacred femininity.[47] Born-again beauty queens engage in a series of packaging and plat-forming maneuvers to justify their pageant participation and purify its corporeal aspects, including following God's design and promoting Christianity. Indeed, the recent post-pageant political visibility afforded ex-beauty queens, such as Carrie Prejean, attests to the power of the throne as a gateway to national prominence. Prejean's recent stand on gay marriage in the Miss USA 2009 pageant has afforded her wide-spread fame on the Christian media circuit including *Focus on the Family* and *The 700 Club*, speaking engagements on Christian college campuses such as Liberty University, and promotion of a recent book, *Still Standing: The Untold Story of my Fight Against Gossip, Hate, and Political Attacks* in which Prejean describes herself as "a sacrificial lamb thrown to the vicious media lions."[48]

Born-again beauty queens have not only revamped the historical relationship between Christianity and beauty pageantry but are generating an unparalleled growth of faith-based, body-centered makeover ministries designed to produce empowered and assertive spiritual femininities. They extol the virtues of beautification, body stewardship, and self-enterprise as strategies for fostering spiritual strength—rather than being merely worldly diversions. They have embraced secular beauty pageants as divine opportunities for professing faith and engaging in both religious recruitment and retail. Many scholars have noted the impact of secularized, gendered, and classed discourses of self-improvement on religiosity.[49] Penny Marler, for example, has observed a growing trend away "from religious homemaker to spiritual self-maker" that has accompanied the shifting gendered patterns of work and faith.[50] The normalization of religion in conventional beauty pageants, along with the establishment of faith-based makeover ministries by born-again beauty queens conjoining beautification and body stewardship with worldly prosperity and spiritual salvation, has fractured and reconfigured conventional binaries of body and soul and the material and spiritual.

The increasing prominence of born-again beauty queens who extol the virtues of their privatized journeys of sacrifice, perseverance, self-improvement, body discipline, and personal gain have thus made inroads into a wide range of beauty pageants. They embrace, embody, and preach emergent normative iterations of otherwise secular and gendered body technologies and middle-class models of self-help as pathways to abundance, salvation, inner beauty, and sacred femininity. On pageant catwalks and in their subsequent ministries, they effectively use contemporary media and market technologies to peddle worldly desires for beautification, financial savvy, self-determination, and entrepreneurialism along with faith, scripture, and miracles. They urge Christian women to embark on an end-less quest to repair and enhance their bodies and lives while traveling on the road to heavenly redemption. Failure becomes a matter of flawed spirits, defeated psy-ches, and sagging bodies; a failure to self-regulate and increase one's personal potency by making capital investments in both the secular and the divine.

Holiness, Higher Education, and Campus Pageants

National trends for bestowing religious righteousness on beauty pageants and their contestants have helped to Christianize campus contests and shape the con-struction of distinction and merit. Drawing upon contradictory and competing discourses of the secular and the spiritual, including inner/outer beauty, body stewardship, public evangelization, salvation, servant-hood, self-betterment, social mobility, and personal empowerment, campus contestants have brought God and Jesus onto campus catwalks. Public affirmations of faith through platforms and proverbs have increasingly become part of many collegiate pageants, and they are grounded in the idea that the power of God can further the project of individual mobility and prosperity and, ultimately, salvation. Embarking upon a spiritual quest through pageantry demands assimilation into a secularized beauty and body culture and as a result contestants offer a variety of cover stories to minimize these contradictions.

One recent Miss Morris Brown College, for example, understood God as a personal safety net: "Live your life for God and that which you will desire will be granted to you. Have faith and believe in His word and you shall never fall."[51] Other campus queens referenced Christian service as their rationales for plat-forming God on stage. Tasha Nicole Askew, Miss Delaware State University and a contestant for the title of Miss MEAC (an HBCU queen competition spon-sored by Fashion Fair Cosmetics), described herself as one who "feeds off of an unwavering faith in the Lord and believes in helping others realize their poten-tial by serving as a product of her testimony."[52] Askew also asserted that the "best way to start and end the day is with a talk with her Lord and Savior." Erin Moss, a Bible and religion major at Andersen University, was featured in a cam-pus publication after winning the title of Miss Michigan 2003. Although Moss had to miss her last year of studies to serve as Miss Michigan, she asserted that it was worth doing since that was part of God's design as well as a "life-changing opportunity to speak about Christian leadership and make a difference in other people's life."[53]

To further their sacred goals of touching others through the word of God, many campus queens herald the importance of engaging in "smile ministries" as the rationale for their participation in campus pageantry. Here, the smile is sancti-fied and serves as a blessed instrument to further one's missionary goals. For example, one UK homecoming queen contender spoke of the power of smiles in her application essay: "God has blessed me with the unbelievable gift of joy. Throughout every situation in my life, whether easy or difficult, I always carry with me happiness in my heart. This gift I want to share with others. I thrive on spreading smiles across campus and filling rooms with laughter."[54] Another UK homecoming queen aspirant who had recently returned from a missionary expedition affirmed that "through my mission experiences, I have already seen what a difference I can make. A helping hand, a hug, even a simple smile can encourage the disheartened and make their lives better. I want happiness to prevail in all people, and I try to spread this attitude daily."[55] Finally, another contestant wrote, "I am very passionate about my faith in God and will be participating in a mission trip with Campus Crusade for Christ to Minsk where I will share my college experience and my Christian faith."[56]

While thanks to God have thus been regularly offered on stage by numerous campus beauty winners, the forcefulness and fervor in which campus contestants evoke God, Jesus, and the Holy Spirit appears to have been strengthened in recent years. In numerous campus contests, contestants now share their personal relationships to God and their deep devotion to their faith and self-maximization to further God's work. Public witnessing and the praise of Jesus have become frequent dimensions of the quest to win campus crowns. Sporting svelte bodies and sweet smiles while professing body stewardship, inner beauty, and spiritual strength, a new assertiveness about Jesus can be seen in campus pageants. This heightened religiosity is helping to refigure notions of feminine worthiness on campus as well as buttressing beliefs that groomed bodies and middle-class aspiration serve sacred causes.

Contestants are expected to reveal their individualized spiritual journeys as well as model Christian virtues and aspirations. In question and answer competitions as well as in their choice of pageant proverbs, platforms, and platitudes, contestants proclaim divine approval for their pageant labors and missions. These faith-based affirmations are typically interlaced with classed grammars for achievement and productivity, as is evident in contestants' biblical advice to their fellow students. One such particularly upbeat and divine dictum for self-creation, success, and empowerment that many students proclaim in various rhetorical forms is "I can be anything I want to be and succeed in everything I try to be, because I'm blessed."[57] I first heard this motto at the 2002 Mr. and Ms. Black UK pageant, which is sponsored by a contradictory patchwork of student organizations that range from the "Black Voices Gospel Choir" to "Hot Girls Athletics." It attracts many contestants who understand their religious commitments as foundational for self-realization and success. Their choice of proverbs reveals their efforts to platform themselves as worldly enterprising subjects yet also devoted spiritual disciples of Christ. One contestant listed her favorite quote as "Seek ye first the kingdom of God, and his righteousness; and all these things shall be added unto you." Another contestant affirmed the importance of tenaciousness and divine blessings for achieving worldly success, noting that "some people succeed because they are destined to, but most people succeed because they are determined to. So therefore, determine to succeed and surely God will bless you."[58] Kristin Gailliard, winner of the 2002 Miss Pride pageant at KSU and president of the Apostolic Lighthouse Campus Ministries, chose as her pageant quote "If you speak it, believe it, then you can achieve it! No matter what, what GOD has for me, it is for me!" Here, the affinities among ascendant neo-liberal and post-feminist rationalities for self-formation and transcendent individualism are linked to such divine proverbs. Salutary logics of God's divine power are coupled with worldly ambition, a blend of faith and fortitude indebted to both biblical and neo-liberal subjectivities. Success, personal empowerment, salvation, and deliverance are in the hands of enterprising individuals and the Almighty. Communalism, as well as an awareness of race and class barriers and burdens, is often sidelined in such divinations.

Both white and black contestants attribute salvation, success, and personal gain to God's providence. However, African American women are especially likely to emphasize the importance of personal endurance and strength in their faith statements. These themes were prevalent at the all-black Miss Pride pageant at KSU in 2002. One contestant conjoined strength and salvation when she wrote "I would like to give glory and honor to my Lord and Savior Jesus Christ. You strengthen me daily and guide my mind, body, and soul down the direct path to heavenly peace and spiritual salvation."[59] Another contestant testified that accomplishment and ecstasy grow out of a non-specific, de-politicized anguish (not referencing the structural dynamics of inequality) by asserting that "character can't be developed in ease and quiet. Only through experiences of trial and suffering, can the soul be strengthened, vision cleared, ambition inspired, and success achieved." Cassandra White-Dodson, the winner of the 2002 Miss Kentucky State University crown, narrated her spiritual journey of suffering and the powerful love of Jesus that inspires endurance and excellence. Raised in her grandparents' home, she said that while "living in a home of God-fearing Christians" she had "learned about and accepted Christ into her life at an early age while attending New Cannon Baptist Church."[60] As an African American woman, she experienced "great trials and tribulations" including navigating the racial difficulties of attending a predominately white Jesuit preparatory high school. Faith in her "Lord and Savior" helped her to persevere. After losing her grandmother, she turned to the "Lord to fight her battle of grief and despair and continued to march in excellence in the name of Jesus." She described herself as one who "performs to succeed and keeps God first," and she "thanked God for all his blessings and especially for his gift of his son Jesus who died for all of our sins." [61] Here, traditional Judeo-Christian discourses of "trials and tribulations" take on deeper resonance when they are also seen as racialized and gendered expressions of the "strong black women syndrome." As Beauboeuf-Lafontant and others have argued, while on the surface claims of black women's strength seem laudatory, they also operate as "prescriptive discourses" that normalize the burdens, suffering, and struggles that black women are expected to manage with strength and forbearance.[62]

The ethos of some campus pageants themselves encourages public proclamations of faith. The Miss Spelman College pageant is a noteworthy example of a Christianized pageant. Originally founded by two white Northern Baptists as a basement church school, Spelman College's early mission included instilling in African American women the importance of embodying Christian womanhood in all aspects of their lives. With a college motto of "Our Whole School for Christ," students received Christian educations that included Bible-reading and prayer meetings. Because the Baptist founders had hoped that such a curriculum would encourage Spelman women to "tell of the love of Jesus in their hearts [and become] converted," records were kept to document the number of student conversions.[63] The present Miss Spelman College pageant reflects this legacy of Christian-inspired education. As one Spelman student acknowledged: "Jesus is a crucial factor in the Miss Spelman pageant competition."[64] Melanie Nicole Bullock, the 2004 Miss Spelman College, for example, "dedicated her reign as Miss Spelman College and her life to letting God's light shine in and through her, touching, and enlightening the lives of many. 'To God be the glory for all the things He has done and continues to do in my life.'"[65] All her attendants that year were forthright about their religious commitments and inspirational missions, including one who simply declared: "For every blink and breath, I give him praise." Most of the eleven contestants for the 2005 Miss Spelman College crown likewise articulated the idea that worldly success demanded not only perseverance and hard work but prayer and faith in the power of the Lord.

Many of the endorsements from family and church members in pageantry programs and publicity emphasize religious sentiments, blessings, and words of inspiration. They highlight the importance of cultivating inner spiritual beauty, the power of hard work, piety and prayer, and heeding divine counsel. In the 2005 Miss Spelman College pageant program, for example, scriptural endorsements fused faith and upbeat, can-do subjectivities, including Matthew 17:20: "If you have faith as small as a mustard seed . . . nothing will be impossible" and "Always remember to let God direct your path and success will follow." Inner spiritual beauty was revered in another contestant endorsement that stated: "What is on the inside shows up on the outside, so continue to let His light shine within you. May you continue to be blessed." [66]

The naturalization of religion and beauty pageantry is further evident in the support contestants receive from their ministers and church congregations. Far from the scathing critiques of the morality of women who participated in Miss America pageants in the 1920s, many ministers have reversed their predecessors' denunciations of beauty pageants as blasphemous spectacles. Instead, they offer their support in a variety of ways, including prayers, endorsements, publicity, and attendance at pageants. So do congregations. Many of the 2005 Miss Spelman College Pageant contestants received endorsements and scriptural advice from their church congregations. The New Life International Family Church in Decatur, Georgia, for instance, endorsed its candidate in a pageant advertisement showing an image of a key opening a symbolic "door of opportunity." The text stated: "For many are called, but few are chosen. Behold, the Lord has set before thee an open door; we pray that this be one of the many doors of opportunity for you." Business cards of the Pastor and the First Lady of the church were also included. St. Marks Baptist Church plugged its favorite Miss Spelman contestant by quoting *Colossians* 3:23: "Whatever you do, work at it with all your heart as working for the Lord, not for men." Another contestant received scriptural advice for her spiritual journey from her "church family," who wrote: "REMEMBER: There's still much work to be done, . . . Trust in the Lord with all thine heart; lean not unto thine own understanding. In all thy ways acknowledge him, and he shall direct thy paths." Such church endorsements reflect new sensibilities about campus pageants as sites offering opportunities for public witnessing and object lessons for exemplary Christian students.

Proverbs alone are often not sufficient to showcase sacred femininity. Miss Howard University 2007–2008, Brittany Brooks, shows how some campus queens express religious convictions by blending spirituality directly into their pageant platforms. Brooks established a student program titled "Full Potential: Focusing on Unparalleled and Limitless Living," which wove together spirituality, healthy bodies, and potentiality.

> An individual can only reach their full potential when they are healthy in every respect. Full Potential will ensure the holistic health of the student body by enhancing students spiritually, physically, mentally, and financially. I have been called to inspire individuals to reach their utmost potential. Hence, I stand upon a platform that will serve as a key to boundless opportunities. . . . Full Potential will redirect students' attention to the old adage that your body is a temple.[67]

In order to further her goal of body stewardship, psychic and spiritual development, and financial well-being, Brooks established faith-based "forums on appreciating ourselves as people" and harnessing spiritual power to foster harmony and individual well-being. She said, "my platform will resurrect the cohesive spiritual unit where we encourage and uplift each other. . . . Howard University's student body varies in thought, willpower, and faith. I would like to host a religious fair where students will be exposed to various theologies and spiritual practices that will help maintain their spiritual wellness."[68] The pageant stage gives Christian-identified queens, such as Brooks, literally a platform from which to spiritualize college campuses and enhance students' bodies. In this case, the body remains an important work site for financial and spiritual fulfillment.

The importance of faith and fortitude, as well as self-techniques for enhancing one's inner core and external appearances, is an integral part of the training at the annual HBCU leadership conferences for kings and queens. Many of its speakers are former beauty queens who have established post-pageant careers as faith-based inspirational and motivational trainers. Theresa McFaddin-Ordell, an ordained minister, has been one of the many conference speakers who fuse entrepeneurship, self-management, bodywork, beauty, and God. Author of *Supernaturally Beautiful*, *Saved/Sexy/Cool*, *No Room for Excuses*, and a "discipleship seminar" called "Me Management," McFaddin-Ordell espouses a Christianized and individualized path for success.

Religion is continually woven through these conferences as the logic for enhancing bodies and souls. Mary Terry Wiley, a regular speaker at the annual conference and one of the founders of Aphesis Outreach Ministry, counsels the queens in her workshop "Food for the Soul" to live by the motto that "blindness is the result of Godless sight."[69] Benecia Williams, the associate director of student affairs at Lincoln University in Missouri also uses God to inspire the queens in her workshop "Crowns and Gowns: How to Plan Your Coronation" by quoting Psalms 139:14, "You are fearfully and wonderfully made," to remind the queens to set high standards for their bodies and souls. Dr. Tonea Steward, a former campus queen from Jackson State University, tells the HBCU queens that the Bible and the Ten Commandments are the catalysts for caring for one's hair and appearance. She urges them to "magnify what God had given" and "enhance one's God given beauty." In her talk, she stressed that

> We must pray for revival. . . . We must know the Bible. . . . We must study the Bible. We must understand the Golden Rule, and we must understand and live the Ten Commandants. We must understand that God gave a promise to us. He promised us all kinds of wonderful things, and He gave us choices. So what choices do we make? We choose to be the best. How do we do that? We look at ourselves in the mirror and say my hair is real short but just because it is short does not mean I should not do anything with it. I can cover it up. I can condition it and wear it the way it is. But I want to make it glorify the halo that is our God-given crown ."[70]

Steward believes that image enhancement can serve both earthly and divine purposes.

Marshawn Evans, a former beauty queen and contestant on Donald Trump's *The Apprentice*, blended etiquette, style, faith, fortitude, and entrepreneurship in her two conference workshops, "Style and Substance" and "Presentation Is Everything." Evans is the president and chief branding officer of *EDGE 3M*, a marketing and management firm for celebrities.[71] She passionately believes that individuals who are motivated to "maximize life's opportunities and make positive choices will have plenteous lives."[72] Nicknamed "Miss Peak Performance," she argues that individuals must "evaluate their attitude, habits, and perception of self to become a peak performer, personally and professionally."[73] Evans began competing in beauty pageants when she was a student at Texas Christian University. Although she never placed higher than second runner-up, she persevered and moved to Washington, D.C., where she won the title of Miss District of Columbia and became eligible to compete in the 2001 Miss America scholarship competition. At the Miss America pageant, she choose to sing "I Will Survive" in order "to inspire the American people with a sense of hope" in the aftermath of 9/11.[74] Evans stated that, given the devaluation of black women's bodies and culture, queens must have faith and stamina to achieve "peak performances" in the quest for beauty pageant titles. Her approach is described as follows:

> Patience was the key to her pageant success since black women do not fit the stereotypical image of a beauty queen. Let's face it we have different body type, different hair, and different experiences. That doesn't mean you can't succeed in pageants or any other area of life. It just means you need to be prepared for the challenges that lie ahead. . . . If she had to narrow her success she has experienced thus far to just three words, she says they would be "faith, focus, and family."[75]

Evans's seminars blend the neo-liberal formula of self-branding, style, and entrepreneurship with biblical and spiritual power as the keys to both worldly bounty and spiritual substance. Her various workshops include "God's Army: Know Your Orders, Accomplish Your Mission," "Faith: Walk on Water Without Getting Wet," "Branding Y.O.U.—the Power and Principles of Personal Branding," "Habitude— Nine Step Peak Performance Training," and "In God We Trust—Biblically-Based Lessons on Business and Leadership." She offers special packages to college students, including "Ooze Success: Dress, Speak, and Act the Part," and "The Six D's: The Recipe for Destiny Driven Success."[76]

In addition to the religious messages given in conference workshops, a variety of faith-based self-help books addressing beauty, renewal, and prosperity are commonly recommended by HBCU conference organizers. These include Mikki Taylor's *Self-Seduction: Your Ultimate Path to Inner and Outer Beauty* and Debrena Jackson Gandy's *Sacred Pampering Principles: An African American Woman's Guide to Self-Care and Inner Renewal* and *All the Joy You Can Stand: 101 Sacred Power Principles for Making Joy Real in Your Life*. In *All the Joy You Can Stand*, Gandy observes that many people are "hemorrhaging spiritually," and she urges her readers to embark on a quest to increase the joy, prosperity, and power in their lives. Her "sacred power principles" include recognition of the ever-presence of God in one's life and the importance of body work as a "divine communication tool."[77]

Marketing Christian Makeovers

A remarkable number of born-again campus beauty queens have launched post-pageant careers as televangelists, makeover coaches, pageant consultants, and inspirational speakers. As emissaries of broad socio-cultural transformations, these contemporary faith healers have enlarged opportunities for evangelical women in beauty and self-help ministries, yet they do so by perpetuating deeply troubling individualistic and unrealistic body-centered standards for the achievement of spiritual renewal and worthiness. They use their beauty queen fame to market a spectrum of God-centered beauty programs and products to help Christian women uplift their sluggish spirits and sagging bust lines. Converting formerly profane pageant stages into pulpits, beauty contestants fuse the sacred and the scriptural with body-centered transformation, materiality, and personal empowerment. They use their tiara celebrity to embody and spread Christian evangelical convictions and class-coded body theologies to increase spiritual vitality and, by extension, personal efficacy. This fusion of spiritual and secular discourses, both on the pageant stage and in entrepreneurial ventures that focus on the enhancement of bodies and the acquisition of earthly bounty and beauty, has proven to be a profitable synthesis—one that has given birth to a new ministerial trajectory, that of the Christian beauty queen entrepreneur. As beauty queen Nancy Stafford asserts, Christian women can now be interested in both "mascara and the ministry."[78]

Although religion has always helped to shape socio-political ideologies and personal identities, new faith-based excursions into beautification, body fitness, and self-renewal are integral parts of contemporary neo-liberal rationalities. Conflating idealized Christian bodies and self presentation with spiritual and economic fulfillment, born-again queens are reshaping normative expectations for sacred femininity, evangelical bodies, and Christian identities in unprecedented ways. Contemporary socio-political rationalities for self-enterprise and personal empowerment through corporeal/spiritual upgrades resonate among evangelical Christian women and have helped to engender new incarnations of normative Christian femininities. As evangelical discourses of worldly self-actualization are increasingly interwoven with neo-liberal and post-feminist projects of self-management, the lines between religious and secular makeover prescriptions become further blurred. The ascendancy of these logics, however, also helps to foster new psychic, spiritual, and body anxieties among Christian women and thus has fueled a market for faith-based programs and products to assist them in disciplining their bodies, improving their selves, and, ultimately, saving their souls. Former Mrs. America Sheri Rose evokes these worldly logics of individual responsibility and a competitive, upwardly mobile subject to encourage body fitness among Christian women. Rose notes, "Do you know that in a race, all the runners run, but only one gets the prize? Run in such a way as to get the prize. Everyone who competes in the games goes into strict training. They do it for a crown that will not last; but we do it to get a crown that will last forever."[79]

Although Christian religion has always issued edicts regarding embodiment, (usually regulating and camouflaging women's bodies to safeguard purity and modesty), gluttony, purification, and worldly prosperity, the shape, scale, and impact of contemporary religious fervor and enterprise for beautification and spiritual/life/bodily conversion is unprecedented. The combination of divine decrees and neo-liberal imperatives for achieving self-renewal, heavenly "temple bodies," and worldly fulfillment has proven to be very good business. Thousands of evangelical women primp, tone, and slim for Jesus, and many born-again beauty queens effectively market Christian makeovers for the flesh and spirit. In such a cultural economy, new formulations of spiritualities, self-determination, and sanctity are closely interlaced with materiality, makeover, and commerce. As beauty queen Nancy Stafford observes: "We have a higher standard as Christians to be creative and celebrate God's creation. We should look for ways to express our uniqueness in what we wear, how we look—broadening the definitions of beauty and fashion."[80]

Faith-based inner/outer beauty and life makeovers have thus become significant parts of Christian self-help and beauty pageant preparation. One speaker at the 2005 HBCU queens' conference was Valorie Burton, a former Miss Black Texas USA, former co-host of the televised ministry *The Potter's Touch with T. D. Jakes*, and author of *Rich Minds and Rich Rewards*. Burton observed that "the makeover craze has been going strong for some time now. At first it was hair and makeup, then wardrobe makeovers. Now we have extreme makeovers, complete with televised plastic surgery. Even homes are getting makeovers these days. It has occurred to me that quite a few of us could use a life makeover."[81] Through her online ministry, "A Better Life Is Calling," she offers faith-based, life-makeover coaching. In her workshop for black queens, "What Is Really Holding You Back?," she emphasizes the importance of faith, positive thinking, and self-renewal for achieving prosperity and spiritual fulfillment.

Many other Christian-identified queens have likewise embarked on lucrative careers as beauteous makeover missionaries. For example, former beauty queen Cynthia Allen and her daughter, Charity Allen Winters, a professional fashion model, have helped to popularize the contemporary cultural mania for body-centered life makeovers among Christians. Allen likens Jesus to a cosmetic surgeon, explaining:

> I turned my inner self over to Jesus Christ—the Great Surgeon who can make over even the hardest cases. He transformed my personality and spirit. I guess that is the appeal of the *Extreme Makeover* show. They take someone and make him or her into someone entirely different. That's what Jesus Christ does for us—He makes us new creations.[82]

In their book *The Beautiful Balance of Body and Soul*, Allen and Winters urge Christian women to embark on their own "makeover miracle" and "soul surgery." They warn that our "bodies are as much us as our thoughts are. This is why calls to ignore our outer appearance as spiritually irrelevant do not help us. Quite the contrary, the more we honor our bodies as us, as intertwined with our spirits, as limbs of Christ, temples of the spirit, and bearers of God's image, the more we understand and manage well the power of physical appearance in our lives."[83] Allen and Winters remind Christian women that they have divine assistance in refining and enhancing their bodies since "the Holy Spirit is our secret weapon as Christians for conquering the old nature, or fleshy will and appetites."[84] Combining skin care principles, scripture, and spiritual beauty, they urge women to "Cleanse by the washing of the Word . . . Freshen with the fellowship of believers . . . Exfoliate by submitting to God and others . . . Moisturize with the oil of the Holy Spirit."[85]

Evoking similar logics that fuse spiritual and corporeal renewal, purification, and pageant readiness, numerous ex–campus queens market scripture to aspiring college women through faith-based ministries/businesses. Monica McKinney, Miss Texas Southern University, for example, implemented a series of self-improvement seminars for students on her campus, including "How to Be a Diva from the Inside Out," which was designed to achieve the following objectives: "Save souls—Learn how to be a spiritual being mastering the human experience—Learn how to be a well-rounded virtuous lady of God." McKinney now operates The Virtuous Crown, a faith-based pageant consulting business based on "the Holy Bible in its entirety and the Trinity."[86] In her talk on stage presence and confidence at the 2004 black campus queen conference, Evans asserted the importance of grooming women beneath the skin to unleash their hidden beauty and spiritual power as well to polish their bodily veneers.

> In the Women's Devotional Bible (Proverbs 31:30), it reads that charm is deceptive and beauty is fleeting, but a woman who fears the Lord is to be praised. In realizing that beauty is skin deep, our first mission is to groom the complete woman from the inside out. Once the light of grace, self-worth, and love shines with luminosity, it will manifest outwardly. In *Ecclesiastes* 3:11 it reads, "God has made everything beautiful in its time." We believe everyone has her time to shine spiritually, socially, emotionally, economically, educationally, as well as physically, whether you are in class or on stage receiving your Virtuous Crown. It is with great boldness that we express our faith, groom you from the inside out, and accentuate your physical beauty so that you will shine as bright as a morning star.[87]

Panache at Your Price is another faith-based, self-help firm that is advertised in the program for the 2005 Miss Spelman College pageant. Panache at Your Price is designed to merge the spiritual, style, and substance. It seeks to "assist all people, primarily females, in knowing, showing, and growing their inner beauty through spiritual style." In order to teach individuals "how we as ordinary people, living ordinary lives can produce Extra-ordinary outcomes," Panache offers training in spiritual style including such topics as "Prince and Princess Social Etiquette," "Dressing the Inner Beauty," and "Ordinary Women Made Whole in Christ." [88]

Sally Gallagher and Christian Smith point out that evangelicalism is an "engaged orthodoxy," one that is increasingly in the world and of the world.[89] Consequently, many born-again beauty queens such as McKinney have effectively engaged the power of media technologies, popular culture, and business savvy to market and popularize religiously guided makeovers. Although some evangelicals distrust the mainstream media and popular culture since they believe them to be inimical to Christian values, many contemporary evangelical women have attempted to purify and reshape media and popular culture for their own purposes. Brenda Brasher has observed that many evangelicals attempt to redefine America culture from within "by converting its most seductive products (rock music, videos, commercial packaging) to Christian purposes",—in this case, beauty, style, and life makeovers.[90]

Religious presence in the beauty, image, and makeover business has escalated rapidly in recent years. Through women-only ministries on the web, television and radio talk shows, devotional advice books, and Jesus-themed retail, numerous faith-based business endeavors have been established to help Christian girls and women enhance their images. Pradip Thomas notes that Christian consumerism helps to create discontent and desire that can be fulfilled by adopting "appropriate behavior, commitments, sociality, and consumption."[91] James Dobson's *Focus on the Family*, for example, is an important forum for distributing gender-specific advice on beauty to Christian girls and women including in *Brio*, its magazine for teen girls that publishes stories of Christian teen beauty contestants.[92] Andrea Stephens, beauty editor of *Brio* and a former beauty pageant contestant, has written numerous Christian beauty books for girls, including *Bible Babes: The Inside Dish on Divine Divas*.

A rash of television programs also peddle and popularize new pedagogies of psycho-spiritual reformation, self-actualization, beauty, consumerism, and conversion. Probably the best-known spokeswoman is the former Miss Black Tennessee and Miss Fire Prevention, Oprah Winfrey, the queen of talk shows. Winfrey introduced spiritualized guidance on her program *Change Your Life TV* in 1998, successfully merging "spiritual counsel with practical encouragement, inner awakenings with capitalist pragmatism."[93] In addition to talk shows that pepper Christian themes such as testimony, conversion, resurrection, and salvation throughout their narratives, reality TV makeover shows fuse religious revitalization and body stewardship as motivating principles for their makeover/conversion regimes.[94]

Body Stewardship

> We are royalty and we are called to honor our King with our bodies. This
> does not mean we have to become "Barbies with Bibles." Our bodies are
> temples of the God's Holy Spirit, and it is time for us to learn to treasure
> those temples. The spirit of the living God has chosen our bodies as his
> dwelling place. He desires that we, the King's princesses, honor him with
> our bodies.[95]

Body stewardship is a foundational component for Christian beautification
and makeover efforts. Christian women are urged to care for their temple-bod-
ies in order to honor God's dwelling place. Forsaking plainness and fat as
ungodly, new body gospels urge Christian women and girls to tend to their
bodies and appearance in order to make radiant testimonies to God's power as
well as to achieve a deeper relational intimacy with God. Flab is not a good wit-
ness to God's glory, nor does it signify a morally disciplined Christian self.
Spiritual accomplishment is understood as well-honed and-maintained outer
bodies that denote inner spiritual stamina, beauty, and strength. Former beauty
queen Cynthia Culp Allen and her fashion model daughter Charity Winters
lament that too often many Christian women "don't understand the concept of
stewardship. All of us are born with so much potential—physically as well as
spiritually—but Christians often think it is more spiritual to ignore their physical selves or dress themselves like the school marm on *Little House on the Prai-
rie*."[96] They state that "a Christ-like Christian is wonderful, no matter what she
looks like. But a sharp-looking Christian, with godly character and a confident
smile, is dynamite!"[97] Christian women, they say, have a responsibility to
"please God with the thoughtful stewardship of all His gifts to us, including
caring for one's God-given fleshy resources."[98] Corporeal gospels, such as those
proclaimed by Allen and Winters, help to reshape constructions of evangelical
feminine worthiness as well as buttress the belief that slim and fashionable
bodies serve sacred purposes, on and off the pageant stage.

Christian weight loss programs and businesses designed to groom worthy
bodies have become increasingly popular. An early forerunner to the recent
upsurge of devotional diet, fitness, and beauty experts marketing God-centered
beauty, diet, and fitness products was beauty queen Deborah Pierce whose 1960
book, *I Prayed Myself Slim*, chronicled her battle to lose weight through prayer. As
R. Marie Griffith has observed, Pierce preached a gospel of self-denial anchored
in a long history of Christian asceticism that has "reaped wondrously modern-day
results, as Pierce embraced the body and beauty standards of American white
middle-class culture as God's will for all, marking deviance from that model as
sin."[99] Since then, many other evangelical spiritual coaches have urged Christian
women to avoid divine disapproval by embarking on rigorous regimes of sweat,

spandex, and sacrifice. Sheri Rose Shepherd, a former Mrs. United States of America, for example, maintains an online ministry, "His Princess Ministries," that promotes her weight loss books, including *Fit for a King* and *Someday My Prince Will Come*. Shepherd gives lectures on her transformation from "a Jewish, drug-addicted teenager from a broken home to a Christian-identified beauty queen."[100] She also offers "His Little Princess Crowning Ceremonies," which crowns young girls with rhinestone tiaras to help them "seal their identity in Christ."[101] Fitness groups such as "Praise Aerobics," "Take Back Your Temple," and "Believercise" have become commonplace, as many women seek slender born-again bodies and spiritual renewal.

Although this contemporary, devotional body-centered culture follows in the footsteps of longstanding and variant forms of Christian body scriptures, Griffith argues that contemporary Christian edicts for shaping the body are distinguished by the willingness of adherents to "accept and even celebrate the most extreme cultural body standards, converting them from social constructs into divine decree."[102] They market normative, body-centered, and secular makeover regimens, imbuing them with higher spiritual purposes. Implicit in these projects are class-coded prescriptions that render lack of class mobility as sinful, not structural.

Cheryl Prewitt is an especially illustrative example of the Christian beauty queen who peddles beauty pageant competition products, such as push-up breast pads, chandelier earrings, double-stick body tape (for binding breasts and buttocks) and pageant swimwear, as part of her ministry. Claiming that the Lord revealed to her the righteousness of marketing pageant bathing suits, she reports:

> When I was a contestant I saw an uneven playing field. I also saw the need for the girls to be able to compete without compromise. It seemed like girls who had a budget had the advantage. But what about the girl next door who had talent, drive, determination, and grit to dig in and do what it takes to win? I knew there was an answer out there so I sought one from the Lord. My pageant business was created out of that prayer.[103]

Prewitt reassures skittish Christian women that it is possible to wear one of her swimsuits and retain their moral virtue. She states:

> When I competed, I was modest, conservative, but I also recognized the necessity of being competitive. I certainly always competed to win, but I was never willing to sacrifice my standards for the sake of the crown. I searched for an answer and the Lord revealed to me how to find the perfect marriage of modesty, competition, affordability, and convenience without compromising yourself or the quality.[104]

Prewitt concludes that in her swimsuits "contestants feel good about themselves and that's really what enhances a true winner; . . . it's what inside that shines through that makes you stand out as a winner. Remember, you shouldn't have to compromise to compete, and you don't have to show skin to win!"[105]

Although Prewitt-Salem has found a way to barter Bibles and bikinis, she hints at the struggles that many contestants face as they juggle the cross-currents of piety, modesty, and sin with swimsuit spectacles of the flesh. Indeed, as we shall see, the corporeality of the swimsuit competition has caused ongoing consternation among pageant contestants, especially among spiritually-identified, academic contenders for the campus throne.

Dilemmas of the Flesh

In recalling her 1951 crowning as Miss America, Yolande Betbezel asserted that "there was nothing but trouble from the minute that crown touched my head."[106] Making a stand for "propriety," she refused to sign the standard Miss America contract that committed the winner to a series of promotional tours for Catalina Swimsuit Company, a key sponsor of the pageant. She declared that she would never again wear a bathing suit in public unless she was going swimming. Betbezel received the support of the Miss America organization, but Catalina withdrew from the Miss America pageant and established the less prudish Miss U.S.A. pageant system. However, Miss America never eliminated the swimsuit competition.

Over the years, the Miss America organization has tussled with how best to publically display women in bathing suits in light of contestants' discomforts with the swimsuit competitions. In 1947, for example, contestants were no longer crowned while wearing their swimsuits. In 1986, pageant officials stopped revealing the physical measurements of contestants. In 1995, viewers and contestants of the Miss America pageant were invited to consider whether or not women should parade in swimsuits to win a scholarship?. Leonard Horn, the pageant's chief executive officer, said that this question had plagued the pageant for over fifty years and that he "personally cannot rationalize putting a young college woman in a swimsuit and high heels."[107] A majority of TV viewers and contestants, however, voted to keep the swimsuit competition.[108] In 1997, new regulations regarding the swimsuit were mandated by Miss America and contestants were allowed to wear two-piece suits with "full coverage" on top and "full-moderate coverage" on the bottom. However, thongs and heels higher than two inches were banned. In 2001, the Miss America pageant changed the name of the swimsuit competition to "lifestyle and fitness" and televised contestants' exercise regimens to showcase their "drive, energy, and charisma." [109] Pageant officials hoped that by highlighting the disciplined body management that accompanies pageant preparation, criticism of swimsuit spectacles as merely exploitative displays of mute feminine corporeality would lessen. Despite the contradictions and discomfort that bikinis ignite, the parade of swimsuit-clad women remains a perennial favorite among TV viewers, and most international and national beauty pageants appraise the flesh of contestants while they wear swimsuits.

This display of flesh, however, has caused even more consternation and contortions among college beauty pageant contestants and recurring opposition from both feminists and a variety of religious Christian, Islamic, and Hindu fundamentalists, including at the 1996 Miss World pageant in India and the 2002 Miss World pageant in Nigeria.[110] Contestants, especially religiously identified women, must navigate deep quandaries about showing skin in beauty contests in light of numerous critics who continue to condemn beauty pageants as indecent spectacles. Ericka Harold, Miss America 2003, however, resolved these tensions by simply asserting that Christians wear bathing suits and the ones worn in pageant competition are more modest than those at the beach. Other born-again queens resolve the paradox of parading in a bathing suit by crusading for modesty and chastity and by attributing a higher Christian purpose to their motives.

The recent ascension of Christian beauty pageants is intelligible in a cultural economy where glamorized made-over bodies are increasingly indexed to signify Christian devotion, despite the persistence of longstanding Christian fears of body exposure and loss of feminine virtue. The Miss Christian International Pageant system attempted to moderate tensions over public exhibitions of women's bodies by banishing the swimsuit competition and by declaring that a beauty pageant is part of a higher purpose: "to spread the Gospel of Jesus by any means necessary."[111] Virtue International Pageants, founded in 2000, also justifies beauty pageants as a pulpit for Christian beauties seeking to use tiaras for evangelical outreach and testimony. To compete, each contestant must submit a character reference from her pastor, be a member of a Christ-centered church, and "confess a personal relationship with Jesus Christ as Lord and Savior."[112] Contestants are required to share their faith and assert their allegiance to Christian goals by "getting baptized or [being] more involved in church, teaching Sunday school, or becoming missionaries."[113] Diane Washington, Ms. Black USA and president of Virtue & Valor Ministries, has also "Christianized" pageant protocols by establishing the Miss Christian America pageant system. Here, contestants give presentations on their outreach ministries, participate in a biblical Q&A, and attend both "virtuous woman self-development seminars and salvation and witnessing training seminars."[114] Nonetheless, the practice of showcasing and appraising women's bodies clad in form-fitting evening gowns has not been banished from these pious pageants.

Bikinis, Speedos, and Higher Education

> The winner of the Miss Pride of KSU Scholarship Pageant will represent
> the university at the Miss Kentucky Pageant, which is a preliminary to
> the Miss America. Each of the contestants will compete in the areas of
> swimsuit, evening gown, interview, and talent. This is a wonderful
> opportunity for our students to demonstrate self-confidence, commu-
> nication skills, and talent. (G. W. Reid, president of KSU)[115]

It is not just conservative or born-again participants in campus pageants who
contend with the issue of bodily exposure. Swimsuit competitions raise dilemmas for many queens of academe. Campus pageants, even non-religious ones, are
not immune to the politics of the flesh. One resolution is that many campus contests no longer require swimsuit competitions. The Black Women of Today contest at the University of Northern Colorado, for example, boasted that its 2005
pageant would be traditional except there would be no swimsuit competition, in
recognition of the fact that "it can be really difficult to participate in pageants and
feel that this portion of the competition can not only be degrading to some, but
also embarrassing."[116] Campus pageants that do require swimsuit competitions,
such as Miss America feeder pageants, struggle to bring respectability to the
spectacle. For example, the Alpha Phi Alpha Fraternity, sponsor of a nation wide
campus beauty pageant for African American college women, requires contestants to wear "a one-piece swimsuit in good taste." While scoring guidelines for
the judges of the swimwear competition are based on the contestants' "form, figure, posture, and carriage," contestants can be penalized for "bodily overexpo-
sure" and are expected to correctly interpret unstated norms of appropriate body
display.[117]

Campus pageant organizers also have employed a variety of tactics to neutralize the swimsuit portion of their pageants. The Miss University of Georgia
contest, a campus-sponsored preliminary pageant for the Miss America Scholarship Organization, for example, attempts to manage the contradictions inherent in sponsoring an explicit beauty/scholarship pageant on campus by
arranging for an emcee to recount contestants' achievements during the bathing suit competition, a strategy that clearly seeks to minimize the display of
mute bodies on stage.[118] The male sponsors of the 2002 UK Black and Gold pageant tried to get off the hook by turning over the responsibility for justifying the
swimsuit competition to a contestan, who was asked in the onstage Q&A.
whether or not she felt the display was degrading to women. This particular student replied that she felt that "it was not problematic since the human body is
beautiful."[119]

The question how to accommodate ambitions for showcasing academic excellence, leadership, spirituality, and middle-class etiquette alongside the exposure

and evaluation of fleshy forms haunts many campus contests. Regardless of whether or not particular campus pageants include swimwear, contestants and sponsors feel compelled to differentiate their contests and participation from accusations that, in the final analysis, all pageants are no more than spectacles of flesh.

Beauty queens continually take pains to assert the decency and tastefulness of their particular pageants. In a study of the Miss America Scholarship Pageant, Sarah Banet-Weiser argues that a "politics of opposition" is operative because it is "crucial for the pageant to define itself in opposition to more debased forms of popular culture for their own legitimation."[120] For example, one of the strategies for bestowing respectability on the corporeal spectacle of the bathing suit competition and for minimizing its sexual content is "to compare it with spectacles that are considered more overt and distasteful in their display of sexuality."[121] Robert Lavenda notes a similar pattern in community queen festivals, where "the most blatant 'unrespectable' markers of the beauty pageant, such as the swimsuit competition, must be downplayed or eliminated, so that the queen pageant is not confused with unwholesome flesh-peddling."[122]

Campus queens themselves struggle over how best to manage the contradictions of parading flesh on the catwalk and participating in campus religious organizations. A few, like Bethany Nesheim, winner of the 2007 Miss North Dakota Miss USA pageant, withdraw. Nesheim decided after much soul searching and prayer to renounce her crown since she felt her effectiveness as a staff member with Campus Crusade for Christ would be compromised. Although she knew that the title would create opportunities to proselytize, she feared that her ability to preach modesty to college women would be impaired since her state title required her to pose in a bathing suit for video clips and photographs for public perusal and online purchase.[123]

Regardless of whether or not they are religious, many college contestants who participate in campus pageants requiring swimsuit competitions express doubts about their participation in displays of sexualized bodies. Although some swimsuit contestants speak of the pleasures and rewards that accompany their determination to make their bodies firm and fit through demanding exercise regimes, a great deal of discomfort is nonetheless attached to collegiate swimsuit competitions. I have interviewed numerous queens who acknowledge the anxieties they feel baring their flesh on stage, especially given their battles against the bulge. One contestant told me that it "was not my favorite part because I do not see what you gain from wearing one since I am not going to walk around the city in one."[124] While some contestants defend the swimsuit competition as a showcase for self-confidence and fitness, they are also quick to catalogue their body flaws. One student queen said, "It's more about being physically fit, it really is. It's not about being the skinny girl up on stage. I will never be teeny, tiny skinny, I have soccer legs. It's about proving you're eating healthy and exercising every day, because being fit is hard work."[125] Another contestant told me that she only competed in her campus pageant because contestants were allowed to wear wraps over their swimsuit, but she regretted having to be on stage in one since she was not "in the best physical state and [her] body needed firming."[126] Several contestants stated that judges could "gain just as much" in their body appraisals by having them model workout clothes rather than swimsuits.

Not all contestants, however, express discomfort with wearing swimsuits on stage. One student contestant told me, "If I win $250 because you want to see me in a swimsuit, that is fine by me."[127] Another contestant offered a popular defense of swimsuits as a stress test, asserting that if "you are not comfortable enough with your body to get on stage for less than a minute, then you are not comfortable with your self overall." Another told me that "there is nothing wrong in judging physical fitness. I know that is not what makes me." Participants also point out how little the swimsuit category counts in the overall scoring of contestants, and they conflate body and character by pointing to the positive personality characteristics signified by disciplined bodywork. One queen contestant confessed to me, "I do not like the swimsuit part myself but I can understand that they want to see that we are disciplined enough to show that we are physically fit. You cannot say you are a disciplined person if you walk out on stage and you are jiggling everywhere."[128] The 2002 winner of the UK Black and Gold pageant told me that she used to watch Miss USA and Miss America on television and she thought, "I would participate if only there were no swimsuit competition involved."[129] She feels differently now, given the constant bombardment of televised images of scantily dressed or nude women.

The director of student life at a historically black university confirmed that many of her students shy away from participating in the campus feeder pageant for Miss America because of the swimsuit. She has a variety of answers to the dilemmas of the flesh. First, she argued that only 20 percent of the score is based on what "one looked like and how they carried themselves."[130] She then equates the swimsuit competition with a job interview and says that if someone could not "carry themselves with confidence, one would not want to hire them for a job." She admits, however, that personally she dislikes the swimsuit competition yet endorses it since it is merely a matter of "showing enough discipline to be fit and into health and wellness." In the interest of recruiting more participants, however, she feels that having contestants model "cute and short" workout clothes would be preferable. Nonetheless, she asserts that once students see how quickly the time goes by while they are standing in a swimsuit on stage, they will change their minds about appearing in swimsuits. She also extols the practice of allowing contestants to wear wraps over their swimsuits but notes that pageant rules require contestants to take off their wraps briefly or else they will be penalized. (One contestant reports that wearing a wrap over her swimsuit was important at black pageants since the "audience was different from white audiences, with all of the screaming and yelling throughout the pageant. Therefore, wearing a wrap was considerate because otherwise you are half-clothed and with the audience hollering, you are uncomfortable.")[131]

A recent past president of the local chapter of the Alpha Phi Alpha fraternity at UK expressed misgivings about showcasing flesh for the fraternity's Black and Gold pageant. He wanted to discontinue the swimsuit competition because he felt that it was a "degrading display." His action caused considerable conflict within the fraternity since many brothers felt that swimsuits were upholding "tradition" and should be maintained. During his tenure as president contestants were allowed to model active wear instead of swimsuits, and they were asked more "socially probing questions."[132] After he graduated, however, the swimsuit competition returned. A recent contestant told me that since women have to wear swimsuits at the regional and national finals they "should get used to doing so at one's home campus so they will have the confidence and strength they need to advance to the next level of competition."

Despite the consternation that bathing suit competitions inevitably arouse, images of half-clad women are circulated and, in some cases, produced by universities. Many campus yearbooks regularly show pageant winners clad only in their swimsuits and others produce official academic calendars that feature their students in bathing suits, most notably Grambling State University. Companies, such as the Student Body University, specialize in college swimsuit calendars. In 2006, this company released a calendar titled "Women of Ohio State University," but it was careful not to use Ohio State logos and trademarks in light of a 1999 lawsuit preventing it from doing so. Rick Van Brimmer, director of Ohio State University's Trademark and Licensing Services, said he did not anticipate a problem with the calendar and trademarks and that he felt that "swimsuit calendars are pretty benign." [133]

Photographs of college women in swimsuits have produced campus protest nonetheless. Massey University, for example, posted a story on its university website about one of its students who competed in the Miss Universe New Zealand pageant and included a photograph of the student frolicking in the surf while wearing a white string bikini. The Association of University Staff protested, declaring it the most "banal news feature emanating from the university this year."[134] After numerous complaints, the image was pulled and replaced with a head and shoulder photograph of the student. University spokesperson James Gardiner said, "We did not wish to offend anyone. Celebrating student achievement in all areas of endeavor, be they academic, sporting, or cultural, has always been encouraged by Massey University."[135] The contestant herself recycled the ever-popular pageant defense line by pointing to the valor of her efforts to discipline her body and hone her inner beauty and spirit. She said, "It's cool to be rewarded for looking after myself, making the most of the beauty I've been given and, most importantly, working on myself from the inside out. I think I am more beautiful inwardly than outwardly." Although Massey University's staff was successful in getting the controversial photograph pulled, campus pageants around the globe continue, by omission and commission, to perpetuate cultural practices that imbue and display women's bodies as essential signifiers of their worth. With or without swimsuit competitions, campus pageants all appraise and allocate value and merit to normative bodies.

In an effort to put God everywhere, evangelical Christian women have struggled to accommodate Bibles, bodies, and beauty pageants. Other contestants have also struggled to reconcile baring the flesh with academic respectability and personal integrity. Regardless of the cover stories used by campus beauty contestants, both the secular, neo-liberal doctrine of body discipline and the display of the body as a strategy for the revelation of divine power, the bathing suit competition in beauty pageantry remains hard to cover up and cover over.

8

Afterword

Class Work/Homework

Not all colleges sponsor beauty pageants, and by no means do all or most students participate in them as contestants, organizers, or audiences. Yet pageants have long tentacles that reach well beyond the pageant stage itself. Although pageants are only one facet of student life, their durability as campus fixtures and their responsiveness to changing campus gender cultures and practices help to make visible the ways students—and institutions of higher education themselves—enact, negotiate, challenge, and affirm hierarchies of gender, class, race, and sexuality in college life across time. The study of pageants helps us to chart substantive shifts and fluidity in both student-generated and officially bestowed hierarchies of student excellence and exclusion. Further, it provides a window on the vicissitudes of class, gender, and race in student cultures throughout the decades. Beyond grades and GPAs, pageants reveal the subtle extracurricular prerequisites for successful self-management and gender presentation that are operative today in campus student cultures including image, style, etiquette, sociability, respectability, and body and emotional regulation. Finally, pageants also reveal the changing ways student bodies have been officially harnessed for college promotion, one indicator of the changing ethos and branding practices of the university itself.

Historically, queens' bodies and faces have had a strong visual presence on campuses throughout the U.S. Queens have been prominently featured in yearbooks, student newspapers, university calendars, and websites. Queens have been dispatched off campus to civic and business beauty competitions, acted as campus tour guides, served as half time sports entertainment, and been appointed as emissaries to campus rituals and alumni events. Like ivy, the images and regalia of queens have decorated many academic walls, not to mention installations in campus museums.

In the past, campus beauty pageants were used to neutralize the threat of women on campus by emphasizing heterosexual desirability, middle-class refinement, and hyper-femininity. On black campuses, pageants were both a vehicle for showcasing class and gender conventionality as well as promoting racial uplift and communal re-representation. Pageants at predominantly white campuses, at times, have served as sites for civil rights activism and provided venues for contesting the exclusion of students of color in campus rituals.

By no means, however, have campus queens become mere museum relics. Beauty pageants have proven to be flexible and enduring collegiate events, not outdated historical remnants of a bygone era relegated to the dusty archives of college life. Today's queens of academe continue to self-platform and navigate shifting cultural hegemonies and norms for campus life as well as the desires and anxieties that such socio-cultural transformation produce. Most recently, neo-liberalism, post-feminism, and body and beauty makeover technologies have reshaped the rationales of campus queens who—no longer mere "campus cuties"—tout discourses of empowerment, girl-power, individual choice, self-control, and personal excellence to legitimate their pageant participation. Women and their tiaras remain key features of the college visual field, reward and recognition structures, and, now, vigorous educational marketing campaigns.

Regarding the latter dynamics of marketing and commercialization, higher education itself has experienced broad transformations in governance, mission, and quotidian practices as pressures to market higher education have intensified. Numerous scholars have noted the escalation of corporate and business discourses and practices designed to increase revenues and profitability, efficiency, and competitiveness in higher education.[1] Faculty face increased demands for productivity, accountability, outcome assessments, and grant-funded research as universities seek to improve their national rankings and increase revenue and enrollments. Students confront increased class sizes and higher tuitions. Such changes have also increased managerialism on campus, the use of strategic and business planning models, corporate partnering and branding, niche marketing campaigns, and the use of private marketing firms. As higher education has increasingly embarked upon expensive capital building, public relations, and recruitment campaigns, many have sought corporate branding opportunities for their campuses.

The University of Kentucky, for example, recently renamed its men's basketball dormitory the "Wildcat Coal Lodge," in order to receive a $7 million donation from coal operators, despite campus protest, and an advocacy group, "Friends of Coal," has sponsored several sporting events on campus. Private marketing firms are increasingly employed by colleges and universities to brand their buildings, students, and mission. Across my own campus at UK, the motto "See Blue" is omnipresent. Much like a beauty competition, UK has engaged in an ongoing campaign to secure a spot as a top twenty Research I institution. A marketing study by the State Higher Education Executive Officers Association reported "higher education needs marketing campaigns unlike any ever seen," including the use of "popular culture, music, video, games, radio, and fashion as a means of reaching potential students."[2]

Campus queens are being asked to play a part in these marketing efforts. One reporter has noted that "from a business perspective, beauty pageants are an extraordinary bit of simultaneous marketing because it targets both women and men. Like music, it is an international language and marketers know its potential."[3] Lincoln University, for example, has used a photograph of their queen to advertise in *Ebony* magazine. But branding goes far beyond campus queens. College women and men in general are increasingly being recruited by numerous corporations as campus "brand ambassadors" and the "face of the brand" on campus.[4] As we have seen, *Sports Illustrated on Campus* and Cool Water cologne have sponsored campus pageants for men not only at Notre Dame University but also at the University of Colorado and University of Virginia. The Ann Taylor company, for example, recently partnered with the Center for Career Education and the Women's Business Society at Columbia University to select two Columbia students to work with student organizations to "provide fashion advice and guidance" throughout the academic year.[5] Marketing firms estimate that as many as 10,000 students are currently being paid to be brand ambassadors, especially those with "good looks and charm." Corporations view such students as highly effective tools for "brand evangelism" and "buzz marketing": the promotion of products to friends without revealing corporate representations.[6] Numerous campuses also sponsor fashion shows and students themselves seek out corporate sponsors to underwrite such events. Howard University, for example, sponsors a homecoming fashion show, an alumni fashion show, a Verde Eco-fashion show, and an African fashion show showcasing "Diaspora designers such as Tribal Immunity."

New media and digital technologies are enlarging the opportunities to promote and package college life. Contestants and queens are making ample use of new virtual performative stages on YouTube, Facebook, personal home pages, and blogs to provide visual galleries of their catwalk victories, to fashion public faces and persona, to narrate post-pageant activities, to create networked identities, to extend social connections and self-marketing, and generally to inflate their post-pageant visibility as campus celebrities. HBCUConnect.com, an online magazine for black college students and alumni, includes a web platform prominently featuring a photograph of each campus queen alongside the school's logo in its web profiles of each HBCU. A longstanding source of visibility for black campus queens, *Ebony* magazine recently intensified the national visibility of black campus queens and the schools they represent with the introduction of a new online, top ten HBCU campus queen contest. The magazine now requires that all the HBCU queens make self-promotional videos to be posted on the *Ebony* website. The photographs of the winning queens continue to have an afterlife on the web since they have been included in *Ebony's* online media and marketing kit.

Queens and kings of academe are not the only ones availing themselves of new opportunities for personal marketing, visibility, and partnerships with fashion magazines and clothing corporations. Numerous college fashion blogs and online college magazines provide yet other sources for student-generated instruction in fashion, style, consumption, and lifestyle that are often supported by corporate interests. *Jayne* is an online lifestyle magazine "devoted to shaping the lives of college women" through "style scholars," since "college life is more than the class-room."[7] Another webzine, *UMagazine*, publishes stories on style and seduction, and *Campus Socialite* caters to men interested in "women, sports, extroverted socializing, and shock humor."[8] There are now so many campus fashion blogs for college women that a list of the top fifty was recently released. *Universitychic.com*, for instance, is sponsored by *Seventeen* magazine and features student bloggers. *Collegefashion.net*, a blog for "stylish college girls," is a student-run online fashion magazine designed to foster discussion of beauty products, lifestyle trends, and shopping. It boasts receiving over one million hits per month and over twenty comments per blog post.

In 2009, two Harvard students launched *Her Campus: A Collegiette's Guide to Life*, which won the Harvard business plan competition in 2009 and has been featured in the *New York Times*, *CNN Money*, and *CBS MoneyWatch*. *Her Campus* partners with *Seventeen* and *Self* magazines, and the *Huffington Post*, and maintains brand relationships with New Balance, Juicy Couture, and Rent the Runway. It individualizes its content on a college by college basis, and it now includes hundreds of campuses with over 1,700 student workers.[9] *Her Campus* recently featured a column explaining "How to Market to College Students" to create a "buzz" on college campuses. It recommended using its successful "Campus Survival Kits" marketing campaign as a model. This campaign consists of giving 500 students free "commoditized care packages" that includes such products as Kate Spade Twirl perfumes, Softlips lip conditioner, and products from the Jack Willis clothing company. The person-to-person distribution of a limited number of care packages did indeed create "a buzz," and generated numerous requests for more of them on Facebook.[10]

Even women who identify as feminists have gotten into the online college fashion business. *Academic Chic.com* was started by a group of "feminist scholars who defiantly wear dresses, fitted jackets, and pointy toe shoes. To teach in. And sometimes just to the library!" In launching this site, they report having struggled to "reconcile the perceived superficiality of our interest in style with our academic commitment to questioning gender and class essentialism." Drawing on the work of feminist theorist Judith Butler, they argue that clothes have the power "to create and constantly recreate identity." Thus, they claim, fashion is not only a powerful tool for identity-making but also for "subverting class and gender norms, performing self, and appreciating aesthetic beauty." Claiming to have resolved the antinomy between superficiality and academic rigor, they "hope to inspire other academics to embrace their love of clothes . . . to engage in a meta-dialogue about art, literature, and garments that can move us all."[11]

But before we get overwhelmed by the latest fusion of student life and con-sumption, what are we to conclude about the durability of campus beauty pag-eantry? On the surface, the rationale that pageants give voice, support, attention, and opportunities for self-expression and communal re-representation to women students can be persuasive for many people. In an unstable economy fraught with uncertainty and dislocation, soaring tuition costs, and a mediated culture of makeover, sexualization, self-improvement, lifelong learning, and personal trans-formation, it is not surprising that many college women continue to perceive pag-eants as viable pathways to enhance self-platforming, self-maximizing, and self-branding—a seductive means of gaining extra credit in a competitive world. As we have seen, many contestants argue that pageant training and "make-up" work help to give them an extra edge that marks them as noteworthy, exceptional, and enterprising neo-liberal college citizens poised for success and personal advancement. Many participants assert that pageants allow students opportuni-ties to learn useful grammars of conduct and style skills, including how to perform with confidence and swagger on and off stage, resources for an empowered and maximized life in the new global and image economy. Their concern with upgrad-ing themselves through style, image, fashion, and taste is shared by many college students and is manifest through dress codes, training in etiquette and image enhancement, and even, the addition of modules on how to dress as part of course-work. Kristina Barnes, a student, has celebrated Tuskegee University's campus-wide preoccupation with aesthetics and self-presentation by observing, in beauty pageant parlance, that on her campus "hallways [are] becoming 'runways,' and our 'yard' the platform."[12]

Not all campus pageants, however, are only about individual advancement and the self-platforming of normative gendered constructions for the body, mind, and soul. If that were the case, it would be easier to dismiss them as anachronistic sites for the objectification of women. Rather, as we have seen, pageants have sometimes served as sites for political contestation, such as the 1960s civil rights battles to challenge racialized constructions of student beauty, worth, and merit. (The sym-bolic politics of canceling homecoming queen ceremonies did indeed galvanize many at Indiana University and around that state.) Following in these footsteps, students of color have mobilized to win university honors by being selected to the homecoming courts of predominantly white campuses. Were such actions effective anti-racist and civil rights strategies, given the time and place? Or were they merely projects of self-commodification and personal packaging, if not in their intent, then in their effects?

Moreover, as we have seen, not all pageant contestants use purely individual-ized discourses of self-maximization and personal empowerment to validate their participation in pageants. Some continue to stress the importance of collec-tive obligation. Many African American contestants continue to point to the importance of black campus pageants as home places—needed rituals of respite, healing, and the celebration of racial solidarities in light of the ever-present dismissals and damages wrought by white racism. They stress the need to save black colleges, many of which face severe funding issues, by showcasing black student excellence. They also underscore the continual necessity of opposing deeply rooted historical legacies of racial exclusion and stigma as well as the need to offset the ongoing demonization and pathologizing of black bodies, culture, and character in the media and in daily life on campus. These contestants rightfully note the ongoing importance of challenging the systematic processes and practices that render African American students on predominantly white campuses as invisible, misrecognized, and disempowered, and they call attention to the racialized fatigue that accompanies such representational and collective responsibilities. One black contestant in a historically white pageant spoke for many students of color attending predominantly white universities when she concluded that "it was an exhaustive burden to have to navigate two worlds." Noting that she had felt constant pressure to avoid giving white contestants, organizers, and audiences any "ammunition" to strengthen racial stereotyping, she articulated the burden that students of color regularly face on college campuses. Many black queens further argue that pageant training in etiquette and image enhancement extends "othermothering," part of a long and important communal self-help tradition needed to survive slavery, segregation, racism, classism, and poverty that remains a vital strategy for self-help and communal advancement. While many of the rationales of black contestants and queens do help to reveal the quotidian politics and practices that perpetuate campus racism, the conventional class and gender politics of pageants nonetheless blunts, it seems to me, their racial critique. Is enhancing cultural pride and education through pageantry, a cultural form teeming with gendered and classed interdictions for the proper management of the self, appearances, and bodies, an adequate political platform from which to launch a challenge to the daily assaults of racism in the academy?

There are many reasons to dispense with campus pageants. Queens still overwhelmingly display slim, "good bodies" and hegemonic versions of racialized femininity and class, perpetuating what Lynn Chancer calls "looks-ism," the "cultivation and maintenance of particular bodily appearances to gain love, status, and recognition."[13] Pageants undoubtedly promote conventional and troubling norms of racialized beauty, femininity, heterosexuality, desirability, and middle-class achievement. As student rituals, they help to affirm collegiate merit based on appearance and visual distinction. Despite the contradictory rhetorics of democracy, social leveling, or elevation and mobility through pageant training and participation, pageants create many more losers and outsiders than winners. Campus pageants function as yet another college entrance exam by helping to create body and psychic prerequisites for campus belonging and success. Clearly, competitive pageant rituals showcasing stylized and preened bodies cannot be the basis for social change on campus.

The tacit approval of such norms, evidenced by university budgets, policies, and officials who directly and indirectly support queen competitions as venues for campus recognition and social marketing, raises important questions. There is a need for the critical interrogation of the institutional supports and roles invested in maintaining such troubling gendered collegiate traditions as well as the relative lack, or lower visibility, of alternative forums and spaces for student recognition and support. Conferring social prestige on women students for how they discipline their bodies and selves to accommodate hegemonic cultural constructions is deeply troubling. There are far better ways for college campuses to enable and acknowledge student achievements, to fight racism and homophobia, to enlarge the parameters of student success, and to produce meaningful celebratory campus rituals other than those that normalize the importance of disciplining student bodies and identities in narrowly defined cultural and class codes. Relying on a contradictory blend of beauty and achievement, pageants limit the possibilities for other forms of campus activism by confining change to a narrow realm of aesthetic visibility and distinction. Collegiate rituals that are deeply and historically implicated in showcasing women's bodies, class-based articulations of self-hood, and restrictive gender/race relations hardly seem like academic traditions worth preserving.

Simply dispensing with campus beauty pageants, however, will not get us off the hook. Nor will characterizing pageant contestants as mere dupes of the glamour and glory of pageants further the project of battling constrictive and deforming gender regulations. A colleague of mine in anthropology recently said that she hoped I would not argue that beauty pageants can be empowering as other scholars have done. Instead of answering yes or no, I argue that as faculty, students, and staff, we have much homework to do. The seductions of neo-liberalism, post-feminism, personal makeovers, and self-transformation extend well beyond the pageant stage and are deeply imbricated in the culture of higher education and the wider socio-political economy. The ongoing exclusions wrought by racism, classism, sexism, and homophobia are ever-present, inside and outside of the classroom, and on and off campus. How do we respond to these challenges in terms of the possibilities for campus activism, teaching for social justice and critical consciousness, and reflecting on educational policies and practices? How can we more explicitly engage with the problematic ways that class, race, gender, sexuality, lifestyle, and consumption are mobilized and braided in student lives and rituals?

What my extended meditations on campus beauty pageants have taught me is that high on the ladder of urgencies is the need for dialogue about class, lifestyle, aesthetics, and consumption on campus and the material and subjective effects of these forces on access, mobility, bodies, emotions, behaviors, aspirations, and identities. While problems posed by gender, race, ethnicity, and sexuality are often addressed in contestants' narratives, nearly all of these narrations negate and mute the importance of class. They rarely mention how class inequalities are at once mobilized and normalized in campus pageants. All campus competitions, including men's pageants, involve resplendent evening gowns, tuxedos, and opulent stage sets, all of which bespeak the desire and fantasy that class can be easily shed and camouflaged by clothing, glamour, attitude, and confidence. Such performances help to displace awareness about the fundamental importance of class and its role in producing student insecurities and vulnerabilities.

Thus I see a great need for collegiate dialogue and action on class privilege, class relations, and daily exchanges "between" classes. The ever-widening gulf between the rich and the poor; the growing insecurities and displacement of poor, immigrant, and working-class people; the issues that students of color and poor and working-class students face in higher education; and the intensification of discourses of personal empowerment, self-enterprise, and individual responsibility that have accompanied neo-liberalism and global capitalism make this class work urgent. Under the auspices of makeover reality TV programming, popular culture offers students a steady diet of self-improvement and lifestyle programming that can blunt their awareness and understanding of class by promising self-help, personal transformation, and the pulling of oneself up by one's bras and bootstraps as the way to success. Class mobility is marketed today as a matter of learning an assemblage of performative technologies for self-presentation including how to enhance one's image, taste, and lifestyle, that is cosmopolitan and elite class proficiencies that include wine, food, art and culture, travel, etiquette, grammar, dress, style, and so on and the corseting of working-class, racialized, and ethnic bodies and behaviors through consumption and makeover technologies.

When Stacy Keaton Brown lassoed that stuffed boar in her performance at Georgetown College's Belle of the Blue pageant in 2002 (see the introduction), I believe she was trying to stretch and enlarge the borders of feminine performativy that could be accommodated within the template of campus beauty pageants. Other academic queens have likewise tried to minimize the gender regulation and confinement required in pageant competition. They have pointed to their enterprising student subjectivites, how they embrace opportunities for skill enhancement and self-promotion, and the opportunity to prove that they are enterprising and ambitious college women. African American students have gone even further in their attempts to reformate and resignify the protocols of campus pageants. They have evoked highly politicized and collective missions for their pageant participation by asserting the importance of challenging and redressing racialized inequalities and exclusions as well as consolidating racial solidarities and excellence through pageant spectacles. In all of these recitations, however, class work has been neglected.

The unrelenting emphases on privatization, self-empowerment, self-surveillance, and body regulation, along with the reduction of structural inequalities to matters of enterprising subjectivities and good choices, call for a much more potent confrontation with the underlying socio-economic forces and desires that propel campus pageants and also shape, position, rank, manage, market, and package the larger student body. As students and faculty, we all have desires for comfort, belonging, and recognition. We seek validation and connection in countless ways in and out of the classroom. We each enjoy the pleasures of self-expression and recognition, whether it is a good haircut, a new outfit, or validation from peers and colleagues. We each do our share of gendered and classed stagecrafting and performing in meetings and classes with our style choices, self-presentation, and interactions. There are no simple remedies for how to resist the myriad of cultural pressures to improve and remake our selves within the highly corseted norms for self and body. Examining and questioning the ways that cultural normalization and structural hierarchies limit our choices and produce our desires and anxieties is an important first step.

Historical struggles by faculty and students have helped significantly to change the landscape of higher education and such battles have engendered numerous outlets and resources for social change. African-American, ethnic, and gender study programs; course offerings in a variety of disciplines on structural inequalities; feminist and LGBTQ student clubs and resource centers; and anti-violence programs help to enlarge the venues from which to question and challenge exclusionary practices in college life. We can choose our campus affiliations, the things we buy and how we spend leisure time, the courses we take, the ways and materials we teach, and the questions and problems we pay attention to. Critical dialogues and collective actions are important antidotes to pressures for conformity, conventionality, and the corporatization of student bodies and higher education. Hopefully, pedagogical practices and reflections about such actions will help us to examine and challenge restrictive and disempowering collegiate and cultural codes and rituals that continue to channel student bodies and behaviors in hegemonic and disempowering directions. Campus pageants provide one such teaching opportunity.

NOTES

Chapter 1

1. Pageant program, "Belle of the Blue: Reach for the Stars," February 23, 2002.
2. Ibid.
3. Author phone interview with Kathy Wallace, February 16, 2002.
4. Greg Kocher, "Georgetown aide arrested after stuffed-pig fracas," *Lexington-Herald*, February 27, 2002.
5. *NPR Weekend Edition*, March 2, 2002.
6. Whitley Arens, "Lindsay Connor Crowned Belle of the Blue," *Georgetonian Online,* available at http://georgetonian.wordpress.com/2009/02/27.
7. David Perlmutter, "Are We Grading on the Curves?," *Chronicle of Higher Education*, December 10, 2004: 13.
8. Ciro Scotti, "Beauty Pageants: What Do They Promote," *Sun-Bulletin*, September 17, 1973.
9. The extracurricular activities of later generations of college women who entered colleges in massive numbers beginning in the 1920s, when college became the norm for middle-class women, remains relatively understudied. More recently, however, there has been more analysis of gender, race, popular culture, and the extracurricular including Donna Freitas, *Sex and the Soul: Juggling Sexuality, Spirituality, Romance, and Religion on America's College Campuses* (New York: Oxford University Press, 2008); Kathleen Bogle, *Hooking Up: Sex, Dating, and Relationships on Campus* (New York: New York University Press, 2008); Amy Wilkins, *Wannabes, Goths, and Christians: The Boundaries of Sex, Style, and Status* (Chicago: University of Chicago Press, 2008); Ritty Lukose, *Liberalization's Children: Gender, Youth, and Consumer Citizenship in Globalizing India* (Durham: Duke University Press, 2009); Julie Bettie, *Women Without Class: Girls, Race, and Identity* (Berkeley: University of California, 2003); S. S. Willie, *Acting Black: College Identity and the Performance of Race* (New York: Routledge, 2003); Paula Fass, *The Damned and the Beautiful: American Youth in the 1920s* (Oxford: Oxford University Press, 1977); Tamara Brown, Gregory Parks, and Clarenda Phillips, *African American Fraternities and Sororities: The Legacy and Vision* (Lexington: University Press of Kentucky, 2005); Diana Turk, *Bound by a Mighty Vow: Sisterhood and Women's Fraternities, 1870–1920* (New York: New York University Press, 2004); Amy Best, *Prom Night: Youth, Schools, and Popular Culture* (New York: Routledge, 2000); Rachelle Winkle-Wagner, *The Unchosen Me: Race, Gender, and Identity Among Black Students in College* (Baltimore: John Hopkins University Press, 2009); C. J. Pascoe, *Dude You're a Fag: Masculinity and Sexuality in High School* (Berkeley: University of California Press, 2007); Natalie Adams and Pamela Bettis, *Cheerleader! An American Icon* (New York: Palgrave-Macmillan, 2003); Helen Lefkowitz Horowitz, *Campus Life: Undergraduate Cultures from the End of the Eighteenth Century to the Present* (Chicago: University of Chicago

Press, 1988); Susan Edgerton, Gunilla Holm, Toby Daspit, and Paul Farber (Eds.), *Imagining the Academy: Higher Education and Popular Culture* (New York: Routledge, 2005); Sunaina Maira and Elisabeth Soep (Eds.), *Youthscapes: The Popular, the National, the Global* (Philadelphia: University of Pennsylvania, 2005); and Nadine Dolby and Fazal Rizvi (Eds.), *Youth Moves: Identities and Education in a Global Perspective* (New York: Routledge, 2008).

10. Many feminist scholars have considered the crosscurrents of gender, race, class, communal empowerment, self-expression, choice, conformity, discipline, and post-feminism in beauty work, fashion and stylization, and body modification, including Sandra Lee Bartky, *Femininity and Domination: Studies in the Phenomenology of Oppression* (New York: Routledge, 1991); Susan Bordo, *Unbearable Weight: Feminism, Western Culture, and the Body* (Berkeley: University of California Press, 1993); Maxine L. Craig, "Race, Beauty and the Tangled Knot of Guilty Pleasure," *Feminist Theory* 7 (2006): 159–77; Shirley Anne Tate, *Black Beauty: Aesthetics, Stylization, Politics* (Farnham, England: Ashgate, 2009); Deborah Rhode, *The Beauty Bias: The Injustice of Appearance in Life and Law* (New York: Oxford University Press, 2010); Lanita Jacobs-Huey, *From the Kitchen to the Parlor: Language and Becoming in African American Women's Hair Care* (New York: Oxford University Press, 2006); Paula Black, *The Beauty Industry: Gender Culture, and Pleasure* (New York: Routledge, 2004); Peg Zeglin Brand, (Ed.), *Beauty Matters* (Bloomington: Indiana University Press, 2000); Ingrid Banks, *Hair Matters: Beauty, Power, and Black Women's Consciousness* (New York: New York University Press, 2000); Noliwe Rooks, *Hair Raising: Beauty, Culture, and African American Women* (New Brunswick: Rutgers University Press, 1996); Naomi Wolf, *The Beauty Myth: How Images of Beauty Are Used Against Women* (New York: Anchor Books, 1991); Lynn Chancer, *Reconcilable Differences: Confronting Beauty, Pornography, and the Future of Feminism* (Berkeley: University of California Press, 1998); Kathy Davis, *Dubious Inequalities and Embodied Difference: Cultural Studies on Cosmetic Surgery* (Lanham, MD: Roman and Littlefield, 2003); and *Reshaping the Female Body: The Dilemma of Cosmetic Surgery* (New York: Routledge, 1995); Brenda R. Weber, *Makeover TV: Selfhood, Citizenship, and Celebrity* (Durham: Duke University Press, 2009); Virginia Blum, *Flesh Wounds: The Culture of Cosmetic Surgery* (Berkeley: University of California, 2003); Debra Gimlin, *Body Work: Beauty and Self-Image in American Culture* (Berkeley: University of California Press, 2002); Victoria Pitts, *Surgery Junkies: The Cultural Boundaries of Cosmetic Surgery* (New Brunswick: Rutgers University Press, 2007); and Kathy Peiss, *Hope in a Jar: The Making of America's Beauty Culture* (New York: Metropolitan Books, 1998).

11. See, for example, Wendy Kozol, "Miss Indian America: Regulatory Gazes and the Politics of Affiliation," *Feminist Studies* 31, 1 (2005): 64–94; Rebecca Chiyoko King-O'Riain, *Pure Beauty: Judging Race in Japanese American Beauty Pageants* (Minneapolis: University of Minnesota Press, 2006); Judy Tzu-Chun Wu, "Loveliest Daughter of Our Ancient Cathay!: Representations of Ethnic and Gender Identity in Miss Chinatown U.S.A. Beauty Pageant," *Journal of Social History* 31, 1 (1997): 5–31; Lok Siu, "Queen of the Chinese Colony: Gender, Nation, and Belonging in Diaspora," *Anthropological Quarterly* 78, 3 (2005): 511–42; Shirley J. Lim, *Feeling of Belonging: Asian American Women's Public Culture, 1930–1960* (New York: New York University Press, 2006); Jennifer Nez Denetdale, "Chairmen, Presidents, and Princesses: The Navajo Nation, Gender, and the Politics of Tradition," *Wicazo Sa Review* 21, 1 (Spring 2006): 9–28; Jon Schackt, "Mayahood Through Beauty: Indian Beauty Pageants in Guatemala," *Bulletin of Latin American Research* 24, 3 (2005): 269–87; Colleen Ballerino Cohen, Richard Wilk, and Beverly Stoeltje (Eds.), *Beauty Queens on the Global Stage: Gender, Contests, and Power* (New York: Routledge, 1996); Susan Dewey, *Making Miss India Miss World: Constructing Gender, Power, and the Nation in Postliberalization India* (Syracuse: Syracuse University Press, 2008); Rupal Oza, "Showcasing India: Gender, Geography, and Globalization," *Signs* 26,

4 (2001): 1067–95; Jean Muteba Rahier, "Blackness, the Racial/Spatial Order, Migrations, and Miss Ecuador, 1995–96," *American Anthropologist* 100, 2 (June 1998): 2421–30; Pamela Thoma, "Of Beauty Pageants and Barbie: Theorizing Consumption in Asian American Transnational Feminism," *Genders* 29 (1999); William Callahan, "The Ideology of Miss Thailand in National, Consumerist, and Transnational Space," *Alternatives: Global, Local, Political* 23, 1 (January, 1998): 29–61; Katarina Mattsson, "Crowning Miss Sweden: Constructions of Gender, Race, and Nation in Beauty Pageants," paper presented at the "Gender and Power in the New Europe" at the European Feminist Research Conference, Lund University, 2003; Pamela Wright, "The Timely Significance of Supernatural Mothers or Exemplary Daughters: The Metonymy of Identity in History," in Jane Schneider and Rayna Rapp (Eds.), *Articulating Hidden Histories: Exploring the Influence of Eric R. Wolf* (Berkeley: University of California Press, 1995), 243–61; Nhi Lieu, "Remembering the Nation" Through Pageantry: Femininity and the Politics of Vietnamese Womanhood in the Hoa Hau Ao Dai Contest," *Frontiers* 21, 1/2 (2000): 127–51; Natasha Barnes, "Face of the Nation: Race, Nationalisms and Identities in Jamaican Beauty Pageants," *The Massachusetts Review* 35 (Autumn 1994): 471–92; Christine Yano, *Crowning the Nice Girl: Gender, Ethnicity, and Culture in the Hawaii's Cherry Blossom Festival* (Honolulu: University of Hawaii Press, 2006); Sarah Banet-Weiser and Laura Portwood-Stacer, "'I Just Want to Be Me Again!': Beauty Pageants, Reality Television, and Post-feminism," *Feminist Theory* 7, 2 (2006): 255–72; Shanti Kumar, "Globalisation, Nationalism, and Feminism in Indian Culture," *South Asian Journal* (2004); M. Cynthia Oliver, *Queen of the Virgins: Pageants and Black Womanhood in the Carribean* (Jackson: University of Mississippi Press, 2009).

12. On labor unions and beauty queens see Joan Sangster, "Queen of the Picket Line: Beauty Contests in the Post–World War Two Canadian Labor Movement, 1945–70," *Labor Studies in Working Class History of the Americas* 5, 4 (2008): 83–106. On beauty pageants in prisons see Karen Tice's film review of *Miss Gulag* and *La Corona*, both of which feature prison beauty pageants, in *Signs: Films for the Feminist Classroom* (Spring 2010) available at http:www.signs.rutgers.edu.

13. Available at http://www.coronationninc.com/DrAmerica/info.htm.

14. Amelia Hill, "TV contest tries to change the face of beauty," *Observer*, October 12, 2008, available at http://www.gauardian.co.uk/media/2008/oct/12/realitytv-television/print.

15. Ibid.

16. Katy Bennett and Samuel Niehaus, "Delta Tau Delta Presents Miss University of Kentucky," October 12, 2011. Available at http://uknow.ukty.edu/node/19594.

17. *East African Weekly*, February 18–24, 1999.

18. *Chronicle of Higher Education*, "There She Is, Miss Akademia," September 14, 2003: A64.

19. Francesc Relea, "The Doll Factory: A Probing Examination of Venezuela's Obsession with Miss Universe," *Hopscotch* 1, 2 (1999): 2–7.

20. Available at http://wmu.or.kr/eng/content.htm.

21. Tomoya Ishikawa and Hiromi Oida, "Cry of Long Live the Queen Resounds on Campus," *Asahi Shimbun*, December 2, 2009.

22. Available at http://iafrica.com/news/worldnews/282738.htm.

23. See Judith Butler, *Gender Trouble, Feminism, and the Subversion of Identity* (New York: Routledge, 1990). For further discussions of performativity and formations of class, race, and gender see Sherry Ortner, *New Jersey Dreaming: Capital, Culture, and the Class of '58* (Durham: Duke University Press, 2003); Julie Bettie, *Women Without Class: Girls, Race, and Identity* (Berkeley: University of California Press, 2003); Candace West and Sarah Fenstermaker, "Doing Difference," *Gender & Society* 9, 1 (1995): 8–37; Gwendolyn A. Foster, *Class Passing: Social Mobility in Film and Popular Culture* (Carbondale: Southern Illinois University Press, 2005); Jaime Lester, "Acting on the Collegiate Stage: Managing

Impressions in the Workplace," *Feminist Formations* 23, 1 (Spring 2011): 155–81; and
Kesha Moore, "Class Formations: Competing Forms of Black Middle-Class Identity,"
Ethnicities 8, 4 (2008): 492–517.

24. Lok Siu, "Queen of the Chinese Colony: Gender, Nation, and Belonging in Diaspora,"
Anthropological Quarterly 78, 3 (Summer 2005): 511–42.

25. Maxine L. Craig, "Race, Beauty, and the Tangled Knot of Guilty Pleasure," *Feminist
Theory* 7 (2006), 166.

Chapter 2

1. *Nutmeg Yearbook*, University of Connecticut (1955): 86.
2. Helen Lefkowitz Horowitz, *Campus Life: Undergraduate Cultures from the End of the
Eighteenth Century to the Present* (Chicago: University of Chicago Press, 1988),
208.
3. Candice Andrews, "Badger Beauties," *On Wisconsin,* available at http://www.uwalumni.
com/onwisconsin/2003_fall/bb1.html.
4. Ibid.
5. "Heyday of the Girlie Galas," *Time,* June 28, 1968, available athttp://www.time.com/
time/printout/0881684133300.html.
6. Ibid.
7. "Fraternity Queens," *Jet,* February 4, 1954.
8. "Miss Average America," *Newsweek,* July 2, 1962, 80.
9. Ibid., "Heyday of the Girlie Galas."
10. *Gopher Yearbook*, University of Minnesota (1950): 84.
11. *Kentuckian Yearbook*, University of Kentucky (1950): 350.
12. *Nutmeg Yearbook*, University of Connecticut (1956): 267.
13. Andrews, "Badger Beauties."
14. Warren Susman, *Culture as History: The Transformation of American Society in the Twentieth Century* (New York: Pantheon, 1984).
15. *Arbutus Yearbook*, Indiana University (1939): 49.
16. Andrews, "Badger Beauties."
17. Alice Smith, "Beauty Insight," *Indiana Daily Student,* November 24, 1964.
18. *Nutmeg Yearbook*, University of Connecticut, 1962.
19. Margaret A. Lowe, *Looking Good: College Women and Body Image, 1875–1930* (Baltimore:
John Hopkins University Press, 2003).
20. Lois Banner, *American Beauty* (Chicago: University of Chicago Press, 1983).
21. David Glassberg, *American Historical Pageantry: The Uses of Tradition in the Early Twentieth Century* (Chapel Hill: University of North Carolina Press, 1999); and Christie Farnham, *Education of the Southern Belle: Higher Education and Student Socialization* (New
York: New York University Press, 1994).
22. Banner, *American Beauty*, 260.
23. Ibid., 258.
24. Mike Donahue, *Portland Rose Festival* (Helena Farcountry Press, 1996).
25. Banner, *American Beauty*, 253.
26. Liz Conor, *The Spectacular Modern Women: Feminine Visibility in the 1920s* (Bloomington: Indiana University Press, 2004).
27. Ibid., 29.
28. Carolyn Kitch, *The Girl on the Magazine Cover: The Orgins of Visual Stereotypes in American Mass Media* (Chapel Hill: University of North Carolina Press, 2004).
29. Karen W. Tice, *Tales of Wayward Girls and Immoral Women: Case Records and the Professionalization of Social Work* (Urbana: University of Illinois Press, 1998).

30. Hazel Carby, "Policing the Black Woman's Body in an Urban Context," *Critical Inquiry* 18 (Summer 1992): 738–55.

31. Daylanne English, *Unnatural Selections: Eugenics in American Modernism and the Harlem Renaissance* (Chapel Hill: University of North Carolina Press, 2004), 17.

32. Daylanne English, "W.E.B. Du Bois 's Family Crisis," *American Literature* 2 (June 2000): 291–319.

33. Kimberly Hamlin, "The First Miss America Pageants, 1921–1927," in Elwood Watson and Darcy Marti (Eds.), *There She Is, Miss America: The Politics of Sex, Beauty, and Race in America's Most Famous Pageant* (New York: Palgrave Macmillan, 2004), 32.

34. "Beautiful but Dumb is True, Says Nichols," *New York Times*, October 2, 1925.

35. Quoted in Hamlin, "The First Miss America," 39.

36. *New York Times*, June 12, 1925.

37. *New York Times*, November 30, 1927.

38. Deborah Wolfe, "Beauty as a Vocation: Women and Beauty Contests in America" (Ph.D. dissertation, Columbia University, 1994).

39. "Two More Spur Beauty Pageant," *New York Times*, September 10, 1925.

40. Susan Dworkin, *Miss America 1945: Bess Meyerson's Own Story* (New York: Newmarket Press, 1987), 101.

41. Ibid.

42. Ibid., 102.

43. Ibid.

44. Sarah Banet-Weiser, *The Most Beautiful Girl in the World: Beauty Pageants and National Identity* (Berkeley: University of California Press, 1999); Elwood Watson and Darcy Marti (Eds.), *There She Is, Miss America: The Politics of Sex, Beauty, and Race in America's Most Famous Pageant* (New York: Palgrave Macmillan, 2004); R. A. Riverol, *Live From Atlantic City: A History of the Miss America Pageant* (Bowling Green: Bowling Green State University, 2002); Candace Savage, *Beauty Queens: A Playful History* (New York: Abbeville Press, 1998); Susan Dworkin, *Miss America 1945: Bess Meyerson's Own Story* (New York: Newmarket Press, 1987); Bryant Simon, *Boardwalk of Dreams: Atlantic City and the Fate of Urban America* (New York: Oxford University Press, 2004); Frank Deford, *There She Is: The Life and Times of Miss America* (New York: Penguin, 1971); Melinda Beck, "A Controversial Spectator Sport," *Newsweek U.S. Edition*, September 17, 1984; and John Canaday, "What Miss America is Made Of," *New York Times*, September 18, 1965.

45. Beretta Smith-Shomade, *Shaded Lives: African American Women and Television* (New Brunswick: Rutgers University Press, 2002); and Shirley J. Lim, *A Feeling of Belonging: Asian American Women's Public Culture, 1930–1960* (Philadelphia: Temple University Press, 2006).

46. "People & Events: Breaking the Color Line," *American Experience*, available at http://www.pbs.org/wgbh/amex/missamerica/peopleevents/e_inclusion.html.

47. "Racial Bias Attacked," *Jet*, May 22, 1952: 5.

48. See Sarah Banet-Weiser, *The Most Beautiful Girl in the World*; and G. Reginald Daniel, *More Than Black: Multiracial Identity and the New Racial Order* (Philadelphia: Temple University Press, 2002) for a discussion of racial containment and accommodation in the Miss America pageant.

49. Maxine L.Craig, *Ain't I a Beauty Queen? Black Women, Beauty, and the Politics of Race* (New York: Oxford University Press, 2004), 32.

50. Noliwe Rooks, *Ladies Pages: African American Women's Magazines and the Cultures That Made Them* (New Brunswick: Rutgers University Press, 2004), 9.

51. Craig, *Ain't I?* Also see Shane White and Graham White, *Stylin:' African American Expressive Culture from its Beginnings to the Zoot Suit* (Ithaca: Cornell University Press, 1998); and Deborah Willis, *Posing Beauty: African American Images from*

1890s to the Present (New York: Norton, 2009), for more on race, beauty, and self-representation.

52. "What Happens to Beauty Queens?," *Jet*, February 26, 1953.
53. Quoted in Joanne Meyerowitz, "Beyond the Feminine Mystique: A Reassessment of Post-War Culture, 1946–1958," *Journal of American History* 79, 4 (March 1993), 1472.
54. Craig, *Ain't I*, 46–47.
55. Ibid, 70.
56. Christine Yano, *Crowning the Nice Girl: Gender, Ethnicity, and Culture in Hawaii's Cherry Blossom Festival* (Honolulu: University of Hawaii Press, 2006); Judy Tzu-Chun Wu, "Loveliest Daughters of Our Ancient Cathay": Representations of Ethnic and Gender Identity in the Miss Chinatown U.S.A Beauty Pageant," in Phillip Scranton (Ed.), *Beauty and Business: Commerce, Gender, and Culture in Modern America* (New York: Routledge, 2001): 278–308; Rebecca Chiyoko King-O'Riain, *Pure Beauty: Judging Race in Japanese American Beauty Pageants* (Minneapolis: University of Minnesota Press, 2006); and Wendy Kozol, "Miss Indian America: Regulatory Gazes and the Politics of Affiliation," *Feminist Studies* 31, 1 (Spring 2005): 64–94.
57. "What Negros Do Not Know About Hawaii," *Jet*, August 20, 1959.
58. Quoted in Yano, *Crowning the Nice Girl*, 62.
59. O. S. Hubbard, "Beauty Contest for High School Girls," *School Life* 1, 18 (September 1932).
60. Maid of Cotton Collection, Auburn University Archives.
61. Lowe, *Looking Good*, 29.
62. Martin and Martin, "The Tainting of the Baby Crop," e *New York Times*, 1915.
63. "Wed College Girls, Miss Thomas Says They Make Better Wives and Have More Children," *The New York Times*, October 28, 1909.
64. For more on the black elite, class, education, and racial uplift see Willard B. Gatewood, *Aristocrats of Color: The Black Elite 1880–1920* (Fayetteville: University of Arkansas, 1990); Linda M. Perkins, "The African American Female Elite: The Early History of African American Women in the Seven Sister Colleges, 1880–1960," *Harvard Educational Review* 67, 4 (Winter 1997): 718–56; Paula Giddings, *When and Where I Enter,: The Impact of Black Women on Race and Sex in America* (New York: Morrow, 1984); Stephanie Shaw, *What a Woman Ought to Be and to Do: Black Professional Workers During the Jim Crow Era* (Chicago: University of Chicago Press, 1996); Kevin Gaines, *Uplifting the Race: Black Leadership, Politics, and Culture in the Twentieth Century* (Chapel Hill: University of North Carolina Press, 1996); Martin Summers, *Manliness and Its Discontents: The Black Middle Class and the Transformation of Masculinity, 1900–1930* (Chapel Hill: University of North Carolina Press, 2004); Evelyn Brooks Higginbotham, "African American Women's History and the Metalanguage of Race," *Signs* 17 (Winter 1992): 251–74; Deborah Gray White, *Too Heavy A Load: Black Women in Defense of Themselves 1894–1994* (New York: Norton, 1999); and Louise Newman, *White Women's Rights: The Racial Origins of Feminism in the United States* (New York: Oxford University Press, 1992).
65. Eunice Fuller Bernard, "The New Freedom of the College Girl," *New York Times*, March 19, 1933.
66. See for example John Kasson, *Rudeness & Civility: Manners in Nineteenth-Century Urban America* (New York: Hill and Wang, 1990); Mary Poovey, *The Proper Lady and the Woman Writer: Ideology as Style in the Works of Mary Wollstonecraft, Mary Shelly, and Jane Austen* (Chicago: University of Chicago, 1984); Alexander Jane Allan, "The Importance of Being a 'Lady': Hyper-femininity and Heterosexuality in the Private Single-sex School," *Gender and Education* 21, 2 (March 2009): 145–58; Jodie Arditi, "The Feminization of Etiquette Literature: Foucault, Mechanisms of Social Change, and the Paradoxes of

Empowerment," *Sociological Perspectives* 39, 3 (1996): 417–34; Cas Wouters, "Etiquette Books and Emotional Management in the 20th Century: The Integration of the Social Classes," *Journal of Social History* 29, 1 (Fall 1995): 107–24; and Cas Wouters, "Etiquette Books and Emotional Management in the 20th Century: The Integration of the Sexes," *Journal of Social History* 29, 2 (Winter 1995): 325–39.

67. Lynn Peril, *College Girls: Bluestockings, Sex Kittens, and Coeds, Then and Now* (New York: Norton, 2006).

68. Rooks, *Ladies Pages*, 9.

69. Katharine Capshaw Smith, "Childhood, the Body, and Race Performance: Early 20th Century Etiquette Books for Black Children," *African American Review* 40 (2007), 3.

70. See Julia Kirk Blackwelder, *Styling Jim Crow: African American Beauty Training during Segregation* (College Station: Texas A&M University Press, 2003); and Kathy Peiss, *Hope in a Beauty Jar: The Making of America's Beauty Culture* (New York: Henry Holt, 1998).

71. Laila Haidarali, "Polishing Brown Diamonds: African American Women, Popular Magazines, and the Advent of Modeling in Early Postwar America," *Journal of Women's History* 17, 1 (2005): 10–37.

72. Lim, *A Feeling of Belonging*, 5.

73. E. Azalia Hackley, *The Colored Girl Beautiful* (Kansas City: Burton Publishing Company, 1916), 71.

74. Ibid., 31.

75. Charlotte Hawkins Brown, *The Correct Thing To Do—To Say—To Wear* (Sedalia, NC: Author, 1940).

76. "Teaching Seniors How To Dress Well," *New York Times*, May 2, 1920.

77. "Residence Halls for Women: Standards of Good Taste," September 1929. Sarah Blanding Papers, University of Kentucky Special Collections.

78. Terry Birdwhistell, "An Educated Difference: Women at the University of Kentucky through World War Two" (Ph.D. dissertation, University of Kentucky, 1995).

79. University of Kentucky Association of Women Students, 1938–39. Box 30, University of Kentucky Special Collections.

80. Stephanie Shaw, *What a Woman Ought to Be and to Do: Black Professional Workers During the Jim Crow Era* (Chicago: University of Chicago Press, 1996).

81. Willard B. Gatewood, *Aristocrats of Color: The Black Elite, 1880–1920* (Fayetteville: University of Arkansas Press, 1990), 265.

82. Stephanie Shaw, *What a Woman Ought to Be and to Do*, 86.

83. Paula S. Fass, *The Damned and the Beautiful: American Youth in the 1920s* (Oxford: Oxford University Press, 1977); Helen Lefkowitz Horowitz, *Campus Life: Undergraduate Cultures from the End of the Eighteenth Century to the Present* (Chicago: University of Chicago Press, 1988); and Dorothy C. Holland, Margaret A. Eisenhart, and R. W. Connell, *Educated in Romance: Women, Achievement, and College Culture* (Chicago: University of Chicago Press, 1992).

84. Martin Summers. *Manliness and Its Discontents: The Black Middle Class and the Transformation of Masculinity, 1900–1930* (Chapel Hill: University of North Carolina Press, 2004), 258

85. Amy McCandless, *The Past in the Present: Women and Higher Education in the Twentieth-Century South* (Tuscaloosa: University of Alabama Press, 1999).

86. Summers, *Manliness and Its Discontents*.

87. Fass, *The Damned and the Beautiful*.

88. Ibid., 199–200.

89. Eunice Barnard, "A New American College Girl Emerges," *New York Times*, March 12, 1933.

90. Ibid.

91. Eunice Barnard, "The New Freedom of the College Girl," *New York Times*, March 19, 1933.
92. Ibid.

Chapter 3

1. Elizabeth B. Boyd, "Southern Beauty: Performing Femininity in an American Region," (Ph.D. dissertation, University of Texas at Austin, 2000); and Karen W. Tice, "Queens of Academe: Campus Beauty Pageantry and Student Life," *Feminist Studies* 31, 2 (Summer 2005): 250–83.
2. Throughout its history, KSU received meager state support relative to predominantly white universities in the state. For example, in 1925, KSU received only $47,250 compared to $877,589 for the all-white University of Kentucky. Disparities in funding persist today.
3. "Black Colleges—Despite Whites Still Project Black Identity," *Kentucky Thorobred*, May 2, 1975. Today, the KSU student body is approximately half African American and half white.
4. In 1993, a Mr. Kentucky State University was established despite the objections of some alumni.
5. Evelyn Brooks Higginbotham, *Righteous Discontent: The Women's Movement in the Black Baptist Church, 1880–1920* (Cambridge: Harvard University Press, 1993), 187. Also see Deborah Gray White, *Too Heavy a Load: Black Women in Defense of Themselves, 1894–1994* (New York: Norton, 1999); Michele Mitchell, *Righteous Propagation: African Americans and the Politics of Racial Destiny After Slavery* (Chapel Hill: University of North Carolina Press, 2004); and Victoria Wolcott, *Remaking Respectability: African Americans in Interwar Detroit* (Chapel Hill: University of North Carolina Press, 2001).
6. See, for example, Maxine L. Craig, *Ain't I a Beauty Queen: Black Women, Beauty, and the Politics of Race* (New York: Oxford University Press, 2002); Patricia Hill Collins, *Black Feminist Thought: Knowledge, Consciousness, and the Politics of Empowerment* (Boston: Unwin Hyman, 1990); and *Black Sexual Politics: African Americans, Gender, and the New Racism* (New York: Routledge, 2004); Beverly Guy-Sheftall (Ed.), *Words of Fire: An Anthology of African American Thought* (New York: New Press, 1995); bell hooks, *Black Looks: Race and Representation* (Boston: South End Press, 1992); and Patricia Morton, *Disfigured Images: The Historical Assault on Afro-American Women* (New York: Greenwood Press, 1991).
7. Lowe, *Looking Good*, 60.
8. Rooks, *Ladies Page*, 74.
9. Gwen Sherard, *Kentucky Thorobred* (March 1933): 3.
10. Gwen Sherard, "Correct, Collegiate, and Casual," *Kentucky Thorobred* 10, 1 (October 1941): 3.
11. Gwen Sherard, "Correct, Collegiate, and Casual," *Kentucky Thorobred* 9, 5 (April, 1941): 4.
12. Phyllis Stovall, "Are You in the Know," *Kentucky Thorobred* 32, 2 (October, 1964): 4.
13. Phyllis Stovall, "Are You in the Know," *Kentucky Thorobred* 32, 4 (December, 1964): 3.
14. Gwen Sherard, "Correct, Collegiate, and Casual," *Kentucky Thorobred* 10, 4 (February, 1942): 4.
15. Gwen Sherard, "Correct, Collegiate, and Casual," *Kentucky Thorobred* 10, 2 (1941): 3.
16. "Miss Kentucky Election," *Kentucky Thorobred* 15, 5 (June, 1948): 1.
17. "Nineteen Past Queens to See Lucille Samuels Crowned," *Kentucky Thorobred* 26, 2 (October, 1958): 1.
18. "Annjo Twines Crowned Miss KSU," *Kentucky Thorobred* 31, 2 (October, 1962): 1.

19. Banet-Weiser, *The Most Beautiful Girl.*
20. Beverly McIntosh, "Greetings from Miss Kentucky State College," *Kentucky Thorobred* (September, 1970): 4.
21. "Get Involved," *Kentucky Thorobred* (August 1974): 1.
22. Frances Wilson, "Campus Sweetheart," *Kentucky Thorobred* 24 (March, 1957): 3.
23. Kathy Peiss, *Hope in a Beauty Jar: The Making of America's Beauty Culture* (New York: Henry Holt, 1998) notes that educational institutions increasingly saw themselves as caretakers of women's appearance.
24. "Freshman Steals Campus Sweetheart," *Kentucky Thorobred* 11, 3 (February 1944): 1.
25. "The Legacy of Miss Maroon and White: Crowns and Gowns: 75 Years of Homecoming at Morehouse College." Anne Ashmore and Brenda Sue Hill reported that they said we "wore our stockings and heels but not our white gloves to the picket lines." DVD produced by Herman Mason, 2004.
26. Gerald Smith, *A Black Educator in the Segregated South: Rufus B. Atwood* (Lexington: University Press of Kentucky, 1994); and George W. Wright, *In Pursuit of Equality: History of Blacks in Kentucky*, vol. 2 (Kentucky Historical Society, 1992).
27. Maxine L. Craig, "The Color of an Ideal Beauty Queen: Miss Bronze 1961–1968," in Evelyn Nakano Glenn (Ed.), *Shades of Difference: Why Skin Color Matters* (Stanford: Stanford University Press, 2009): 81–94; Shirley Ann Tate, *Black Beauty, Aesthetics, Stylization, and Politics* (Farnham, England: Ashgate, 2009); and Bianca Taylor, "Color and Class: The Promulgation of Elitist Attitudes at Black Colleges," in Marybeth Gasman and Christopher Tudico (Eds.), *Historically Black Colleges and Universities: Triumphs, Troubles, and Taboos* (New York: Palgrave Macmillan, 2008): 189–206.
28. Audrey Elisa Kerr. "The History of Color Prejudice at Howard University," *Journal of Blacks in Higher Education* 54 (Winter 2006): 82–87.
29. Judy Klemesrud, "There's Now Miss Black America," *New York Times*, September 9, 1968: 54.
30. Craig, *Ain't I*, 35.
31. Chandra Thomas, "Scared Straight," *Essence* (November 2009): 126.
32. Cathy Ferguson, "World of Color," *Kentucky Thorobred* (October 1973): 1.
33. Wayne Green, "Constance Hunter, Miss BSU," *Kentucky Thorobred* (December 1972): 2.
34. *The Kentuckian Yearbook*, 1943:56.
35. *Kentucky Kernel* 17 (January 1930).
36. *Kentucky Kernel* 7 (November 1930).
37. *Courier Journal*, Box 53, University of Kentucky Special Collections, October 8, 1939.
38. "35 Coeds Compete for Queen," *Kentucky Kernel* 31 (October 1963).
39. *The Kentuckian Yearbook*, 1944: 144.
40. Today, women's fashion magazines and beauty retailers increasingly sponsor campus programming in beauty and fashion. For example, *Glamour* magazine holds annual glamour days in conjunction with Pennsylvania State University, and Howard University hosts the Essence College tour that distributes free makeup to students. How students are recruited for corporate marketing and branding efforts on campus is discussed more fully in Chapter 8.
41. "Residence Halls for Women," Box 6, Sarah Blanding Papers, University of Kentucky Special Collections, September, 1939.
42. "Women's Building on the U of K Campus," Box 6, University of Kentucky Special Collections.
43. *Kentucky Kernel*, October 27, 1939: 2.
44. "News Release," Dean of Women Students Office, 1939, University of Kentucky Special Collections; and "U.K. Dating Bureau, Now a Week Old, Boasts of Its Success in Promoting Acquaintance," *Herald Leader*, November 19, 1939.

45. "A Clearinghouse for Date-Seekers," *Kentucky Kernel*, November 28, 1939: 3.
46. Yvonne Eaton, "Attention UK Gals: You Each Have Two and Half Boys to Choose From, So Get Going," *Lexington-Leader*, December 4, 1956: 2.
47. *Kentucky Kernel*, 1964.
48. Sarah Blanding to Frank McVey, September 29, 1936, Box 28, Frank McVey Papers, University of Kentucky Special Collections.
49. Sarah Blanding to Frank McVey, October 21, 1939, Box 28, Frank McVey Papers, University of Kentucky Special Collections.
50. *Report of the Campus Queens Committee*, Kentucky Association of Deans of Women, October 13, 1939, Box 28, Frank McVey Papers, University of Kentucky Special Collections.
51. Sarah Blanding to Frank McVey, March 22,1940, Box 28, Frank McVey Papers, University of Kentucky Special Collections.
52. "Beauty Demands Rise! Dean Fails to Name Co-ed to Court of Kentucky Tobacco Queen," *Cincinnati Enquirer*, October 10, 1939.
53. Although Kentucky did not secede from the Union, it sent many soldiers to fight for the Confederacy and a separate Confederate capital operated in the western portion of the state.
54. *The Kentuckian Yearbook*, 1958: 294–95.
55. Ibid., 72.
56. "The U of K Has No Difficulty In Assimilating Negro Students," *Louisville Courier Journal*, July 17, 1948.
57. "The Students Pick," *Time*, November 19, 1951.
58. Trisha Bracken, *Herstories*, Indiana University Archives, 5.
59. "Congratulations, Miss I.U.," *Indiana Daily Student*, May 16, 1959: 4.
60. Bracken, *Herstories*, 6.
61. Ibid., 6.
62. Correspondence, Herman B. Wells Papers, University of Indiana Archives, May 20, 1959.
63. Ibid., May 26, 1959.
64. Ibid., May 21, 1959.
65. In 1960, Marlene Owens Rankin was crowned as Ohio State University's first African American homecoming queen. She noted that "politically, the time was right and people were in a mood to make a statement." Monica Torline, "Homecoming Reunion Unites Former Courtiers," *Lantern*, October 16, 2000. In 1967, numerous African American women sponsored by various black campus organizations won pageants at predominantly white campuses including Northwestern University, the University of Michigan, Morehead University, and University of Illinois-Chicago Circle. Daphne Maxwell, the winner at Northwestern University, believed that "some whites voted for her thinking she would not win since they wanted to show their tolerance. Maybe this was the year of the Negro" (quoted in "Black Beauty Queens," *Jet*, November 30, 1967). In 1973, Governor George C. Wallace, a proponent of school segregation, crowned Terry Points as the first African American queen at the University of Alabama. Available athttp://www.sa.ua.edu/osm/coralla/26.html.
66. Craig, *Ain't I*, 71.
67. Ibid., 70.
68. In 1958, Nancy Streets was considered for the lead role in the film version of Mary Hastings Bradley's book *I Passed for White*.
69. Joint Committee on Discriminatory Practices, University of Indiana Archives., 1968.
70. "Statement Presented to JCDP," October 11, 1968, University of Indiana Archives, 1.
71. Ibid., 2.
72. Letter to the Academic Community, "Opinion on Queen Contests," Indiana University Archives, 1968.
73. Ibid., 2.
74. "Committee Opinion on Queen Contests," Indiana University Archives, 1968.

75. *Lebanon Reporter*, October 18, 1968: 4.
76. Herman Wells Correspondence, October 14, 1968, Indiana University Archives.
77. Ibid., November 27, 1968.
78. "Interdepartmental Communication from Lester Wolfson Dean's Office," Herman Wells Papers, March 14, 1969.
79. "Minutes of Student Affairs Committee Meeting," March 26, 1969, Indiana University Archives.
80. "Students for a Democratic Society," March 17, 1969, Indiana University Archives.
81. Telegrams sent to South Bend campus, March 29, 1969, Indiana University Archives.
82. "Homecoming Edition," *Indiana Daily Student* (December 14, 1996): C1.
83. Pete Adams, "A Queen Uncrowned," *Griot* (November–December 1996):1; and Patrick Kaster, "*Griot*: You Should Be Ashamed of Yourself," *Griot* (January 1997): 7.
84. "Black Beauty Queens at White Schools," *Jet*, 30 (November 1967): 44.
85. *Kentucky Kernel*, October 29, 1979: 1.
86. *Kentucky Kernel*, November 2, 1979: 3.
87. An exception, however, to the pattern of racial hegemony on predominantly white campuses is the University of North Carolina at Chapel Hill. Due to the organizing efforts of the Black Student Union there, from 1979 through 1995, all of the homecoming queens were African American, though not without white protest and harassment. *Daily Tar Heel* 5 (November, 1998): 1.
88. Judith Duffett, "WLM vs. Miss America," *Voice of the Women's Liberation Movement*, October, 1968. Available at http://www.uic.edu/orgs/cwluherstory/CWLUArchive/vioces/voices4-1.html.
89. Charolette Curtis, "Miss America is Picketed by 100 Women," *New York Times*, September 8, 1968.
90. Judy Klemesrud, "There's Now Miss Black America," *New York Times*, September 8, 1968.
91. Ruth Lovell, "Male Homecoming Queen Signs Book," *Daily Beacon*, May 31, 1996.
92. Elizabeth Davis, "Columnist Almost Became Queen in 1970," *Daily Beacon*, September 29, 1995.
93. Terry McWilliams, "Male Homecoming Queen? Student Center Board Votes to Allow Men," *Kentucky Kernel* 3 (September 1975): 1; and Mary Amidon, "De-sex Decision: Student Board at UK Votes to Allow Males," *Courier-Journal*, September 4, 1975.
94. Susan Jones, "Male Queen Candidate Threatened," *Kentucky Kernel*, October 15, 1975.
95. Kitty Hundley, "Campus Views," *Lexington Leader*, May 3, 1962.
96. *Kentucky Kernel*, November 2, 1979.
97. *Kentucky Kernel*, October 5, 1984.
98. Banet-Weiser, *The Most Beautiful Girl*, 44.

Chapter 4

1. Melissa LaPinta, "Contestants for Homecoming Queen Blend Academics, Leadership, Talent," *Alligator Online*, October 20, 1999. Available at http://www.alligator.org/edit/issues/99-fall/991020/bo2pageant20.htm.
2. Cody Kees, "Miss UA not Just a Beauty Pageant," *Arkansas Traveler* (2009). Available at http://www.thetraveleronline.com/home/index.cfm?event.
3. Crystal Allen, "Miss Howard Represents for 'the Mecca,'" *Hilltop*, September 25, 2009. Available at http://www.thehilltoponline.com/miss-howard-represents-for-the-mecca-1.1914519.
4. Available at http://www.missamerica.org/scholarships/purpose.aspx.
5. Amie McLain, "Pageant Winners Gear Up for Mr. and Miss Howard Competition," *Hilltop*, September 17, 2002.
6. *Kansas State Collegian*, December 3, 2001.

7. Miss Purdue University Pageant video, 1999.

8. Ibid.

9. Matt Hosapple, "Talent Key to Nursing Major's Win at Miss Purdue Pageant," *Journal and Courier*, March 26, 2001: C2.

10. "Campus Happenings: More Than Just a Gown," *Purdue Alumnus* (May/June, 2001):11.

11. Evelyn Barge, "Pepperdine Beauty Pageant Contestants Reveal the Ins and Outs of the Pageant System," available at htpp://graphic.pepperdine.edu/ane/2005/2005-03-31-pageant.htm.

12. Meredith Shamburger, "Students Demonstrate Talents, Diversity at First Annual Miss Purple and Gold Pageant," *Daily Campus*, April 4, 2008, available at http://www.smudailycampus.com/home/index.cfm?event.

13. Author interview, Miss Purdue University, March 25, 2001.

14. Mike Redmond, "Pageant is Queen of Un-reality TV," *Indianapolis Star*, August 21, 2000. One queen wrote Redmon and stated that "I am insulted to be grouped into the ever-so-old-and-annoying stereotypical bubblehead pageant contestant group. I think it's important to let a bitter journalist who has nothing better to do than pick on young women know he's the bubblehead." Email correspondence, "Pageant Slamming news article." After receiving numerous outraged emails, Redmond wrote another column, "Non-pageant Hits the Non-funny List," *Indianapolis Star*, August 31, 2001.

15. Available at http://web.ics.purdue.edu/~Misspu/site/home.html.

16. Available at http://web.ics.purdue.edu/~Misspu/site/home.html.

17. Liza Pitts, "A Year in the Life," April 30, 2008, available at http://www.uga.edu/campuslife/missuga/year/04_08.html.

18. Miss UGA 2009 also held a Miss UGA tiara tea party.

19. Pitts, "A Year in the Life."

20. "Who Are We?," available at http://www.clubs.psu.edu/misspennstate/whoarewe.html.

21. 2001 Miss Pennsylvania State University pageant video.

22. Author interview, Debi Swarner, Executive Director, Miss Penn State Scholarship Organization, March 12, 2001.

23. "The 2005 Miss Maroon & White Pageant," *Morehouse Quarterly*, April 8, 2005.

24. Annette Kuhn, *Family Secrets: Acts of Memory and Imagination* (London: Verso, 2002), 117.

25. Kelly Simmons, "Scholarship Attracts Many to Pageants," *Atlanta Constitution*, April 16, 2006.

26. Herman Mason, "The Miss Maroon & White Court Reunion: Diamond Reflections of Feminine Pulchritude," Morehouse College pageant booklet, October 28, 2004.

27. Lee Haven Monet Cooper, "Beauty in the Eye of the Historian," *Morehouse Magazine* (Fall 2004).

28. *Daily Mississippian*, November 16, 1996.

29. Author interview, Miss Maroon and White, April 7, 2005.

30. Author interview, queen participant at the HBCU Leadership Conference for Queens and Kings, July 2004.

31. In 2009, the University of Kentucky, for example, posted on its main campus web site a feature story, "Pageantry to Pharmacy," as well as photographs of the winner and links to various Miss America web sites. University of Alabama president Robert Witt also honored student beauty pageant winners at his university in his e-letters to the campus community. Many campuses, such as Howard University, regularly send out press releases praising students who have won local, state, and national beauty competitions.

32. Robert Lavenda, "'It's Not a Beauty Pageant': Hybrid Ideology in the Minnesota Community Queen Pageants," in C. Ballerino, R. Wilk, and B. Stoeltje (Eds.), *Beauty Queens on the Global Stage: Gender, Contests, and Power* (New York: Routledge, 1996), 31.

33. Hans Gerth and C. Wright Mills, *Character and Social Structure: The Psychology of Social Institutions* (New York: Harcourt and Brace, 1964).

34. *Miss Congeniality* (2000).

35. Jamie Teibel, "Miss Purdue Stands by Her Cause, Prepares for Scholarship Program," *Purdue Exponent,* 2001.

36. Kelly Simmons, "Scholarship Attracts Many to Pageants," *Atlanta Constitution,* April 16, 2006.

37. Chelsea Cook, "For University Queens, Beauty is More than Skin Deep," posted February 5, 2009, to http://www.redandblack.com./home/index.cfm?event+display.

38. Author interview, 1997 University of Kentucky homecoming queen, September 20, 2001.

39. Many male participants in homecoming pageantry observe that personal appearance is more important for women competing in campus queen pageants. A male member of the University of Kentucky 2000 royalty court admitted that "there is some ground to stand on" for those who critique homecoming royalty as being nothing more than beauty and popularity contests, yet he believes that there is more at stake, including "personality and friendliness" for men. He denies getting votes based on his looks, as is the case for the "girls." Instead, he asserted that "achievement and personality matter more" for men.

40. 2008 Application for the Miss Mississippi State University Scholarship Pageant, Office of Student Affairs, Mississippi State University.

41. *Minnesota Daily Online,* October 23, 2000.

42. *Daily Trojan,* October 29, 1996.

43. Kelly Simmons, "Scholarship Attracts Many to Pageants," *Atlanta Constitution,* April 16, 2006.

44. Cody Kees, "Miss UA Not Just a Beauty Pageant," available at http://thetraveleronline.com/home/index.cfm?event.

45. Author interview, Miss Black and Gold, February 15, 2002.

46. Ian Rosales Casocot, "Truth and Reality in the Miss Silliman College Pageant," available at http://www.silliman.com/reality_vs_perception.php.

47. Cook, "For University Queens."

48. Alex Weininger, "PA Pageant Looking for Contestants," *Digital Collegian,* September 22, 2000.

49. Author interview, 1992 Homecoming queen, University of Kentucky, March 24, 2000.

50. *Signal,* February 1, 2000.

51. Ibid.

52. Chakita Holmes, no title, *Xavier Herald Online,* posted 2003.

53. Ibid.

54. Cook, "For University Queens."

55. 2005 Miss Spelman Pageant Walk of Fame program.

56. Author interview, 1997 Homecoming queen royalty court, April 17, 2000.

57. Author interview, 2004 Kentucky Derby Princess, May, 2004.

58. According to Meredith Clark, Mr. FAMU spent more than $3,700 on his campaign. "Costly Campaigns Near End," *Tallahassee.com,* February 19, 2005.

59. Shannon Colavecchio, "Pageant Finalists Break Away from Stereotypes," available at http://www.alligator.org/edit/issues/96-fall/961011/b04pagea.htm.

60. Author interview, President of the UK Alpha Phi Alpha Fraternity, February 25, 2002.

61. Allen, "Miss Howard Represents for 'the Mecca.'"

62. Author interview, Miss Purdue University pageant organizer, March 25, 2001.

63. Stephanie Abrams, "A History of Feminist Activism at Miami University, Oxford Campus, 1969–1993," available at http://www.libmuohio.edu/epub/abrams.

64. D. Erickson, "Miss Miami Returns to Campus," *Miami Student,* February 15, 2002.

65. Author interview, University of Kentucky Vice-President for Student Affairs, 2006.

66. Eboni Graham and Robert Saucedo, "Drop-Dead Gorgeous: Aggies Find Both Confidence and Condemnation in Beauty Pageants," *Battalion,* February 7, 2005. Available at http://www.thebatt.com/2.8488/drop-dead-gorgeous.

67. Ibid. Also see Erica York, "Beauty Secrets,", *Battalion,* October 16, 2002. Available at http://www.thebatt.com/beauty-secrets.

68. Sharon Haddock, "UVSC Panel Asks: Do Pageants Hurt or Help?" *Deseret Morning News,* June 9, 2005.

69. Available at www.uca.edu/facultysenate/document/missuacpageant_inquiry.pdf.

70. Ian Rosales Casocot, "Truth and Reality in the Miss Silliman Pageant," available at http://www.silliman.com/reality_vs_perception.php.

71. Donelle Ruwe, "I Was Miss Meridian 1985: Sororophobia, Kitsch, and Local Pageantry," in Elwood Watson and Darcy Martin (Eds.), *There She Is, Miss America* (New York: Palgrave Macmillan, 2004), 137.

72. Ibid., 146.

73. Ibid., 148.

74. Author interview, Debi Swarner, Executive Director, Miss Penn State Scholarship Organization, March 12, 2001.

75. Graham and Saucedo, "Drop-Dead Gorgeous."

76. Nakeisha Rowe, "Crowning Achievements," *University of Evansville Crescent Online,* March 28, 2008. Available at http://www.uecrescent.org?articles/stories/public/200803/28/04fd_lifestyle.

77. Elliot, "Protesters storm."

78. William Lee Adams, "A British Row Over College Beauty Pageants," *Time,* December 11, 2008.

79. Vanessa Allen, Sophie Borland, and Rachel Porter, "The Frilly Feminists: Uni Students Fighting to be Beauty Queen," *Mail Online,* December 4, 2008. Available at http://dailymail.co.uk/femail/article-1091533/The-frilly-feminist.

80. Beth Evans, "Global Perspective," *On Campus with Women,* available at http://www.aacu.org/ocww/volume38_3/global.cfm.

81. Miss-Ogynist University London. Facebook public group.

82. Eleanor James, "Miss-Ogynist UL vs. Sunday Times: v V. un-stylish," In response to "The new feminists: lipstick and pageants," *Sunday Times,* December 21, 2008. Available at http://www.miss-ogynist.org/wp/.

83. For more on the purported extinction and irrelevance of feminism in mainstream media see "Requiem for the Women's Movement"(*Harper's,* 1976); "Feminists Have Killed Feminism" (*LA Times,* 1992); "When Feminism Failed" (*New York Times,* 1988); "Feminism—A Lost Cause" (*Vogue,* 1983); "Is Feminism Dead?" (*Time,* 1998); "Women's Issues a Tough Sell" (*Florida Sun Sentinel,* April 2002); and Susan Bolotin, "Voices from a Post-feminist Generation" (*New York Times Magazine,* October 17, 1982). For scholarly analyses of the paradoxes and micro-politics of post-feminism, third-wave feminism, second-wave feminist backlash, and image and consumption, see Mary Hawkensworth. "Semiotics of Premature Burial: Feminism in a Post-Feminist Age," *Signs* 29, 4 (2004): 961–85; Stephanie Genz, "Third Way/ve: The Politics of Post-Feminism," *Feminist Theory* 7, 3 (2009): 333–53; Rosalind Gill, "Post-Feminist Media Culture: Elements of a Sensibility," *European Journal of Cultural Studies* 10, 2 (2007): 147–66; and "From Sexual Objectification to Sexual Subjectification: The Resexualization of Women's Bodies in the Media," *Feminist Media Studies* 3, 1 (2003): 100–106; Jennifer Pozner, "The '"Big Lie"': False Feminist Death Syndrome, Profit, and the Media," in Rory Dicker and Alison Piepmeier (Eds.), *Catching a Wave: Reclaiming Feminism for the 21st Century* (Boston: Northeastern University Press, 2003): 31–56; Susan J. Douglas, "Manufacturing Postfeminism," April 26, 2002. Available at http://www.inthesetimes.com/main/article/1466; Angela McRobbie, "Post-Feminism and Popular Culture," *Feminist Media Studies* 4, 3 (2004): 255–64; Angela Robbie, "Notes on Post-Feminism and Popular Culture: Bridget Jones and the New Gender Regime," in Anita Harris (Ed.), *All About the Girl: Culture, Power, and Identity* (New York: Routledge, 2004): 3–14; and Yvonne Tasker and Diane Negra (Eds.), *Interrogating Post-Feminism: Gender and the Politics of Popular Culture* (Durham: Duke University Press, 2007).

84. Gemma Soames, "The New Feminists: Lipstick and Pageants," *Sunday Times,* December 21, 2008. Available at http://women.timesonline.co.uk/tol/life_and_style/women.

85. Ellie Levenson, *The Noughtie Girl's Guide to Feminism* (Oxford: OneWorld Publications, 2009).

86. Bonnie Dow, "Feminism, Miss America, and Media Mythology," *Rhetoric & Public Affairs* 6, 1 (2003), 129.

87. Ibid., 129.
88. Claire Ellicott, "Protesters Storm 'Sexist' Miss University London Beauty Pageant and Set Off Stink Bombs," *Mail Online,* March 11, 2009.
89. Emine Saner, "Betraying the Student Body?" *The Guardian,* December 5, 2008. Available at http:www.guardian.co.uk/education/2008/dec/05/students-gender/.
90. Rosalind Gill, "Post-Feminist Media Culture: Elements of a Sensibility," *European Journal of Cultural Studies* 10, 2 (2007), 151. Also see Robert Goldman, *Reading Ads Socially* (London: Routledge, 1992).
91. Susan Douglas, *Enlightened Sexism: The Seductive Message that Feminism's Work is Done* (New York: Times Books, 2010), 10.
92. Holly Thompson, "The Great Debate Beauty Pageants: Male Domination or Free Choice?," October 21, 2009. Available at http://www.london-student.net/2009/10/21/the-great-debate-beauty.
93. Allen, Borland, and Porter, "The Frilly Feminists," December 4, 2008. Available at http://dailymail.co.uk/femail/article-1091533/The-frilly-feminist.
94. Available at http://www.popmatters.com/pm/tools/print/40156.
95. Susheel Bal, "I Won a Beauty Contest. Now Get Over It." *Independent,* March 13, 2009.
96. Ellicott, "Protesters storm."
97. Gill, "Post-Feminist Media Culture," 154.
98. Ibid., 165.
99. Porter, "The Frilly Feminists."
100. Thompson, "The Great Debate."
101. Ibid.
102. Brenda R. Weber, "Beauty, Desire, and Anxiety: The Economy of Sameness on ABC's *Extreme Makeover,*" *Genders* 41 (2005), available at www.genders.org.
103. Carole Leathwood and Barbara Read, *Gender and the Changing Face of Higher Education* (Berkshire: Open University Press, 2009); and Katherine Sender, "Queens for a Day: Queer Eye for the Straight Guy and the Neoliberal Project," *Critical Studies in Media Communication* 23, 2 (June 2006): 131–51.
104. Robert Goldstein, "What Queer Eye? Are the Fab Five a Breakthrough or a Stereotype?," *Village Voice.* Retrieved April 5, 2009, from http://villagevoice.com.
105. Susan Faludi, *Stiffed: The Betrayal of the American Man* (New York: Morrow, 1999).
106. Toby Miller, "Metrosexuality: See the Bright Lights of Commodification Shine! Watch Yanqui Masculinity Made Over," in Dana Heller (Ed.), *The Great American Makeover: Television, History, Nation* (New York: Palgrave, 2006).
107. Nathan Thornburgh, "Taming the Toga," *Time,* February 20, 2006: 2.
108. I attended the fifteenth annual charm school in 2008. MIT participants total up the number of charm credits they earn based on their attendance at the various workshops throughout the day. Unfortunately, I failed to earn enough credits to reach my goal of personally earning a Ph.D. from MIT, but I did manage to receive a Masters of Charm degree.
109. Malniquia Evans, "Black Star Power Brings BET College Tour to CAU," *Clark University Panther,* September 20, 2010. Available at http://www.thecaupanther.com/home.
110. Available at www. kingsruletogether.com; and Janice Richardson, "MTV Personality Keeps it Classy," September 30, 2010, available at www.hustonianonline.com.
111. "The Come Up 2009 Recognition Ceremony," Office of Diversity Programs at Western Kentucky University. Also see "The Come Up Scholar," available at http://www.wku.edu/odp/tcu.html accessed 1/28/2010.
112. Nancy Salem, "Pretty Funny: Omega Man Beauty Pageant is Unconventional," available at http://www.abqtrib.com/news/2006/nov/16/pretty-funny.
113. Kate Gales, "Cool Water, SI Sponsor Pageant," available at http://www.ndsmcobserver.com/home/index.cfm?event.
114. Anna Friedman, "Currier Claims Mr. Harvard," *Harvard Crimson,* May 16, 2005.
115. "Delta Zeta Presents the Mr. UK Pageant," April 23, 2003.
116. Ibid.

117. Ibid.

118. Author interview, May 1, 2003.

119. Other kings made similar comments about "girls" and "razz." Mr. Black UK 2001, for example, said that his fraternity brothers would razz him by yelling "lay away the king is coming." He also told me that many more people now approach him after his win including some women he was hoping he could ask out on a date.

120. Weintana Abraha, "Mr. Vassar Candidates Walk on the Wild Side," available at http://misc.vassar.edu/archives/2007/02/mrvassarcandi1.html.

121. Tendai Musakwa, "Mr. Vassar Pageant Reinforces Male Stereotypes," available at http://misc.vassar.edu/archives/2007/02/views on vassar11.html.

122. "The University Wants its Queens to be Women," *Chronicle of Higher Education*. Available at http://chronicle.com/weekely/v46/i13/13a01201.htm; and Chris Schurtz, "Man Makes Statement as Homecoming," available at ../../../Local Settings/Temporary Internet Files/Content.Outlook/DC8KRFLW/%3Ca href=http://www.studentadvantage.com/article/0,1075,cl-i76-t0-al6874,00.html.

123. Loretta Panichi, "He dreams of becoming a homecoming queen," *Daily University Star*, available at http://www.studentadvantage.com/article/0,1075,c3-i64-t0-a16758,00.html.

124. Sarah Kershaw, "Gay Students Force New Look at Homecoming Traditions," *New York Times*, November 26, 2004. Available at http://www.nytimes.com/2004/11/27/national/27homecoming.html?_.

125. Ibid.

126. Ibid.

127. Gabrijel Gelic, "Miss Gay IU Hits Campus Friday," *Indiana Daily Student*, April 18, 2008.

128. Annie Gowen, "GMU's Choice of Homecoming (Drag) Queen Sparks Campus Debate," *Washington Post*, February 20, 2009: B01.

129. Andrew Hall, "Female Excluded from Mr. MWC Contest," available at http://www.thebullentononline.com/2003-10-30/news5.html.

130. 2006 Mr. Collegiate African American Pageant. Available at http://www.prnewsnow.com/Public Release/Public Relations/84318.html.

131. Mishawn Dubose, *Gazette*, February 8, 2006.

132. "Lincoln University to Host Mr. HBCU Leadership Conference and Competition," available at http:www.blackcollegevoice.com, February 25, 2005. Fonzworth Bentley was a featured speaker.

133. "Fourth Annual Mr. HBCU: Official Candidate's Guide," 2008.

134. DeShanee Miner, "Suttle to Compete in National Pageant," available at http://media.www.tsumeter.com/media/storage/paper956/news/2004/11/15/campus news.

135. Ibid.

136. Kevin Chappel, "A Modern Morehouse: Are HBCU Traditions at Odds with Freedom of Expression," *Ebony* (September 2010): 96–98.

137. Layla Schlack, "Mr. and Miss Black UCONN Pageant Celebrates Black History Month," *Daily Campus*, February 24, 2003. Available at http://dailycampus.com/home/index.cfm?event.

Chapter 5

1. Author interview, 2004 Miss Florida A&M University, July 16, 2004.

2. Jennifer Koehmstedt, "2010 Miss Native American University of Arizona Approaches," March 24, 2010. Available at http://wildcat.arizona.edu/news/2010-miss-native-american-ua-pageant-approaches.

3. Ian Rosales Casocot, "Truth and Reality in the Miss Silliman Pageant," available at http://www.silliman.com/reality_vs_perception.php.

4. Ibid.

5. See Maxine L. Craig, *Ain't I a Beauty Queen: Black Women, Beauty, and the Politics of Race* (New York: Oxford University Press, 2002), for an excellent discussion of beauty and the politics of race.

6. See for instance Darryl Fears, "Growing Number of Ethnic Beauty Pageants Restyle American Beauty Contests," *Courier-Journal*, October 30, 2005: E6; Pamela Wright, "The Timely Significance of Supernatural Mothers or Exemplary Daughters: The Metonymy of Identity in History," in Jane Schneider and Rayna Rapp (Eds.), *Articulating Hidden Histories: Exploring the Influence of Eric R. Wolf* (Berkeley: University of California Press, 1995): 255–61; Nhi Lieu, "'Remembering the Nation' Through Pageantry: Femininity and the Politics of Vietnamese Womanhood in the Hoa Hau Ao Dai Contest," *Frontiers* 21, 2/1 (2000): 127–51; Natasha Barnes, "Face of the Nation: Race, Nationalisms and Identities in Jamaican Beauty Pageants," *Massachusetts Review* 35 (Autumn, 1994): 471–92; Christine Yano, *Crowning the Nice Girl: Gender, Ethnicity, and Culture in the Hawaii's Cherry Blossom Festival* (Honolulu: University of Hawaii Press, 2006); Wendy Kozol, "Miss Indian America: Regulatory Gazes and the Politics of Affiliation," *Feminist Studies* 31, 1 (2005): 64–94; Rebecca Chiyoko King-O'Riain, *Pure Beauty: Judging Race in Japanese American Beauty Pageants* (Minneapolis: University of Minnesota Press, 2006); Judy Tzu-Chun Wu, "Loveliest Daughter of our Ancient Cathay!: Representations of Ethnic and Gender Identity in Miss Chinatown U.S.A. Beauty Pageant," *Journal of Social History* 31, 1 (1997): 5–31; Lok Siu, "Queen of the Chinese Colony: Gender, Nation, and Belonging in Diaspora," *Anthropological Quarterly* 78, 3 (2005): 511–42; Shirley Jennifer Lim, *A Feeling of Belonging: Asian American Women's Public Culture, 1930–1960* (New York: New York University Press, 2006); Jon Schackt, "Mayahood Through Beauty: Indian Beauty Pageants in Guatemala," *Bulletin of Latin American Research* 24, 3 (2005): 269–87; and Colleen Ballerino Cohen, Richard Wilk, and Beverly Stoeltje (Eds.), *Beauty Queens on the Global Stage: Gender, Contests, and Power* (New York: Routledge, 1996).

7. Author interview, Miss Maroon & White, April 7, 2005.

8. For more on black colleges and popular culture see Adam Parrott-Sheffer, "Not a Laughing Matter: The Portrayals of Black Colleges on Television," in Marybeth Gasman and Christopher Tudico (Eds.), *Historically Black Colleges and Universities: Triumphs, Troubles, and Taboos* (New York: Palgrave-Macmillan, 2008): 207–39.

9. Leadership conference for historically black college and university queens, Nashville, Tennessee, July 15–17, 2004. Author in attendance.

10. Anthony Jones, "Making it a Night to Remember: Planning the Perfect Coronation," leadership conference for historically black college and university queens, July 15–17, 2004.

11. Dale Williams, *Leadership for Queens: A Guide and a Journal* (self-published, 2010). Available at http://hbcukingsandqueens.com/main-hbcu/www.hbcukingsandqueens.com.

12. *Brownite*, Morris Brown Yearbook, 2000.

13. Author in attendance, Mr. and Miss Kentucky State University pageant, October 11, 2002.

14. Andrea Uhde, "Queen Never Got Royal Treatment," *Kentucky Kernel*, October 12, 2001: B4.

15. The National Black College Alumni Hall of Fame Foundation, Inc., "Competition of Black College Queens," April 15, 2008: 3.

16. Ibid., 7.

17. Ibid., 16–17.

18. "Miss UVI to Compete for Crown in South Africa," University of the Virgin Islands news release, November 27, 2000.

19. Available at http://www.missmalaikauk.co.uk.

20. Dahleen Glanton, "Black College Queens Hang on to Homecoming Tradition," *Tallahasee.com*, November 14, 2004.

21. *Brownite*, Morris Brown College Yearbook, 1994: 38.

22. Author interview, 2003 Miss Maroon & White, April 7, 2005.

23. Glanton, "Black College Queens Hang On."

24. Ibid.

25. This pageant was established by Frank Meracado-Valdes and his Kappa Alpha Psi fraternity brothers in order to recruit more black women to come to the University of Miami campus. See Wendy Harris, *Against All Odds: Ten Entrepreneurs Who Followed Their Hearts and Found Success* (New York: Wiley, 2001).

26. C. C. Campbell-Rock, "Campus Royalty Goes to Hollywood," *Black Collegian* 23, 1 (September 1992).

27. Ibid.

28. Sarah Poole, *The Onyx: Berea College Black Cultural Center Newsletter*, 2004.

29. Shirley Henderson, "It's Great to be a Queen," *Ebony*, September 2010: 105.

30. Author interview, Miss Maroon & White, April 7, 2005.

31. Dr. Tonea Steward, "What Does it Mean to Be a Campus Queen," Leadership Conference for Kings and Queens, July 15–18, 2004. Author in attendance.

32. Jamie Jenkins, "Beauty Queens: What They Are, What They Should Be," *Clark Atlantic Panther*, April 4, 2006. Available at http://www.thecaupanther.com/home/index.cfm?event.

33. Author interview, Miss Maroon & White, April 7, 2005.

34. Jenny Telwar, "My Experience/My Advice," 2004 HBCU Leadership Conference for Kings and Queens, July 15–18, 2004. Author in attendance.

35. Author interview, Miss Maroon & White, April 7, 2005.

36. Ibid.

37. Ibid.

38. Ibid.

39. Ibid.

40. Author interview, 2001 Mr. Black University of Kentucky, December 9, 2001.

41. 2002–2003 Mr. and Ms. Black UK Pageant, October 23, 2002. Author in attendance.

42. Maxine L. Craig, "Race, Beauty, and the Tangled Knot of Guilty Pleasure," *Feminist Theory* 7, 2 (2006): 167.

43. Author interview, March 1, 2002.

44. Author interview, Miss Maroon & White, April 7, 2005.

45. The 2005 Miss Maroon & White Pageant, *Morehouse Quarterly,* April 8, 2005.

46. Ibid.

47. Office of Communications and Public Affairs, "33rd Annual Miss Calendar Girl Pageant," Grambling State University, March 20, 2001.

48. "Presidential Introduction to the 2004 Activity Calendar," Grambling State University home page, July 8, 2004.

49. Valerie Felita Kinloch, "The Rhetoric of Black Bodies: Race, Beauty, and Representation," in Elwood Watson and Darcy Martin (Eds.), *There She Is, Miss America: The Politics of Sex, Beauty, and Race in America's Most Famous Pageant* (New York: Palgrave Macmillan, 2004), 104.

50. Ibid., 55.

51. "Blacks Winning Six Campus Wueens at White University Stirs Controversy," *Jet* 14 (November 1994): 55.

52. Ibid.

53. Amy Cappiello, "Voting for Royalty or Race," *Daily Tar Heel Online*, November 5, 1998.

54. Ibid.

55. Ibid.

56. "Minority Students Upset by U. Arizona Homecoming Nominations," available at wysiwyg://92/http://www.grandcmcsa.com/casczinc/stories/articlc-307.html.

57. Alison Fischer, "Homecoming Queen Selection Continues Despite Racial Turmoil," available at http://www.unc.edu/dth/archives/1995/10/101695/div.html.

58. Author interview, 2001 University of Kentucky Homecoming queen candidate, October 4, 2001.

59. Ashley Boyd, "Queen joins long UA tradition," *Tuscaloosanews.com*, October 31, 2008.

60. Author interview, 2004 Kentucky Derby Princess, May 2004.

61. Available at http://www.latino.uconn.edu/news/fall00/page1.html.

62. Author interview, 2001 University of Kentucky Homecoming queen candidate, October 4, 2001.

63. Jessica Johnson, "Martin Makes History with Landslide Victory," *Thorobred News*, April 30, 2009.

64. Merlene Davis, "White Miss KSU at Her 'Dream College': Victory Shows How Diverse School Is," *Lexington Herald-Leader*, May 19, 2009.

65. Author interview, Miss Kentucky State University, December 17, 2009.

66. Ibid.

67. Ibid.

68. Available at http://www.congress.org/congressorg/bio/userletter/?letter_id=406651.

69. In an online forum on Churchill's crowning, comments included "We know who is racist. Some blacks are!" "It is about time that this Racist College fixed their ways," and "poor little black girls didn't win and now they throw a hissy fit about it. Get over it. What part of the double standard do you not understand?" Available at http://www.topix.net/forum/source/wtkr/TASBOPD5JBCMP6D0A3. In another forum, similar sentiments were expressed, including "Why is this girl going to a black school? Does she not know that this is the deal with these people?" and "This is so unfair but it is real life that whites must endure when blacks do not get their way." Available at http://www.floppingaces.net/2009/10/20/the-racism-ignored.

70. Author interviews, 2002 Miss Black and Gold contestants, February 15, 2002.

71. Dave Gorman, "UK Student Wins Pageant," *Kentucky Kernel Online*, September 23, 1999.

72. Allison Leigh Bourg, "Minority Pageant Crowns King, Queen," *Lantern*, October 13, 2000.

73. Kiran Sood, "Asian-Pacific Community Celebrates History Month through Beauty Pageant," *Daily Illini*, March 7, 2005.

74. Ibid.

75. "Pageant Application: 2001 Miss Asian America, University of Washington Scholarship Program, " Asian Student Commission.

76. Ibid.

77. Pamela Wright, "The Timely Significance of Supernatural Mothers or Exemplary Daughters: The Metonymy of Identity in History," in Jane Schneider and Rayna Rapp (Eds.), *Articulating Hidden Histories: Exploring the Influence of Eric R. Wolf* (Berkeley: University of California Press, 1995): 243–61, notes similar processes of reformulation in pageants in Belize. Although ethnic knowledge is the main criterion and national legitimation of various ethnic groups the goal, the beauty contest format transforms the ethnic content into an individualized performance that can be evaluated by the judges. Also see Nhi Lieu, "'Remembering the Nation' Through Pageantry: Femininity and the Politics of Vietnamese Womanhood in the Hoa Hau Ao Dai Contest," *Frontiers* (2000):,127–51; and Natasha Barnes, "Face of the Nation: Race, Nationalisms and Identities in Jamaican Beauty Pageants," *Massachusetts Review* 35 (Autumn 1994): 471–92, for discussions of ethnicity, representation, and identity in beauty pageants.

78. Natalie Cheng, "African Students Association Crowns Miss Africa Mizzou 2010," *Maneater*, Missouri University, November 9, 2010; and Jordane Fraizer, "African Students' Association Crowns Royalty at Pageant," *Hilltop*, February 27, 2011.

79. Miss Black and Gold pageant, Clemson University, available at http://virtual.clemson.edu/groups/APAFRAT/apaweb/pageant.html.

80. Aimee Harris, "Pageant Salutes Black Women," *Digital Collegian*, February 24, 1997.

81. 2002 and 2003 Mr. and Ms. Black UK pageants, October 10, 2001, and October 23, 2002. Author in attendance.

82. Ann Ducille, "Black Barbie and the Deep Play of Difference," in Morag Shiach (Ed.), *Feminism and Cultural Studies* (New York: Oxford University Press, 1999): 106–32.

83. Alpha Phi Alpha Fraternity, Inc., "2003 Miss Black and Gold Pageant: Official Score Sheets."

84. 2002–3 Miss Black and Gold Pageant: Herstory in the Making," February 7, 2002. Author field notes.

85. Layla Schlack, "Mr. and Miss Black UConn Pageant Celebrates Black History Month," *Daily Campus*, February 24, 2003.

86. Talia Tsosie and Cher Thomas, "Meet Ms. Indian Arizona State University," February 8, 2010. Available at http://www.nativeyouth magazine.com/index.php?option.

87. Miss Native American University of Arizona Pageant: 2006–2007 Contestant Application, available at http://missnativeua.edu/.

88. Hanh Quach, "Ethnic Pageants Shed Light on Age-Old Tradition," *Arizona Daily Wildcat*, April 12, 1996.

89. *Kentucky Kernel*, October 28, 1997.

90. Lisa Gentry, "Seven Compete for Ms. Black UK," *Kentucky Kernel* 14, October 1997.

91. Author interview, 2002 Miss Black and Gold University of Kentucky, February 15, 2002.

92. See, for example, "Minorities Protest Coverage by Northern Illinois Paper," *Chronicle Online*, November 6, 1995; "Our Take: R&B not Racist," *Red and Black Student Newspaper*, University of Georgia, October 27, 1998; and Hank Johnson, "Letters Accusing Racism Show Need for Open Dialogue," *Online Athens*, October 25, 1998.

Chapter 6

1. "College Queens Striving for Excellence," 2004 HBCU Leadership Conference for Kings and Queens handout.

2. Dale Williams, "Top Ten Things Every College Queen or King Should Know," 2004 HBCU Queen Leadership Conference.

3. Author interview, Elisabeth Martin, 2009 Miss Kentucky State University, December 17, 2009.

4. Coletta Reid, "Recycled Trash," *Furies* 1, 5 (June–July 1972): 8.

5. Helen Merrell Lynd, *On Shame and the Search for Identity* (New York: Harcourt Brace, 1958), 40.

6. Rita Felski, *Doing Time: Feminist Theory and Postmodern Culture* (New York: New York University Press, 2000), 43.

7. Frank Deford. *There She Is: The Life and Times of Miss America* (New York: Viking Press, 1971), 54.

8. Ibid.

9. Angela Taylor, "Her Name is Ophelia Devore and her Specialty is Polishing Black Diamonds," *New York Times*, August 20, 1969. See also Laila Haidarali, "Polishing Brown Diamonds: African American Women, Popular Magazines, and the Advent of Modeling in Early Postwar America," *Journal of Women's History* 17, 1 (2005): 10–37.

10. See for example, bell hooks, *Where We Stand: Class Matters* (New York: Routledge, 2000); Vivyan Adair and Sandra Dahlberg (Eds.), *Reclaiming Class:Women, Poverty, and the Promise of Higher Education* (Philadelphia: Temple University Press, 2003); Helen Lucey, June Melody, and Valerie Walkerdine, "Uneasy Hybrids: Psychosocial Aspects of Becoming Educationally Successful for Working-Class Young Women," *Gender & Education* 15, 3 (September 2003): 285–99; Michelle Tokarczyk and Elizabeth Fay, *Working-Class Women in the Academy: Labors in the Knowledge Factory* (Amherst: University of Massachusetts Press, 1993); Pat Mahony and Christine Zmroczek (Eds.), *Class Matters: Working-Class Women's Perspectives on Social Class* (New York: Taylor & Francis, 1997);

Lorraine Lopez, *An Angle of Vision: Women Writers on their Poor and Working Class Roots.* (Ann Arbor: University of Michigan Press, 2009); Stephen Muzzatti and C. Vincent Samarco, *Reflections from the Wrong Side of the Track: Class, Identity, and the Working Class Experience in Academe* (Lanham, MD: Rowman and Littlefield, 2006); Michael Zweig (Ed.), *What's Class Have To Do With It?: American Society in the Twenty-First Century* (Ithaca: Cornell University Press, 2004); Jenny Stuber, "Talk of Class: The Discursive Repertoires of White Working Class and Upper Middle Class Students," *Journal of Contemporary Ethnography* 35, 3 (June 2006): 285–318; Valerie Hey, "Joining the Club? Academia and Working-Class Femininities," *Gender & Education* 15, 3 (September 2003): 319–35; Diane Reay, "A Risky Business? Mature Working-Class Women Students and Access to Higher Education," *Gender & Education* 15, 3 (September 2003): 301–17; and Renny Christopher, *A Carpenter's Daughter: A Working-Class Woman in Higher Education* (Rotterdam: Sense Publishers, 2009).

11. Author interview with former homecoming queen who wished to remain completely anonymous.

12. Helen Lucey, June Melody, and Valerie Walkerdine, "Uneasy Hybrids: Psychosocial Aspects of Becoming Educationally Successful for Working-Class Young Women," *Gender & Education* 15, 3 (September 2003), 293.

13. Gwendolyn Foster, *Troping the Body* (Carbondale: Southern Illinois University Press, 2000), 9.

14. John Kasson, *Rudeness & Civility: Manners in Nineteenth-Century Urban America* (New York: Hill and Wang, 1990), 180; and T. O. Beidelman, *Moral Imagination in Kaguru Modes of Thought* (Washington, DC: Smithsonian, 1993), 61.

15. Radhika Parameswaran, "Global Queens, National Celebrities: Tales of Feminine Triumph in Post-Liberalization India." *Critical Studies in Media Communication* 21, 4 (December, 2004), 422.

16. Shirley Henderson, "Black College Queens: Then & Now," *Ebony*, April 2005.

17. Kelly Simmons, "Scholarship Attracts Many to Pageants," *Atlanta Constitution*, April 16, 2006.

18. Miss America, American Experience, available at http://www.pbs.org/wgbh/amex/missamerica/filmmore/pt.html.

19. William Cromie, "The Whys and Woes of Beauty Pageants," *Harvard University Gazette*, June 8, 2000.

20. See Janny Scott, "New Respectability for Manners: Scholars Tackle a Topic Long Thought Too Trivial for All but Fussbudgets," *New York Times*, February 28, 1998, for scholarship on class and etiquette.

21. John Hartigan, *Odd Tribes: Towards a Cultural Analysis of White People* (Durham: Duke University Press, 2005), 18.

22. Ibid., 3.

23. Kasson, *Rudeness & Civility*, 67.

24. Peter Miller and Nikolas Rose, *Governing the Present: Administering Economic, Social, and Personal Life* (Cambridge: Polity Press, 2008), 202.

25. Nikolas Rose, *Powers of Freedom: Reframing Political Thought* (Cambridge: Cambridge University Press, 1999), 162.

26. Michael Apple, "Comparing Neo-Liberal Projects and Inequality in Education," *Comparative Education* 37, 4 (2001), : 416.

27. Rosalind Gill, "Postfeminist Media Culture: Elements of a Sensibility," *European Journal of Cultural Studies* 10, 2 (2007), : 164.

28. Nikolas Rose. "Governing "Advanced" Liberal Democracies," in Andrew Barry, Thomas Osborne, and Nikolas Rose (Eds.), *Foucault and Political Reason: Liberalism, Neo-liberalism, and Rationalities of Government* (Chicago: University of Chicago Press, 1996), 41.

29. Nikolas Rose, *Inventing Ourselves: Psychology, Power, and Personhood* (Cambridge: Cambridge University Press, 1996), 154.

30. Valerie Walkerdine, "Reclassifying Upward Mobility: Femininity and the Neo-Liberal Subject," *Gender and Education* 15, 3 (September 2003): 242.

31. Paul Du Gay, *Consumption and Identity at Work* (Thousand Oaks: Sage, 1996).

32. Heidi Marie Rimke, "Governing Citizens Through Self-Help Literature," *Cultural Studies* 14, 1 (2000): 61–78.

33. Lisa Atkins and Beverley Skeggs, *Feminism after Bourdieu* (Oxford: Blackwell, 2004), 91.

34. L. S. Kim, "Race and Reality TV," *FlowTV* (November 19, 2004). Available at http://flowtv.org.

35. Walkerdine, "Reclassifying Upward Mobility," 240.

36. Judith Martin, *Star-Spangled Manners: In Which Miss Manners Defends American Etiquette (For a Change)*. (New York: Norton, 2003), 20.

37. Alexandra Jane Allan, "The Importance of Being a Lady: Hyper-femininity and Heterosexuality in the Private, Single-sex Primary School," *Gender & Education* 21, 2 (March 2009): 145–58.

38. See for example Laurie Ouellette and James Hay, *Better Living Through Reality TV* (Malden: Blackwell, 2008); Dana Heller (Ed.) *The Great American Makeover: Television, History, Nation* (New York: Palgrave Macmillian, 2006); Dana Heller (Ed.) *Makeover Television: Realities Remodeled*. (New York: Palgrave Macmillian, 2007); Jessica Ringrose and Valerie Walkerdine, "Regulating the Abject: The TV Makeover as Site of Neo-liberal Reinvention Towards Bourgeois Femininity," *Feminist Media Studies* 8, 3 (2008): 227–45; Judith Franco, "Extreme Makeover: The Politics of Gender, Class, and Cultural Identity," *Television/New Media* 9, 6 (2008): 471–86; Diane Negra and Yvonne Tasker (Eds.) *Interrogating Post-Feminism: Gender and the Politics of Popular Culture* (Durham: Duke University Press, 2007); Brenda R. Weber., *Self-hood, Citizenship, and Celebrity* (Durham: Duke University Press, 2009); and Susan Murray and Laurie Ouellette, *Reality TV: Remaking Television Culture* (New York: New York University Press, 2004).

39. Beverley Skeggs, "The Moral Economy of Person Production: The Class Relations of Self-Performance on Reality Television," *Sociological Review* 57, 4 (2009): 628.

40. Martin Roberts, "The Fashion Police: Governing the Self in *What Not to Wear*," in Diane Negra and Yvonne Tasker (Eds.), *Interrogating Post-Feminism: Gender and the Politics of Popular Culture* (Durham: Duke University Press, 2007), 228.

41. Author interview, Veleashia Smith, February 24, 2010.

42. Ibid.

43. Laura Holson, "A Finishing School for All, Disney Style," *New York Times*, October 4, 2004.

44. Libby Copeland, "Glamour Babes: At Glittery and Glossy Club Libby Lu," *Washington Post*, March 25, 2006; and Peggy Orenstein, "What's Wrong with Cinderella," *New York Times Magazine*, December 24, 2006.

45. Marina Jimenez, "Venezuela's Rouged Revolution," *Globe and Mail*, December 6, 2006.

46. Juan Forero, "A Bevy of Teeny Beauties, Minds Set on Being Queens," *New York Times*, April 15, 2005.

47. Ibid.

48. *Giridharadas International Herald Tribune*, 2007. Similarly, in the Philippines, see Patty Betita, "High on E (Tiguette): It's Beauty Pageant Season Once Again!," *Global News Bites, Manila Times*, February 16, 2006.

49. Huma Ahmed-Ghosh, "Writing the Nation on the Beauty Queen's Body," *Meridians: Feminism, Race, and Transnationalism* 4, 1 (2003): 219.

50. Karal Ann Marling, *Debutante: Rites and Regalia of American Debdom* (Lawrence: University of Kansas Press, 2004); Amy Best, *Prom Night: Youth, Schools, and Popular Culture* (New York: Routledge, 2000); Lawrence Graham, *Our Kind of People: Inside America's Black Upper Class* (New York: Harper Collins, 1999); Susan Baer, "'I Have to Dance?':

Kids and Cotillions," available at http://www.washingtonian.com; and Michele Salcedo, *Quinceanera! The Essential Guide to Planning the Perfect Sweet Fifteen Celebration* (New York: Henry Holt, 1997).

51. Delta Sigma Theta Sorority, Inc., 2004 Debutante Scholarship Ball, Lexington, Kentucky. Author in attendance.
52. Eilene Zimmerman. "Smart? Fine, But Do You Know What to Do With the Olive Pits?," *New York Times*, May 8, 2005.
53. Molly Sevin, "Using the Right Fork for the Job," *Los Angeles Times*, November 13, 2007.
54. Wellesley College, "Dress for Success Fashion Show," 2007. Author in attendance.
55. Available at www.bennett.edu/pdf/student%handbook%20 2008–2009.
56. Debi Dozier, "Personal Style Analysis," 2004 HBCU Leadership Conference for Kings and Queens.
57. Dale Williams, "Responsibilities of Kings and Queens," 2004 HBCU Leadership Conference for Kings and Queens.
58. Author interview with Dale Williams, May 2004.
59. Candace Johnson, "A Royal Gathering: HBCU Queens Prepare for Their Reign," Tennessee State University, *Meter*, September 2, 2003.
60. In 2010, a book *Leadership for Queens: A Guide and a Journal* was published and is available through the conference web site.
61. Available at http://www.tiedtogreatness.org/alex.
62. Williams, "Responsibilities of Kings and Queens."
63. Beverley Skeggs, *Formations of Class and Gender: Becoming Respectable* (London: Sage Publications, 1997), 98.
64. Patricia Williams, "On Being the Object of Property," *Signs* 14, 1 (Autumn 1988): 5.
65. Author interview with Morehouse College's Miss Maroon and White, April 2005.
66. Ibid.
67. Author interview with Dale Williams, May 2004.
68. Pat Hill Collins, *Black Sexual Politics: African Americans, Gender, and the New Racism* (New York: Routledge, 2004); Kimberly Springer, "Divas, Evil Black Bitches, and Bitter Black Women: African American Women in Postfeminist and Post-Civil-Rights Popular Culture," in Diane Negra and Yvonne Tasker (Eds.), *Interrogating Post-Feminism: Gender and the Politics of Popular Culture* (Durham: Duke University Press, 2007), 249–76; bell hooks, *Black Looks: Race and Representation* (Boston: South End Press, 1992); and Beretta Smith-Shomade, *Shaded Lives: African American Women and Television* (New Brunswick: Rutgers University Press, 2002).
69. Pat Hill Collins, *Black Sexual Politics: African Americans, Gender, and the New Racism* (New York: Routledge, 2004), 140.
70. Tonea Steward, "What Does It Mean to Be a Campus Queen," 2004 HBCU Leadership Conference for Kings and Queens.
71. Sandra Isley, "HBCU Queens, Kings Met in City for Unique Conference," *Chronicle* 32, 47, July 20, 2006: 1.
72. Dale Williams, "College Queens Striving for Excellence," 2004 HBCU Leadership Conference for Kings and Queens.
73. Dale Williams, "Top Ten Things Every College Queen or King Should Know," 2004 HBCU Leadership Conference for Kings and Queens.
74. Benecia Williams, "Crowns and Gowns: How to Plan your Coronation," 2004 HBCU Leadership Conference for Kings and Queens.
75. Author interview with Morehouse College's 2003 Miss Maroon and White, March 2005.
76. Sandra Lee Bartky, "The Pedagogy of Shame," in Carmen Luke (Ed.), *Feminisms and Pedagogies of Everyday Life* (Albany: State University of New York Press, 1996), 225–41; Rita Felski, *Doing Time: Feminist Theory and Postmodern Culture* (New York: New York University Press, 2000); and Gareth Palmer, "Video Vigilantes and the Work of Shame," *Jump Cut: A Review of Contemporary Media* 48 (Winter 2006), http://www.ejump.cut.org/archive.

77. Tonea Steward, "What Does It Mean to Be a Campus Queen," 2004 HBCU Leadership Conference for Kings and Queens.
78. Many former campus queens now work at HBCUs and some have been successful in securing funds from their universities in order to properly adorn their queens and attendants. Tennessee State University, for example, allots $5,000 to enhance its queens' closets.
79. Dale William, "College Queens Striving for Excellence," handout at the 2004 HBCU Leadership Conference for Kings and Queens.
80. Foster, *Troping the Body*, 1.
81. Helen Wood and Beverley Skeggs, "Notes on Ethical Scenarios of Self on British Reality TV," *Feminist Media Studies* 4, 2 (2004): 205–8.
82. Ibid., 82.
83. Dale Williams, "Dos and Don'ts for College Queens and Kings.," handout at the 2004 HBCU Leadership Conference for Kings and Queens.
84. Williams, *Leadership for Queens*, 74.
85. Beverley Skeggs, "(Dis)Identifications of Class: On Not Being Working Class," in D. Robbins (Ed.), *Pierre Bourdieu: Sage Masters of Social Thought* (Thousand Oaks: Sage, 2005), 207–44.
86. Jocey Quinn, "The Corporeality of Learning: Women Students and the Body," in S. Ali, S. Benjamin, and M. Mauthner (Eds.), *The Politics of Gender and Education: Critical Perspectives* (New York: Palgrave-Macmillan, 2004), 180.
87. Author interview with Morehouse College's 2003 Miss Maroon and White, March 2005.
88. Debbie Dozier, "Personal Style Analysis," handout at the 2004 Leadership for HBCU Kings and Queens, July 2004.
89. Available at http://www.etiquette.com/denise.html.
90. Denise Marcia, Conference Program for the 2006 HBCU Leadership Conference for Kings and Queens.
91. Candace Johnson, "A Royal Gathering: HBCU Queens Prepare for Their Reign," *Tennessee State University, Meter*, September 2, 2003.
92. Available at www.thefillies org and kdf.org.what-is-the-princess-program-html.
93. The nomination form for the Fillies includes spouse's occupation and friends and family that have been members of the organization.
94. Author interview with the 1996 Kentucky Derby Festival Queen, November 2003.
95. Ibid.
96. Ibid.
97. Author interview with 2004 Kentucky Derby Princess, May 2004.
98. "KSU Senior is a Derby Princess," *Louisville Defender*, February 15, 1996: 10.
99. Author interview with 2004 Kentucky Derby Princess, May 2004.
100. Author interview with the 1996 Kentucky Derby Festival Queen, November 2003.
101. Ibid.
102. Author interview with 2004 Kentucky Derby Princess, May 2004.
103. William Stucky, "Mountain Laurel Pageant in Old Feuding Country," *New York Times*, May 9, 1948.
104. "Festival Draws Thousands to Celebrate the Blooming of Mountain Laurel,"*Pineville Sun*, May 25, 2000: C2.
105. John Hevener, *Which Side Are You On? The Harlan County Coal Miners, 1931–39* (Urbana: University of Illinois Press, 1978).
106. Available at http://www.kmlf.org.
107. "Festival Draws Thousands to Celebrate the Blooming of Mountain Laurel," *Pineville Sun*, May 25, 2000: C2.
108. Thomas Tolliver, "UK Queen Hopes Public Opinion Will Change Rules for Pageant," *Lexington Herald-Leader*, May 4, 1991: B1; Spencer Healey, "Single Mom Takes on Miss UVU

Pageant," *UVU Review*, October 17, 2011. Available at www.uvureview.com/2011/10/17/single-mom-takes-on-miss-uvu.

109. Brian Johns, "Transylvania Student Wins Crown," *Lexington Herald-Leader*, May 28, 1928: B1.
110. Michele Roan, Letter to Prospective Contestants, February 2000.
111. Kentucky Mountain Laurel Festival Operating Guidelines, 1987.
112. Barbara Ward, "Student Models Small-Town Values," *Lexington Herald-Leader*, June 26, 1997: B1.
113. Author attended the 2000 KMLF including the coronation, the coronation ball, the governor's breakfast, and receptions. I interviewed contestants, escorts, and pageant sponsors.
114. Sarah E. Hargis, "From Queen to Real Life," available at http://www.centre.edu/mycentrellife0607.
115. Beverly Fortune, "Laurel Candidate has 'Royal' Lineage," *Lexington Herald-Leader*, May 19, 2002: J4.
116. Author interview with KSU queen, March, 3, 2004.

Chapter 7

1. Rebecca Grace, "Miss America Crowns Purity as Priceless Message," *ChristiansUnite.com*, February 15, 2005.
2. Leslie McKellar, "Beauty by the Book," *Christian Health* (September, 2002): 17.
3. "Should Christians Participate in Beauty Pageants?," Available at http://sheworships.com/2009/07/11.
4. Special Cable, "Miss Europe Warned Against Texas Show," *New York Times*, April 7, 1929: N3.
5. Jean Comaroff, "The Politics of Conviction: Faith on the Neo-Liberal Frontier," *Social Analysis* 53, 1 (Spring 2009): 20.
6. Neil Swidey, "God on the Quad," *Boston Globe*, November 30, 2003. Available at http://www.boston.com/news/globe/magazine. Also, see Donna Freitas, *Sex and the Soul: Juggling Spirituality, Romance, and Religion on America's College Campuses* (Oxford: Oxford University Press, 2008); and Alan Finder, "Matters of Faith Find a New Prominence on Campus," *New York Times*, May 2, 2007.
7. John Turner, *Bill Bright and the Campus Crusade for Christ: The Renewal of Evangelism in Post-War America* (Chapel Hill: University of North Carolina Press, 2008).
8. Author in attendance, "Reach for the Stars," Belle of the Blue pageant, Georgetown College, February 23, 2002.
9. Eliza Tychonievich, "McClain Crowned Belle of the Blue," *Georgetonian*, February 21, 2007: 1.
10. Heather Lowhorn, "Changing the World a Continent Away," available at http://www.anderson.edu/au-eastafrica/article.html.
11. Ibid.
12. Pamela Podger, "Beauty Queen Glad to Honor Her Faith," *Roanoke Times*, October 14, 2005.
13. Pamela Podger, "College Beauty Queen Wears Tiara over Her Hajib," *Spartanburg Herald-Journal*, October 15, 2005.
14. Available at http://www.howard.edu/currentstudents/studentlifeactivities/Student Activities/Mr.andMiss.
15. The 80th Annual Coronation, "A Royal Affair," Kentucky State University, October 16, 2009: 11.
16. Ibid., 9.

17. Author interview, Miss Kentucky State University, December 17, 2009.
18. Katharine Wasson, "Students Elect First White Queen," *State Journal*, April 30, 2009. Available at http://www.state-journal.com/news.
19. Kimberly Hamlin, "The First Miss America Pageants, 1921–1927," in Elwood Watson and Darcy Marti, (Eds.), *There She Is, Miss America: The Politics of Sex, Beauty, and Race in America's Most Famous Pageant* (New York: Palgrave-Macmillan, 2004), 27–52.
20. Deford, *There She Is*, 151.
21. Ibid., 149.
22. Ibid., 68.
23. Vonda Kay Van Dyke, *That Girl in the Mirror* (Westwood, NJ: Fleming Revell Company, 1966), preface.
24. Ibid., 121.
25. Ibid., preface.
26. See, for example, Barbara Brasher, *Godly Women: Fundamentalism and Female Power* (New Brunswick: Rutgers University Press, 1998); Kristin Aune, "Evangelical Christianity and Women's Changing Lives," *European Journal of Women's Studies* 15, 3 (2008): 277–94; and Michael Hamilton, "Women, Public Ministry, and American Fundamentalism: 1920–1950," *Religion and American Culture* 3, 2 (Summer 1993): 171–96.
27. Jennifer Heller, "Marriage, Womanhood, and the Search for 'Something More': American Evangelical Women's Best-Selling 'Self-Help' Books, 1972–1979," *Journal of Religion and Popular Culture* 2 (Fall 2002), http://www.uask.ca/relst/jrpc/article-selfhelp.html.
28. Shirlee Monty, *Terry* (Waco: Word Books, 1982), 33.
29. Terry Meeuwsen, available at http://terrymeeuswsen.com. Accessed July 21, 2007.
30. Cheryl Prewitt with Kathryn Slattery, *A Bright Shining Place: The Story of a Miracle* (Tulsa: Praise Books, 1981), 193.
31. Prewitt, *Bright*, 127.
32. Ibid., 210.
33. Ibid., 245.
34. Ibid., 255.
35. Ibid., 255.
36. Available at www.salemfamilyministries.org/shop/web/cheryl.asp.
37. Charles Reagan Wilson, *Judgment and Grace in Dixie: Southern Faiths from Faulkner to Elvis* (Athens: University of Georgia Press, 1995), 158.
38. Kara Briggs, "Postcard from Miss America: Faith Becomes a Miss America Theme," *Oregonian*, August 15, 2002: E01.
39. Elizabeth Kastor, "Winning with Tradition: The New Miss America: Modesty before Swimsuit," *Washington Post*, September 16, 1984: B1.
40. Lynn Norment, "Here She Is, Miss America! Black, Beautiful, Brainy, and Born-Again," *Ebony* (December 1989): 132.
41. John Kennedy, "Miss (Christian) America," *Today's Christian* 6. Available at http://www.christianity.com/Christian%20Living/Features/11622493/.
42. Ibid., 5.
43. Tara Christensen, "Journey with Christ," available at http://www.taradawn.net.
44. Kennedy, "Miss (Christian) America," 2.
45. Ibid., 4.
46. Wilson, *Judgment & Grace in Dixie*, 158.
47. Karen W. Tice, "Queens of Academe: Campus Beauty Pageantry and Student Life," *Feminist Studies* 31, 2 (2005): 250–83; and Maxine L. Craig, *Ain't I a Beauty Queen: Black Women, Beauty, and the Politics of Race* (New York: Oxford University Press, 2002).
48. Alicia Cohen, "Carrie Prejean's Book Urges Women to Stand Up for their Beliefs," November 10, 2009. Available at http://blog.christianitytoday.com/women/2009/11.
49. Kristin Aune, "Evangelical Christianity and Women's Changing Lives," *European Journal of Women's Studies* 15, 3 (2008): 281.

50. Penny Marler, "Religious Change in the West, Watch the Women," in K. Aune, S. Sharma, and G. Vincent (Eds.), *Women and Religion in the West: Challenging Secularization* (Aldershot, England: Ashgate, 2008): 23–56.

51. 1992 *Morris Brown Brownite Yearbook*, Robert Woodruff Library, Atlanta University Archives.

52. Available at http://www.designalkhemy.com/contest-alt/msmeac/bio.php?cod=dsu.

53. Joy Sherman, "Moss Fulfilling Duties as Miss Michigan," available at http://www.andersen.edu/signatures/spring03/valley/valley3.html.

54. Available at http://www.uky.edu/SAB/homecoming/hcqueen.html. Accessed November 11, 2000.

55. UK Homecoming 2001, available at http://web.uky.edu/~cbramb0/hcqueen.html. Accessed October 7, 2001.

56. Available at http://www.uky.edu/SAB/homecoming/hcqueen.html. Accessed November 11, 2000.

57. 2002 Mr. & Ms. Black UK pageant.

58. Ibid.

59. Miss Pride Pageant Program, Kentucky State University, 2002.

60. Ibid.

61. Miss Kentucky State University program, 2002: 6.

62. Tamara Beauboeuf-Lafontant, *Behind the Mask of the Strong Black Women: Voice and the Embodiment of a Costly Performance* (Philadelphia: Temple University Press, 2009), 71.

63. Margaret Lowe, *Looking Good: College Women and Body Image, 1875–1930* (Baltimore: John Hopkins University Press, 2003), 59.

64. Author interview, April 7, 2005.

65. 2005 Miss Spelman Pageant Program: Walk of Fame.

66. Ibid.

67. Available at http://misshowarduniversity2007.com/default.aspx. Accessed June 2, 2008.

68. Ibid.

69. HBCU Leadership Conference for newly elected Kings and Queens. Available at http://hbcukingsand queens.com/gpage3.html 2009.

70. Tonea Steward, "What Does It Mean to Be a Campus Queen?" 2004 HBCU Queen Leadership Conference.

71. Available at http://alumni.georgetown.edu/site/PageServer?pagename=spotlight_evans.

72. Ibid.

73. Available at http://bureau.espeakers.com/bsol/speaker.php?sid=8259.

74. Marshawn Evans, "No Trouble Finding Work," *Mortar Board Forum* (Spring 2006).

75. Valorie Burton, "Marshawn Evans Vies to be Donald Trump's Apprentice," available at http://blackamericaweb.com/site.aspx/Praise/challenge/mars.

76. Available at http://www.standpointmanagementgroup.com/MarshawnEvans-ProfessionalPrograms.html.

77. Debrena Jackson Gandy, *All the Joy You Can Stand: 101 Sacred Power Principles for Making Joy Real in Your Life* (New York: Random House), 101.

78. Nancy Stafford, *Beauty by the Book: Seeing Yourself as God Sees You* (Sisters, OR: Multnomah, 2002), 22.

79. Shepherd, "Fit for a King," available at http:/www.hisprincess.com/Resources/Articles/122744.aspx.

80. Jeanette Thomason, "More Than a Pretty Face," *Aspire* (April 1997), 25.

81. Valorie Burton, "Five Signs You Need a Life Makeover," June 20, 2005. Available at www.valorieburton.com.

82. Margaret Feinberg, "Makeover Mania," *Christianity Today* 42, 5 (2005): 24.

83. Cynthia Allen and Charity Allen Winters, *The Beautiful Balance for Body and Soul* (Grand Rapids: Fleming H. Revell, 2003), 18.

84. Ibid., 90.

85. Ibid., 91–92.
86. Monica McKinney, "Stage Presence and Confidence." Presentation at the HBCU Leadership Conference for Kings and Queens, Nashville, Tennessee, 2004.
87. Ibid.
88. 2005 Miss Spelman Pageant program: "Walk of Fame."
89. Sally Gallagher and Christian Smith, "Symbolic Traditionalism and Pragmatic Egalitarianism: Contemporary Evangelicals, Families, and Gender." *Gender & Society* 13, 2 (April 1999): 211–33.
90. Brasher, *Godly Women*, 167.
91. Thomas Pradip, "Selling God/Saving Souls: Religious Commodities, Spiritual Markets and the Media," *Global Media and Communication* 5, 57 (2009): 59.
92. Jennifer Hilde as told to Martha Krienke, "Christ Before the Crown," *Brio*, June 20, 2005.
93. Kathryn Lofton, "Practicing Oprah; or, The Prescriptive Compulsion of a Spiritual Capitalism," *Journal of Popular Culture* 30, 4 (2006): 599–621.
94. Brenda R. Weber and Karen W. Tice, "Are You Finally Comfortable in Your Own Skin?: The Raced and Classed Imperatives for Somatic/Spiritual Salvation in *The Swan*," *Genders* 49 (2009), http://www.genders.org/recent.html.
95. Sheri Rose Shepherd, "His Princess Devotionals," available at http://www.hisprincess.com.
96. Feinberg, "Makeover Mania," 24.
97. Allen and Winters, *A Beautiful*, 21.
98. Ibid., 91.
99. R. Marie Griffith, *Born Again Bodies: Flesh and Spirit in American Christianity* (Berkeley: University of California Press, 2004), 162.
100. Sheri Rose Shepherd, *Who Would Have Thought* (Scottsdale, AZ: Shepherd Marketing, 1995).
101. Sheri Rose Shepherd, "My Introduction to the Ministry," available at http:/www.hisprincess.com.
102. Griffith, *Born-Again Bodies*, 204.
103. Cheryl Prewitt Salem, available at http://www.cpannie.com/aboutus.asp 2007.
104. Ibid.
105. Ibid.
106. Owen Edwards, "American Idol: Once Upon a Time Miss America Reigned Supreme," *Smithsonian Magazine*, January, 2006.
107. Larry Sutton, "Sink or Swim—You Decide," *Daily News*, July 13, 1995.
108. Frank Bruni, "Here She Is, Miss America, Whose Ideal?" *New York Times*, September 16, 1995.
109. Mark Armstrong, "Miss America Outwit-Outprimp," available at http://fr.eonline.com. August 16, 2001.
110. See Rupal Oza, "Showcasing India: Gender, Geography and Globalization," *Signs* 26, 4 (2001): 1067–95, for an excellent analysis of the 1996 Miss World pageant held in Bangalore, India, which took a police security force of over 7,000 to ensure a peaceful pageant. Miss World supporters included both the state and business enterprises that heralded the pageant as an opportunity to showcase Indian modernity and a way to promote tourism and investment. On the other hand, right-wing Hindu fundamentalists and progressive feminist activists opposed pageants as a pernicious Western import that contaminated Indian life. One right wing legislator, Pramila Nesargi, said, "Today it is Miss World; tomorrow it is electrolysis, liposuction, artificial eyes, and face-lifting" (Barry Bearak, "India Sees Ugly Side of Pageant," *LA Times*, November 15, 1996: C1). Many Hindu fundamentalists fumed that beauty pageants threatened to undermine traditional womanhood, whereas the feminist activists challenged the pageant on the basis of imperialism. In order to quell the religious and feminist strife, the pageant held its swimsuit competition on an offshore island to ensure the

safety of the contestants. Despite the beauty conflicts of 1996, Indian beauty pageants continue to be an attraction. In 2001, 6,500 women applied for the Miss India contest. Chosen to host the 2002 Miss World pageant, Nigeria braced itself for the expected wrath of its Muslim citizenry. Nigeria also was a site of religious conflict over the Miss World pageant in 2002. In hopes of avoiding the ire of Muslims, organizers not only postponed the pageant until after Ramadan but also dispensed with the bathing suit competition (*Liberian Orbit*, 2002, available at http://www.liberiaorbit.org/lonewspageantthreats.htm). However, the pageant still produced religious conflict. Four contestants protested a Shariah court verdict to stone an unwed mother to death for adultery and boycotted the pageant. Then when an incendiary article appeared in the Christian newspaper *This Day* suggesting that Mohammed would have likely taken one of the ninety-two contestants for his wife, riots ensued and left more than 200 people dead. The pageant was subsequently moved to London (Tom Masland, "A Pageant Turns Ugly," *Newsweek*, December 2, 2002).

111. Available at http:/misschristianinternational.org/home2.html.
112. Virtue International Pageants, available at http://virtueinternationalpageants.com/.
113. Ibid.
114. Available at http://www.christianpageants.com/html_files/pageant_fact_sheet.html.
115. The 10th Annual Miss Pride of Kentucky State University Scholarship Pageant program, February 21, 2002.
116. Black Women of Today Beauty Pageant, University of Northern Colorado, available at http://www.unco.edu/garvey/Pageant.html 2005.
117. Orientation Guide for the Alpha Phi Alpha Fraternity, Inc. Miss Black and Gold Pageant, available at http://www.thasigma1960.net/Miss_Black_and_Gold_Contestant_Packet.doc
118. 2001 Miss University of Georgia pageant video.
119. 2002 University of Kentucky Black and Gold pageant. Author in attendance.
120. Banet-Weiser, *The Most Beautiful Girl in the World*, 85.
121. Ibid., 80.
122. Robert Lavenda, "It's Not a Beauty Pageant: Hybrid Ideology in the Minnesota Community Queen Pageants," in *Beauty Queens on a Global Stage*, 42.
123. Sarah Freyermuth, "Choosing between the Crown and the Campus," Campus Crusade for Christ. Available at http://www.ccci.org/ministries/college/miss-nd-crown-and-campus-print.html.
124. Author interview with 2002 Kentucky State University Miss Pride pageant contestant.
125. Chelsea Cook, "For University Queen, Beauty is More than Skin-Deep," http://redandblack.com May 2, 2009.
126. Author interview with 2002 Miss Black and Gold, University of Kentucky, February 15, 2002.
127. Author interview with Krista Kober, Miss Purdue University, March 25, 2001.
128. Ibid.
129. Author interview with 2002 Miss Black and Gold, University of Kentucky, February 15, 2002.
130. Author interview, Director of Student Life, Kentucky State University, March 1, 2002.
131. Author interview with 2002 Miss Black and Gold, University of Kentucky, February 1, 2002.
132. Author interview with President of Alpha Phi Alpha Fraternity, University of Kentucky, April 3, 2002.
133. Don Howard, "Women of OSU Pose for Calendar to be Released in Fall," available at http://thelantern.com/home/index.cfm?. July 13, 2006.
134. Martha McKenzie-Minifie, "Academics in a Flap over Beauty Queen Grad," available at http://www.nzherald.co.nz/topic/print.cfm?c. May 2, 2008.
135. Sarah Robinson, "Association of University Staff Offended by Massey's Beauty Queen," available at http://www.salient.org.nz/news/aus-offended-by-massey. May 12, 2008.

Chapter 8

1. Gaye Tuchman, *Wannabe U: Inside the Corporate University* (Chicago: University of Chicago Press, 2009); Randy Martin (Ed.), *Chalk Lines: The Politics of Work in the Managed University* (Durham: Duke University Press, 1998); Shelia Slaughter and Gary Roades, *Academic Capitalism and the New Economy* (Baltimore: John Hopkins University Press, 2004); and Ellen Schrecker, *The Lost Soul of Higher Education: Corporatization, the Assault on Academic Freedom, and the End of the American University* (New York: New Press, 2010).
2. Malaika Mckee-Culpepper, "Social Marketing in Higher Education," 2005. Available at www.sheeo.org/pubs.
3. Maria Alaguru, "Marketing with Miss Universe," available at http://asiamediamonitors.com.
4. Leah Chernikoff, "Ann Taylor Goes Ivy League, Partners with Columbia," available at http://fashionista.com/2011/02.
5. Elizabeth Foydel, "Ann Taylor Puts in an Order for Columbia Student Models," *Columbia Spectator,* February 8, 2011.
6. Sandra Schweiitzer, "Building a Buzz on Campus," *Boston Globe,* October 24, 2005.
7. Available at http://www.jayemag.com.
8. http://www.campussocialitemedia.com.
9. http://hercampus.com/about-us. Also see Simmi Aujla "Wired Campus," http://chronicile.com/blogPost. September 19, 2009.
10. "How to Market to College Students," *HuffPost College,* April 14, 2011, http://www.huffingtonpost.com/her-campus/how-to-market-to-college.
11. http://www.academicchic.com.
12. Ian Evans, "The dress code," http://www.blackcollegian.com. September 19, 2008.
13. Lynn Chancer, *Reconcilable Differences: Confronting Beauty, Pornography, and the Future of Feminism* (Berkeley: University of California Press, 1998), 83.

SELECTED BIBLIOGRAPHY

Archival Collections

Atlanta University Center Archives, Robert Woodruff Library
Morehouse College
Kentucky State University Archives and Special Collections
Indiana University Archives
University of Connecticut Archives
University of Kentucky Special Collections and Archives

Secondary Sources

Adair, Vivyan, and Sandra Dahlberg (Eds.) (2003). *Reclaiming Class: Women, Poverty, and the Promise of Higher Education*. Philadephia: Temple University Press.

Adams, Natalie, and Pamela Bettis (2003). *Cheerleader! An American Icon*. New York: Palgrave Macmillan.

Ahmed-Ghosh, Huma (2003). Writing the nation on the beauty queen's body: Implications for a "Hindu" nation. *Meridians: Feminism, Race, and Transnationalism* 4(1): 205–27.

Allan, Jane A. (2009). The importance of being a 'lady': Hyper-femininity and heterosexuality in the private single-sex school. *Gender and Education* 21(2): 145–58.

Allen, Cynthia, and Charity Allen Winters (2003). *The Beautiful Balance for Body and Soul*. Grand Rapids: Fleming H. Revell.

Apple, Michael (2001). Comparing neo-liberal projects and inequality in education. *Comparative Education* 37(4): 409–23.

Arditi, Jodie (1996). The feminization of etiquette literature: Foucault, mechanisms of social change, and the paradoxes of empowerment. *Sociological Perspectives* 39(3): 417–34.

Atkins, Lisa, and Beverley Skeggs (2004). *Feminism after Bourdieu*. Oxford: Blackwell.

Aune, Kristin (2008). Evangelical Christianity and women's changing lives. *European Journal of Women's Studies* 15(3): 277–94.

Banet-Weiser, Sarah, (1999). *The Most Beautiful Girl in the World: Beauty Pageants and National Identity*. Berkeley: University of California Press.

Banet-Weiser, Sarah and Laura Portwood-Stacer (2006). I just want to be me again! Beauty pageants, reality television, and post-feminism. *Feminist Theory* 7(2): 255–72.

Banner, Lois (1983). *American Beauty*. Chicago: University of Chicago Press.

Bartky, Sandra Lee (1991). *Femininity and Domination: Studies in the Phenomenology of Oppression*. New York: Routledge.

Banks, Ingrid (2000). *Hair Matters: Beauty, Power, and Black Women's Consciousness.* New York: New York University Press.

Barnes, Natasha (1994). Face of the nation: Race, nationalisms and identities in Jamaican beauty pageants. *Massachusetts Review* 35: 471–92.

Bartky, Sandra Lee (1996). The pedagogy of shame. In Carmen Luke (Ed.), *Feminisms and Pedagogies of Everyday Life,* 225–41. Albany: State University of New York Press.

Beidelman, T. O. (1993). *Moral Imagination in Kaguru Modes of Thought.* Washington, DC: Smithsonian.

Best, Amy (2000). *Prom Night: Youth, Schools, and Popular Culture.* New York: Routledge.

Bettie, Julie (2003). *Women without Class: Girls, Race, and Identity.* Berkeley: University of California Press.

Black, Paula (2004). *The Beauty Industry: Gender, Culture, and Pleasure.* New York: Routledge.

Blackwelder, Julia Kirk (2003). *Styling Jim Crow: African American Beauty Training during Segregation.* College Station: Texas A&M University Press.

Blum, Virginia (2003). *Flesh Wounds: The Culture of Cosmetic Surgery.* Berkeley: University of California.

Bogle, Kathleen (2008). *Hooking Up: Sex, Dating, and Relationships on Campus.* New York: New York University Press.

Bordo, Susan (1993). *Unbearable Weight: Feminism, Western Culture, and the Body.* Berkeley: University of California Press.

Boyd, Elizabeth B. (2000). *Southern Beauty: Performing Femininity in an American Region.* Ph.D. dissertation, University of Texas, Austin.

Brand, Peg Zeglin (Ed.) (2000). *Beauty Matters.* Bloomington: Indiana University Press.

Brasher, Barbara (1998). *Godly Women: Fundamentalism and Female Power.* New Brunswick, NJ: Rutgers University Press.

Brown, Tamara, Gregory Parks, and Clarenda Phillips (2005). *African American Fraternities and Sororities: The Legacy and Vision.* Lexington: University Press of Kentucky.

Butler, Judith (1990). *Gender Trouble, Feminism and the Subversion of Identity.* New York: Routledge.

Callahan, William (1998). The ideology of Miss Thailand in national, consumerist, and transnational space. *Alternatives: Global, Local, Political* 23(1): 29–61.

Capshaw Smith, Katherine (2007). Childhood, the body, and race performance: Early 20th century etiquette books for black children. *African American Review* 40: 795–811.

Carby, Hazel (1992). Policing the black woman's body in an urban context. *Critical Inquiry* 18(4): 738–55.

Chancer, Lynn (1998). *Reconcilable Differences: Confronting Beauty, Pornography, and the Future of Feminism.* Berkeley: University of California Press.

Christopher, Renny (2009). *A Carpenter's Daughter: A Working-Class Woman in Higher Education.* Rotterdam: Sense Publishers.

Cohen, Colleen Ballerino, Richard Wilk, and Beverly Stoeltje (Eds.) (1996). *Beauty Queens on the Global Stage: Gender, Contests, and Power.* New York: Routledge.

Collins, Pat Hill (2004). *Black Sexual Politics: African Americans, Gender, and the New Racism.* New York: Routledge.

Comaroff, Jean (2009). The politics of conviction: Faith on the neo-liberal frontier. *Social Analysis* 53(1): 17–38.

Conor, Liz (2004). *The Spectacular Modern Women: Feminine Visibility in the 1920s.* Bloomington: Indiana University Press.

Craig, Maxine L. (2006). Race, beauty and the tangled knot of guilty pleasure. *Feminist Theory* 7(2): 159–77.

Craig, Maxine L. (2009). The color of an ideal beauty queen: Miss Bronze, 1961–1968. In Evelyn Nakano Glenn (Ed.), *Shades of Difference: Why Skin Color Matters,* 81–94. Stanford, CA: Stanford University Press.

Craig, Maxine L. (2002). *Ain't I a Beauty Queen: Black Women, Beauty, and the Politics of Race.* New York: Oxford University Press.

Daniel, G. R. (2002). *More Than Black: Multiracial Identity and the New Racial Order.* Philadelphia: Temple University Press.

Davis, Kathy (2003). *Dubious Inequalities and Embodied Difference: Cultural Studies on Cosmetic Surgery.* Lanham, MD: Rowman and Littlefield.

Davis, Kathy (1995). *Reshaping the Female Body: The Dilemma of Cosmetic Surgery.* New York: Routledge.

Deford, Frank (1971). *There She Is: The Life and Times of Miss America.* New York: Viking Press.

Denetdale, Jennifer Nez (2006). Chairmen, presidents, and princesses: The Navajo nation, gender, and the politics of tradition. *Wicazo Sa Review* 21(1): 9–28.

Dewey, Susan (2008). *Making Miss India Miss World: Constructing Gender, Power, and the Nation in Postliberalization India.* Syracuse: Syracuse University Press.

Dolby, Nadine, and Fazal Rizvi (Eds.) (2008). *Youth Moves: Identities and Education in Global Perspective.* New York: Routledge.

Douglas, Susan (2010). *Enlightened Sexism: The Seductive Message That Feminism's Work Is Done.* New York: Times Books.

Dow, Bonnie (2003). Feminism, Miss America, and media mythology. *Rhetoric & Public Affairs* 6(1): 127–60.

Ducille, Ann (1999). Black Barbie and the deep play of difference. In Morag Shiach (Ed.), *Feminism and Cultural Studies*, 106–32. New York: Oxford University Press.

DuGay, Paul (1996). *Consumption and Identity at Work.* Thousand Oaks, CA: Sage.

Dworkin, Susan (1987). *Miss America 1945: Bess Meyerson's Own Story.* New York: Newmarket Press.

Edgerton, Susan, Gunilla Holm, Toby Daspit, and Paul Farber (Eds.) (2005). *Imagining the Academy: Higher Education and Popular Culture* New York: Routledge.

English, Daylanne (2004). *Unnatural Selections: Eugenics in American Modernism and the Harlem Renaissance.* Chapel Hill: University of North Carolina Press.

Faludi, Susan (1999). *Stiffed: The Betrayal of the American Man.* New York: William Morrow.

Farnham, Christie (1994). *Education of the Southern Belle: Higher Education and Student Socialization.* New York: New York University Press.

Fass, Paula (1977). *The Damned and the Beautiful: American Youth in the 1920s.* New York: Oxford University Press.

Felski, Rita (2000). *Doing Time: Feminist Theory and Postmodern Culture.* New York: New York University Press.

Foster, Gwendolyn (2005). *Class Passing: Social Mobility in Film and Popular Culture.* Carbondale: Southern Illinois University Press.

Foster, Gwendolyn (2000). *Troping the Body.* Carbondale: Southern Illinois University Press.

Franco, Judith (2008). Extreme makeover: The politics of gender, class, and cultural identity. *Television/New Media* 9(6): 471–86.

Freitas, Donna (2008). *Sex and the Soul: Juggling Sexuality, Spirituality, Romance, and Religion on America's College Campuses.* New York: Oxford University Press.

Gaines, Kevin (1996). *Uplifting the Race: Black Leadership, Politics, and Culture in the Twentieth Century.* Chapel Hill: University of North Carolina Press.

Gallagher, Sally, and Christian Smith (1999). Symbolic traditionalism and pragmatic egalitarianism: Contemporary evangelicals, families, and gender. *Gender & Society* 13(2): 211–37.

Gatewood, Willard B. (1990). *Aristocrats of Color: The Black Elite, 1880–1920.* Fayetteville: University of Arkansas Press.

Genz, Stephanie (2009). Third way/ve: The politics of postfeminism. *Feminist Theory* 7(3): 333–53.

Giddings, Paula (1984). *When and Where I Enter: The Impact of Black Women on Race and Sex in America.* New York: Morrow.

Gill, Rosalind (2007). Postfeminist media culture: Elements of a sensibility. *European Journal of Cultural Studies* 10(2): 147–66.

Gill, Rosalind (2003). From sexual objectification to sexual subjectification: The resexualization of women's bodies in the media. *Feminist Media Studies* 3(1): 100–106.

Gimlin, Debra (2002). *Body Work: Beauty and Self-Image in American Culture*. Berkeley: University of California Press.

Glassberg, David (1999). *American Historical Pageantry: The Uses of Tradition in the Early Twentieth Century*. Chapel Hill: University of North Carolina Press.

Goldman, Robert (1992). *Reading Ads Socially*. London: Routledge.

Graham, Lawrence (1999). *Our Kind of People: Inside America's Black Upper Class*. New York: Harper Collins.

Griffith, R. Marie (2004). *Born Again Bodies: Flesh and Spirit in American Christianity*. Berkeley: University of California Press.

Hackley, E. Azalia (1916). *The Colored Women Beautiful*. Kansas City: Burton Publishing Company.

Haidarali, Laila (2005). Polishing brown diamonds: African American women, popular magazines, and the advent of modeling in early postwar America. *Journal of Women's History* 17(1): 10–37.

Hamilton, Michael (1993). Women, public ministry, and American fundamentalism: 1920–1950. *Religion and American Culture* 3(2): 171–96.

Hamlin, Kimberly (2004). The first Miss America pageants, 1921–1927. In Elwood Watson and Darcy Martin (Eds.), *There She Is, Miss America: The Politics of Sex, Beauty, and Race in America's Most Famous Pageant*, 27–52. New York: Palgrave-Macmillan.

Harris, Wendy (2001) *Against All Odds: Ten Entrepeneurs Who Followed Their Hearts and Found Success*. New York: John Wiley.

Hartigan, John (2005). *Odd Tribes: Towards a Cultural Analysis of White People*. Durham: Duke University Press.

Hawkensworth, Mary (2004). Semiotics of premature burial: Feminism in a post-feminist age. *Signs* 29(4): 961–85.

Hawkins, Charlotte Brown (1940). *The Correct Thing To Do—To Say—To Wear*. Sedalia, NC: Author.

Heller, Dana (Ed.) (2006). *The Great American Makeover: Television, History, Nation*. New York: Palgrave-Macmillan.

Heller, Dana (Ed.) (2007). *Makeover Television: Realities Remodeled*. New York: Palgrave-Macmillan.

Heller, Jennifer (2002). Marriage, womanhood, and the search for "something more": American evangelical women's best-selling "self-help" books, 1972–1979. *Journal of Religion and Popular Culture* 2 (Fall), http://www.uask.ca/relst/jrpc/article-selfhelp.html.

Hevener, John (1978). *Which Side Are You On? The Harlan County Coal Miners, 1931–39*. Urbana: University of Illinois Press.

Hey, Valerie (2003). Joining the club? Academia and working-class femininities. *Gender & Education* 15(3): 319–35.

Higginbotham, Evelyn Brooks (1992). African American women's history and the metalanguage of race. *Signs* 17: 251–74.

hooks, bell (2000). *Where We Stand: Class Matters*. New York: Routledge.

hooks, bell (1992). *Black Looks: Race and Representation*. Boston: South End Press.

Horowitz, Helen Lefkowitz (1988). *Campus Life: Undergraduate Cultures from the End of the Eighteenth Century to the Present*. Chicago: University of Chicago Press.

Huey, Lanita Jacobs (2006). *From the Kitchen to the Parlor: Language and Becoming in African American Women's Hair Care*. New York: Oxford University Press.

Kasson, John (1990). *Rudeness & Civility: Manners in Nineteenth-Century Urban America*. New York: Hill and Wang.

Kerr, Audrey Elisa (2006). The history of color prejudice at Howard University. *Journal of Blacks in Higher Education* 54: 82–87.

King-O'Riain and Rebecca Chiyoko (2006). *Pure Beauty: Judging Race in Japanese American Beauty Pageants*. Minneapolis: University of Minnesota Press.

Kinloch, Valerie Felita (2004). The rhetoric of black bodies: Race, beauty, and representation. In Elwood Watson and Darcy Martin (Eds.), *There She Is, Miss America: The Politics of Sex, Beauty, and Race in America's Most Famous Pageant*, 93–110. New York: Palgrave-Macmillan.

Kitch, Carolyn (2001). *The Girl on the Magazine Cover: The Origins of Visual Stereotypes in American Mass Media*. Chapel Hill: University of North Carolina Press.

Kozol, Wendy (2005). Miss Indian America: Regulatory gazes and the politics of affiliation. *Feminist Studies* 31(1): 64–94.

Kuhn, Annette (2002). *Family Secrets: Acts of Memory and Imagination*. London: Verso.

Kumar, Shanti (2004). Globalisation, nationalism, and feminism in Indian culture. *South Asian Journal* 4 (July–September).

Lafontant, Tamara Beauboeuf (2009). *Behind the Mask of the Strong Black Woman: Voice and the Embodiment of a Costly Performance*. Philadelphia: Temple University Press.

Lavenda, Robert (1996). It's not a beauty pageant: Hybrid ideology in the Minnesota community queen pageants. In Colleen Ballerino Cohen, Richard Wilk, and Beverly Stoeltje (Eds.), *Beauty Queens on the Global Stage: Gender, Contests, and Power*, 31–46. New York: Routledge.

Leathwood, Carole, and Barbara Read (2009). *Gender and the Changing Face of Higher Education*. Farnham, England: Open University Press.

Lester, Jamie (2011). Acting on the collegiate stage: Managing impressions in the workplace. *Feminist Formations* 23(1): 155–81.

Levenson, Ellie (2009). *The Noughtie Girl's Guide to Feminism*. Oxford: One World Publications.

Lieu, Nhi (2000). "Remembering the Nation" through pageantry: Femininity and the politics of Vietnamese womanhood in the Hoa Hau Ao Dai contest. *Frontiers: Journal of Women's Studies* 21(1/2): 127–51.

Lim, Shirley J. (2006). *Feeling of Belonging: Asian American Women's Public Culture, 1930–1960*. New York: New York University Press.

Lofton, Kathryn (2006). Practicing Oprah; or, the prescriptive compulsion of a spiritual capitalism. *The Journal of Popular Culture* 30(4): 599–621.

Lopez, Lorraine (2009). *An Angle of Vision: Women Writers on Their Poor and Working Class Roots*. Ann Arbor: University of Michigan Press.

Lowe, Margaret (2003). *Looking Good: College Women and Body Image, 1875–1930*. Baltimore: John Hopkins University Press.

Lucey, Helen, June Melody, and Valerie Walkerdine (2003). Uneasy hybrids: Psychosocial aspects of becoming educationally successful for working-class young women. *Gender & Education* 15(3): 285–99.

Lukose, Ritty (2009). *Liberalization's Children: Gender, Youth, and Consumer Citizenship in Globalizing India*. Durham: Duke University Press.

Lynd, Helen Merrell (1958). *On Shame and the Search for Identity*. New York: Harcourt Brace.

Mahony, Pat, and Christine Zmroczek (Eds.) (1997). *Class Matters: Working-Class Women's Perspectives on Social Class*. New York: Taylor & Francis.

Maira, Sunaina, and Elisabeth Soep (Eds.) (2005). *Youthscapes: The Popular, the National, the Global*. Philadelphia: University of Pennsylvania Press.

Marler, Penny (2008). Religious change in the West: Watch the women. In K. Aune, S. Sharma, and G. Vincent (Eds.), *Women and Religion in the West: Challenging Secularization*, 23–56. Aldershot, England: Ashgate.

Marling, Karal Ann (2004). *Debutante: Rites and Regalia of American Debdom*. Lawrence: University of Kansas Press.

Martin, Judith (2003). *Star-Spangled Manners: In Which Miss Manners Defends American Etiquette (For a Change)*. New York: Norton.

Martin, Randy (Ed.) (1998). *Chalk Lines: The Politics of Work in the Managed University*. Durham: Duke University Press.

Mattson, Katarina (2003). *Crowning Miss Sweden: Constructions of Gender, Race, and Nation in Beauty Pageants*. Paper presented at Gender and Power in the New Europe at the European Feminist Research Conference, Lund University, Lund, Sweden.

McCandless, Amy (1999). *The Past in the Present: Women and Higher Education in the Twentieth Century South*. Tuscaloosa: University of Alabama Press.

McRobbie, Angela (2004). Postfeminism and popular culture. *Feminist Media Studies* 4(3): 255–64.

McRobbie, Angela (2004). Notes on postfeminism and popular culture: Bridget Jones and the new gender regime. In Anita Harris (Ed.), *All About the Girl: Culture, Power, and Identity*, 3–14. New York: Routledge.

Meyerowitz, Joanne (1993). Beyond the feminine mystique: A reassessment of post-war culture, 1946–1958. *Journal of American History* 79(4): 1455–82.

Mitchell, Michele (2004). *Righteous Propagation: African Americans and the Politics of Racial Destiny*. Chapel Hill: University of North Carolina Press.

Miller, Peter, and Nikolas Rose (2008). *Governing the present: Administering economic, social, and personal life*. Cambridge: Polity Press.

Miller, Toby (2006). Metrosexuality: See the bright lights of commodification shine! Watch Yanqui masculinity made over. In Dana Heller (Ed.), *The Great American Makeover: Television, History, Nation*, 105–24. New York: Palgrave.

Monty, Shirlee (1982). *Terry*. Waco: Word Books.

Moore, Kesha (2008). Class formations: Competing forms of black middle-class identity. *Ethnicities* 8(4): 492–517.

Murray, Susan, and Laurie Ouellette (2004). *Reality TV: Remaking Television Culture*. New York: New York University Press.

Muzzatti, Stephen, and C. Vincent Samarco (2006). *Reflections from the Wrong Side of the Track: Class, Identity, and the Working Class Experience in Academe*. Lanham, MD: Rowman and Littlefield.

Newman, Louise (1992). *White Women's Rights: The Racial Origins of Feminism in the United States*. New York: Oxford University Press.

Oliver, M. Cynthia (2009). *Queen of the Virgins: Pageants and Black Womanhood in the Caribbean*. Jackson: University of Mississippi Press.

Ouellette, Laurie, and James Hay (2008). *Better Living Through Reality TV*. Malden, MA: Blackwell.

Oza, Rupal (2001). Showcasing India: Gender, geography and globalization. *Signs* 26(4): 1067–95.

Palmer, Gareth (2006). Video vigilantes and the work of shame. *Jump Cut: A Review of Contemporary Media* 48 (Winter), http://www.ejumpcut.org/archive.

Parameswaran, Radhika (2004). Global queens, national celebrities: Tales of feminine triumph in post-liberalization India. *Critical Studies in Media Communication* 21(4): 346–70.

Pascoe, C.J. (2007). *Dude You're a Fag: Masculinity and Sexuality in High School*. Berkeley:University of California Press.

Peiss, Kathy (1998). *Hope in a Jar: The Making of America's Beauty Culture*. New York: Metropolitan Books.

Perkins, Linda M. (1997). The African American female elite: The early history of African American women in the Seven Sister Colleges, 1880–1960. *Harvard Educational Review* 67(4): 718–56.

Pitts, Victoria (2007). *Surgery Junkies: The Cultural Boundaries of Cosmetic Surgery*. New Brunswick, NJ: Rutgers University Press.

Poovey, Mary (1984). *The Proper Lady and the Woman Writer: Ideology as Style in the Works of Mary Wollstonecraft, Mary Shelly, and Jane Austen*. Chicago: University of Chicago.

Pozner, Jennifer (2003). The "Big Lie": False feminist death syndrome, profit, and the media. In Rory Dicker and Alison Piepmeier (Eds.), *Catching a Wave: Reclaiming Feminism for the 21st Century*, 31–56. Boston: Northeastern University Press.

Pradip, Thomas (2009). Selling God/saving souls: Religious commodities, spiritual markets and the media. *Global Media and Communication* 5(57): 157–76.

Prewitt, Cheryl, and Kathryn Slattery (1981). *A Bright Shining Place: The Story of a Miracle*. Tulsa: Praise Books.

Quinn, Jocey (2004). The corporeality of learning: Women students and the body. In S. Ali, S. Benjamin, and M. Mauthner (Eds.), *The Politics of Gender and Education: Critical Perspectives*, 174–88. New York: Palgrave-Macmillan.

Rahier, Jean M. (1998). Blackness, the racial/spatial order, migrations, and Miss Ecuador, 1995–96. *American Anthropologist* 100(2): 2421–30.

Reay, Diane (2003). A risky business? Mature working-class women students and access to higher education. *Gender & Education* 15(3): 301–17.

Reid, Coletta (1972). Recycled trash. *Furies* 1(5): 8.

Rhode, Deborah (2010). *The Beauty Bias: The Injustice of Appearance in Life and Law*. New York: Oxford University Press.

Rimke, Heidi Marie (2000). Governing citizens through self-help literature. *Cultural Studies* 14(1): 61–78.

Ringrose, Jessica, and Valerie Walkerdine (2008). Regulating the abject: The TV make-over as site of neo-liberal reinvention towards bourgeois femininity. *Feminist Media Studies* 8(3): 227–45.

Riverol, R.A. (2002). *Live From Atlantic City: A History of the Miss America Pageant*. Bowling Green: Bowling Green State University.

Roberts, Martin (2007). The fashion police: Governing the self in *What Not To Wear*. In Yvonne Tasker, and Diane Negra (Eds.), *Interrogating Post-Feminism: Gender and the Politics of Popular Culture*, 227–48. Durham: Duke University Press.

Rooks, Noliwe (1996). *Hair Raising: Beauty, Culture, and African American Women*. New Brunswick, NJ: Rutgers University Press.

Rooks, Noliwe (2004). *Ladies Pages: African American Women's Magazines and the Cultures that Made Them*. New Brunswick NJ: Rutgers University Press.

Rose, Nikolas (1999). *Powers of Freedom: Reframing Political Thought*. Cambridge: Cambridge University Press.

Rose, Nikolas (1996). Governing "advanced" liberal democracies. In Andrew Barry, Thomas Osborne, and Nikolas Rose (Eds.), *Foucault and Political Reason: Liberalism, Neo-liberalism and Rationalities of Government*, 37–65. Chicago: University of Chicago Press:.

Rose, Nikolas (1996). *Inventing Ourselves: Psychology, Power, and Personhood*. Cambridge: Cambridge University Press.

Sangster, Joan (2008). Queen of the picket line: Beauty contests in the post–World War Two Canadian labor movement, 1945–70. *Labor Studies in Working Class History of the Americas* 5(4): 83–106.

Savage, Candace (1998). *Beauty Queens: A Playful History*. New York: Abbeville Press.

Schackt, Jon (2005). Mayahood through beauty: Indian beauty pageants in Guatemala. *Bulletin of Latin American Research* 24(3): 269–87.

Schrecker, Ellen (2010). *The Lost Soul of Higher Education: Corporatization, the Assault on Academic Freedom, and the End of the American University*. New York: New Press.

Sender, Katherine (2006). Queens for a day: Queer eye for the straight guy and the neoliberal project. *Critical Studies in Media Communication* 23(2): 131–51.

Shaw, Stephanie (1996). *What a Women Ought to Be and to Do: Black Professional Workers During the Jim Crow Era*. Chicago: University of Chicago Press.

Shepherd, Sheri Rose (1995). *Who Would Have Thought*. Scottsdale, AZ: Shepherd Marketing.

Shomade, Beretta Smith (2002). *Shaded Lives: African American Women and Television*. New Brunswick, NJ: Rutgers University Press.

Simon, Bryant (2004). *Boardwalk of Dreams: Atlantic City and the Fate of Urban America*. New York: Oxford University Press.

Siu, Lok (2005). Queen of the Chinese colony: Gender, nation, and belonging in diaspora. *Anthropological Quarterly* 78(3): 511–42.

Skeggs, Beverley (1997). *Formations of Class and Gender: Becoming Respectable*. London: Sage.

Skeggs, Beverley (2009). The moral economy of person production: The class relations of self-performance on reality television. *Sociological Review* 57(4): 626–44.

Skeggs, Beverley (2005). (Dis)identifications of class: On not being working class. In Derek Robbins (Ed.), *Pierre Bourdieu: Sage Masters of Social Thought*, 207–44. Thousand Oaks, CA: Sage.

Slaughter, Shelia, and Gary Roades (2004). *Academic Capitalism and the New Economy*. Baltimore: John Hopkins University Press.

Springer, Kimberly (2007). Divas, evil black bitches, and bitter black women: African American women in postfeminist and post-civil-rights popular culture. In Y. Tasker and D. Negra (Eds), *Interrogating Post-Feminism: Gender and the Politics of Popular Culture*, 249–76. Durham: Duke University Press.

Stafford, Nancy (2002). *Beauty by the Book: Seeing Yourself as God Sees You*. Sisters, OR: Multnomah.

Stuber, Jenny (2006). Talk of class: The discursive repertoires of white working class and upper middle class students. *Journal of Contemporary Ethnography* 35(3): 285–18.

Summers, Martin (2004). *Manliness and Its Discontents: The Black Middle Class and the Transformation of Masculinity, 1900–1930*. Chapel Hill: University of North Carolina Press.

Tasker, Yvonne, and Diane Negra (Eds.) (2007). *Interrogating Post-Feminism: Gender and the Politics of Popular Culture*. Durham: Duke University Press.

Tate, Shirley Anne (2009). *Black Beauty: Aesthetics, Stylization, Politics*. Aldershot, England: Ashgate.

Taylor, Bianca (2008). Color and class: The promulgation of elitist attitudes at black colleges. In Marybeth Gasman and Christopher Tudico (Eds.), *Historically Black Colleges and Universities: Triumphs, Troubles, and Taboos*, 189–206. New York: Palgrave-Macmillan.

Thoma, Pamela (1999). Of beauty pageants and Barbie: Theorizing consumption in Asian American transnational feminism. *Genders* 29. Available at www.genders.org.

Tice, Karen W. (2005). Queens of academe: Campus beauty pageantry and student life. *Feminist Studies* 31(2): 250–83.

Tice, Karen W. (1998). *Tales of Wayward Girls and Immoral Women: Case Records and the Professionalization of Social Work*. Urbana: University of Illinois Press.

Tokarczyk, Michelle, and Elizabeth Fay (1993). *Working-Class Women in the Academy: Labors in the Knowledge Factory*. Amherst: University of Massachusetts Press.

Tuchman, Gaye (2009). *Wannabe U: Inside the Corporate University*. Chicago: University of Chicago Press.

Turner, John (2008). *Bill Bright and Campus Crusade for Christ: The Renewal of Evangelism in Post-war America*. Chapel Hill: University of North Carolina Press.

Turk, Diana (2004). *Bound By a Mighty Vow: Sisterhood and Women's Fraternities, 1870–1920*. New York: New York University Press.

Walkerdine, Valerie (2003). Reclassifying upward mobility: Femininity and the neo-liberal subject. *Gender and Education* 15(3): 237–48.

Watson, Elwood, and Darcy Marti (Eds.) (2004). *There She Is, Miss America: The Politics of Sex, Beauty, and Race in America's Most Famous Pageant*. New York: Palgrave-Macmillan.

Weber, Brenda R., and Karen W. Tice (2009). Are you finally comfortable in your own skin? The raced and classed imperatives for somatic/spiritual salvation in *The Swan*. *Genders* 49. Available at www.genders.org.

Weber, Brenda R. (2009). *Makeover TV: Selfhood, Citizenship, and Celebrity*. Durham: Duke University Press.

Weber, Brenda R. (2005). Beauty, desire, and anxiety: The economy of sameness on ABC's *Extreme Makeover*. *Genders* 41. Available at www.genders.org.

West, Candace, and Sarah Fenstermaker (1995). Doing difference. *Gender & Society* 9(1): 8–37.

White, Deborah Gray (1999). *Too Heavy a Load: Black Women in Defense of Themselves 1894– 1994*. New York: Norton.

White, Shane, and Graham White (1998). *Stylin' African American Expressive Culture from its Beginnings to the Zoot Suit*. Ithaca: Cornell University Press.

Wilkins, Amy (2008). *Wannabes, Goths, and Christians: The Boundaries of Sex, Style, and Status*. Chicago: University of Chicago Press.

Williams, Patricia (1988). On being the object of property. *Signs* 14(1): 5–24.

Willie, S.S. (2003). *Acting Black: College Identity and the Performance of Race*. New York: Routledge.

Wilson, Charles Reagan (1995). *Judgment & Grace in Dixie*. Athens: University of Georgia Press.

Winkle-Wagner, Rachelle (2009). *The Unchosen Me: Race, Gender, and Identity Among Black Students in College*. Baltimore: John Hopkins University Press.

Wolcott, Victoria (2001). *Remaking Respectability: African Americans in Interwar Detroit*. Chapel Hill: University of North Carolina Press.

Wolf, Naomi (1991). *The Beauty Myth: How Images of Beauty Are Used Against Women*. New York: Anchor Books.

Wolfe, Deborah (1994). *Beauty as a Vocation: Women and Beauty Contests in America*. Ph.D. dissertation, Columbia University.

Wood, Helen, and Beverley Skeggs (2004). Notes on ethical scenarios of self on British reality TV. *Feminist Media Studies* 4(2): 205–8.

Wouters, Cas (1995). Etiquette books and emotional management in the 20th century: The integration of the social classes. *Journal of Social History* 29(1): 107–24.

Wouters, Cas (1995). Etiquette books and emotional management in the 20th century: The integration of the sexes. *Journal of Social History* 29(2): 325–39.

Wright, Pamela (1995). The timely significance of supernatural mothers or exemplary daughters: The metonymy of identity in history. In Jane Schneider and Rayna Rapp (Eds.), *Articulating Hidden Histories: Exploring the Influence of Eric R. Wolf*, 243–61. Berkeley: University of California Press.

Wu, Judy Tzu-Chun (2001). "Loveliest daughters of our ancient Cathay": Representations of ethnic and gender identity in the Miss Chinatown U.S.A. beauty pageant. In Phillip Scranton (Ed.), *Beauty and Business: Commerce, Gender, and Culture in Modern America*, 278– 308. New York: Routledge.:

Van Dyke, Vonda Kay (1966). *That Girl in the Mirror*. Westwood, NJ: Fleming Revell.

Yano, Christine (2006). *Crowning the Nice Girl: Gender, Ethnicity, and Culture in the Hawaii's Cherry Blossom Festival*. Honolulu: University of Hawaii Press.

Zweig, Michael (Ed.) (2004). *What's Class Have To Do With It?: American Society in the Twenty-First Century*. Ithaca: Cornell University Press.

INDEX